FORTU...ᴸ

THE RISE AND RISE OF AFRIKANER TYCOONS

Ebbe Dommisse

Translated by Linde Dietrich

JONATHAN BALL PUBLISHERS
JOHANNESBURG · CAPE TOWN · LONDON

To Daléne, Ebbe Jan, Jacques and Melinda and their families,
the most loyal stalwarts.

---*---

JONATHAN BALL PUBLISHERS
A division of Media24 (Pty) Ltd
PO Box 33977
Jeppestown
2043

Reprinted in 2021

ISBN 978-1-86842-754-3
ebook ISBN 978-1-86842-755-0

Website: www.jonathanball.co.za
Twitter: www.twitter.com/JonathanBallPub
Facebook: www.facebook.com/JonathanBallPublishers

Translated by Linde Dietrich
Cover by Michiel Botha
Design and typesetting by Martine Barker
Printed and bound by CTP Printers, Cape Town
Set in Adobe Garamond Pro

Contents

Money is a great servant
but a bad master.

— FRANCIS BACON

Author's note

The New South Africa that was ushered in by the transition of 1994 has produced a number of outcomes that were not generally foreseen. One of these is the rise of a dozen or two Afrikaner businesspeople who have achieved unprecedented success. A handful of them have become billionaires, with fortunes equalling the earlier success stories of English-speaking and Jewish entrepreneurs.

In agriculture, technological advances have been instrumental in the success of ten or so big commercial farmers who started excelling at large-scale farming despite the enormous challenges South Africa poses as an agricultural country. They have become known as mega-farmers, some of whom could really be described as 'ultrapreneurs'.

The focus of the book falls on Afrikaners who rose as a group, although individuals in other cultural groups have also built successful businesses. Since 1994, a number of Indian and black businesspeople have come to the fore as ingenious entrepreneurs. The richest black businessman, Patrice Motsepe, also notes the earlier examples of great black entrepreneurs who founded successful businesses in defiance of the apartheid laws that restricted them in various ways.

In my research I did not come across Afrikaans-speaking coloured people who can be described as super-rich, although they occupy key leadership positions in scholarly and professional fields. Besides the curbs of the apartheid era that held coloured entrepreneurs back, the coloured people as a cultural group for a great part displayed the same pattern that prevailed among other Afrikaners: the pioneering leading lights mostly turned to the professions, making their mark as teachers, public servants and clergymen in particular.

The book, which was three years in the making before the outbreak of the Covid-19 pandemic, is the account of a journalist who has been a long-time observer of developments in the related fields of the South African economy and politics. Most of these Afrikaner businesspeople and mega-farmers started out with little, but have distinguished themselves as entrepreneurs who rose to the top in business through daring and drive. The aim was to describe the activities of these person-alities and their interrelationships as impartially as possible.

The core of the book is based on interviews and e-mail correspon-dence with leading figures in business and mega-agriculture. My son Jacques wrote the section on the mega-farmers as ultrapreneurs.

Since the book is not meant to be an academic dissertation, the issue of footnotes and endnotes, which many readers find intrusive, is all the more problematic in an era where virtually all references can be located fairly easily via search engines. 'Googling' has become common parlance, as we know. In many cases, a source is already in-dicated in the text, while formal particulars about many institutions are readily available on websites on the internet. Quotations that may raise doubt were checked with the individuals concerned.

Accordingly, it was decided in consultation with the publisher to provide only a list of sources and a list of interviews, while pointers on supplementary reading are also given. More citations than these acknowledgements are simply impractical and may come across as superfluous. Readers who would like to trace specific references are welcome to direct queries to me via the publisher.

Thank you to Jonathan Ball, who encouraged me to write a book about the rise of Afrikaner businesspeople, a phenomenon that has long struck both of us. Annie Olivier and Louis Esterhui-zen proficiently took care of the text editing, while the talented Fred Mouton provided the portrait sketches. Linde Dietrich expertly handled the English translation, with Karin Schimke contributing to the final editing.

A big thank you, too, to my son Jacques who dealt with the mega-farmers, and still greater thanks to my wife, Daléne, for her love and solicitude, and especially for her patience with my slogging away on a computer.

Ebbe Dommisse

Introduction: Reach for the stars

ONE OF THE MOST remarkable features of the transition to a full-fledged democracy in South Africa in 1994 when an Afrikaner-controlled government surrendered power to a black liberation movement has been the rise of Afrikaners in business under a totally new dispensation.

Despite successive Afrikaner-controlled governments having wielded the sceptre for many years, white English speakers and Jewish entrepreneurs dominated the South African business world. In the post-1994 era, however, a number of Afrikaans-speaking business-people in the private sector have taken the lead.

Of the Afrikaners who started excelling in business since the takeover by Nelson Mandela's government, several have become billionaires, some with huge international firms spread far beyond the country's borders. A few of them rank among the wealthiest individuals in South Africa and are included in the lists of billionaires – the super-rich with assets in excess of R1 000 million. A handful have become dollar billionaires whose names appear in global rankings.

The most phenomenal ascent has been that of Koos Bekker, who became the chief executive and later chair of Naspers. Under Bekker's leadership, the former media company that had been founded in 1915 to advance Afrikaner interests was transformed into a global investment holding group focused on e-commerce and the internet. After the mining giants Anglo American and Billiton moved their head offices offshore, Naspers has come to dominate the Johannesburg Stock Exchange (JSE) to such a degree that Naspers shares make up more than a fifth of the JSE's total market capitalisation.

Johann Rupert, heir to the business empire founded by his father Dr Anton Rupert in the university town of Stellenbosch, has strengthened the global footprint of the Rupert tradition at the helm of Richemont, the world's second-biggest luxury-goods group.

Two former residence friends at Stellenbosch University, Christo Wiese and Whitey Basson, have gained renown as the uncrowned kings of retail. The two lifelong friends grew Pepkor and Shoprite into Africa's biggest clothing and food retail groups, respectively.

1

Jannie Mouton, shortly after being fired by his partners in a stock-broking firm in Johannesburg, started off with practically nothing and within a few years built PSG into one of the largest financial services groups in the country.

PSG supplied the start-up financing for the Capitec founder Michiel le Roux who, with his exceptional success story as a young entrepreneur in banking, has become another of Stellenbosch's billionaires. Capitec, which provided thousands of South Africans in the low-income bracket with banking services for the first time, has grown to the country's largest banking group by customer numbers (13 million).

Another player in the financial services industry is Coronation co-founder Thys du Toit, who has carved out a niche in Stellenbosch with the concept of family offices that manage the assets of wealthy families.

Elsewhere in banking, two other Afrikaners, GT Ferreira and Laurie Dippenaar, founded a relatively small enterprise in Johannesburg together with Paul Harris, and eventually built it into the country's biggest banking group, FirstRand.

Two Afrikaners, both former pupils of Hoërskool Jan van Riebeeck in Cape Town, have accomplished outstanding feats in separate fields of the modern economy overseas. The fascinating story of Roelof Botha, grandson of South Africa's longest-serving minister of foreign affairs, Pik Botha, stretches from his schooldays in Cape Town to Silicon Valley in California where he is now one of the leading lights in the United States' venture capital industry. Hendrik du Toit is another Capetonian who has made a name for himself in foreign parts. As founder of Investec Asset Management, he moved to London to expand the group internationally from there.

A pacesetter from the insurance industry, former Sanlam chair Johan van Zyl consolidated a close association with South Africa's foremost black businessman Patrice Motsepe and his African Rainbow Capital to establish ARC as a heavyweight in the economy.

Another leader from the insurance industry who forged close ties with a black leader is Douw Steyn, a maverick among the Afrikaner businesspeople. With the phenomenally successful Meerkat advertising campaign, Steyn, founder of the insurance giant Auto &

General, established one of the biggest insurance companies in Britain. The meerkat symbol was a connection with South Africa that was enhanced by his friendship with the late former president Nelson Mandela, who was housed by Steyn while the ANC leader completed his autobiography *Long Walk to Freedom*.

Many of the super-rich have also demonstrated that South Africa is a country of givers. François van Niekerk of the Mergon Group, for instance, was named Africa's top philanthropist by *Forbes* magazine in 2011.

Beyond the business sector there have consistently been outstanding achievers in agriculture, a sector regarded by the ANC government as a key future job creator, along with mining and tourism.

Though South Africa does not have Africa's most fertile farmland by a long chalk, accomplished Afrikaans-speaking farmers play a crucial role in keeping the country at the forefront of the continent's food chain. They help ensure that food security is maintained domestically while agriproducts are also exported on a large scale.

In the industry, a number of them are referred to as ultrapreneurs: mega-farmers who, as innovative agriculturalists, use state-of-the-art techniques to ensure large-scale and sustainable production. The ten or so mega-farmers discussed in this book cannot be viewed merely as farmers. Rather, they are market leaders and creative businesspeople who run their farming operations like a multinational company.

But the rise of Afrikaners as trendsetting figures in business has not just been a one-way trajectory. The fall of one of their number dominated the news for weeks, even amid sensational revelations of state capture under the corrupt administration of former president Jacob Zuma.

The leading figure in the Steinhoff scandal which stunned the South African business community, was Markus Jooste, around whose head a fraud bombshell exploded on 6 December 2017. On that day Jooste, also a resident of Stellenbosch, resigned out of the blue as CEO of Steinhoff International due to 'accounting irregularities'. The global furniture and clothing retailer's share price plummeted overnight by more than 90 per cent to a paltry R6, eventually dropping to below R1 as the shock waves of South Africa's biggest corporate scandal continued to ripple outward.

The collapse in the share price severely damaged the pensions of millions of South Africans and almost wiped out the fortunes of quite a few of Jooste's business acquaintances. Among them was Christo Wiese, who resigned as chair of Steinhoff and lodged a R59-billion claim against the company. Prior to the Steinhoff scandal – through which Wiese lost fifty years' work, by his own account – he had been labelled the richest man in South Africa.

Jooste was one of the businessmen associated with the 'Stellenbosch Mafia'. An appellation used in jest by the fund manager David Shapiro in a radio interview in 2003, this term was subsequently weaponised by politicians as a slur against a collective of Stellenbosch businessmen who in many respects differ with, and are very different from, one another.

The reference to the 'Stellenbosch Mafia' derives from the fact that the town, formerly mainly known for its university, has become the domicile of a generation of billionaires. In late 2017, business figures with intimate knowledge of the town calculated that between 30 and 35 billionaires lived in and around Stellenbosch.

The 'Mafia' generalisation was coupled with a propaganda campaign against so-called 'white monopoly capital' which was devised in London by the discredited public relations agency Bell Pottinger in collaboration with the Zuma clique in the ANC and the Gupta state capturers. Even after Bell Pottinger collapsed in disgrace, notably as a result of criticism that it had inflamed racial tensions in the sensitive South African situation, 'white monopoly capital' has remained a target for race-baiting politicians who plundered state coffers, and their hangers-on.

The post-1994 rise of Afrikaners in the private sector was indirectly boosted by the ANC government's intention to wholly dominate the public service and parastatals. In 1998, this hegemonic goal was spelled out in the ANC mouthpiece *Umrabulo*: 'Transformation of the state entails, first and foremost, extending the power of the National Liberation Movement over all levers of power: the army, the police, the bureaucracy, intelligence structures, the judiciary, parastatals, and agencies such as regulatory bodies, the public broadcaster, the central bank and so on.'

Prior to the election of 2019, Deputy President David Mabuza reaffirmed this policy. According to a report in the *Sowetan*, he stated that there were 'other options' for those who failed to make the ANC's national and provincial candidate list – which boasted the names of notorious state capturers. Mabuza referred to a wide scope of deployment 'so that we occupy every important point and every important institution in the country'.

The intention to control 'all levers of power' as part of the National Democratic Revolution, an old communist term that was dusted off and harnessed anew, entailed cadre deployment in terms of which large numbers of card-carrying ANC members were 'deployed' to the public sector. This went hand in hand with 'demographic representivity', a form of social engineering that was based on the apartheid regime's racial classification and had been expanded into one of the largest projects of its kind in the world. The staff composition of all institutions had to transform in accordance with the race-based formula of 80-9-9-2: 80 per cent black, 9 per cent white, 9 per cent coloured and 2 per cent Indian.

'Jobs for pals' instead of a professional public service became the order of the day. Thousands of white public servants departed with retrenchment packages. In many cases, their posts were filled by inexperienced ANC cadres, while the number of public servants increased from 1,57 million at the time of the change of government in 1994 to 2,04 million in 2017. Their remuneration packages were considerably better than those in the private sector – in some cases up to 40 per cent higher.

The social engineering impelled Afrikaners who left the deteriorating public service to enter the private sector instead. Clem Sunter, who gained prominence as Anglo American's scenario planner, remarked that the ANC government's affirmative action had the unintended consequence that a great number of Afrikaners started successful businesses and therefore mostly benefited from that policy.

On the other hand, the government's attempts at intervention in the economy advantaged a small black elite, while the unemployment rate, by the expanded definition that includes 'people no longer seeking work', rose to nearly 40 per cent under the Zuma regime – from 3,2 million unemployed in 1994 to more than 10 million in

2019. Another consequence was that the Gini coefficient, which measures inequality in a country, declined between 2006 and 2015, according to Statistics South Africa. But inequality among black South Africans – the unemployed poor versus a well-off minority – had increased despite social grants being paid out to 18 million recipients.

External factors, too, inhibited the South African economy, notably the financial crisis of 2008 that rocked the global economy and resulted in a widespread recession. The crisis started when the housing market in the United States collapsed because thousands of subprime mortgage loans had been granted. The bankruptcy of Lehman Brothers ignited distrust in the international banking system, and massive bailout packages had to rescue other banks from a similar fate. In South Africa, however, the sophisticated banking system remained stable.

Confidence in the country was dented after the ANC officially resolved during President Cyril Ramaphosa's election as leader in 2017 to expropriate property without compensation and nationalise the Reserve Bank. The risk of a debt trap and policy uncertainty were the main reasons why rating agencies downgraded South Africa's sovereign credit rating to junk status. In early 2020, the deadly coronavirus outbreak, which sparked a global economic crisis and forced the South African government to declare a national state of disaster, was a further blow to the jugular for the country's economic prospects.

Although the Steinhoff scandal tarnished the reputation of the business sector and increased concern as to whether the government had the will and the ability to resuscitate the economy, the overwhelming majority of Afrikaner entrepreneurs were still leading the task of keeping the faltering national economy afloat.

Compared with 30, 40 years ago, since the transition of 1994 it has been mostly Afrikaner or black businesspeople who have made the headlines. Christo Wiese reckons this is because Afrikaner or black businesspeople are to some extent second-generation entrepreneurs who descended from businesspeople that already established themselves years ago. 'They had good teachers, grew up in a commercial environment and built on what they had inherited,' he said.

The country's turbulent history has continued to be characterised by the historian CW de Kiewiet's often-quoted observation: 'South Africa advanced politically by disasters and economically by windfalls.'

The rise of Afrikaner business leaders after 1994 was preceded by a long and sustained struggle to secure a place for the Afrikaner community in the spheres of commerce and industry as well. In the pursuit of that ideal, a number of far-sighted businesspeople were defining trailblazers.

Among them were role models who could also inspire a younger generation of business leaders when their time came to reach for the stars.

1

The ancestors

RELATIVELY FEW Africans feature on the lists of the world's richest people. Most of the billionaires in Africa, with its abundance of natural resources, hail from South Africa. This country's vast mineral resources, particularly gold and diamonds, laid the initial foundation for its emergence as a modern industrial state.

Yet an African is believed to have been the richest person in history. He was Mansa (emperor) Musa I of Mali, whose 14th-century wealth has been estimated at $400 billion; nearly double the estimated fortune of the wealthiest of all modern families, the Rothschilds. Moreover, it is almost triple the wealth of the frontrunner among the super-rich of today, the American Jeff Bezos, founder and CEO of Amazon, the world's largest internet retailer.

Bezos, with a net worth of $112 billion, topped *Forbes* magazine's list of the richest billionaires on the planet in 2018, followed by Bill Gates of Microsoft ($90 billion) and the ace investor Warren Buffett ($84 billion). In January 2021, however, Bloomberg reported that Bezos had been surpassed by South African-born Elon Musk who, with assets of $184 billion, had become the richest man in modern history, according to the group's Billionaires Index.

Mansa Musa (1280–1337) was the ruler of the Malian Empire, an Islamic state the size of Western Europe that included modern-day Ghana and Mali in West Africa. He owed his fabulous wealth to the production of more than half of the world's salt and gold, in which a flourishing trade was conducted with Egypt in particular. Mansa Musa achieved legendary status when he undertook a pilgrimage to Mecca across the desert in 1324, accompanied by a caravan unlike any other. Part of his retinue consisted of 12 000 servants all clad in brocade and Persian silk, while Mansa Musa rode on horseback behind a procession of some 500 servants who each carried a gold staff weighing about 3 kg on their shoulders.

He built libraries and a university in Timbuktu, which became a centre of learning and a trade hub of exceptional cultural significance, as well as large mosques of which some were still standing 700 years later. After his death, his kingdom and wealth faded away, however, because his successors were unable to fend off a civil war and invading conquerors. Advanced trade routes and trade links were therefore already well established in the north of Africa centuries ago.

In the south of the continent there were likewise signs of sophisticated economic activities, as evidenced especially by the ruins of Great Zimbabwe and the remains of the hilltop city of Mapungubwe in Limpopo in South Africa. Scholars believe that from about AD 1200 to AD 1300 Mapungubwe (Hill of the Jackal) was the centre of a kingdom that traded gold and ivory with China, India and Egypt. One of the artefacts found at the site, a golden figurine of a rhinoceros, shows that the inhabitants were smelting gold hundreds of years ago.

As for the ruins of the city of Great Zimbabwe, the majority of archeologists are of the view that the most significant settlement took place there between AD 1200 and AD 1500. Though there is still some uncertainty about who erected the stone structures, there is now reasonable consensus that the builders were Shona speakers, and that they traded gold, among other commodities, with foreign traders. The famous soapstone sculpture of the Zimbabwe Bird that was found in the ruins appears on the national flag of modern-day Zimbabwe.

The inhabitants of both Mapungubwe and Great Zimbabwe eventually abandoned these sites and moved away, most likely as a result of climate change that made it harder to grow crops and feed animals.

South Africa's first capitalist

Bartering and communal farming were prevalent in South Africa before the first Europeans settled at the Cape in 1652 on the arrival of Jan van Riebeeck, commander of the Dutch East India Company (the Vereenigde Oost-Indische Compagnie, or VOC), to establish a maritime replenishment service. The VOC was in effect the world's first stock exchange in that shares were issued to the general public. For almost two centuries, the VOC, which was also the world's first limited-liability company, paid out highly profitable dividends. The trading ships' voyages to the East were in fact an early process of globalisation.

The demand for fresh meat, vegetables and water was the original reason for the integration of the Cape of Storms, later renamed the Cape of Good Hope, into the trade route between the East and the West. On the long voyages between Europe and the East, the strategic location of the Cape settlement founded by Van Riebeeck provided a stopover during which ships replenished their stocks of fresh water and supplies.

Although the Cape sea route was one of the world's most vital trade routes up to the opening of the Suez Canal in 1869, South Africa was by 1870 still predominantly an agricultural country, with only 20 towns that had more than 1 000 residents. From about 1681, several butchers ran their own businesses under the VOC administration, which allowed free burghers to farm.

In fact, South Africa's first capitalist was a butcher: Henning Hüsing (sometimes spelled Huising or Huisen), who became the richest man at the Cape.

Hüsing, who had come to the Cape from Hamburg as an ordinary soldier, first worked as a farm *knecht* (foreman) and cattle herder after receiving his military discharge. By 1678, he had started raising cattle in the Hottentots-Holland Mountains as a free burgher. As heemraad (member of the local governing board) of Stellenbosch, he concluded a contract with the VOC to supply the local hospital and visiting ships with meat, and subsequently obtained, together with his partner, the meat contract for the garrison.

He supported Adam Tas in the burgher revolt against Governor Willem Adriaan van der Stel in 1706 and was arrested as one of the conspirators. After the VOC authorities in Amsterdam ruled in favour of the settlers, Hüsing settled on his farm Meerlust, the later showpiece farm of eight generations of Myburghs, where he had 100 000 vines.

The inventories of deceased estates of other farmers at the Cape, especially in the period of the Dutch occupation until 1806, attest to a society that was much more affluent than some historians have believed. Their lifestyles were so ostentatious that in 1755 Governor Ryk Tulbagh imported the so-called sumptuary laws from Batavia to the Cape of Good Hope to restrict extravagance ('splendour and pomp') among Company officials and burghers.

Although there were indeed destitute farmers, particularly among the frontier farmers, Professor Johan Fourie of Stellenbosch University, in an analysis of 2 500 probate inventories of the assets of farmers, compared those who produced for the market with residents of parts of England, the Netherlands and the Chesapeake region in North America. In the 18th century these Cape farmers, who established the Cape Dutch style of architecture, among other things, not only owned more sheep and cattle than their counterparts in the above regions but also possessed books and paintings.

Besides demonstrating a notable cultural heritage, this evidence serves as an important rebuttal of views about the supposed backwardness of Afrikaners who could devise the racist apartheid policy of the 20th century. An example of such views is provided by Allister Sparks, who wrote: '[T]he mind of the Afrikaner was shaped during the six generations they were lost in Africa: a people who missed the momentous developments of eighteenth-century Europe, the age of reason in which liberalism and democracy were born and which had its climax in the great revolution of the French bourgeoisie; a people who spent that time instead in a deep solitude which, if anything, took them back to an even more elementary existence than the seventeenth-century Europe their forebears had left; a people who became, surely, the simplest and most backward fragment of Western civilization in modern times.'

Like many other English-speaking historians, Sparks probably did not have sufficient access to historical sources written in Dutch, which is the oldest written language in South Africa. Along with such gross generalisations, he also failed to note that a British colonial governor, Sir Theophilus Shepstone, is considered the architect of segregation in South Africa. There were similar racial views in other countries too, and the segregation policy in the United States persisted until the second half of the 20th century.

Cape farmers cultivated their land to meet their own needs and those of the passing maritime traffic. Because they obtained the guarantee under British occupation that their rights and privileges would be recognised and that private landownership would be respected, they sold more and more products to visiting ships. The economy, which was basically agrarian but which retained features of a subsistence economy and bartering, became fully transformed only once diamonds were discovered in 1867 and gold in 1886. Prior to the discovery of diamonds, 94 per cent of the exports had comprised agricultural and animal husbandry products.

Following the British occupation of the Cape in 1806, business and politics in the Cape Colony were initially dominated by English speakers until the Afrikanerbond of Onze Jan Hofmeyr started making an impact. At that stage the entrepreneurs who founded sophisticated industries and financial companies were mainly of British and East European Jewish origin, whereas Afrikaners in the Boland focused on wine and wheat farming.

The diamond- and gold-mining industries were likewise controlled by mining magnates who were mostly of British and East European Jewish origin. Some of the best-known Jewish tycoons were George Albu, Barney Barnato, Alfred Beit, Solly and Woolf Joel, Sammy Marks, Harry Mosenthal, Lionel Philips and Ernest Oppenheimer. Cecil John Rhodes was the most prominent Englishman, followed by Abe Bailey, JB Robinson, Thomas Cullinan and the American John Hays Hammond. Collectively they became known as the Randlords, in part because quite a few of them were awarded hereditary baronetcies by the British government.

Towards the end of the 19th century, however, widespread poverty increased among Afrikaners. The rinderpest of 1896 that decimated cattle herds was followed by the disastrous Anglo-Boer War and the British 'scorched earth' policy that left tens of thousands of Afrikaners destitute. Hamstrung by a lack of professional skills and shut out of the industrialisation process, large numbers were forced into dependence on charity.

Early entrepreneurs: Jannie Marais and Sir David Graaff

One eminent Afrikaner did make a fortune from diamonds: Jannie Marais from Stellenbosch, who with his brothers owned a large number of diggings in and around Kimberley.

In 1870, Johannes Henoch Marais, commonly known as Jannie,

and three of his brothers along with other relatives set out for the alluvial diamond diggings on the banks of the Harts and the Vaal rivers. They toiled day and night, digging and sorting diamonds. They kept buying additional claims until they eventually had to oursource work at Dutoitspan, Bultfontein, De Beers and Kimberley.

Marais Brothers became a well-known concern, with their work-force increasing in time to twenty supervisors and a great many temporary manual labourers. Jannie was the planner among the brothers, the one who had to solve the problems. He was inventive, too: the man who built the pontoon over the river at Gong Gong and launched the first boat. His brother Pieter was the public figure and organiser, while Christian, the financial guru, was in charge of diamond sales.

Mining became increasingly expensive, and only those with suf-ficient capital could make a living from it. By the end of the decade, the realisation dawned that the only solution lay in consolidation of the claims, a process on which the Marais brothers had already embarked in 1877. In 1880, all the Marais claims, except for 190 belonging to Christian Marais, were consolidated in the Kimber-ley Central Mining Company. The brothers owned 40 of the 1 490 shares in the company. According to a map from 1882, the company owned a significant portion of the Kimberley Mine that had become known worldwide as the Big Hole.

Following further mergers, fierce competition erupted between Barney Barnato and Cecil John Rhodes. Rhodes ultimately persuaded Barnato to merge his interests in Kimberley Central with De Beers in 1889. This ensured that Rhodes, who in 1890 also became prime minister of the Cape Colony, acquired a diamond monopoly that was to make him the richest man in the British Empire. The Marais brothers were opposed to the merger but were unable to prevent it. Though they retained their stake in De Beers they became resolute opponents of Rhodes, so much so that they subsequently ranged themselves with the Afrikanerbond of Onze Jan Hofmeyr and the National Party.

Jannie Marais returned to Stellenbosch in 1891. He and his brother Frikkie bought the farm Coetzenburg, today the university's sports grounds, from their mother. Later he bought Frikkie out and put 90 morgen of Coetzenburg under cultivation with fruit orchards and vines, added a dairy of his own, and a wine cellar in which wine was aged in wooden barrels and sold in bulk.

Marais entered the wine industry when he co-founded the Lions Distillery on the Vlottenburg estate with Bruckner de Villiers. He was also the director and majority shareholder of the Riebeeck Mineraalwatermaatskappy and owner of the Shepherds Jam Factory, which provided employment to a hundred people. Besides making money from farming and companies, he owned several properties in the town on top of his lucrative diamonds interests.

He was the wealthiest client of the Stellenbosch District Bank, of which he became a director in 1906. In time, he became the bank's biggest shareholder by constantly buying up new shares.

Marais, who gained renown as a major benefactor of Stellenbosch and the Afrikaners, was elected MP for Stellenbosch in 1910 as a member of General Louis Botha's South African Party (SAP). In 1915, he made a decisive contribution to the founding of *De Burger*, later known as *Die Burger*, which was launched as an 'independent Christian-National daily paper'. He is equally renowned as the person who made the founding of Stellenbosch University possible in 1918, with an exceedingly generous donation of £100 000 on condition that Dutch (Afrikaans) would occupy 'no lesser place' than English at the institution – in other words, equal status for the two languages.

An Afrikaner contemporary of Jannie Marais was Sir David Graaff, who became known as the pioneer of cold storage in South Africa. As in the case of Marais, his entrepreneurship differed considerably from that of the mining magnates who made their fortunes from the country's mineral riches.

David Pieter de Villiers Graaff was born in 1859. As an eleven-year-old herdboy with little schooling and from a poor family on a farm in Villiersdorp, he left for Cape Town to start working at the butchery of a relative, Jacobus Arnoldus Combrinck. He showed an exceptional brain for business from an early age, and was only eighteen when he took over the management of Combrinck & Co.

Graaff extended his innovations in the field of refrigeration and new developments in the meat industry with a countrywide distribution network for frozen products, inter alia by means of refrigerated railroad trucks he personally bought for transport on the growing South African rail network. When meat was in short supply in South Africa after the rinderpest of 1896, he was able to supply the market with imported meat. Large-scale refrigeration of meat, fruit and other products, hitherto undreamt of in the country of his birth, made him a fortune. During the Anglo-Boer War, Graaff's South African Cold Storage Company, which developed out of Combrinck & Co, supplied meat to the British troops as well as to the people in the interior and the concentration camps.

Graaff, who became a member of the first cabinet after Unification in 1910, was a confidant of the Boer generals Louis Botha and Jan Smuts, the first two premiers of the Union of South Africa.

As entrepreneur, Graaff did not limit himself to South Africa, but expanded his business interests internationally to Europe, South America and to South Africa's neighbouring countries. After the Anglo-Boer War, his meat interests were merged with the Imperial Cold Storage Company (ICS), a company originally begun by Rhodes in opposition to him. Graaff had remained a major shareholder in ICS, of which he regained full control in the 1920s.

At the end of World War 1, Graaff was instrumental in the transfer of the German diamond interests in South West Africa (Namibia) to Consolidated Diamond Mines, the diamond company of which he was a director, with Sir Ernest Oppenheimer as managing director. The transaction enabled Oppenheimer to take over the later world-famous De Beers in 1929. Graaff resigned as chair of ICS on account of his deteriorating health in 1928, but at the time of his death in 1931 he was regarded as the wealthiest man in the Cape Colony.

Afrikaner poverty and the Helpmekaar movement

Although Graaff and the Marais brothers were affluent people in the Cape Colony, most Afrikaners had been hit hard by the Anglo-Boer War. A great number of Afrikaners had been left destitute after the war, also in the Cape Colony where the colonial government disenfranchised the rebels who had fought on the side of the Boer republics. The destruction wreaked in the two Boer republics (the

Orange Free State and Transvaal) in the course of the three-year war spilled over the borders, with the northern and eastern Cape Colony particularly affected.

The concentration camps, in which a great many black people had been interned as well, were the primary cause of the bitterness that prevailed after the war – even more so than the British chief commander Lord Roberts's 'scorched earth' policy, as a result of which some 30 000 farmhouses were burnt down, large numbers of cattle herds and other farm animals were killed, and food supplies in the vicinity of farmsteads were destroyed. Of the 27 927 Boer civilians who died in the camps, the overwhelming majority (26 251) were women and children.

According to Professor Jan Sadie's calculations, the consequences of the destructive war were that 70 per cent of the Afrikaners' assets were destroyed. Large-scale urbanisation was the only option for impoverished Afrikaners, but urbanisation did not offer a way out of poverty. In the cities and towns the migrants encountered an urban economy that was dominated by English-speaking South Africans and which had been ravaged by the depression and drought of the 1930s.

In his book *'n Volk Staan Op* ('A Nation Stands Up'), the journalist EP du Plessis summed up the situation as follows: 'While foreign entrepreneurs with superior technical and management knowledge amassed fortunes from South African gold and diamonds, the Afrikaner became a foreigner, and in many cases a struggling foreigner, in his own country. The urban, capitalistic structure born out of mining gained the upper hand over the Boer.'

As employers, Afrikaners could at this stage for the most part hold their own in their traditional occupation of farming; in the cities to which hundreds had migrated, they were mainly employees in the predominantly English and often unsympathetic business sector. A sense of inferiority was exacerbated by many English speakers' condescending attitude. The English elite showed little empathy for the distress of poor Afrikaners and very little understanding of the deeper nature of the trauma their compatriots had experienced.

Sir Carruthers Beattie, vice chancellor of the University of Cape Town, was for instance quoted by the writer ME Rothman (MER) as casually telling a public meeting that 'poor whites' were 'intellectually backward' and that 'something inherent in the Afrikaners' was the reason why the phenomenon of poverty was taking on such alarming dimensions in their case. The Carnegie Commission on the Poor White Problem in South Africa, however, found in 1932 that the intelligence levels of the poor whites were on a par with those of the rest of the population. According to the commission's statistics, some 300 000 out of a white population of 1 800 000 could be classified as poor whites. The Stellenbosch economist Professor CGW Schumann calculated that the per capita income of Afrikaners in 1936 averaged £86, as opposed to the £142 of other South African whites. The English speakers' advantage was considerable.

In ethnically divided societies there is a tendency that people do not compete individually but as members of groups. Hence a headstart in the inter-group economic competition is exceptionally valuable, being the key ingredient of the politics of empowerment. Sadie illustrates this with a striking example in his study *The Fall and Rise of the Afrikaner in the South African Economy*. An English-speaking businessman who from 1900 onwards was in a position to invest £1 000 annually at a rate of return of 12,5 per cent would have been £3 241 000 strong by 1950.

Sadie adds: 'He would have been that much ahead of an Afrikaner starting a venture in the latter year, and he would, in all probability, have been able to finance maximum education and training opportunities for his descendants, affording them a headstart over contemporary Afrikaner generations.'

South Africa's remarkable economic development in the 20th century was nonetheless initially mainly due to English-speaking entrepreneurs who had immigrated to South Africa and had made the country their home. Michael O'Dowd describes how these English speakers brought with them all the competencies required for industrial development – from financial and business expertise to the skills of mineworkers, artisans and railway workers. This gave rise to an indigenous body of entrepreneurs, the most important asset a country can have. The entrepreneurs were instrumental in ensuring that, like the United States, South Africa did not remain an exploited colony that lapsed into underdevelopment under governments that nationalised industries or sought to control them.

After Unification in 1910, when the former four South African colonies were unified as provinces in the Union of South Africa, Afrikaner empowerment gained momentum when the Helpmekaar movement was established in 1916 in the aftermath of the Rebellion of 1914–15. (The name of this mutual aid movement means 'help one another').

Following the outbreak of World War 1, about 11 000 rebels had revolted against Louis Botha's government's decision to invade the German-controlled South West Africa at the behest of Britain, the recent adversary in the Anglo-Boer War. The rebels, who were poorly organised, had looted shops and commandeered cattle. After their defeat, many faced financial ruin on account of claims and fines for damages that had been imposed on them.

The Helpmekaar movement set up branches in all four provinces with the aim of raising funds to pay the claims and fines. The fundraising campaign gathered steam after JE de Villiers of Paarl, who became known as Oom Japie Helpmekaar, promised in a letter to the newly established *De Burger* to donate £500 provided that 500 other people each contributed £100. After enough funds had been collected to settle the rebels' debt, the surplus of £92 000 was divided among the provincial associations to be used for study loans.

The historian Anton Ehlers describes the Helpmekaar movement, which has continued to provide study loans for tertiary education to this day, as an important enabler in Afrikaners' upliftment and their sense of self-esteem and respectability – an early contributor that helped pave the way for 'the eventual creation of a substantial Afrikaner middle class that came into its own, especially from the 1960s onwards'. The Helpmekaar movement was therefore a catalyst in the economic upliftment of Afrikaners.

Moreover, the fund's financial success story – in itself an indication that there was also a significant number of affluent Afrikaners who had compassion with their compatriots and a sense of responsibility towards them – had a positive influence on Afrikaners' stance towards the financial and business world. An economic inferiority complex to which the poor white problem had contributed was alleviated by the success of the Helpmekaar movement. In addition, the Helpmekaar

Study Fund played a significant role in promoting education and training – a further incentive for parents to have their children educated.

The formation in 1915 of De Nationale Pers, Beperkt (later Naspers), the parent company of the oldest Afrikaans-language daily, *Die Burger*, arose from the upsurge of Afrikaner nationalism that was sparked by the Helpmekaar movement. Its great success in mobilising Afrikaner capital – spearheaded by moneyed, nationalist-minded Afrikaners in the western Cape to advance the interests of the wider Afrikaner community – was also the inspiration for the establishment of the insurance companies Suid-Afrikaanse Nasionale Trust en Assuransie Maatskappy (Santam) and the Suid-Afrikaanse Nasionale Lewens Assuransie Maatskappy (Sanlam) in 1918. In the same year, the Ko-operatiewe Wijnbouersvereniging (Cooperative Wine Farmers Society, KWV) was founded, and the Victoria College achieved full university status as the University of Stellenbosch, the oldest Afrikaans university. This was also the year of the *Groot Griep* (the deadly 1918 Spanish flu pandemic) and the birth year of the undertaker Avbob (Afrikaanse Verbond Begrafnis Onderneming Beperk), which buried hundreds of victims of the pandemic. A century later, all of these institutions were still in existence.

In the arduous post-World War 1 process of building initially modest enterprises that would grow into giants, two businessmen stood out: Willie Hofmeyr of Nasionale Pers and Tienie Louw of Sanlam. Through their hard work, dedication and perseverance in the face of fierce competition and scant resources, these trailblazers set an example for subsequent success stories.

WA Hofmeyr

William Angus Hofmeyr, a clergyman's son from Montagu, was simultaneously the first chair of Nasionale Pers, Sanlam and Santam. Having practised law in Johannesburg before the outbreak of the Anglo-Boer War, he joined the Boer commandos and returned to Cape Town after the war, where he became a partner in the later well-known legal firm of Bissett and Hofmeyr. As a result of family connections with Onze Jan Hofmeyr and Professor NJ Hofmeyr, as well as his friendship with a group of idealistic 'Victorians', he ventured into business and politics as well.

He assumed a leading role in the establishment of Nasionale Pers and was elected the company's first chair. In 1915, he persuaded the later prime minister Dr DF Malan to leave the ministry and his congregation in Graaff-Reinet to become the first editor of *De Burger*, later renamed *Die Burger*. Willie Hofmeyr was actively involved in setting up the Cape Helpmekaar, whose cause was, in turn, strongly promoted by Malan and his paper, which had become increasingly influential in South African politics.

Hofmeyr was initially also party secretary of the Cape National Party, but his mounting interest in business activities continued to expand. Besides chairing the board of Nasionale Pers, he became the first chair of Santam and Sanlam to boot.

He often related that his uncle, Professor Nicolaas Hofmeyr of the Stellenbosch Theological Seminary, had told him the Afrikaans language would receive recognition only once it acquired commercial value. Hence his focus on the Afrikaans-speaking community for whom opportunities were beckoning in the insurance industry, trust affairs and financial services. Hofmeyr stated that an Afrikaner selling Sanlam's insurance policies in Afrikaans to other Afrikaners was in fact engaged in a cultural mission. He considered it a mission that carried more weight than all the political speeches delivered in the country.

As a man of culture, Hofmeyr was co-founder and first secretary of the Afrikaanse Taalvereniging (Afrikaans Language Society) and a co-founder of the Zuid-Afrikaanse Akademie voor Taal, Letteren en Kunste (now the Suid-Afrikaanse Akademie vir Wetenskap en Kuns, South African Academy for Science and Art) as well as of Hoërskool Jan van Riebeeck in Cape Town. He became a senator in 1929 and was active in politics throughout his career, though operating in the inner circles rather than in the limelight.

He was attached to Sanlam and Nasionale Pers in various capacities until his death in 1953 at the age of 84. When the University of Stellenbosch conferred an honorary doctorate on him in 1947, it was stated that Hofmeyr could lay claim to the title of leader of the first economic upsurge among Afrikaans speakers.

MS (Tienie) Louw

The Ladismith-born Dr Marthinus Smuts Louw was also the son of a clergyman. He was the first Afrikaner to qualify as an actuary and, together with Hofmeyr, he achieved success in business.

In 1907, Tienie Louw obtained a BA Honours degree with a major in physics at the then Victoria College. Having worked as a schoolteacher before being appointed at Sanlam on the founding of the new company in 1918, he qualified as actuary in Edinburgh, Scotland, in 1921.

In 1927, he was appointed general manager and actuary of Sanlam, which had opened its doors with capital of just £25 000. Louw recognised that if something were to be done towards the economic upliftment of his people, it had to happen through the mustering of own resources that lay frozen in building societies, trust chambers and insurance companies. More productive employment of these interest-bearing assets would offer job opportunities to young people in commerce and industry.

Under his leadership, Sanlam, of which he later became managing director, was at the cutting edge of product development in the long-term insurance market. Engaging in product innovation since the early 1920s with the aim of increasing its market share, Sanlam followed strategies that established it firmly in the market that had traditionally been dominated by British companies. While the manifestly marginalised position of the Afrikaans segment of the population presented Sanlam with an opportunity, its strategic business plan was also inclusive to the extent that in time the company gained the confidence of non-Afrikaans speakers. The competitive advantage that Sanlam acquired laid the foundation for subsequent expansion and diversification.

Louw campaigned tirelessly for Afrikaans to enjoy its rightful share in the commercial world as well. Santam's and Sanlam's documents were available in both official languages, while the companies also endeavoured to shed an exclusively Cape image by appointing directors from other provinces. Furthermore, one of Sanlam's first steps was the appointment of coloured agents to recruit customers in the coloured community.

The establishment of a solid staff structure was rooted in the heart of the Afrikaner nation, but English speakers had been welcomed at the company from the start-up years. The company's motto *'Uit die volk gebore om die volk te dien'* ('Born from the Afrikaner nation to serve the Afrikaner nation') could therefore readily be reformulated as: 'Principally, but not wholly, born from the Afrikaner nation to serve the South African nation.'

In the course of his long business career, Louw was associated with various large Afrikaner organisations, in some cases as chair and in others as a director – including Sanlam, Bonuskor, the Industrial Development Corporation (IDC), Sasol, Saambou Building Society, and others. He died in 1979.

His namesake, CR Louw, Sanlam's second chair, served uninterruptedly as a director of the company from 1918 to 1966 – the last thirteen years as chair – besides also serving as a director of Nasionale Pers for many years. His goal with Sanlam was to provide his *volk* with a foothold in the economy.

Having grown into giants among South African insurers, both Sanlam and Santam would in time also embark on extensive empowerment initiatives in which black South Africans started playing a major role. Under the leadership of Johan van Zyl, Sanlam was at the time of its centenary in 2018 a diversified international financial services group with a footprint in 36 countries.

HH van Rooijen

Hendrikus Hermanus van Rooijen, the first chief executive of Avbob, was a founder member of the Afrikaanse Verbond (Afrikaans Alliance) that established the AV Spaar en Voorskot Kas during the Spanish flu pandemic of 1918 to assist members financially in the event of the death of a loved one. Estimates for deaths globally during that year vary between 20 and 50 million; in South Africa, the death toll is believed to have been about 350 000.

In these dismal conditions the Dutch-born Van Rooijen, a partially blind teacher from Bloemfontein who was involved in various church and charitable organisations, became convinced that every human being was entitled to a dignified funeral. Three years later, the AV took over a struggling funeral parlour in Bloemfontein and founded a limited-liability company called the Afrikaanse Verbond Begrafnis Onderneming Beperk (Avbob).

Van Rooijen was appointed managing director of Avbob in 1922. His approach was to put people first; the money would follow. As a mutual-benefit society, the firm gradually came to offer a full service from death to burial, a free funeral with coffins, hearses, wreaths and other accessories, as well as a cash payout for other necessities.

Prior to Van Rooijen's death in 1952, Avbob became the first Afrikaans organisation to sell funeral policies to all racial groups from 1947 onwards. The first coloured representatives were appointed in 1952.

Avbob's first state funeral dates back to 1922: that of the Boer general Christiaan de Wet, who had been a co-founder of the Afrikaanse Verbond along with the Reverend JD Kestell (also known as Father Kestell) and the Reverend Willem Postma. Since then, Avbob has been involved in the state funeral of every South African head of state or head of government. In 2013, Avbob was the official undertaker at the funeral of former president Nelson Mandela, and a year later the company also conducted the funeral of the 98-year-old Epainette (MaMbusi) Mbeki, the mother of former president Thabo Mbeki. By this time nearly 96 per cent of Avbob's policyholders were black South Africans.

Unlike insurance companies, Avbob has not chosen to demutualise and offer shares to policyholders. Profits, including those from investments, are transferred to policyholders instead. On the occasion of Avbob's centenary celebrations in 2018, when its net asset value stood at R17 billion, the chief executive, Frik Rademan, announced the allocation of R3,5 billion to policyholders as a fifth special bonus.

A nation rescues itself

Prior to the outbreak of World War 2, the progress of the Afrikaner businesspeople had been slow and laborious. At the same time there was mounting concern about the large number of impoverished and demoralised Afrikaners, coupled with the realisation among the business elite that they dare not leave this underclass to their fate. The effects of the Great Depression that continued into 1933, and the consequences of a severe drought, were aggravated by General JBM Hertzog's government's refusal to abandon the gold standard. The crisis was so grave that Hertzog and Smuts merged their political parties in 1933 and formed the United Party as government.

The Carnegie Corporation in New York funded a comprehensive investigation into the poor white question. The 1932 report found that poor whites numbered 300 000, which amounted to 17 per cent of the white population.

The result was a landmark initiative, the *Eerste Ekonomiese Volkskongres* (First National Economic Congress) of 1939, where the appeal of the esteemed Reverend JD Kestell for the economic upliftment of the Afrikaners resounded: *''n Volk red homself'* ('a nation rescues itself'). The congress resolved to follow the free-market approach by mobilising capital for an Afrikaner finance house, managed by Sanlam, to pave the way for Afrikaner investment in business enterprises. The intellectuals spearheading the economic struggle advocated a variant of capitalism that became known as *'volkskapitalisme'* (national capitalism). As Professor LJ (Wicus) du Plessis put it, the new economic movement had as its aim 'no longer to tolerate the Afrikaner nation being devastated in an effort to adapt itself to a foreign capitalist system, but to mobilise the nation to conquer this foreign system by transforming it and adapting it to our national character'.

Two influential thinkers, Sanlam's Tienie Louw and Professor CGW Schumann, founder of the University of Stellenbosch's commerce faculty, advocated the school of thought that cash-rich enterprises be supported to strengthen the position of the Afrikaner in commerce and industry. Nevertheless, there was much support for a quota approach after the National Party assumed power in 1948, as revealed by an unpublished study by Stellenbosch historian Ernst Stals on the history of the Afrikaner Broederbond. 'Broederbond' means 'league of brothers'. A decisive meeting was that of the Broederbond's *Bondsraad* in 1956, where it became clear that the most prominent Afrikaner business leaders (who were also members of the Broederbond) were opposed to a quota system favouring Afrikaner enterprises. Andreas Wassenaar from Sanlam warned that the

Afrikaners' own misconceptions about their economic problems were the major obstacle. Stals's study shows convincingly that the Broeder-bond was surprisingly ineffective in its efforts to either coordinate or manipulate the Afrikaner's advancement in business.

Tienie Louw, a founder member and later chair of the Economic Institute of the Federasie van Afrikaanse Kultuurvereniginge ('Feder-ation of Afrikaans Cultural Associations', often referred to simply as the FAK), was appointed the first president of the Afrikaanse Handels-instituut (AHI, Afrikaans Institute of Commerce), the mouthpiece of organised Afrikaans business that was registered in 1943 as a non-profit organisation. A liaison committee was set up between the AHI and the Kamer van Koophandel (Chamber of Commerce) to coordinate joint action in matters of common interest.

Louw was later chair of Federale Volksbeleggings ('Federal National Investments', shortened to FVB), an investment house founded as a direct outcome of the 1939 congress for the purpose of mobilising Afrikaner capital. By the end of World War 2, the FVB had substantial investments in the fishing industry, wood, steel, chemicals and agricultural implements.

The accelerated mobilisation of Afrikaner capital following the *Volkskongres* was accompanied by an active policy of secondary in-dustrialisation where the state took the lead, as in the development of the Iron and Steel Corporation of South Africa (Iscor), the Elec-tricity Supply Commission (Escom), South African Coal and Oil Company (Sasol) and the Phosphate Mining Corporation (Foskor). Michael O'Dowd writes about these parastatals: 'The primary credit [for the policy of state-backed projects] belongs to the Afrikaners, and it was in effect opposed by many, if not all, English-speaking South Africans.'

The pioneering figure who laid the foundation for the country's expanding industrial development was Dr Hendrik van der Bijl, an electrical engineer who had returned to Pretoria from the United States in 1920 to establish Escom (later Eskom) and Iscor. He was able to realise his ideal of supplying inexpensive electricity and steel as the basis for industrial development.

Another Afrikaner who created empowerment and job opportu-nities for Afrikaners in parastatals in the early 20th century was the chemical engineer Dr Hendrik van Eck. Under his chairmanship of the IDC, important state-backed institutions such as Sasol, Foskor, the shipping entity Safmarine and the aluminium smelter Alusaf were established and financed.

Other leading figures who were involved in parastatals that contributed to the country's economic development were people such as Frikkie Meyer (Iscor), who, as chair of the council of the University of Pretoria, established the first business school in the world after that of Harvard University, GSJ Kuschke (IDC), SM Naudé (Council for Scientific and Industrial Research, CSIR), David de Villiers, Joe Stegmann and Paul Kruger (Sasol), AM Jacobs, JJ Hattingh and John Maree (Eskom).

The first significant entry of an Afrikaner into the gold-mining industry took place in the 1930s. This pioneer, WB (Willem) Boshoff from Krugersdorp, was an entrepreneur who bought up worked-out mines and mined gold using methods more economical than the conventional ones. He also reclaimed gold from mine dumps, and probably became the first Afrikaner millionaire in the gold-mining sector.

As a result of the calls for economic mobilisation in the 1940s, many new enterprises in the private sector sprung up among Afrikaners, most of which failed. In Johannesburg alone some fifty such fledgling ventures folded.

Ultimately, out of the initiatives of those years two private-sector enterprises in particular were to grow and flourish. The one was Anton Rupert's Rembrandt Group, which developed out of the tobacco company Voorbrand. The other was Veka, subsequently known as Veka/Bertish, a clothing manufacturing company established by Albert Wessels. Wessels, later the founder of Toyota South Africa, would make a fortune in the automotive industry.

Elsewhere in the private sector other prominent names emerged in time: Albert Marais (Nasionale Bouvereniging), Frikkie Neethling (Brown & Neethling), Piet Badenhorst (United Group/National Building Society), George Huysamer (a stockbroker), Jan S Marais (Trust Bank), Jan Pickard (Picardi), Gerrie van Zyl (fisheries and various companies) and Phil Morkel (Morkel Group).

Anton Rupert

Doctor Anton Rupert was the foremost figure who entered the private sector with great success after the *Volkskongres* of 1939. He grew up as a Karoo child in Graaff-Reinet where, during the Great Depression, the annual income of his father, an attorney, dropped from £3 000 to £120, and the family automobile had to stand idle in the garage for several years. After abandoning his original plan to study medicine because the costs were too high, he obtained a master's degree in chemistry at the University of Pretoria (UP). What had attracted to him to UP was his desire to study in Afrikaans.

Rupert's first enterprise was a dry-cleaning business in Pretoria with three partners before he joined the small-business section of the Reddingsdaadbond. 'Reddingsdaad' means 'act of rescue'. This organisation, which was an outcome of the *Volkskongres*, dispensed funds to suitable Afrikaner applicants who wanted to venture into business. His experience as a child of the Depression led him to conclude that an entrepreneur keen on entering the business world should sell products that were depression proof, notably tobacco and liquor. In 1941, an opportunity arose to take over an insolvent tobacco company in Johannesburg, which soon led to his next important step in business: the establishment of the Voorbrand Tabakmaatskappy.

Voorbrand, which Rupert started with only £10 that he could personally contribute and two loans of £2 500 each received from the FVB and Kopersbond (a big wholesale concern), was established at a time when the South African business world was dominated by English speakers. Ninety per cent of the tobacco industry was controlled by the giant United Tobacco Company. In trade, industry, finance and mining, the turnover of Afrikaner enterprises made up only 5 per cent of the total in 1938–39; in industry, a mere 3 per cent. The few established Afrikaans companies included the insurance companies Sanlam and Santam, the media companies Nasionale Pers (later Naspers) in the south and Voortrekkerpers (later Perskor) in the north, the undertaker Avbob, and Volkskas, the first Afrikaans commercial bank, founded in 1934.

War-time quota allocations and import restrictions that prohibited the importation of cigarette machines severely inhibited the expansion of Voorbrand, which initially could focus only on pipe tobacco while cigarettes were the big money-spinner. The underperformance of Voorbrand made Rupert realise at an early stage of his career that he would have to diversify. In this he exhibited a typical trait of entrepreneurs: they are restless people who embrace experimentation and are never wedded to a specific industry.

He then launched a small investment company, Tegniese en Industriële Beleggings (TIB, Technical and Industrial Investments), which would become his vehicle for gaining access to the liquor industry. From 1943 on, TIB would expand and become the parent company of the later Rembrandt Group after Rupert moved to Stellenbosch.

The only way to enter the liquor industry was to buy a Cape company, Forrer Brothers. Rupert, who had acquired a 50 per cent interest in Forrer Brothers, crisscrossed the Boland in his little car to sell TIB shares to the more established, wealthier wine and export-grape farmers in the western Cape, who were to become the mainstay of his business empire. 'I showed them a few labels for wine bottles and sold them my idea. I sold them a dream,' he said afterwards. This enabled him to establish Distillers Corporation, which was registered on 11 June 1945 – the first Afrikaans company to be listed on the Johannesburg Stock Exchange.

In 1948, he started a cigarette factory in Paarl, but was faced with the problem that the war-time quota system for cigarette tobacco was reimposed by the new National Party (NP) government. Established manufacturers benefited, while the restrictions prevented new entrants from competing on a level playing field. Hence Rupert, who throughout his career received few favours from the government, launched a protest against the quota system, which outraged the NP government. He even threatened to send female employees in Voortrekker dresses to demonstrate outside Parliament with posters reading: 'Quotas are killing us!' The quota system was subsequently ameliorated. Voorbrand would be absorbed in the Rembrandt Tabakvervaardigingskorporasie van Suid-Afrika (Rembrandt Tobacco Manufacturing Corporation of South Africa), the name that Rupert chose for his expanding business empire inspired by the famous Dutch painter.

At the time of the listing of Distillers there was a second event besides the Depression that would fundamentally shape Rupert's worldview. It was the world's first war-time nuclear explosion: the atom bomb that destroyed Hiroshima on 6 August 1945. 'I realised that the human race had become like scorpions in a bottle, with the power to destroy one another totally,' he stated. In future, he realised, humanity could save itself only through coexistence: 'People simply have to learn to live together.'

Coexistence subsequently became the core concept that was to inspire Rupert all his life, the vision with which he developed his business philosophy of co-partnership. On this philosophy of coexistence, or partnerships forged from country to country, he built a global business chain long before globalisation became a buzzword in the 21st century.

In his view, a business enterprise had a three-pronged responsibility: to its employees, to its shareholders, and to society. When he was later asked about his involvement in Lesotho to which he sent 'flying doctors', among other initiatives, he replied: 'In southern Africa you cannot escape being your brother's keeper; we cannot sleep peacefully if our neighbour has no food.' Years after his death these words would still reverberate.

Aware of the fact that a price war could damage his group, Rupert decided to extend his operations abroad in order to build up profitable new markets. During his first overseas trip in 1945 he had met Sidney Rothman, head of the celebrated tobacco house Rothmans of Pall Mall, in London. He would later take over this group, and succeeded with the takeover bid thanks to a loan granted to him by the Afrikaans companies Volkskas and Sanlam and their subsidiaries after he had addressed Sanlam's board as an outsider. Rupert was exceedingly proud of what had been achieved with Rothmans.

'We built that business – a great achievement, but we South Africans built it,' he declared in a lecture to commerce students of the University of Pretoria in 1972. 'Today .... we are the biggest exporters of cigarettes in the world. Young South Africans did the groundwork, the planning, and the product design, and it was done at Stellenbosch.'

An appreciation of the need for diversification prompted Anton Rupert to enter the luxury-goods market as well. The acquisition of a controlling stake in Cartier – 'the jeweller of kings and the king of jewellers' – along with Rothmans laid the foundation for the consolidation of Rembrandt's international interests under the umbrella of Richemont, the second-largest luxury-goods group in the world (after LVMH, the French multinational corporation).

Rupert experienced political pressure from both the left and the right. The ANC launched a boycott campaign targeting Rembrandt's products, while the Verwoerd government thwarted his plans to set up factories in the Transkei and to start a factory in partnership with coloured people at Dal Josafat in Paarl. In 1963, he also elicited antagonism from both the government and some in the business sector when he sent shockwaves through the country by introducing a minimum wage of R2 per day, besides fringe benefits, for all of Rembrandt's workers. Another of his innovations was the establishment of the first South African company owned and set up entirely by women: Eerste Nasionale Tee- en Koffiefabrieke Beperk (First National Tea and Coffee Factories Limited), which manufactured products such as Braganza Tea and Senator Coffee.

Although Rupert generally kept a low profile, especially because of the threat of sanctions against South Africa in the apartheid years, he nevertheless acquired a reputation in the media as the 'king of luxury', the 'secretive marketing giant', the 'shy king of snob smokers' and the 'true gentleman of the business world'. He was linked to some of the most prestigious international trademarks, a terrain he concentrated on. In the building and protection of trademarks, he focused in the finest detail on the advertising and packaging of products, including the colour, typeface and 'feel' of labels – so much so that he was described as the 'oracle of trademarks'.

His perfectionistic attention to branding and marketing went hand in hand with a great emphasis on distribution. This was due to a lesson learnt as a student during the 1938 centenary celebrations of the Great Trek when thousands of unsold copies of a jubilee newspaper published by him had to be burnt because of poor distribution. He made sure that his sales organisation and distribution network functioned smoothly so that products would be available in time and in sufficient quantities at retail outlets.

While Rupert always kept aloof from party politics, he did not neglect to give an account of himself when it came to politics. In a letter to President PW Botha dated 24 January 1986, he expressed his concern that Botha was not prepared to renounce apartheid – 'that word for which we have been crucified'. Rupert said he believed apartheid jeopardised the survival of white people. He directed an impassioned personal appeal to Botha: 'Reaffirm your rejection of apartheid. It is crucifying us, it is destroying our language [Afrikaans], it is degrading a once heroic nation to be the lepers of the world. Remove the burden of the curse of a crime against humanity from the backs of our children and their children.'

Botha responded negatively, but Rupert's thinking increasingly resonated with other Afrikaners and formed the breeding ground for FW de Klerk's speech on 2 February 1990 in which he announced the unbanning of the liberation movements and outlined a vision for a wholly new South Africa.

For several years now, the Ruperts have appeared on the *Forbes* business magazine's list of the world's 500 richest people, the billion-aires with estimated assets of more than one billion American dollars. Besides the Ruperts, *Forbes* has for many years listed only one other family from Africa: the Oppenheimers, the heirs of the South African mining magnate Sir Ernest Oppenheimer, his son Harry and his grand-son Nicky.

To many among the succeeding generations of Afrikaner busi-nesspeople, Anton Rupert, who died in 2006, was a role model par excellence. The poet Dirk Opperman described him as the 'Prince of Commerce', someone who reconciled commerce, science and the arts in his activities. Rupert illustrated what could be achieved if one was prepared to stand on one's own feet and work hard. Above all, he inculcated the notion that businesspeople have a responsibility to-wards the communities they serve – an idea that has gained ground in the 21st century as the global success of the free market showed that unfettered capitalism without a social conscience was detrimental to humanity.

Albert Wessels

Rupert's contemporaries included Albert Wessels, who would become a heavyweight in the South African economy with Toyota vehicles.

Wessels, a farmboy from Dealesville in the Free State, initially set his sights on becoming a clergyman. When his parents could no longer afford his study costs during the depression years, he accepted a position at the Bank van die OVS Onderwysersvereniging (The Bank of the Orange Free State Teachers' Union, later Sasbank). The process of Afrikaner urbanisation was in full swing as a result of the drought of the 1930s. Wessels moved to Johannesburg to start a correspondence college with two partners, and later gained a BCom degree.

Wessels, who married the poet Elisabeth Eybers in 1937, found only three sizeable Afrikaner enterprises in the business hub of Johannesburg on his arrival in the city that same year. In 1940, Sasbank offered him the position of manager of the Volkshemde- en Klerefabriek (Veka). Veka, which manufactured men's clothing and school uniforms, soon had a large turnover.

Not all Wessels's business ventures were successful; a construction company he owned with a partner ran into financial difficulties because of insufficient control over the artisans. For two long years they battled to repay that debt, he related.

In time, he became keen to diversify out of the clothing trade. On a visit to Japan to acquire textiles for women's clothing, he negotiated with the motor vehicle manufacturer Toyota. In 1961, he obtained a permit from the government to import ten Toyota bakkies. These ten Toyopet Stouts heralded the start of the astounding success story of Toyota South Africa, which soon dominated the market for commercial vehicles. A year later, 30 Toyota dealers sold 384 vehicles, and in 1963 the first Toyota shares were sold to the public.

By 1968, Toyota – which was chosen as Company of the Year by the financial press that year – had become Africa's largest producer of commercial vehicles. Before long, the Japanese agreed to allow Wessels to produce the vehicles under licence in South Africa. The Wessels family held their interests under the umbrella of Wesco (which listed on the Johannesburg Stock Exchange in 1971) and Metair. A new assembly plant, Motor Assemblies, was built in Prospecton near Durban at a cost of R15 million. Greatly impressed by the Japanese's devotion to their work, Wessels strove to emulate them by putting productivity on a par with quality.

The company gradually produced more models than just commercial vehicles. When the Corolla series was launched in South Africa in 1975, Toyota's combined sales came to 250 000. The

Corolla, probably the global motor industry's biggest success story, with more than 45 million vehicles sold worldwide since 1966, became the jewel in Wessels's crown. More than a million Corollas were sold in South Africa before the Hilux bakkie and the Fortuner sport utility vehicle became Toyota's mainstays.

By 1980, Toyota was the South African market leader in the automotive industry. A reputation for quality and reliability was encapsulated in a slogan devised by a later chief executive with a knack for advertising, Colin Adcock: 'Toyota – everything keeps going right'.

Wessels and Eybers divorced in 1961, and he died in 1991. His daughter Elisabeth Bradley, a businesswoman in her own right, was regarded the richest woman in South Africa when she sold Wesco's last remaining shares (a 25 per cent stake) in Toyota SA back to the Japanese parent company in 2008.

The advertising luminary Len van Zyl, at one time the executive chair of the country's largest advertising agency, came to know Albert Wessels and Anton Rupert well, particularly as far as image building was concerned. He says both men always put the company and the brand first. The person behind the company and brand was secondary. He believes this to be the reason why Marius Jooste of Perskor and later Louis Luyt, as well as Jan Marais of Trust Bank, were less successful: they emphasised personality over business.

Van Zyl considers Rupert and Wessels to have been true gentlemen who acted honourably and put a premium on loyalty. Wessels, for instance, retained the horse on Toyota's logo until his son took over from him. Both businessmen kept their companies out of party politics: Wessels because of the sensitive political relationship with Japan (Japanese people were classified as 'honorary whites' in South Africa), and Rupert on account of opposition to the apartheid regime.

Renier van Rooyen

The first Afrikaner entrepreneur to make a major breakthrough in the retail clothing industry was Renier van Rooyen, the founder of Pep Stores, the forerunner of Pepkor, the biggest retail clothing group in Africa.

Van Rooyen grew up in poverty in the Northern Cape town of Kenhardt. As the top academic achiever in his class at school, he was encouraged by his headmaster to pursue tertiary studies.

His first job was that of a clerk at the office of the Receiver of Revenue in Kuruman. With the help of a loan of £250 from a farmer from Kuruman, he enrolled at the University of Stellenboch in 1950, but realised after three months that the BA course was not for him. Van Rooyen was then re-employed in the office of the Receiver of Revenue, this time in Upington. He also worked as secretary of a tungsten mine and as a messenger of the court, where his experiences with debtors and repossessions gave him insight into the dangers of buying and selling on credit. In time, he established a private book-keeping firm and an agency for agricultural supplies.

In 1955, he took over a general dealership in Upington in partnership with an attorney, Gawie Esterhuyzen. Here Van Rooyen was initiated into the secrets of the retail trade. He received much help from a seasoned coloured shop assistant, Piet Strauss, whose knowledge, salesmanship, competence and tact in dealing with their clients – mainly poor coloured people – proved to be a major asset to the 23-year-old rookie entrepreneur. Strauss would become his right-hand man.

Van Rooyen soon grasped that he should focus on clothing – by selling it efficiently and profitably at a lower price than any other store. His motto was: 'We don't sell cheap clothing, we sell clothing cheaply.' He believed that poor people were not stupid; they wanted to buy quality clothes and cared about their appearance. He obtained supplies by driving down to Cape Town on the gravel road once or twice a month, loading up the car with clothing and returning on the same day.

A year later, he bought out Esterhuyzen's stake and established a private company, Bargain Stores Pty Ltd. Further expansions followed, including a store called Upington Volksklere, managed by his wife, Alice, while he also increased the workforce by appointing other family members. After merging the two stores under a new name, BG Bazaars, in 1960, he expanded to Kuruman, Beaufort West and De Aar.

One of Van Rooyen's innovations was that he allowed customers to select and try on clothing and shoes. Everyone could use the same dressing rooms – in defiance of the then apartheid policy. This was the start of Van Rooyen's clashes with the NP government, while he also battled local authorities to obtain trading licences. He often criticised the apartheid policy at a time when few business leaders did. In 1973, for example, he stressed the need for all measures that 'harmed the dignity of black and brown people' to be scrapped.

By 1965, his enterprise had made such strides that he founded a new company: Pep Stores, the precursor of Pepkor. The first Pep Store opened in De Aar in that year, and the number of stores increased to ten. Van Rooyen insisted that employees take up shares in the company, thereby ensuring their commitment in that they were effectively working for themselves.

With a view to further expansion, Van Rooyen and his family moved to Cape Town a year later, and a new head office and warehouse were opened in Kuils River in 1967. In that year, Christo Wiese, a cousin of Van Rooyen's wife who used to work in the Upington store during his holidays, joined Pep Stores as company secretary and second-in-command. When Pep listed on the JSE in 1972, Van Rooyen appointed a young accountant, Whitey Basson, as financial director. In 1979, he entrusted Basson with the responsibility of taking over eight stores from Shoprite. In his later capacity as CEO, Basson would also take over OK Bazaars and Checkers and build Shoprite into a giant among grocery retailers.

Van Rooyen stepped down shortly before his 50th birthday in 1981. He felt he needed a break from business and the associated pressure, as he had not allowed himself to take any time off. Save for 200 000 shares, he sold his stake in Pep for R7 million to Christo Wiese, who became the new chair. Van Rooyen stayed on as a director for a while.

By 1981, a quarter of a century after Van Rooyen's humble beginnings in a small store with a single employee in Upington, Pep Stores had grown into a retail colossus with 500 stores, 10 factories, 12 000 employees and a turnover of close to R300 million. His credo was: faith, positive thinking, hard work, enthusiasm and compassion. 'You must select a market, know the product you are selling, and you must believe in what you are doing. You must be single-minded and prepared to work day and night. In other words, you must eat, sleep and drink your business,' Van Rooyen explained.

After emigrating in 1985, Van Rooyen and his wife spent ten years in Portugal and England. In 1996, he returned to his home country 'to help build the new South Africa'. In November 2018 he died at the age of 86 at a retirement home in Durbanville.

Louis Luyt

Another poor boy from the Karoo became a fertiliser tycoon who once ranked among Johannesburg's richest residents. The Britstown-born Louis Luyt, who started his career as a railway clerk, excelled at rugby and eventually captained the Free State rugby team. Aided by his rugby connections, he achieved a breakthrough in the business world and made a fortune with Triomf Kunsmis, the company he founded to sell fertiliser to farmers countrywide.

Luyt also ventured into the beer market, which was dominated by SA Breweries (SAB). Anton Rupert, who regarded Luyt as one of the few true Afrikaner entrepreneurs of that era, once obtained shares in Louis Luyt Breweries, but the differences between the two unlikely partners proved too big. There was no 'chemistry' between the courteous, sophisticated Rupert and Luyt, who described himself as a beer-drinking street fighter. They parted ways and Rupert sold his beer interests to SAB.

Luyt often became embroiled in controversy, for instance when – as a central figure in the Information Scandal under John Vorster's administration – he agreed to start an English-language daily, *The Citizen*, into which state funds were funnelled. He emerged relatively unscathed from the scandal, and afterwards even met with the banned ANC leaders outside the country.

As president of the South African Rugby Union, he hosted the 1995 World Cup tournament won by François Pienaar's Springboks. A subsequent court case, which stemmed from an inquiry into racism and nepotism in rugby, took an unpleasant turn when Luyt summoned then president Mandela to testify in court. Luyt later entered politics by founding his own party but made little headway, and ultimately joined the Freedom Front of the Mulder brothers. He died in 2013.

Hard-earned success

The economic advance of Afrikaners in the first three decades after the 1939 *Volkskongres* was attributed by some liberal and radical historians to state patronage extended to Afrikaner business by the NP government, while Afrikaner historians took the view that the Afrikaners had pulled themselves up by their own bootstraps.

According to Stellenbosch professor of economics Jan Sadie's calculations, by 1954, at a time when Afrikaners made up 58 per cent of the electorate, they controlled only 1 per cent of the mining sector, 6 per cent of manufacturing and construction, and 10 per cent of the financial sector – not much more than in the case of black South Africans today.

It goes without saying that the state assisted white-owned businesses on a large scale, but with a few relatively minor exceptions there is little evidence that the state deliberately favoured Afrikaner firms. In the early 1960s, however, the Verwoerd government did take the northern Afrikaans press companies under its wing in an inappropriate manner, at the expense of Naspers and other publishers with, for instance, printing contracts for telephone directories.

During the 1960s, the South African economy was characterised by boom years from which both English and Afrikaans entrepreneurs benefited. A massive capital outflow in the aftermath of the Sharpeville massacre on 21 March 1960 was soon followed by unprecedented economic growth after the Pan Africanist Congress (PAC) and the ANC were banned by the Verwoerd government and Nelson Mandela and his co-accused in the Rivonia Trial were jailed. The economy recovered rapidly, money streamed into the country and, with an average growth rate of 6 per cent, South Africa fared better than almost all Western countries during the rest of the 1960s. Thanks to improved education, there was a trend among Afrikaners away from unskilled or semi-skilled labour to skilled and better remunerated positions.

A new class of financial and industrial capitalists emerged, such as CR Louw of Sanlam and Santam, CH Brink of Federale Volksbeleggings and Jan S Marais, a flamboyant banker who, with Trust Bank, created a new image of banking. Trust Bank in particular was emblematic of the new entrepreneurial spirit. Clients were greeted by young tellers and attactive receptionists with beehive hairdos instead of the traditional stiff, conservative banking officials. Within a decade, the bank with its brisk, modern appearance expanded quickly and by 1964 had 50 branches, more than 2 000 employees and assets in excess of R200 million.

One of the academics who imputed political motives to the advance of Afrikaners in business, Dan O'Meara, was parrotted by a number of other authors and English journalists. In his book *Volkskapitalisme* (National capitalism), O'Meara presented a rigid class analysis to prove collusion between Afrikaner capital and the Afrikaner working class in order to secure political power. The economic and business historian Grietjie Verhoef, however, regards this view as a 'distorted ideology-driven perspective'. She points out that O'Meara never consulted any primary company archives but instead served up material from secondary sources that fitted into his class-based analysis of the dominance of capitalists.

In an internal memorandum of the Rembrandt Group, Anton Rupert's partner Dirk Hertzog denied that the group donated money to either the NP or the HNP (the Reunited National Party of the 1940s). In fact, in 1959 Rupert placed countrywide advertisements declaring that Rembrandt was not under any government control and practised no discrimination. Hertzog also responded to O'Meara's allegation that the group's Broederbond connection 'was vitally important to the early development of Rembrandt'. He rejected as 'nonsense' the notion that Rembrandt had been founded by the Broederbond.

Another much-discussed case of alleged favours to Afrikaner businesspeople related to the mining sector, where Gencor came under Afrikaner control. The historian Hermann Giliomee notes that in the academic literature and in the English press it was often alleged that Afrikaners owed their major economic breakthrough in the 1960s to the goodwill of Harry Oppenheimer, who headed the Anglo American Corporation. He had supposedly allowed the sale of the Anglo-controlled mining house General Mining to the Sanlam-controlled company Federale Mynbou 'at a fraction of its value'.

In response to inquiries from Giliomee, two Anglo directors, Michael O'Dowd and Michael Spencer, together with business historian Grietjie Verhoef, dismissed this version as a fabrication. Not only was General Mining sold at a market-related price but Oppenheimer also secured an important concession: that Sanlam not proceed with the development of its diamond interests. Anglo's ulterior motive was that Oppenheimer wanted to protect his interest in De Beers, the progenitor of the diamond industry. After all, De Beers had a virtual monopoly in the diamond market as a result of its sole control of worldwide marketing through the Central Selling Organisation.

In fact, it is hard to find any example of English companies that advantaged Afrikaner competitors. While Giliomee was working on his book *The Afrikaners*, a remark made to him by Anton Rupert, who often expressed his aversion to English superciliousness in private, had set Giliomee thinking. He asked Rupert if he knew of any Afrikaans company that had been 'empowered' by an English company. His reply was: 'I cannot think of any, and I am very grateful for that.'

The statement alerted Giliomee to the value a business giant like Rupert attached to the fact that Afrikaner companies had to achieve success without state or English support. It was the only route through which Afrikaners would gain recognition for their economic achievements from the English business elite.

This was confirmed by Albert Wessels, who wrote: 'I felt I had to succeed in order to show my fellow Afrikaners that we could become the equals of our English-speaking fellow citizens. Only on the basis of hard-earned economic success could a sense of equality between the two white communities be created.'

For the generation of post-1994 Afrikaner businesspeople, these successful pioneers served as lodestars: leaders who exemplified what could be achieved with a spirit of enterprise, gumption, ingenuity and perseverance. After the democratic transition, however, the emphasis on the Afrikaans market would gradually fade away as the new generation spread their wings more widely and shifted their focus to the largest possible diverse market, locally as well as internationally.

2

Ten cents become billions

Koos Bekker

IN THE 21ST CENTURY, the most spectacular growth of a South African company since the exploitation of the country's mineral wealth came from a media company. A century after Naspers was born in 1915, out of the distress of Afrikaners in the wake of the devastating Anglo-Boer War (1899–1902), the company had repositioned itself to such a degree in the technological era that it dominated the Johannesburg Stock Exchange with more than 20 per cent of the total market capitalisation.

In hindsight, many observers found it hard to believe that such an enterprise would become the country's first trillion-rand company and Africa's leading media group. The extraordinary feat was brought about by a young entrepreneur, Koos Bekker, who transformed Naspers from a media company into a global investment giant. He made a fortune in the process, becoming one of the five richest people in South Africa. In 2020, he appeared as number 11 on the *Forbes* list of Africa's dollar billionaires with a net worth of $2,5 billion, or close to R42 billion.

Jacobus Petrus Bekker, who prefers being called Koos, was born and went to school in the Gauteng town of Heidelberg. He was headboy at the local Hoër Volkskool. His father, Cor Bekker, was in the intelligence business, serving as a high-ranking official in the Department of National Security (later renamed the National Intelligence Service) under the National Party (NP) government. Cor had previously been a lecturer at the Teachers' Training College in Heidelberg and also owned a cattle and maize farm in the district. Koos's mother was an Afrikaans teacher.

Cor Bekker's boss at National Intelligence, Dr Niël Barnard, describes him in his memoirs as 'a man with gravitas and a strong personality'. Barnard, who was very closely involved in the secret talks with the ANC prior to 1994, sums up the influence of Bekker, his deputy director-general, as follows: 'He is a progressive thinker who, as time went by, came to play a significant role in making me think along the lines of a new and strategic solution for the country's political problems.'

The young Koos Bekker studied law and literature at Stellenbosch, where he was editor of the student paper *Die Matie*. After completing his LLB degree at the University of the Witwatersrand, he obtained an MBA at Columbia University in New York in the 1980s. The topic he researched for a project paper in the United States was pay television, an industry that was in its infancy at the time. Shortly after graduating, he approached Ton Vosloo, managing director of Naspers, with a proposal for developing a pay-television venture in South Africa. Bekker believed he had a solution to the print media's struggle against the SABC's television monopoly that deprived newspapers of advertising revenue.

Vosloo agreed. He appointed Bekker as his personal assistant with a confidential mission, a budget of R50 000 and an office with a secretary in Johannesburg. Over the next three decades, they would work together very closely – with Bekker embarking on a variety of initiatives, and Vosloo backing him strongly as chair of the board.

In 1985, the 32-year-old Bekker joined a company with an organisational culture he considered himself to be 'slightly to the left' of. Nationale Pers, Beperkt, which was later renamed as Naspers at Bekker's insistence, had been founded in 1915. The group's flagship paper *Die Burger* had been described in its first editorial as a 'child of

sorrow and of hope'. Its mission at inception had been to help mobilise a demoralised Afrikaner nation that had been crushed by British
imperialism a decade before.

In the 1980s, Naspers was the leading Afrikaans media company, with subsidiaries and publishing houses distributing newspapers,
magazines and books countrywide. Despite its dominant position in
the limited Afrikaans-language market, Naspers was compelled to
spread its wings wider since the print media were increasingly under
pressure in a changing media landscape that needed new strategies.

Vosloo initially sought an Afrikaans partner for the new pay-
television venture Bekker wanted to launch but had no luck. He
wanted to approach Anton Rupert, who was unwell at the time
and, on medical advice, virtually inaccessible. Vosloo asked Rupert's
brother Koos to take the matter to Anton. Though Anton regarded
the project an excellent business opportunity, he had reservations. He
believed M-Net would be strongly focused on entertainment, while
he was more concerned about job creation. He suggested that Vosloo
approach other press groups instead.

Pay television, which would also mean competition for the
state-controlled South African Broadcasting Corporation (SABC),
required government approval. Vosloo started lobbying members of
the government with a view to obtaining a licence. He knew that
President PW Botha, in spite of his frequent attacks on the press, was
an avid newspaper reader. So Vosloo's strategy was to spell out clearly
how SABC TV, which benefited from advertising revenue that was
lured away from the print media, was choking newspapers to death.

What they were requesting was not a state subsidy, Vosloo explained, but merely the right to compete. 'As a result, daily papers
could have a future: not only those that supported the government,
but from across the political spectrum. In this way, one would keep
the country's broad democratic conversation alive,' he wrote.

Vosloo's idea also found acceptance with foreign affairs minister
Pik Botha, who was in charge of the SABC. The SABC was opposed
to the proposal, but Pik welcomed the initiative as a fresh influence
on the media landscape that would keep the SABC on its toes. He
advocated the idea that all daily papers in the country be included in
a consortium.

Negotiations with the other press groups were successful. The requisite licence, subject to a string of conditions, was eventually awarded to the consortium. Among other restrictions, they were prohibited from broadcasting news. The new pay-television service was called M-Net, an abbreviation for Electronic Media Network, and was listed on the JSE. Naspers, with a stake of 26 per cent, obtained management control. The other shareholders were the old Argus group (now Independent Media), Times Media (since then Tiso Blackstar, later Arena Holdings) and the unbundled Perskor, each with a 23 per cent stake, as well as the smaller *Natal Witness* from Pietermaritzburg and the *Daily Dispatch* from East London.

In 1986, M-Net was one of the first two pay-television operators outside the United States. In time, its services would expand to Supersport and then MultiChoice. Later, the group entered markets in the rest of Africa.

The television licence in South Africa was granted only to daily papers, not to Sunday papers or magazines. 'Our standpoint was that daily papers were vitally important to the discourse in the country. They had a watchdog function, encouraged open conversation and endeavoured to open doors. They were the oxygen of public life: indeed, this is still the case. The success of M-Net meant a huge financial boost for all our partners and shareholders,' Vosloo wrote in his memoirs. Years later, the promise to keep newspapers alive would resurface when the envisaged unbundling and listing of MultiChoice was announced in 2018.

A year after the establishment of M-Net, Naspers donated R150 000 to the NP for its election campaign. A further donation of R220 000 followed in 1989. On that occasion, Vosloo wrote in a letter to the NP's national leader, FW de Klerk: 'We trust that the donation will help to defray expenses and put the NP on the path to a solid victory in the general election.'

When asked to comment on the donations in 2017, Vosloo replied that the historical connection between the two entities was well documented. 'Naspers, like other business enterprises, from time to time made donations to the NP on request. Since the advent of full democracy in South Africa in 1994 Naspers has made donations to various political parties, including the ANC, on condition that donations go to parties that subscribe to the Constitution and are represented in Parliament.'

M-Net and a joint venture with the Ruperts

From the outset, Bekker made his own style felt in the new enterprise. At M-Net's head office, the dress code was informal, there were no parking bays reserved for management, and no colour or gender discrimination was tolerated. Everyone had to call the managing director 'Koos', not 'Mr Bekker'. He was intent on appointing young people, and also continuously endeavoured to attract young talent.

In its start-up years, M-Net also launched the cellphone group MTN in collaboration with partners that included Telkom and Nail.

Vosloo views the establishment of M-Net as the biggest and most radical initiative in the history of Nasionale Pers up to that point. In this regard, he refers to a quotation from Professor Lizette Rabe's 'Naspers 100: Chronicle of a company, its people, its country and its world' (a manuscript commissioned by Naspers in celebration of the company's 2015 centenary and which has, controversially, remained unpublished). She writes that the founding of M-Net 'can be regarded as the actual quantum leap at the end of Nasionale Pers's seventh decade. With that, Naspers launched itself from a print-media company into the electronic age, and thereby amassed enough financial muscle to enable it to ride the wave with the advent of the digital age.'

The group expanded to Europe in 1991 with the acquisition of the struggling pay-television operator FilmNet. The deal was made possible by means of a joint venture with Richemont, the Ruperts' international luxury-goods group. The collaboration came to an end when the business was sold to Canal Plus in France in 1997.

There were allegations later that the joint venture had soured relations between Bekker and Vosloo on the one side and the Ruperts on the other. Bekker denies this: 'I have a lot of respect for the Ruperts, both father and son.'

He points out that M-Net and Canal Plus were 'early movers' as the first two pay-television experiments outside the US. 'By 1991 we wanted to spread our wings wider. FilmNet, an ailing pay-TV company in Europe, was for sale.' With M-Net unable to take any money out of the country due to exchange control regulations, Bekker approached Anton Rupert about starting a joint venture. Eventually they entered into a 50/50 partnership with Richemont, with Johann Rupert as chair of the joint company, Nethold.

'For five years we worked together very well, and the cooperation produced billions of rands for both companies,' Bekker recounts. 'The alleged dispute was about the sale of Nethold. By 1996, there were two offers on the table: one was a generous bid from DirecTV in the US to inject $1 billion into Nethold for a one-third stake. But this scared the bejesus out of the French, and out of fear for American entry into "their" European TV market, they offered us as much as $2,2 billion to buy Nethold. It was a very rich price, probably too much.'

Bekker had earlier been impressed by DirecTV, which had launched digital television technology in America. This gave rise to his decision to switch MultiChoice from analogue to digital at a very early stage. The multiple benefits of digital proved to be a winning recipe, also against the SABC, which remained stuck in analogue.

A contract with DirecTV was ready for signing, but when Bekker and his team arrived in America with Johann Rupert, the latter raised serious objections to the contract. He detected a perceived threat in the fine print and crossed swords with DirecTV's CEO, John C Malone, a dollar billionaire who had overtaken CNN's Ted Turner as the biggest landowner in the US. After the deadlock, Rupert told the board of MultiChoice International Holdings (MIH, the new holding company for M-Net and MultiChoice) that he had a better option: an offer from the French TV group that was almost too good to be true, as Bekker also indicates.

Rupert maintained afterwards that he had spared Naspers huge embarrassment by selling Nethold to the French. It was even whispered from the Rupert camp that Naspers had been saved from bankruptcy.

According to Bekker, they could take two views: continue to expand the Nethold business with American money, or cash in. Some Naspers directors preferred the former route, and Richemont the latter. 'Looking back today, I have no regrets that in the end the collective decision was to cash in. In that way, we realised a huge profit, and for the first time got our own dollars to invest in the internet. Of course, Richemont made just as much.'

MultiChoice is established and Naspers lists

In 1993, Hans Hawinkels was appointed at M-Net, which had just become profitable. The business was subsequently split in two. Hawinkels became chief executive officer of the newly established MultiChoice. M-Net, with Cobus Stofberg as chief executive, concentrated on subscriber management and signal distribution, while MultiChoice would offer a variety of channels that catered for entertainment, sport, lifestyle topics, movies and music.

'MultiChoice was Koos's idea; he had the vision also of digital television, going forward. So, initially, the objective of MultiChoice was to go and expand our interests in Africa,' Hawinkels relates. After a gradual start, their expansion drive into Africa proceeded increasingly successfully as they branched out from Namibia and Botswana to elsewhere in Africa.

Bekker and Stofberg, who was also chief executive of the holding company MIH, moved to Amsterdam with a view to international expansion, particularly in Europe. MIH was only the second company in the world to launch digital satellite television after the Hughes Corporation in the United States.

Hawinkels was excited about their competitive advantage: 'It was fantastic. Koos had magic vision, it was really great. But we were always looking at doing deals … because Koos was a very entrepreneurial guy, and that's the mindset I had as well.'

Bekker used a colourful image to describe their entrepreneurial approach: 'We throw spaghetti at the ceiling and see what sticks.'

From Amsterdam there were rapid expansions under the leadership of Bekker and Stofberg, to the other Benelux countries, Central Europe, Italy and elsewhere. Bekker returned to South Africa after the deal with Canal Plus. He asked Hawinkels, who had helped launch DStv with its multiple channels and options in digital format successfully in South Africa and elsewhere in Africa, whether he'd be willing to be transferred to Hong Kong in order to exploit pay-television opportunities in Asian markets.

M-Net was an important factor in the listing of Naspers in 1994. The broker Mof Terreblanche, an ardent campaigner for the listing, was among the investment experts who advised Vosloo. He had previously been involved in the listing of both Richemont and Medi-clinic. One of the corporate experts who was subsequently involved in the spadework, Murray Louw, devised the entrenched-control structure through which fears that the group could fall prey to hostile takeovers were allayed.

On 12 September 1994, Naspers listed on the JSE with an open-ing price of R17,50. Even small shareholders who did not sell too soon would in time make a small fortune.

Although Naspers was doing well with pay television at the time, other affordable investment opportunities in the sector were thin on the ground. A few investments were made in print media, but most of those lost the group money, notably Abril in Brazil. The advent of television, and then of the internet and social media in the late 1990s and early 2000s, negatively impacted the revenue sources of newspapers and magazines in particular – in short, all the mainstays on which Naspers had built its success in the past. Falling advertising revenue and plunging circulation figures had become a threat to their survival. Globally, similar media companies were all in decline.

As a result, from the beginning of the 2000s, Naspers concentrated increasingly on the internet and e-commerce.

At the end of 1997, Bekker succeeded Vosloo, who became the Naspers chair, as managing director. Bekker, who had already made a small fortune at MIH, said he would take no salary or benefits but wanted to be paid in shares. His contract stipulated that he could be summarily dismissed without a golden handshake if he failed to deliver.

Vosloo agreed to this arrangement and awarded him a generous number of share options for his first five-year contract. The exact number is not known, as it was not disclosed in Naspers's annual report. For the second of his three five-year contracts in 2002, Bekker received 4,2 million Naspers shares at between R22 and R29 each. For the third contract in 2008 he was given considerably more: 11,6 mil-lion shares at between R141 and R185, hence about 3 per cent of the company's issued shares.

By March 2014 he held 16,38 million Naspers shares. During Bekker's seventeen-year stint as managing director, the market capital-isation had increased from about $600 million to $45 billion. In 2015, before taking over the chairmanship, he reportedly sold 70 per cent of his Naspers shares, which yielded an estimated R30 billion.

In a country where major companies often draw flak for exorbitant executive remuneration packages, Bekker is in a league of his own.

After taking over as managing director, Bekker took the lead in buying out other press groups in M-Net/MultiChoice, inter alia in exchange for Naspers's shares in the cellphone company MTN. The decision not to continue with the cellphone licence was taken despite the view that cellphones were a cash cow with champion status: a business with a regular monthly revenue stream.

According to Bekker, the decision was motivated by the fact that Naspers did not control any of the electronic businesses when he became CEO at the end of 1997. There was simply not sufficient capital for both the television and the cellphone industry. Naspers had a small minority stake of about 10 per cent in MTN, which in time expanded into Africa and internationally.

Although MultiChoice started the business, it had to take on partners along the way, explains Bekker, who regarded cellphones as a 'mono product'. On the other hand, they had a 26 per cent stake in M-Net/MultiChoice. 'Steve Pacak (financial director) and I recommended to the Naspers board that since we would never be able to afford a majority in MTN, we sell that stake and use the proceeds to acquire a majority of M-Net/MultiChoice. Today the maths shows that we were fortunate.'

Bekker came in for much criticism about his decision at the time, but Ton Vosloo reckons he had the last laugh later: 'Thanks to digitisation, the DStv service could connect with cellphones, laptops and tablets – so, today, the cellphone companies are major rivals of the DStv offering in its various forms and industries worldwide.'

Spaghetti against the Chinese wall

Bekker had long harboured a desire to enter the vast Asian markets, especially China with its population of 1 300 million. He and other senior executives of Naspers visited China in the late 1980s. But after the 1989 massacre on Tiananmen Square in Beijing, with its ironically named Gate of Heavenly Peace, where Chinese troops mowed down hundreds of demonstrators, there was huge uncertainty and concern about investments in China.

The Tiananmen Square massacre was the most sensational outrage against the Chinese population since Mao Zedong's disastrous rule. Historians estimate that Mao's 'Great Leap Forward', a campaign aimed at catching up with the economies of Western countries, led to the death of up to 40 million Chinese due to starvation, executions, torture and forced labour. Bekker maintained, however, that in recorded history China had more often been the leading economy than any Western country, and predicted that the historical pattern would recur.

This would eventually lead to Naspers's best investment in the electronic era: a one-half stake in the Chinese communications company Tencent. The investment flowed from Bekker's strategy to unlock and exploit the commercial potential of the nascent telecommunications and information technology purposefully and with enormous drive.

The market capitalisation of the Chinese internet giant, in which Naspers still had a one-third stake in 2019, had risen to $525 billion in March 2018 when Tencent's massive customer base exceeded 1 000 million subscribers for the first time. By then, the group's messaging platform WeChat, known as Weixin in China, had become that country's dominant social media app for messages and other functions. Tencent had become the Cullinan Diamond among Naspers's crown jewels, the basis on which the company, with its Cape Town head office, dominated the JSE with more than 20 per cent of the value of the entire local market.

The person who did the groundwork for the crucial deal with Tencent at the turn of the millennium was Hawinkels, who was appointed CEO of MIH in Asia in 1998. Hawinkels and his team embarked on expansions in Asia, looking for investment opportunities in pay televison as well as in the rapidly developing internet sphere. This was where the thrilling saga of the acquisition of Tencent would unfold.

In Hong Kong, MIH was approached by some Asian companies about digital satellite television with a view to using the group's Irdeto technology. One of these was IBC in Bangkok, which had successfully launched pay television in Thailand. Hawinkels negotiated with the IBC owner Thaksin Shinawatra and bought a 36 per cent stake in the company. A partnership was also entered into with a Chinese company called IDG Ventures as a minority shareholder to establish an internet service provider, 21 Vianet, in Beijing.

One day, Hawinkels received a call from 21 Vianet: they also had a stake in Tencent, whose executive team was unhappy about their other partner, PCCW, a company in Hong Kong. Each partner had a 25 per cent shareholding in Tencent. The team from 21 Vianet suggested that Hawinkels fly to Shenzhen to meet Tencent's chair, Pony Ma, and talk to him about a new deal. If PCCW could be persuaded to sell its shares to MIH, Tencent's founders would support the deal and IDG would likewise sell its stake to MIH.

Tencent had been founded by a small group of university friends in November 1998. Like the e-commerce company Alibaba and the internet company NetEase, Tencent was typical of the modern technology entrepreneurs with an emerging business model: a bunch of enterprising risk-takers who started small and hoped to strike gold.

Hawinkels departed for Shenzhen and started negotiating with the four founders of Tencent, who he came to know as Pony, Charles (Chen Yidan), Daniel (Xu Chenye) and Tony (Zhang Zhidong). Pony is Ma Huateng, a software developer and executive chair of Tencent. He is widely regarded as the main rival of the Alibaba founder Jack Ma, or Ma Yun.

Pony Ma could speak English, as could some of the three other Tencent founders.

The name 'Tencent' is connected with Pony Ma, whose nickname derives from the English translation of his surname, which means 'horse'. The pronunciation of one of the Chinese characters in his name sounds almost like 'Ten', while 'cent' is connected with his previous company, Runxun, where the 'xun' sound was converted into the English 'cent'.

Hawinkels recounts that he got on well with the founders and convinced them that MIH would be a good partner. They were working out of cramped offices in a ramshackle old building in Shenzhen and wanted another kind of partner, one that could back them properly. In other words, not like PCCW 'who were drip-feeding them capital, not getting anywhere, and giving them no direction, no leadership, nothing'.

After he informed IDG that the meeting had gone well, they recommended that he speak to PCCW, the business owned by Richard Li, son of the very wealthy Li Ka-Shing, a prominent property developer in Hong Kong. Hawinkels's discussion with Li resulted in months-long negotiations during which PCCW kept on asking what his business model was, why he wanted to buy 'this thing', and what he planned to do with it.

Tencent was actually regarded as a communications company, not a typical internet business. PCCW was reluctant to sell their shares, but Hawinkels kept pushing and prodding.

While Tencent had 22 million users who could communicate with each other thanks to its messaging service, it had no revenue. But Hawinkels was itching to take the gamble. After several failed attempts, he again phoned Mika Chung, the manager of PCCW with whom he had been negotiating. By this time, they knew each other well. 'He said, Hans, you've pestered me so much; this is the deal. The valuation [of Tencent] is $66 million; I'm not giving you any time to do due diligence; that's it, take it or leave it.'

Although Naspers's war chest was depleted by this time, Hawinkels relied on Bekker's backing. He was the only one among the top management who was keen to risk the bet after their past mistakes. After all, these were testing times for the technology industry. In the period from 2000 to 2002, internet-related companies declined dramatically after the dotcom bubble burst. Many companies went bankrupt and closed down – including some in which MIH had an interest – while a few, such as eBay and Amazon, rebounded and surpassed their initial highs.

To Naspers's entrepreneurs, the failures must have felt like spaghetti that had boiled over and landed on their faces. In a contribution to Ton Vosloo's memoirs, Charles St Leger Searle, later the CEO responsible for the group's listed internet assets, tells of the disastrous investments in China such as the Shanghai-based financial portal Eefoo and the internet sports portal Sportscn. Another failure was Maibowang, an internet connectivity service provider launched in 1998 that was brought to its knees by the tough competition from capable Chinese entrepreneurs with intimate knowledge of the local market. Losses of $46 million had to be written off. According to Searle, the string of doomed investments 'was a huge cost to the group in both financial and human terms'.

But the Chinese proverb that every crisis is also an opportunity proved true.

Hawinkels considers the acquisition of Tencent as having been decisive for the group: 'Koos backed me. It was a tough decision he had to make. He made that call; I have to give him credit for that. He persuaded Cobus (Stofberg) and Steve (Pacak). If he hadn't backed it, we would have been dead.'

Bekker negotiated a loan of $33 million (about R275 million at the time) with Absa, firstly to buy out the 25 per cent shares held by PCCW and then to acquire the other 25 per cent from IDG.

In September 2001, amid the turmoil and uncertainty caused by the dotcom crash, Naspers suddenly acquired a controlling stake of 50 per cent in a relatively obscure Chinese company that would blossom into one of the world's largest technology groups.

In an interview with Hanna Ziady of Moneyweb, Bekker spoke philosophically about this difficult period: 'People usually talk about their successes but, if you think about it, success doesn't teach you anything. All you learn is how smart you are and that doesn't take you anywhere. But if you fail you can actually improve yourself and the next time do it slightly better.'

When they went to China with their internet investments in 1997, their first three ventures all failed – 'not marginally, totally,' Bekker said. 'We lost all our money, which was $80 million, and we fired 150 people and closed the doors.

'Then we sat down and we said okay, why did we collapse in such a spectacular fashion? Well, number one, we had five Western managers. They don't work on Friday evenings or Saturdays like the Chinese, they cost three times as much as the Chinese, they were not as smart and so on and so on. So we analysed what we did and the next time we did exactly the opposite.

'So we said, instead of leading in China, let's follow, let's find smart entrepreneurs, local people who hardly speak English and let's follow them, support them with money, comment when they need a comment. Our biggest success actually in China was that we failed so early and so spectacularly and that caused a certain humility in us to change our policy. Had we succeeded with the first ventures we would have done what all Western companies do, and we probably would have got nowhere.'

At a certain point, Naspers's share price plummeted from a high of R100 to a mere R12. Profits fell from R3,3 billion in 2000 to a loss of R1,9 billion in 2002. For Bekker, these were tough times and he managed to get by only thanks to what he had earned at MIH.

After assuming the chairmanship of Naspers in 2015, Bekker reflected in an interview on his seventeen years as CEO when he received no salary and had to rely on his share options: 'I don't recommend it to everyone, because it's high risk.'

Hawinkels, who after the effective takeover of Tencent was still involved for the next six months with Pony Ma's management team working on a business plan to be presented to the Naspers board, became one of the casualties of these anxious times. In 2002, his tenure at MIH came to an abrupt end. 'My contract was not renewed, and Koos said: "Thank you very much, goodbye."'

A deeply upset Hawinkels believes that he 'was made the scapegoat for all the losses and kicked out'. He was not able to share in the benefits of the acquisition; there was no golden handshake, and he had to forfeit his Naspers shares. As Ton Vosloo put it in his memoirs, Hawinkels 'fell victim to Koos's guillotine. The affable, friendly Koos could be implacable once he had made up his mind about an individual or an issue. As this was a management matter, far away from Naspers and light years away from the giant that Tencent would become, the board did not ask many questions.'

Hawinkels returned to South Africa where he started his own venture and was also appointed non-executive director of Tiso Blackstar (formerly Times Media, a competitor of Naspers's Media24). Years later, he found himself on the same flight to China as Bekker. They started talking about apple cider, because Hawinkels was helping Distell with a cider project in China and Bekker also made cider on his farm in the English county of Somerset. 'So we had a good chat,' Hawinkels relates, 'and when we left the plane, we walked out together towards customs. I said to Koos: "You know, you were wrong; you know what has happened between then and now." And he didn't say a word.'

Hawinkels still feels that Bekker and the others gave him no credit for what he had achieved, and there was no discussion about it either. Nonetheless, he regards Bekker as a brilliant businessman who is adept at handling the regulatory requirements of governments: 'Koos was good at that; he manages the regulator. Even here [in South Africa], he was fantastic.'

Like Bekker, Cobus Stofberg and Steve Pacak became billionaires. On the 2018 *City Press* Wealth Index, Pacak was ranked 25th with a gross worth of R1,93 billion and Stofberg 34th with a gross worth of R1,3 billion.

Tencent and Naspers go from strength to strength

In the case of Tencent, the bones thrown by the goddess of fortune like an African sangoma had indeed fallen in the right places. Two years after Hawinkels's dismissal, on 16 June 2004, Tencent was listed on the Hong Kong Stock Exchange with an opening price of HK$4. By mid 2018, the share had grown spectacularly to a high of HK$470, and that after a subdivision at HK$600. The effective value of a Tencent share had therefore increased from HK$4 to more than HK$1 000 (about R1 700 per share).

Tencent became by far the best investment in the history of Naspers, the first share on the JSE to break through the R4 000 mark. Some analysts reckon that at one stage Tencent represented nearly 140 per cent of Naspers's value, which meant that all other Naspers subsidiaries were regarded as loss-makers.

Hawinkels was succeeded by Antonie Roux, who had become chief executive of M-Web, the company's internet service provider, before being transferred to Thailand to replace Hawinkels as chief executive of MIH. According to Ton Vosloo, Roux did 'stellar work' in Tencent on behalf of Naspers: 'Quarter after quarter, he would bedazzle the board with images of rising growth charts and mind-boggling predictions of future growth. The predictions were all realised.'

After the listing of Tencent, Roux received one of the biggest bonuses in the history of Naspers. He had been earmarked to succeed

Bekker as the new group CEO when Bekker would take over from Vosloo as chair, but died of pancreatic cancer in 2012. The succession plans were put on hold for a year until it was decided to appoint Bob van Dijk, a Dutch-born e-commerce specialist who had previously worked at eBay, as the new CEO.

Naspers had been under Afrikaner control for a hundred years, and Van Dijk was the first foreigner to head the group. On taking over the reins in 2014, he stressed that he aimed to retain Naspers's character 'as a group that can change and test new things before they become mainstream'. This was widely interpreted as adherence to the Bekker playbook: 'We will keep on throwing spaghetti at the ceiling,' newspaper headlines read when Van Dijk announced the company's annual financial results for the first time. In time, as more offshore expansions followed and more foreign than South African managers were appointed, people started calling the Naspers senior team Van Dijk's 'eBay B-team' in the corridors of the Media24 building (as the head office in Cape Town was renamed).

Bekker and Charles St Leger Searle became directors of Tencent. Bekker remained a member of the Tencent board, also during the two periods at Naspers during which he went on sabbaticals. Each time he had taken time off and travelled the world to explore new possibilities; to see whether 'the next big thing' would pop up somewhere. During his sabbatical leave he also sold some of his Naspers shares, in other words, within a timeslot where JSE rules did not require directors to disclose their share dealings. According to the company's 2016 annual report he still owned a total of 4 688 691 Naspers shares, which, according to Meloy Horn, head of investor relations at Naspers, made him one of the twenty largest shareholders in the group.

Tencent, one of China's largest internet companies, owns the country's most popular messaging app, WeChat, and is also the world's largest video games company. The services and products offered by its various subsidiaries include social networks, music, web portals, e-commerce, internet services, mobile games, payment systems, smartphones and multiplayer online games. In 2017, Tencent, the first Asian company to reach a market capitalisation of $500 billion, became the world's fifth-largest company when it overtook Facebook.

As a result of its investments, Naspers, now a global internet group and technology investor, operates in more than 120 countries and directly or indirectly employs almost 70 000 people. The board of directors, previously dominated by Afrikaans speakers, has undergone an identity change with English-speaking entrants as well as directors from China, Singapore, the United States, Brazil and the Philippines. On Vosloo's recommendation, the lingua franca of the board was changed to English in 2014.

Pony Ma has become the richest Asian entrepreneur. He was ranked 20th on *Forbes'* Rich List for 2019, with a net worth of $41,2 billion. In Tencent's 2016 annual report it was stated that he owned shares worth $29 billion in the company, which amounted to 8 per cent of Tencent's total shares. The shareholdings of the South African non-executive directors, Koos Bekker and Charles St Leger Searle, were not disclosed.

During Ton Vosloo's tenure as chair, the Naspers board resolved to award Pony Ma the group's highest accolade for performance, the Phil Weber Award. He declined the prize, however, because he sets great store by a good relationship with the Chinese authorities and did not want to attract attention in China with this foreign tribute.

Pony Ma in any case makes no bones about publicising his close association with the Communist Party of China and its leader Xi Jinping, for whom the way has been paved to remain president of the authoritarian state for life. On the day of the Chinese president's address to the party congress in October 2017, Tencent released a new mobile game titled 'Clap hands for Xi Jinping'.

Yet the close ties with the Chinese Communist Party did not deter Xi Jinping's government from clamping down on video games. Amid concerns about online addiction and the impact of gaming on children's eyesight, licences were revoked and no new licences were granted. Tencent's share price was badly hit and slumped by more than 30 per cent.

By 2019, the Chinese government resumed the process of awarding licenses for new games. When the government announced its intention to obtain a stake in technology giants, Tencent and Alibaba expressed support for the proposal. The year before, the Chinese Communist Party had further tightened its grip on all forms of freedom of expression in that the party's central department of propaganda took over all agencies that regulate the mass media, including any collaboration with foreign organisations.

Tencent has its own internal control system to ensure compliance with the strict statutory censorship requirements. Staff use keywords to monitor or to block messages or articles. Popular blogs focusing on celebrity scandals and the intrigues of the rich and famous have been forced to close because discussion of such matters has been deemed to be not in keeping with 'core socialist values'. Moreover, private entities that run social media platforms are required to enforce content restrictions and report those who violate them to the 'relevant authorities'. Even Winnie the Pooh is banned, since the fictional teddy bear has been used as a caricature of Xi Jinping.

Google withdrew from China on account of the censorship regime. The websites of Amnesty International, Facebook and Twitter are inaccessible to most Chinese, except if they are able to use a virtual private network (VPN). But such networks have also been banned, and Apple was requested to remove VPN apps from its Chinese App Store. Apple acquiesced in order to, like Naspers, retain access to the enormous Chinese market.

Meanwhile, gaming has surged again. Tencent's big money-spinners are League of Legends and the similar Honor of Kings, which is based on historical Chinese characters. Much revenue is derived from the sale of virtual clothing, weapons, explosives and the like to blow opponents to smithereens, while substantial investments are made in non-Chinese game developers and publishers.

Apart from the fact that Tencent is an exceptionally profitable investment, the Chinese technology group holds its internet operations in a structure known as a variable interest entity (VIE). This distinctive Chinese measure offers foreign shareholders such as Naspers a contractual claim on profits and dividends of Tencent, but no claim on the Chinese group's assets that are situated on the Chinese mainland. The VIE structure, which also applies to Alibaba and other Chinese groups, is deemed to be risky by some analysts – something like the Chinese version of the approach to colossuses that are 'too big to fail'. As far as the Chinese investment is concerned, it helps that 'South Africa has no enemies' and are more welcome than, say, the United States in countries such as China, Russia and Brazil, says Meloy Horn.

Naspers's biggest investment is indeed in communist China. Ton Vosloo writes that during his years as Naspers leader, he was 'bombarded' with more questions about this stake than about any other aspect of the group's activities. 'I would simply reply that China, with its 1,5 billion people, was currently in a development phase. There was still an enormous amount of blue sky left, and if Tencent maintained its course with good management, I saw no reason why it would not flourish.'

The threat of a takeover

Over the years, covetous eyes were cast on Naspers by competitors as well as businesspeople who were keen to obtain a slice of the burgeoning conglomerate. One such case was a South African takeover bid by Jannie Mouton and Chris Otto of PSG in 2008. In this instance, Bekker took the initiative to fend off a possible hostile raid.

While he was a partner at the stockbroking firm Senekal, Mouton & Kitshoff (SMK), Mouton had built up a considerable portfolio of unlisted shares in the group prior to Naspers's listing in 1994. While on holiday, Mouton thought up a scheme and returned with his Keerom plan, a deal which referred to the then Naspers headquarters in Keerom Street in Cape Town, a 'controversial but exciting deal'. A consortium led by PSG discovered that Naspers's shareholder register was outdated and started phoning shareholders with a view to buying up shares. They were particularly interested in A-shares, which had higher voting rights, as well as in the shares in the other unlisted companies – such as Keeromstraat Beleggings and Nasbel in Naspers's voting control structure – that had been retained after the company listed.

In the course of their takeover bid, the PSG-led consortium had a number of discussions with a key figure in the tug of war: Dr Johan van Zyl, the then MD of Sanlam, the company that was one of the largest shareholders in Naspers subsidiaries. Van Zyl believed it would be unfair not to talk to Bekker in order to ascertain his reaction. During their conversation, Bekker, who sought to protect Naspers's control structure, gave him a 'very good rationale as to why control was necessary, especially because of the Tencent story'. Van Zyl regarded his eventual decision as an economic consideration that was not only in the interest of Sanlam's clients but also in the national interest.

He would support the formation of a 50/50 partnership provided Bekker was able to get together a consortium made up of 'the right people' with a long-term perspective. Bekker responded that he and Cobus Stofberg were prepared to do it themselves.

Van Zyl explained that Sanlam had 'two pots of money': the company's own money, and the clients'. He undertook to approach the individuals concerned about taking over their Naspers controlling shares under Sanlam's control and entrenching them with 'people who get the picture' (of the importance of retaining control of the company). Many of the Sanlam clients were willing to go along with this, also because they received a more favourable offer than the nominal value of the shares. Sanlam obtained a 50 per cent stake in Wheatfields 221, a dormant company that was taken over by the new partnership. Bekker and Cobus Stofberg paid a combined R135 million for a 25 per cent stake each in Wheatfields. Bekker sold N-shares worth R63 million to acquire A-shares with the higher voting rights.

Vosloo writes in his memoirs that Wheatfields was regarded as the white knight and that the board of Naspers was notified of the deal with the explanation that a raid had been fended off. Wheatfields' partners agreed to consult one another beforehand about important decisions, and that Sanlam would not vote against Naspers's vote. In the event of a disagreement, they had to decide jointly on the course to be followed. Thus a block vote was established that lay outside Naspers's control structure, but which would serve as an obstacle to a hostile takeover.

Van Zyl still regards the investments in Wheatfields as good value for Sanlam's clients. Jannie Mouton and company have since sold their shares. Vosloo, in whose mind questions about the future of Wheatfields arose, nonetheless believes 'it can be accepted that Bekker and Stofberg will deal with this valuable instrument in the best interests of the company. I am fully satisfied that the matter will be dealt with in such a way that the independence of Naspers is cemented.'

Some people think Wheatfields now controls Naspers, but this is not the case. Wheatfields 'is not and has never been part' of the control structure. 'It is a private investor, not a Naspers company, and it effectively votes some 12 per cent of the aggregate Naspers vote,' according to David Tudor, general counsel of Naspers.

Tudor explained on inquiry that 'Naspers's issued share capital presently comprises 438 656 059 Class-N Ordinary Shares and 907 128 Class-A Ordinary Shares. The N-shares are listed on the JSE and have one vote per share. The A-shares are unlisted and have 1 000 votes per share.' The control structure, he said, was achieved in the following way: 'Heemstede Beleggings Proprietary Limited ("Heemstede"), a wholly owned subsidiary of Naspers, holds 49 per cent of Naspers Beleggings (RF) Limited ("Nasbel"). The latter, in turn, holds 49 per cent of the Class-A Ordinary Shares and they carry approximately 33 per cent of the total voting rights in respect of Naspers's ordinary shares. The remaining 51 per cent of the shares of Nasbel are widely held by another 2 611 shareholders. Keeromstraat 30 Beleggings (RF) Limited ("Keerom") holds around 31 per cent of the Class-A Ordinary Shares, which represents around 21 per cent of the total voting rights in respect of the company's ordinary shares. Keerom has 2 843 shareholders, none of whom is a controlling shareholder.

Nasbel and Keerom thus collectively hold an absolute majority of 53,9 per cent of the voting rights in respect of Naspers. This is the control structure of Naspers. If Nasbel and Keerom vote together, they can determine the majority of the total voting in Naspers, including in respect of an unfriendly raid or takeover attempt. Nasbel and Keerom have agreed to exercise their voting rights in consultation with one another in terms of a voting pool agreement.'

Tudor confirmed that the group's complex voting control structure had been in place since Naspers had listed on the JSE in 1994. Its aim is to ensure the independence of the group and to prevent a raid or unfriendly takeover. Naspers operates in more than 120 countries, and 'when entering foreign countries in the media sphere, and when dealing with regulators, it is critical that we are able to give an assurance of continuity of identity: i.e. that we are not susceptible to takeover by unknown and possibly unacceptable parties'.

This guarantee of identity is crucial for partners and regulators.

Tudor pointed out that many other international media and technology companies (such as Google, Facebook, LinkedIn, Schibsted Media, News Corporation, Groupon, Zynga, Snap, Liberty Global, Discovery Media, and others) have control structures with similar aims. The voting control structure was continued when Naspers was listed offshore as Prosus in Amsterdam in 2019.

Quality journalism and the print media under pressure

Although Naspers's leap onto the electronic highway was a spectacular success, for the print media that had begun ailing with the advent of television it meant an accelerating decline, as was also the case elsewhere in the world. When Bekker joined Naspers, the group's newspapers, magazines and book publishers were still in the golden age of the print media. Their success was the foundation on which M-Net was able to develop pay television.

All print publications felt the impact of the changing media landscape, but digital competition was not the sole factor. Television, the internet, and the rise of social media caused publications to decline. And then there was also an internal circulation debacle at Media24 in 2010–11.

Management had decided to implement a sophisticated new electronic customer management system called Cycad. The distribution responsibility for the various publications was consolidated at On the Dot, an entity within Media24 that was a successful distributor of, among other things, books, in order to run a centralised distribution operation.

It was the kind of technology-driven innovation to which Bekker has always been devoted. But the implementation dragged on too long for his liking. The CEO of Media24, François Groepe, confidently promised that the system would be operational by the end of July 2011, or he would resign. Though the software engineers warned him that the system was not ready, Groepe was determined to make the deadline. When the start button was pushed, chaos ensued – all the circulation figures of Media24's publications plummeted, and subscribers cancelled in droves.

At a management meeting where the disaster was discusssed,

Bekker looked around the boardroom: 'Didn't someone say he would resign if this system didn't work?' Groepe did resign a while later. He was subsequently appointed deputy governor of the Reserve Bank.

The cumulative effects of the logistical nightmare and the disruptive electronic competition were falling newspaper circulations, and magazines that became thinner as advertising moved to new media. Inevitably, staff reductions followed. Editorial posts were cut and journalists lost their jobs.

Even Media24's investigations unit, which included Jacques Pauw, author of the best-seller *The President's Keepers,* got the chop. 'Naspers is one of the richest media companies in the world. They don't give a fuck about their papers,' he declared. At the very time that the free press's investigative journalists, along with an independent judiciary, constituted the most important bulwark against corrupt politicians and the abuse of power, Africa's largest media company was without a team of investigative journalists.

After his retirement as chair of Naspers, Vosloo tried to save the pieces. He and his wife Anet donated R3,5 million in 2019 for the establishment of a non-profit company, Waarheid Eerste/Truth First, to promote investigative journalism. Media24's online news service News24 had begun using the services of amaBhungane, the private sector-funded investigative team that has produced numerous exposés about the Gupta scandals.

Meanwhile, juniorisation of newsrooms continued due to the loss of the experience and the institutional memory of senior journalists who had seen the writing on the wall. As these publications languished, the focus on the electronic media increased, with centralised gathering of news that was channelled to the digital news services Netwerk24 and News24. A form of 'assembly-line journalism' emerged where publications and websites could select from the news offering and choose what prominence they would give to reports.

Concerns kept mounting about the declining newspaper industry. When it was announced in 2018 that MultiChoice, which controls pay television in 48 countries in Africa, would be unbundled and listed separately from Naspers, some recalled that M-Net had been founded to help newspapers survive. Several commentators referred to the original motive for the establishment of pay television, among them the columnist Johannes Froneman, professor in journalism at North-West University, who reckoned newspapers were owed a debt of honour, and that some of the money of MIH could be deposited in a trust for newspapers.

On inquiry, Bekker, who had previously said that newspapers were the place where a society entered into conversation with itself, responded to this as follows: 'Over the years, Naspers has transferred large amounts to Media24, which have been used to extend the life of printed newspapers, even those that were already running at a loss, as well as to move newspaper titles online. Dividends from MultiChoice have often been employed for this purpose. Naturally it is up to the board to decide, but I would suspect that future help is not excluded either.'

Bekker, who assumes that this kind of support on the part of the board will continue, also points out that in the past the South African print-media landscape was dominated by local media, apart from the occasional imported magazine here and there. Then television came with overseas programmes, and later also overseas channels via satellite. In the internet era, however, competition has become global. Google and Facebook separately have larger audiences in South Africa than all the local internet media combined. Each of them, according to him, takes more advertising revenue out of the country than the entire South African industry combined.

Media24 no longer competes with local internet players, but with Google, Facebook and Amazon, three of the five largest companies in the world. 'Our regulators have not quite grasped that yet. They want to subject local players to all kinds of regulations. If that happens, we are in deep trouble because there is no way that local regulations can impose those same rules on the international giants. The local guys will only fall further behind,' he has stated.

Bekker added that in a few years' time newspapers would be a thing of the past, just as the telegram no longer exists. 'Our task is to convert print media successfully and in good time into digital versions.'

Bekker, a regular Davos-goer, encountered similar views among influential media leaders at a meeting of the World Economic

Forum in Davos in Switzerland in January 2019. By then, he had been attending the annual gathering, where he rubs shoulders with world leaders, the global business elite and celebrities, for sixteen years. This time he was seated next to the head of the *New York Times* and the editor-in-chief of the *Financial Times*.

'Both of them accept this technological evolution philosophically, and point to outstanding recent growth in their digital news services, particularly paid news services. I believe that is also where our future lies: in free, advertising-funded news as well as in subscription news services,' he said.

All the same, the disappearance of newspapers is by no means an unmixed blessing. In the United States, research already found that the demise of so many community newspapers has exacerbated polarisation among Americans. Social media platforms offer extremists, loonies and malcontents the opportunity to distribute their fake news, hate speech and dangerous prejudices worldwide at lightning speed, while cybercriminals are able to manipulate data, as in the case of Cambridge Analytica during the Brexit referendum.

For digital news services, the timeless criteria that quality newspapers still ought to meet have in fact become all the more compelling. Maintenance of these standards mainly hinges on experienced and well-informed journalists: reporters who report accurately, subeditors who evaluate the sifting and weighting of news in a balanced way and do rigorous verification, and editors who comment with authority and insight on the fast-moving global and local events.

Although Bekker has put a lot of money into digital media, staff cuts that were seen as business decisions have resulted in the company losing dozens of good journalists. In the long term, this may bode ill for sustainable quality journalism in South Africa.

Naspers under fire

The future of quality journalism was not the only worrying question that preceded the unbundling of MultiChoice. As more and more revelations leaked out about the 'Zupta' corruption scandal that caused a stir during the Zuma administration, Naspers, too, incurred unsavoury publicity with regard to the Gupta-controlled TV channel

ANN7 that was carried by MultiChoice as one of its news channels.

ANN7 became known as the Gupta channel, the way the *New Age* was seen as the Gupta newspaper. The *New Age*'s main source of revenue was advertising from government departments, while ANN7 was harnessed as a propaganda machine for the Zuma and Gupta families. State-owned entities such as Eskom, Transnet and Telkom splurged millions of rands on ANN7's business breakfast briefings that were also televised by the SABC.

Journalists from the Naspers subsidiary Media24 broke the story that the #GuptaLeaks emails revealed MultiChoice had made an allegedly questionable one-off payment of R25 million to ANN7. In addition, MultiChoice increased its annual payment to the con- troversial Gupta-linked channel from R50 million to R141 million. This happened shortly before an important government decision about encrypted versus unencrypted set-top boxes for the country's transition from analogue to digital terrestrial television was due to be taken.

The negotiations, which were conducted with Nazeem Howa of ANN7's holding company, had taken place under the supervision of the then MultiChoice group CEO, Imtiaz Patel, who declared at the launch of the channel that ANN7 would not get a cent from it. While MultiChoice pays all television channels for their content, questions were asked, also in Naspers publications, as to whether ANN7 had been overpaid in exchange for influence over the government's policy on set-top boxes.

MultiChoice preferred unencrypted set-top boxes, as this could keep competitors out of the pay-television space. It was indeed adopted as policy a while later by the then communications minister Faith Muthambi, a Zuma acolyte whom Cyril Ramaphosa left out of his cabinet when he became president.

Various commentators sharply criticised the payments to ANN7 by MultiChoice, which in December 2017 still sponsored the gala dinner at the ANC's election conference at Nasrec. One of the critics was Shane Watkins, the chief investment officer of the fund manager All Weather Capital, who wrote to Bekker that there were legitimate concerns over the relationship between ANN7 and Naspers and MultiChoice. He emphasised that Bekker was responsible for corporate governance at Naspers and for the protection of the group's reputation.

Bekker initially responded that the board would discuss the matter along with many other issues, but later merely stated: 'Multi-Choice is a separate company to Naspers.'

Watkins remarked that Naspers owned 80 per cent of Multi-Choice, but he was unable to get an undertaking that the matter would be investigated independently. Bekker reportedly concluded his last email to Watkins with: 'I'm afraid I can't help you and am terminating the discussion.'

Eventually an internal inquiry was conducted, led by Multi-Choice's audit and risk committee. The findings were announced in January 2018 by Naspers CEO Bob van Dijk and MultiChoice CEO Calvo Mawela. Mawela, son-in-law of the ANC's national chair Gwede Mantashe, had at that stage only been in his new position for two months after succeeding Imtiaz Patel.

Van Dijk and Mawela admitted that 'mistakes' had been made in their dealings with ANN7, but said the internal inquiry had found no evidence of corruption or illegal activity in respect of the ANN7 contract. While any involvement in state capture was denied, the company acknowledged that it had not performed proper due diligence, had not responded soon enough when concerns were first raised about ANN7, and had not communicated sufficiently with all stakeholders, including the public, about the matter.

Mawela also announced that only the findings and recommendations would be released and not the full report, as it contained sensitive commercial information. Furthermore, ANN7's contract would be terminated by August 2018, and they would call for proposals from interested media groups for a new black-owned channel to replace ANN7 on the DStv bouquet.

Two other contentious issues that gave rise to polemics prior to the unbundling of MultiChoice were Naspers's executive pay policy and the valuation gap between the group itself and its stake in Tencent. The debate about executive pay shed light on Bekker's implacable attitude in certain situations.

A robust debate about these issues had long been raging among stockbrokers and technical analysts. On the one hand, it was argued that Naspers shareholders should be better rewarded from the dividends of Tencent, whose share price was at one point valued at almost R400 billion more than that of Naspers. On the other hand, objections were raised, in particular, about the remuneration paid to Naspers's new CEO Bob van Dijk, since it was believed he was being rewarded for Tencent's performance without having had any hand in it. Among the protestors against the remuneration policy was the investment management group Allan Gray.

Matters came to a head at the Naspers annual general meeting in Cape Town in August 2016.

The shareholder activist Theo Botha sought to gain access to the trust deeds of a new share incentive scheme that would be used to attract and retain staff with critical skills. His questions, however, caused a former director to jump up and walk out in protest. Koos Bekker, as chair, even threatened at one point to have Botha removed from the meeting.

Bekker said that remuneration was important to Naspers: 'We want to attract the best engineers and give them the best remuneration to retain them.'

Responding to Botha's questions about the targets set for remuneration, Professor Rachel Jafta, a Naspers director and member of the group's audit and risk committee, explained that a part of the remuneration scheme related to financial targets, but the part about strategic targets was confidential, as it contained commercially sensitive information.

Bekker's conduct raised eyebrows when he refused to take further questions from Botha and said: 'I've ruled. That's the end of it.'

Botha, who regularly questions the remuneration of executives and directors, said afterwards that he had never been so disappointed. This was the first time in a shareholder meeting that he had been threatened with being kicked out: 'It never happened to me before.'

The remuneration policy was approved despite the fact that a majority of Naspers's ordinary N-shareholders had voted against it. It had the support of the A-shareholders whose shares carry a thousand votes each, however, and their higher voting rights were decisive. As chief executive, Bob van Dijk was paid an annual salary of $2,2 million after a pay rise of 32 per cent. He was also awarded long-term share options worth $10,4 million. Naspers's lavish remuneration of top executives and directors would continue to be a much-discussed and controversial topic in many media and other circles.

Two years later, a totally different atmosphere prevailed at the AGM of August 2018. At a three-hour meeting, during which the group's activities were elucidated on flashing video screens, shareholders were afforded ample opportunity to interact with directors and executives and ask questions.

Still, the disgruntlement on the part of N-shareholders about the value of Tencent that had not been fully unlocked for them was probably a factor in Naspers's decision in early 2018 to sell 2 per cent of its shares in Tencent. Although Naspers's stake in the Chinese internet giant was thereby reduced to 31,2 per cent, Tencent still indicated on its website that Naspers was the owner.

The sale raised almost $10 billion, which enabled Van Dijk to continue with the established 'spaghetti' tradition. He said he regarded Naspers primarily as an online enterprise concentrating on consumer internet business, hence investments would be made in classified ads, online food delivery (such as Delivery Hero, which operates in more than 40 countries), and financial technology.

On 27 February 2019, MultiChoice listed on the JSE as MCG, with an opening price of R95. With a market capitalisation of R44 billion, the company, which would thenceforth be run separately from Naspers, on its debut immediately entered the ranks of the top 40 companies listed on the local bourse.

Internal censorship

Bekker's retirement as CEO of Naspers in 2014, when he was replaced by Van Dijk, and his assumption of the chairmanship of the group after a year-long sabbatical, was accompanied by controversy. Although he and Vosloo had worked closely for many years, relations between them soured over the envisaged publication of a history of Naspers to mark the company's centenary in 2015. Bekker absolutely refused that the commemorative book be published.

A few years earlier, Vosloo, then still chair of Naspers, had commissioned Professor Lizette Rabe, head of the journalism department at Stellenbosch University, to write the book that was due to be published during the centenary year of 2015. She had to sign a contract that prohibited her from publishing the manuscript elsewhere. Vosloo, who was pleased with the final product, writes in his memoirs that the clash of opinions about the publication was the most vehement disagreement in his relationship with Bekker.

Bekker, who succeeded Vosloo as chair in 2015, was concerned that the book would, in his view, have negative implications for Naspers and that it did not contain enough information about the digital era and the Chinese investment. Since Rabe had been unable to gain access to Pony Ma and his team from Tencent, Bekker – then still CEO, although he was on sabbatical leave – asked two members of his top management team to compile contributions on the Chinese investment for the book. At some stage, Bekker sent three envoys to Vosloo in an attempt to persuade him to drop the project – his confidant Cobus Stofberg, the financial director Steve Pacak, and the company secretary Gillian Kisbey-Green. But Vosloo, who thought 'with all due respect' that none of the three envoys had detailed knowledge of Naspers's past prior to the more recent phases of its century-long existence, dug in his heels.

Although staunchly Afrikaans by birth, Bekker believes that in the business world, one should put business interests first, not sentimental considerations that may hamper one's success. He would terminate discussions about difficult decisions that affect employees' careers with an abrupt: 'It's a business decision.'

In 2000, he instructed that an exhibition of front pages from the past with which *Die Burger* was commemorating its 85th anniversary, which included posters that celebrated National Party election victories, be removed from the foyer of the Naspers Centre. In 2015, he was present as chair at the centenary celebrations of the company in front of the same building, which was renamed the Media24 Centre at the event, but did not address the gathering. On that occasion, the Media24 CEO Esmaré Weideman issued a formal apology for Naspers's role in apartheid.

By the time Bekker returned to work in May 2015 in the capacity of Vosloo's successor as non-executive chair, he had decided against publishing the book for which Naspers held the copyright. According to Vosloo, Bekker's reason was Naspers's thousands of black employees: 'If they were to read about the company's past, it would draw the attention of the ANC government to the company, which could be prejudicial to its regulated businesses, such as DStv and the digital expansions.' In Vosloo's opinion, Bekker's fears were excessive because the company's past was public knowledge.

In his farewell speech in February 2016, Vosloo appealed to Bekker to reconsider his decision about the history book. Bekker only dropped his head. When Vosloo asked him after the speech whether he had embarrassed him with his appeal, Bekker just said no and smiled.

In January 2019, Bekker – who since his assumption of the chairmanship has not pronounced on the dispute – responded via email to an inquiry about the rationale behind his decision.

'It is relatively simple. I respect both Ton and Lizette and have worked well with both of them for years. But about the book Lizette wanted to publish as an 'official history' of the company, we differ politely. In my view, the events are depicted purely from an Afrikaner perspective, whereas the Naspers river was later joined by various tributaries that did not originate from the Afrikaner source of 1915. Today we have businesses (big and small) in 120 countries, many of them created by entrepreneurs, and the majority of our employees won't identify with some of the views in the book. Which doesn't mean to say that she is wrong (I, too, come from an Afrikaans background); just that different people in different cultures can honestly see things in diverse ways. The modern Naspers wants to be a house with many mansions, a place where all cultures and languages and creeds can feel equally at home.'

Rabe is adamant that the manuscript was not written from an 'Afrikaner perspective', but presents a balanced, comprehensive overall picture of Naspers's century and its innovations and development trajectory over decades.

Many other companies, including media groups, have allowed their histories to be written 'warts and all'. It is doubtful that Bekker's explanation, which sounds incongruous coming from the chair of a company with extensive media interests that propagate media freedom and freedom of expression, will be the last word on this matter. For if the publication of a book is stopped because it may harm a media company's commercial interests, the question arises whether other publications, including newspapers, magazines and news websites, also run the risk of being censored.

Listing in the Netherlands

The persistent criticism that Naspers was not unlocking enough value from its stake in Tencent led to a further step after the unbundling of M-Net and selling off a small stake in Tencent: the announcement about listing on the Euronext stock exchange in Amsterdam in 2019. Naspers spokespeople were at pains to explain that the foreign listing was not a move to quit South Africa.

The new group would hold Naspers's international internet assets, while Naspers's interests in Media24 and related companies would remain on the JSE. The Naspers part comprises Media24, Takealot, Autotrader, Property24 and webuycars.co.za. In the Netherlands, Prosus would control all of Naspers's international assets: the 31,2 per cent stake in Tencent, as well as its shares in OLX, Swiggy (an Indian online food-delivery company), and two large Russian companies (Avito, an online classifieds and property platform, and Russia's biggest internet company, Mail.ru, with large gaming, social media and e-commerce businesses).

Prosus was chosen as the new name for the group after the generic name NewCo was initially used. The group said in a statement that 'Prosus is a Latin word, with various meanings. Its use in this case is inspired by the meaning "forwards".' Other meanings include absolutely, completely, in any event, utterly or briefly.

Shareholders could choose between receiving new Prosus shares or increasing their Naspers shares. Naspers would retain a holding of 73 per cent of the Prosus business, and the existing voting control structure would remain in place.

Van Dijk stated that the Amsterdam listing provided 'a strong foundation for our future growth ambitions', and that they believed it would help them maximise shareholder value over time. His strategy for Prosus was to focus on growing global businesses in online classifieds, food delivery, and payments and fintech.

One of his first forays under the Prosus umbrella was, ironically, to throw spaghetti at food-delivery vehicles. Prosus made an offer of R93 billion to take over the British online food-delivery business Just Eat. Its bid failed, however, to the relief of some shareholders.

Along with the stake of 31,2 per cent in Tencent and its stake in Mail.ru in Russia, Naspers owns or is in partnership with an array of e-commerce groups in more than 120 countries, ranging from Eastern Europe, Latin America and Africa to Asia. Naspers is the largest media group outside the United States and China by market capitalisation, and the largest consumer internet company in Europe.

At President Cyril Ramaphosa's investment conference in October 2018, Naspers announced an investment of R4,6 billion in South Africa and the establishment of the Naspers Foundry, a funding initiative which would back technology start-ups in South Africa that seek to address major societal needs.

In 2019, the 48-year-old Phuthi Mahanyele-Dabengwa, known for her long career in corporate leadership and her close ties with Ramaphosa, became the first black woman to lead Naspers's activities in South Africa. Prior to her appointment as CEO of Naspers SA, she had been the executive chair of the majority-black-owned investment group Sigma Capital. Her stepmother was Sankie Mthembi-Mahanyele, minister of housing in the Mbeki cabinet and later deputy secretary-general of the ANC.

During the state of disaster that was declared as a result of the Covid-19 pandemic in 2020, Naspers donated R1,5 billion in emergency aid to the government's response plan. This was shortly after the Rupert and Oppenheimer families, as well as Patrice Motsepe's foundation, had each donated R1 billion. Naspers's donation comprised a contribution of R500 million to the Solidarity Response Fund, and R1 billion that would be used to buy personal protective equipment and other medical supplies from China – in partnership with the Chinese government and Tencent – to support South Africa's health workers.

Interland and life lessons

The Naspers head office in Cape Town is in a tower block with an enviable view over Table Bay and the majestic Table Mountain. Bekker, arguably the most active non-executive chair in South Africa, does not spend most of his working time at the head office, but rather on planes in what he calls 'a kind of interland'. His colleagues are in agreement about the fact that he works extremely hard, often till late at night, and that he pays meticulous attention to the finest details of the various businesses. It is said jokingly about his subordinates that they are somewhat wary of the 'big boss' and conclude instructions in memos with 'KSS', which stands for 'Koos says so'.

Bekker was a winner of the South African chapter of Ernst & Young's World Entrepreneur Award and was honoured by the *Sunday Times* with its Lifetime Achievement Award. He was also a member of the South African bid committee that ran a successful campaign to host the Fifa World Cup in South Africa in 2010. Naspers bestowed its Phil Weber Award on him when he stepped down as CEO in 2014.

Bekker has few personal friends; he believes such friendships may influence business decisions. Many of the leading Afrikaner business-people know each other fairly well, but he responded as follows when asked how important such mutual connections are to him: 'Language is not a factor in international business: many of my best business acquaintances are Argentinians or Chinese or Poles. Besides, doing business with social friends is not a good idea: it undermines your objectivity.'

According to him, political considerations do play a significant role in decision-making in his businesses both nationally and inter-nationally, 'because we often work in regulated sectors'.

The great emphasis Koos Bekker places on adaptability in business in order to stay ahead of the pack stems in part from his study of the ideas of Charles Darwin, author of the pioneering work *On the Origin of Species*. 'People quote Darwin saying that it is the strongest that survive, the fittest. But that is not what he said: he said it is those who are the most flexible, those who can adapt to change, who survive.'

He does not follow any fixed recipe for achieving success in his businesses. 'I think recipes, like "principles", are dangerous. Both imply a certain timelessness in your views, an unshakeable truth with which you are born and with which you will die. But in reality a human baby enters the world with virtually nothing in its head – one advantage your brain has over that of an ant is precisely that it is reprogrammable. You learn from events. As John Maynard Keynes purportedly said: "When the facts change, I change my mind – what do you do, sir?"'

Bekker has a special interest in history. In response to a question about his reading habits and influences on his life, he replied: 'I read quite a lot of history. It teaches you to recognise patterns, and when one day you see a similar theme unfolding again, you recognise it and you are better able to assess what remedies may succeed. All history is actually Harvard Case Studies. Learning from another guy's mistakes is the methodology on which all MBAs are based. When it comes to fiction, I like Leo Tolstoy, Guy de Maupassant and Somerset Maugham. All three had razor-sharp insight into human motivations; taught me a lot.'

Nowadays globalisation, political issues and rapid techological and scientific advances demand exceptionally resourceful and visionary leadership, and he expanded on what he regarded as the foremost requirements for constructive business leadership: 'As a student I was presumptuous enough to believe that if I thought long and deeply enough about something, I would be able to anticipate its future. Today I realise that's rubbish: there is no way anyone could have anticipated the advent of Twitter (140 characters; a throwback to the 19th-century telegraph, who knew he needed *that*?).

'So if the future is unknowable, your best tool is adaptability. Unfortunately this trait declines as managers get older. Secondly, it is also important to be honest with yourself – there are many things you don't know, and some things that are impossible to know. Entertain the possibility that many of your own ideas might be wrong. You'd best re-evaluate them every day.'

As for significant technological developments that would change the world radically, Bekker said he had a hunch, although he admitted that he might be wrong: 'The most important technology in our economy over the past half-century has been electromagnetic impulses (the computer, internet, etc). Today, the five most valuable companies in the world all come from this sector (hence no banks, oil companies, etc). But I suspect this sector will run out of steam within years, and that the biological sciences will take over: manipulation of plants and animals and humans.'

In response to a question about what advice on achieving sustainable economic growth he would give the South African government, he replied sardonically: 'They haven't yet asked me for advice, and I wouldn't like to offer unsolicited advice.'

But he does have advice for the youth of South Africa: 'There are so many interesting things a young person can tackle today! Try something, and if you fail – which is likely – stand up and try the next thing. I wish I was 30.'

3

Legends of luxury

Johann Rupert

IN 2018, Johann Rupert was the richest Afrikaner in the country, with a net worth of $7,2 billion (about R92 billion). Only one other South African outranked him on *Forbes*'s Rich List for Africa: Nicky Oppenheimer, heir to the Oppenheimer dynasty, with an estimated fortune of $7,7 billion.

Such rankings of the super-rich vary from year to year. According to the *Sunday Times* list of the richest South Africans, which was no longer published after 2017, Christo Wiese was still the richest person in South Africa in 2016, with a net worth of R81,2 billion.

A year later, Rupert had overtaken Wiese on *Forbes*'s Africa list. At the time, his net worth was recorded as $6,1 billion, compared with Wiese's $5,6 billion. This was before the spectacular collapse of Steinhoff shares in December 2017 when Wiese, in his own words, lost fifty years' work. He then barely made it into the ranks of dollar billionaires, with a net worth of $1,1 billion. Nicky Oppenheimer was at that stage number 202 and Rupert number 228 on *Forbes*'s list of the world's thousand richest people.

Both Rupert and Oppenheimer enjoyed the advantage of having

taken over family businesses that had already made their mark on global markets – Oppenheimer as the third generation in control of De Beers and Anglo American, and Rupert as the second generation in control of the former Rembrandt Group.

In business circles, Rupert commanded respect particularly for the way in which he consolidated and expanded the group's luxury-goods interests. It was at his insistence that the international assets of the former Rembrandt Group were spun off and restructured under the umbrella of Richemont. From the time that he effectively took over the control in 1988, Richemont's market capitalisation in Swiss francs had increased from CHF3,2 billion to CHF48 billion.

An outspoken business leader who has often waded into the political terrain where other business leaders fear to tread, he has been a voice governments had to listen to in spite of themselves. At the same time, he has elicited paroxysms of fury from radical elements that peddle scare stories about 'white monopoly capital'.

The founding of Richemont

Johann Peter Rupert, who is named after the Rupert progenitor in South Africa, is the elder son of Dr Anton Rupert, the legendary entrepreneur who built the Rembrandt Group into an international business empire after starting off with a small tobacco company, Voorbrand, in Johannesburg. Established in the 1940s, the group owned significant interests in the tobacco, financial services, wines and spirits, gold- and diamond-mining industries as well as in luxury goods. Thereby Rupert senior became a role model for many among the younger generation of Afrikaner businesspeople.

Johann grew up in Stellenbosch where his parents lived for decades in the same house at 13 Thibault Street. He and his younger brother Anthonij were pupils at the local Paul Roos Gymnasium, a parallel-medium public school for boys, while his sister Hanneli, later a well-known singer, attended the neighbouring Bloemhof girls' high school.

Johann started off studying commerce and law at Stellenbosch University, but did not complete his degree. As a sports enthusiast, he was a keen cricketer who played a few times for the Western Province

B team while at university until he had to give up the game because of a knee injury. At that stage, the idea of working for his father did not appeal to Johann. One of his lecturers, the political scienctist Professor Ben Vosloo, who would later become head of the Small Business Development Corporation, reminded him of an old Zulu proverb: 'Nothing grows beneath a big tree.'

He needed just two subjects to complete his degree and had been admitted to write both examinations, but the university (which was to award him an honorary doctorate in 2004, causing him to quip that they were honouring a dropout) insisted that he repeat both courses. Consequently, he suspended his studies and, at the instigation of their family friend David Rockefeller, departed for New York to develop his business acumen there. After two years at Chase Manhattan Bank, he joined the investment bank Lazard Frères, where he worked for three years. There he learnt, in his own words, to work very hard, a fourteen-hour day, six days a week – 'and to my surprise, I found I enjoyed it'.

On his return to South Africa in 1979, he started Rand Merchant Bank (RMB) and worked in Johannesburg for a few years, where he renewed ties with old Stellenbosch friends such as GT Ferreira and Paul Harris. The banking licence Johann obtained would in time become very valuable to them.

He was still not keen to join Rembrandt. But in 1984 a situation arose that upset the Rupert family terribly. While Johann was on a business visit to London with friends, they called on his father at his regular suite in Grosvenor House. They found Anton Rupert in an agitated state – 'he was as white as a sheet'. He told them he had just been informed by the chair of Rothmans, Sir Robert Crichton-Brown, that in future he would only be welcome at Rothmans as a shareholder, not as part of management.

The presumptuous conduct of Crichton-Brown, an Australian formerly known as Bobby Cohen, was evidently a consequence of anti-South African sentiments that had intensified in the 1980s as a result of the anti-apartheid campaign. The sanctions campaign was the very reason why Rembrandt had sold half its shares in Rothmans to the tobacco company Philip Morris a few years earlier, a transaction in which Johann Rupert had been involved. As a result, the two companies each owned 34 per cent of Rothmans. The motivation had been that Rothmans operated in countries like Malaysia where South Africans were not admitted at all.

Johann was incensed at such treatment of his 68-year-old father. 'The man tells my father (and my father had appointed him), "You're no longer welcome here as part of the management ..." I thought my father was going to suffer a heart attack.' The younger Rupert decided there and then that the time had come for him to join Rembrandt.

His dilemma was that he did not want to sell his colleagues at RMB out to a larger bank or leave them at the mercy of their competitors. He did have three friends he felt he could trust completely, although they were also major competitors: GT Ferreira, Paul Harris and Laurie Dippenaar at Rand Consolidated Investments (RCI), who had long been unable to secure a banking licence. At Johann's suggestion, Rand Merchant Bank merged with RCI. The merger benefited both parties: RCI could at last obtain the banking licence that was the prelude to the further success story of the financial services group FirstRand, while Johann could leave for Stellenbosch.

Johann was initially appointed as an executive director of Rembrandt. He had set only two conditions on which he would join the group. The first was that his father would permit him to transfer all Rembrandt's international assets to a separately listed company abroad, which made sense in view of the growing threat of sanctions that in 1986 resulted in South Africa's credit facilities being withdrawn by Chase Manhattan and other banks. He also had reservations about the management control of the international assets.

The second condition was that he be given the use of the company plane, because 'I wanted to see my wife and children and there was no chance that I would be constantly flying all over the world if I could not use that plane'. No salary was discussed, just the two conditions. Both requests were granted, and Johann duly moved to the Cape.

By that time, Edwin Hertzog, the son of Anton Rupert's partner Dirk Hertzog, had also started working at Rembrandt. Edwin, a medical doctor, would eventually become the founder of the Mediclinic hospital group.

Johann played a crucial role in reshuffling Rembrandt's international structure under the umbrella of Richemont, for which his father gave him full credit. When Anton Rupert was named *Die Burger*'s Business Pioneer in 1999, he stated in his speech that Johann's commitment and attention to detail had been decisive factors in the formation of Richemont.

Johann himself came up with the name for the new overseas luxury-goods conglomerate. After a late-night business conference in Geneva, he caught a few hours' sleep at the Hotel Le Richemond, which marketed itself as 'one of the real palace hotels of Switzerland and Europe as a whole'. He'd only got to bed at 2 am and needed to catch a flight at 6 am. He was shocked at the bill of 1 400 Swiss francs for a stay of a few hours. The cashier's response was that Le Richemond was a luxury hotel. Mulling over the incident on the plane, Johann thought of the name he was looking for a conglomerate manufacturing and selling luxury goods. He decided that Richemont, ending with a *t* instead of a *d*, was a good name. Besides, it started with the essential *R* that was used in so many Rupert and Rembrandt businesses.

Rembrandt's international interests were transferred to Compagnie Financière Richemont AG – a newly constituted group that focused on luxury goods but also held strategic interests in the tobacco industry – in 1988. The globally renowned jewellery group Cartier and the Rothmans tobacco company were some of the top brands in the new overseas group, along with Alfred Dunhill, Chloé and Montblanc. All Rembrandt Group shareholders obtained one share in Richemont for every Rembrandt share they owned. Richemont is controlled by the Rupert family via a holding company, Compagnie Financière Rupert. In 2004, the family bought out the minority stakes in the holding company, some of which had been passed to the third generation of the original Rembrandt founders.

Shortly after Johann Rupert's arrival at Rembrandt in Stellenbosch, a controversial Cartier board meeting took place overseas that was to give rise to an intense battle at board level. Once again, the Rothmans chair Sir Robert Crichton-Brown was the mischiefmaker and tried to edge out the South Africans. Cartier's two major shareholders, Rembrandt and Rothmans, each held 47,5 per cent, with the remaining 5 per cent owned by Sofina, a company in Belgium.

Sketching the background, Johann related that it was December; his parents were already at their holiday home in Hermanus. 'I was in New York on business when I got a call from our former colleague Joe Kanoui [a partner from Cartier]. In tears, he told me they had just come out of a board meeting of Cartier where Crichton-Brown had told them that henceforth they would be reporting to Rothmans; they had nothing to do with Rembrandt or the Ruperts – because of sanctions, etcetera – and no communication with Stellenbosch was allowed.

'Well, I had been involved with Cartier from 1975. Among other things, I went out with our partner's daughter [Nathalie Hocq] for years, so I know the family, I know Joe Kanoui … We are all friends, but again as a result of sanctions, etcetera we endeavoured to have third parties as shareholders in order to protect Cartier.

'Murray Louw [the South African dealmaker], who had been present at the meeting, also called me and told me Sir Robert Crichton-Brown had further said that all jewellers were thieves – he would be watching them, for he had learnt in Australia that people in the jewellery industry stole. This he said to the most sophisticated French board members, and he claimed to be saying it 'with Dr Rupert's knowledge and consent'. I phoned my father in Hermanus and told him: "You now have two options: you either lose the cooperation and the support of the entire Cartier team, or you rein Sir Robert Crichton-Brown in."'

Eventually Johann came up with another plan: an ingenious move to ensure control of Rothmans. He and Kanoui flew to Belgium and, together with Sofina, established a new company called Luxco and registered it in Luxembourg. It became the holding company for Rembrandt's 47,5 per cent interest and Sofina's 5 per cent interest in Cartier.

Sofina was given 10 per cent of Luxco and Rembrandt 90 per cent, which gave Rembrandt a controlling interest in Cartier. 'We then informed Rothmans, "By the way, this is the new structure." The news hit the Rothmans board like a bombshell. Johann stood his ground: unless Crichton-Brown was removed as chair, he would listen to no further communication from them.

When Johann finally spoke to Crichton-Brown, 'he kept on

calling me "my boy" and treated me like a child. He proposed that Rembrandt should trust the management and sell their shares in Rothmans to Rothmans Australia ... So I said, but why would we do something like that? We don't want to sell. He then tried to work South Africa out of the system.

'I did some research on Crichton-Brown and found out he had done the same thing to another family in a firm of insurance brokers he had headed in Australia, and he'd engineered a similar reverse takeover when he arrived in England.'

Johann informed the Rothmans board in England that he wanted to convene an extraordinary shareholders' meeting to ask for Sir Robert's resignation. 'I was in my mid thirties at the time, and I'll never forget it: the head of the merchant bank and the senior legal partner told me I couldn't do it. So, I asked, but why not?'

A senior director of Rothmans, John Mayo, replied: 'But you are South Africans.' He retorted: 'Mr Mayo, where in the Companies Act does it say that South Africans are not allowed to vote?' According to Johann, that was when the board saw 'we were serious, very serious, and Sir Robert Crichton-Brown was replaced by Sir David Montagu'.

Johann went ahead with the plans for the establishment of Richemont. At his father's insistence, he informed his colleagues at Rembrandt of the project. Anton Rupert had cautioned his son that 'I don't want to get a reputation for acting unpatriotically. You have to convince all of your colleagues.' Some refused to back the formation of a separately listed company because they saw they would be relinquishing their power. 'The argument was: Why should we give away our assets? Of course, these were not management's assets in the first place, they belonged to the shareholders.'

Overseas they needed to obtain the consent of Philip Morris (to whom Rembrandt had sold half its stake in Rothmans) to the transaction, but problems also arose in this regard. At the next meeting of the Rothmans board, Johann was duly put through his paces. In the first place, he received the documents for the meeting less than 24 hours before it was due to start. Only then did he learn that Rothmans London was planning to buy out Rothmans Australia and Rothmans Singapore.

'By then the share price had already gone through the roof; there had evidently been a leak,' Johann recalled. But the chair, Sir David Montagu, refused his request that the proposals not be submitted because he had had no time to study them. 'There were fourteen directors, and – that was when I learnt how these things work – he let me sit directly opposite him, but started with the director on my right. One by one, the directors around the table thought we should approve the proposed deal. When I put up my hand, the chair said, "I'll get to you last ..." Then my turn came and now it was one out of fourteen, and I knew exactly why they wanted to do it.'

In the first place, Johann told the board, he did not believe the figures that had been submitted. Questioning the financial sense of the purchase of Rothmans Australia, he exposed spurious arguments based on a discrepancy between Australian and German interest rates as well as the strength of the Deutschmark (with which the Australian assets would be bought) as opposed to the Australian dollar. In response to the directors' retort that they thought the Australian dollar would appreciate, he asked whether they thought the Australian interest rates would fall while the currency would simultaneously strengthen.

'I started to get the board's attention. Then I said: "Apples and pears are being compared here." Thank God I had spent those years at Lazard Frères and had had my own bank ... because these chaps were told to push through the deal, however unlucrative financially, simply to make it impossible for Rembrandt to buy out the Philip Morris shares. That was the sole reason.'

One of the directors, Henry Keswick, asked the chair: 'Mr Chairman, is it correct that you did not ask your proprietor and you are going against his wishes?' When Johann demurred that they did not own all the shares and were not the proprietor, Keswick, a close friend of Montagu's, said firmly: 'Young man, you *are* the proprietor.'

Johann then expressed his surprise that they would be using the assets of a German pension fund, in other words, German workers' money, to buy assets in Australia. The upshot was that the proposal was turned down. In 1989, Rembrandt finally bought out Philip Morris's shares in Rothmans after negotiations that lasted for months.

Richemont's establishment outside of South Africa in 1988 raised suspicion among some politicians. Johann was confronted about Richemont by Cyril Ramaphosa in 1990, the then secretary-general of the South African trade union federation Cosatu who subsequently became the ANC's chief negotiator at the Kempton Park negotiations on the country's transition to democracy. At a dinner at a Cape Town restaurant where the two men met for the first time, Ramaphosa wanted to know why they had established the new company overseas.

At the time, the ANC still had strong communist leanings and nationalisation was in the air. Johann gave a straight answer: 'Cyril, it's actually very simple, and you can tell that to your stakeholders. I have to protect the assets of *my* stakeholders, the shareholders, against your stakeholders – so that if they want to steal them, they won't be able to do so. No capital has left the country; no capital *will* ever leave the country; and all the revenue still returns to South Africa. I've given my word to Dr Gerhard de Kock [former president of the Reserve Bank], and over all the years we have not taken out a single penny.'

Ramaphosa then nearly 'split his sides' and said: 'Oh, you Afrikaners!' When Johann asked what he meant by this, Ramaphosa said he had just put the same question to Julian Ogilvy-Thompson, chair of Anglo American, and that Ogilvy-Thompson had told him all kinds of stories about marketing agreements with Russia, etcetera. Johann said such talk was just nonsense, and he and Ramaphosa subsequently became good friends. Ramaphosa even served for a while as a director of the Peace Parks Foundation founded by Anton Rupert.

In the early 1990s, Johann Rupert was also involved in the negotiations about the last remaining sticking points of South Africa's final new constitution, which was finalised in 1996 to establish the new dispensation as a constitutional state in which the exercise of governmental power is constrained by the law. He was invited to a conference of negotiators aimed at reaching agreement about the last two controversial issues: the right of trade union members to prevent lockouts, and property rights.

As a proponent of small business, Rupert was strongly opposed to the envisaged lockout clause that would prohibit employers from locking trade union members out of the workplace in the event of strikes. He had been warned against this by the former British prime minister Lady Margaret Thatcher, who had told him that the scrapping of this clause constituted her greatest victory over the militant British trade unions. The clause could favour trade union members to such an extent that they could occupy factories and workplaces and break down everything on the premises if they did not get their own way.

About sixty people attended the meeting that was chaired by President Nelson Mandela, including the secretary-general of Cosatu, Mbhazima (Sam) Shilowa, a member of the central committee of the South African Communist Party who would become premier of the Gauteng province in 1999. Mandela started the proceedings by addressing the younger Rupert directly: 'Johann, I know that you have reservations about the lockout clause. But you have to trust the government in this matter.'

Johann was equally direct in his reply: 'Mr Mandela, you know I have great respect for you and that I love you like a father. But it's not you that I have to trust. Because I don't trust Sam (Shilowa).'

He continued by pointing out that four workers of his group had been murdered by trade union members during a strike at Heidelberg. Ramaphosa confirmed the veracity of his statement. Rupert then said that if the lockout clause were to be enforced, he would close down all his factories and mines in South Africa the next day. An uneasy silence followed, and the meeting was adjourned. Outside, Ogilvy-Thompson came up to him and muttered: 'A bit aggressive, a bit aggressive …'

When the meeting finally resumed, Ramaphosa, as chief negotiator of the ANC, said that they had struck a 'deal' with the National Party about property rights. Afterwards Marinus Daling of Sanlam walked up to Roelf Meyer, the chief negotiator of the NP, and said he heard they had entered into a 'deal' with the ANC. Meyer replied: 'No, not a "deal", an understanding.' Daling retorted: 'Roelf, I'm not a politician, but could you explain to me what the difference is between a deal and an understanding?'

Meyer failed to provide an answer.

Ultimately, the lockout clause was not included in the final constitution while property rights enjoyed constitutional protection – until the ANC threw the continuation of such protection into doubt at its congress in December 2017.

Two decades after the final constitution was signed into law in 1996, Rupert was still critical of the negotiations phase in which De Klerk's side, in his view, had committed many blunders. These included the 'concession' of an election date being set before either the negotiations or the constitution had been finalised. 'I mean, I got to know Cyril, and he laughed his head off about this. The National Party was gullible and naive during the negotiations – they had children at the negotiating table.'

Restructuring of the Rembrandt Group

Johann had taken over from his father as non-executive chair of the Rembrandt Group as far back as 1992. Anton Rupert died in 2006, a few months after the death of his wife Huberte.

In time, Johann's international experience became a major asset for the Rembrandt Group. Through his network of international friends and acquaintances, he kept abreast of global economic and political developments. He impressed colleagues with his incisive analyses and relevant examples from other situations that could affect the group, or which were of significance to business enterprises.

A former colleague recounts: 'Johann was the master questioner: with sequential questions he could get to the heart of a complex problem. And just when everyone thought it was the end of his questions, he would start with a new series from a different angle. Of course, he had been a citizen of the world from an early age; he was widely travelled, well read and aways well informed.

'This, together with an exceptional memory, enabled him to illustrate his standpoints with relevant stories and anecdotes. Then there were of course also the times when he was unable to assert or impose his standpoint and would challenge the other party to a bet, sometimes with comical and even bizarre consequences.'

The restructuring of the Rembrandt Group advanced a further step in 2000 when the holding company was split in two: Remgro, as an investment company holding tobacco, financial services, mining and industrial interests, and the venture capital company VenFin, which housed the technology and telecommunication interests. From its inception in 2000 up to 2006, the group declared four large special dividends with a total value of R13 per share, over and above the ordinary interim and final dividends that were declared annually.

In 2008, Remgro unbundled its investment in British American Tobacco to its shareholders by way of an interim dividend in specie. In 2009, Remgro and VenFin, which had disposed of a 15 per cent stake in the cellphone group Vodacom, merged again, adding media and technology interests to the group's investments. Remgro, with Jannie Durand as chief executive, has investments in about thirty companies, including MBH, FirstRand, Mediclinic (which was headed for many years by the Rupert partner Edwin Hertzog), RCL Foods and Distell, as well as a number of unlisted companies.

In 2015, Mediclinic made a bad investment in Al Noor in Dubai, and the share price dropped from a peak of R218 to R93 in 2016. Rupert subsequently told the *Financial Mail* the problem was not that Mediclinic had made an investment overseas, but that it had used the wrong financial structure. 'You can't blame Mediclinic for looking abroad. Here [in South Africa] it was facing an industry that was becoming more regulated and highly politicised.' But such deals had to be structured properly, he said.

Meanwhile Richemont had continued to expand abroad. The subsidiary companies of the parent group Richemont jointly constitute the second-biggest manufacturer of luxury goods in the world, with only Louis Vuitton Moët Hennessy (LVMH) a bigger competitor. Richemont, which was established on the foundations of Cartier and Rothmans International, is in fact one of the few South African firms that has achieved great success by moving to new fields of business by means of a radical adjustment – from tobacco and liquor to luxury goods.

The Specialist Watchmakers segment in the Richemont group comprises some of the most sought-after brands. A stake of 60 per cent in the Swiss watchmaker Piaget, which had been acquired in 1988, was pushed up to 100 per cent in 1993. The oldest Swiss watchmaker still in operation, Vacheron Constantin, was taken over in 1996. The following year the Italian watchmaker Officine Panerai with its luxury watches was added to the group.

Another three famous watchmakers, the German firm A. Lange & Söhne and two Swiss firms, Jaeger-LeCoultre of Le Sentier and IWC of Schaffhausen, were acquired in 2000. In the watch segment, Richemont also entered into a joint venture with Ralph Lauren. In 2018, Watchfinder.co.uk, a marketplace for premium pre-owned watches that operates both online and through its boutiques, was added to the group.

Richemont's Jewellery Maisons segment includes several of the most prestigious names in the luxury industry. The flagship is the iconic and profitable Cartier, which accounts for an estimated two-thirds of the group profits. In 1999, the group acquired a 60 per cent stake in the Parisian jewellers Van Cleef & Arpels, which was increased to 80 per cent in 2000. Giampiero Bodino is the third jewellery company in this segment.

A third segment is made up of other businesses such as Azzedine Alaïa, Chloé, Dunhill, Montblanc, Peter Millar, and the venerable British institution Purdey, the firm of gunsmiths whose exclusive, hand-engraved shotguns and sporting rifles have a tradition dating back to 1814. In the 2018 financial year, the group increased its stake in the duty-free retailer Dufry and made a bid for the shares in the online luxury retailer Yoox Net-a-Porter (YNAP), which the group did not yet own.

Richemont had divested itself of its holdings in the tobacco industry as far back as 2008 through the establishment of the investment vehicle Reinet Investments in Luxembourg, the principal asset of which was at that stage Richemont's interest in British American Tobacco. A decade after its founding, Reinet still held substantial tobacco interests, while other investments had been made. Remgro, like other ageing companies, started showing signs of decelerating growth, with share prices that had lost their sheen.

Of relevance in this regard is the well-known sigmoid curve, which describes many other phenomena besides business organisations. The curve, which corresponds to the phases of the human life cycle, is characterised by a period of rapid growth, followed by a maturity phase where growth slows down and eventually stops. Questions about the group's performance were reflected in a front-page report in the *Financial Mail* of 7 February 2019, which speculated whether Johann Rupert might have lost his mojo.

Johann had indicated a few years earlier, however, that he did not intend to keep up the same pace. In 2013, he announced at Richemont's annual general meeting that he would take a year-long sabbatical. 'After 25 years I'd like a bit of a break,' the 62-year-old Rupert said, adding that he planned to travel to Antarctica and get through a backlog of more than fifty books. 'I want to be master of my own time for a while.'

On his return, he revealed at the *Financial Times* Business of Luxury Summit in Monaco that he couldn't sleep at night because of global concerns. The most important issue for the luxury industry and economies globally was the structural unemployment and growing wealth gap caused by technological advances. He feared that 'envy, hatred and social warfare' against the winners in the new economy would destabilise the world. It was 'unfair' that the accelerating inequality was destroying the middle classes. People with money would not wish to flaunt it by buying luxury goods. 'We can't have the 0,1 per cent of the 0,1 per cent taking all the spoils. Now folks, these are our clients. But it's unfair and it's not sustainable. This is really what keeps me up at night.'

Since the establishment of the luxury group, Rupert had taken action to stabilise and strengthen Richemont's market position on an number of occasions. In 2009, he returned for the third time as executive head to lead the group through a financial crisis. In a sweeping overhaul at the end of 2016, he changed the board radically and also brought younger people into the management team to meet changing customer demands. Heads of individual brands would in future report directly to the chair of the board.

In the 2018 year-end results, it was announced that while the group's sales had grown by 3 per cent and the operating profit was up 5 per cent, the results had been negatively affected by a buyback of unsold watches from shops that amounted to more than €200 million. Manufacturers of luxury goods were changing their strategy by moving to e-commerce as a younger generation of customers increasingly purchased digital watches and did their shopping online.

Johann Rupert's son Anton was appointed to the board of Richemont in 2017 after eight of the older directors retired. 'Anton

Rupert's proposed appointment to the board will bring further insight into the changing consumer behaviour of our target markets, particularly in digital marketing and web-based commerce. Anton has had extensive exposure to all of the group's businesses over the past eight years,' Johann Rupert announced. A cousin, Jan Rupert, also serves on the board.

In 2018, Richemont's increasing focus on e-commerce was confirmed in that the group acquired full control of Yoox Net-a-Porter, an online luxury retailer, in a €2,69 billion deal. YNAP, which was established after a merger between Net-a-Porter, a British-based online fashion retailer, and Yoox, an Italian fashion and technology company, sees itself as 'the world's biggest online luxury fashion store'.

Amazon had tried earlier to enter the luxury market, but without success. With the aim of keeping the retail giant out of this market, Rupert offered his competitors like LVMH stakes in the YNAP platform in exchange for a commitment that they would sell their brands on the site. He continued the established Rembrandt pattern by retaining the CEO of the business they had taken over, and he expressed his full confidence in YNAP's management team.

In October 2018, a further expansion of YNAP followed when a joint venture with China's biggest e-commerce company, Alibaba, was announced. This would enable Richemont to take on the Chinese market on a much larger scale since its online store obtained access to Alibaba's 600 million users. The CEO of Alibaba, Daniel Zheng, said the partnership 'would bring Chinese customers unprecedented access to the world's leading luxury brands'.

Rupert has also campaigned strongly for the preservation and celebration of master craftsmanship, particularly the European tradition of classic artisans who have been handcrafting valuable designer products and utilitarian objects for hundreds of years. Together with Franco Cologni, he founded the Michelangelo Foundation as a platform to support craftspeople. The foundation introduces such specialist firms, family businesses in which artisanal skills have been transferred from generation to generation, and unique ateliers to an international network of discerning buyers. Expensive shoes, knitwear, ceramic stoves, watches and leather saddles and boots are among the wide variety of select products made by craftspeople that benefit from the foundation established in 2018.

'What can Europe sell to the rest of the world?' Rupert asked rhetorically at the time. 'Culture. History. Taste.'

Rupert has often reaffirmed his confidence in investments in luxury brands: 'Anniversaries, birthdays and girlfriends are always going to be there.' And he has quoted the French fashion designer and businesswoman Coco Chanel: 'Money is money is money. It's only the pockets that change. We've got to find those pockets.' His business philosophy, one shared by virtually all luxury-goods billionaires, is succinct: 'The only way we know how to maintain a sustainable competitive advantage is to grow the brand equity … because that brand equity creates demand and will result in pricing power.'

When Rupert received the *Sunday Times* Top 100 Companies Lifetime Achievement Award in 2016, he said the biggest mistake he'd made in business was 'being too conservative and not doing deals I could have done because I listened to other people'. A missed deal he regretted was that he could have bought Gucci for $175 million, but his board advised against it and he listened to them. In 1997, he bought Panerai for $1,1 million against the advice of his board, and in 2016 the company was worth about $1,5 billion.

'We have created wealth,' he said in his acceptance speech. 'By the way, for all of you civil servants here – even Minister Gordhan says we've got to be "caring". We mustn't make too much money." I've got news for you. The Public Investment Corporation owns two-and-a-half times the number of shares in both Richemont and Remgro that our family owns. Now remember, that's *your* pension fund, you may wish to reconsider the "caring" bit.'

Rupert on apartheid and Afrikanership

At Remgro's annual general meeting in December 2017, Johann Rupert once again felt obliged to defend his company against accusations that it was an apartheid beneficiary. He pointed out that his father had started the Small Business Development Corporation (SBDC, now Business Partners). The initiative came about as a result of Rupert senior being egged on by Johann, a fervent proponent of small business. From the time of its inception, this institution that finances and supports small and medium-sized enterprises (SMEs) has helped create around 700 000 jobs in South Africa.

He estimated that the value created by Remgro from 1994 to 2017 topped R327 billion in capital growth and R29,8 billion in dividends. Along with Richemont, dividends and distributions repatriated topped R81,5 billion, while excise duties and taxes amounted to R197 billion. 'So we pay tax. We have 152 000 employees working for us, we create jobs. We bring money back to South Africa, we don't take it out. You'd think people would say "thank you". But no.'

Rupert said it was time for serious people to get together and discuss serious national issues: growing unemployment and almost zero economic growth. 'People get poorer and poorer and poorer, and there's a huge disparity in wealth. And I hate to tell you that it will get worse globally. The 0,1 per cent will take more and more in the future, because where an Amazon or an Apple is created you realise that information technology is replicable at virtually zero marginal cost.

'In the old days a bricklayer who laid 60 bricks an hour compared with someone who could lay 100 bricks an hour still had a job. He did not get paid the same, but he had a job. Today a guy who writes software at 60 bricks an hour compared with one who writes 100 doesn't have a job. The best one gets everything. It's a winner-takes-all economy.'

He explained a new skills policy adopted in Richemont. 'When we appoint anyone, that individual in the factories is advised that they should be multiskilled since I can no longer guarantee a job. Because they can become redundant within five years as a result of new machinery, new techniques and artificial intelligence. So, a polisher has to be multiskilled. We help to train them so that they are not replaced by machines.' He took a swipe at radicals. 'Here [in South Africa] they want to take the land. To do what with?'

He pleaded for the education system to be fixed. 'My heroes are not the rock stars, the movie stars or the golf players I meet. My heroes are the teachers. They are missionaries. But we can't reach those young people in schools because Sadtu [the teachers' union] says it owns them from Monday to Saturday. Now please believe me, we as a society did not build schools to provide jobs for teachers.

We've created schools to educate children; not to give teachers permanent jobs. So, we have critical problems like that, and we sit and debate nonsense.'

It made him boiling mad, Rupert said, because the rest of the world was doing better. There were countries that were doing very well and companies that were doing very well in those countries, because they had made the right choices. Those were the places to which money and brainpower flowed. Money and brainpower did not go to regions where they were not welcome; they went to where they were welcomed.

Rupert has on occasion showed himself to be a champion of the Afrikaans language. In September 2005, he decided to withdraw millions of rands' worth of advertising from the international decor magazine *Wallpaper*. In the magazine, one of its writers had written that the architect Jan van Wijk erected the Taal Monument in Paarl in 1975 'in honour of one of the world's ugliest languages' [Afrikaans] – a monument which, if appreciated for nothing else, was a fine picnic spot on the way to Franschhoek and the Stellenbosch Winelands.

He responded to this incident as follows: 'The magazine humiliated my mother tongue and I've now had enough of my culture being constantly belittled. I'm not going to sit idly by while my language and culture are dragged through the mud. What they had to say about Afrikaans was the biggest load of rubbish I'd seen in a long time, and I decided that it called for action.'

At the time of the centenary of the Afrikanerbond in 2018, Rupert was one of a number of prominent South Africans interviewed about their attitude towards the Bond and Afrikaners for the purposes of a commemorative volume titled *Broederskap*. He was never a member of the Afrikanerbond or its predecessor the Afrikaner-Broederbond, although his father had belonged to it at an early stage of his career. Anton Rupert's membership lapsed as he gradually saw less need for such an organisation after 1948, 'when our own people had come to power'. He became uncomfortable with participation in the secret society, feeling it had become 'an absurdity' and 'counterproductive' over time.

Asked whether he considered himself an Afrikaner, the younger Rupert replied firmly: 'Absolutely! But you need to understand that there is an enormous difference between the Transvaal Afrikaner who wanted to put the coloured people in homelands, and the Cape Afrikaner. I'm much closer to Russel Botman [the late theologian and former rector of Stellenbosch University] who speaks Afrikaans and is coloured. Well, is he an Afrikaner or not? Not according to the logic of the Broederbond and rightists. Not at all. I'm much closer to the coloured people of the Cape than to those who expound their crazy right-wing views in *Beeld* and *Rapport*.

'These people resent FW de Klerk for the steps he took in 1990; they believe if FW hadn't done that, we would still have had the 'good life'. He amputated the gangrenous leg and saved the patient. We wouldn't have existed today if it hadn't been for the drastic steps taken in 1990.'

In his opinion, apartheid was a tragedy for the Afrikaner. 'It made us the polecat of the world. I'm glad it was an Afrikaner [De Klerk] who got rid of it. Better still, that it wasn't determined by a war, but that it was the first time in human history where a group of people voluntarily surrendered power. FW saved us, even though he knew beforehand he would be vilified by many – he pressed on regardless.'

The Guptas and the 'white monopoly capital' campaign

In the last years of former president Jacob Zuma's administration, Rupert was an early target of the propaganda campaign against 'white monopoly capital', a smear campaign against the South African business sector that was funded by the Indian-born Guptas and led by the British PR firm Bell Pottinger from March 2016. The three Gupta brothers, Ajay, Tony and Atul, amassed a fortune by leveraging their close relationship with Zuma, bullying government officials and wangling government contracts for their sprawling network of interests in mining, media, energy, armaments and railways. They even offered cabinet positions to ANC members such as Mcebisi Jonas – in his case, an offer of R600 million in cash to become minister of finance.

The Guptas became stinking rich. At the end of 2016, Atul Gupta, chair of Oakbay Investments, was listed as the seventh wealthiest South African and the top-earning black businessman on the *Sunday Times* Rich List, with a net worth of R10,7 billion – at the time more than that of both Johann Rupert and Patrice Motsepe. As criticism and concern about state capture mounted, the sell-out of state assets and governance was finally confirmed by the damning findings about the Zuma regime in Public Protector Thuli Madonsela's 'State of Capture' report.

The 'Zuptas', as the notorious alliance between President Zuma, the Guptas and their holding company Oakbay Investments was increasingly called, needed the PR equivalent of a stun grenade to deflect the attention of their many critics and direct it towards their enemies. In consultation with Victoria Geoghegan from Bell Pottinger, Zuma's son Duduzane, who was employed by the Guptas, devised a propaganda campaign to be harnessed against 'white monopoly capital'. Geoghegan's consultation with Duduzane Zuma involved a 'project fee' of £100 000 (about R2,3 million).

The younger Zuma was so influential that critics took to calling the president uBaba kaDuduzane, the father of Duduzane. The inciting use of 'white monopoly capital' stirred up racial tensions in the already sensitive South African situation by claiming that whites acquired their wealth by stealing land and resources from blacks who were deprived of jobs and education.

To Rupert, it was a bitter irony that he of all people was targeted by the campaign; by then he had been a Bell Pottinger client for about fifteen years. The British prime minister Margaret Thatcher had told him about the company's founder, Tim Bell, who had helped her Conservative Party secure an election victory in 1979 thanks to an advertising campaign with the slogan 'Labour isn't working'. According to mutual friends of Rupert's and Lady Thatcher's, Rupert once silenced her at a dinner during one of their intense discussions with: 'Stop interrupting me while I'm interrupting you!'

Bell Pottinger was paid 12 000 Swiss francs a year for basically distributing Richemont's annual reports in London. Rupert commented on this as follows at Richemont's AGM in December 2017: 'And whilst they were still in the employment of Richemont they started working for the Guptas. Their total task was to deflect attention [from state capture allegations involving the Guptas]. Guess who they took as a target? A client of theirs ... me!'

Tim Bell tried for a while to keep up the pretence that there was nothing amiss with the reprehensible campaign. 'Morality is a job for priests,' he stated emotionlessly in an interview with the *New York Times*, 'not PR men.'

In a BBC programmme, Bell related that Rupert had threatened to close his account if the company did not ditch the Gupta account, since he had become a target of the Gupta campaign. 'Johann Rupert wrote to me and said if you want to handle me, you can't handle the Guptas.'

The instruction to drop the Gupta account was ignored, however, after which Rupert and several other clients, including Richemont and Investec, withdrew their accounts. Rupert tweeted under his Twitter handle, Cutmaker: 'Very illuminating. The term #White-MonopolyCapital didn't exist on Google prior to the #Gupta appointment of #BellPottinger.'

Rupert, the first high-profile businessman to go on the warpath against Bell Pottinger, said the real story about Bell Pottinger was that the company used the inflammatory 'white monopoly capital' and 'radical economic transformation' narratives to cover up their clients' looting. On 6 September 2017, Cutmaker tweeted: 'Reason Zuptas hired Bell Pottinger to destroy critics of theft/corruption? BP campaign of lies/hatred followed.'

Some time before, during one of the biggest furores under the corruption-plagued Zuma regime, Rupert was implicated by the then president in an alleged conspiracy against him. This was in December 2015, shortly before Bell Pottinger's propaganda campaign was launched. Zuma summarily axed the minister of finance, Nhlanhla Nene, and replaced him with a virtually unknown parliamentary back-bencher, Des van Rooyen. After the rand plummeted, Zuma made a U-turn in the space of four days and reappointed the experienced Pravin Gordhan as finance minister.

Zuma claimed that Rupert had specially flown from London to South Africa to scheme behind his back. He had supposedly met with a senior ANC leader and demanded that Van Rooyen's appointment be reversed. In a speech to a meeting of the ANC's national executive committee in March 2016, an irate Zuma declared that people should tell him directly if he should step down, rather than stabbing him in the back. Zuma's eldest son, Edward, even opened a case of corruption against Rupert at the Nkandla police station.

In response, Rupert said if Zuma's information had been correct and had not come from the Guptas, he would have known that Rupert was attending a graduation ceremony of Stellenbosch University in his capacity as chancellor; he had not flown in from London. He was fed up with the way Zuma managed the country, and it was time for people to make their voices heard. Business leaders should be prepared to be unpopular, as they had been with the previous regime, he said. International investors had warned him that South Africa's credit rating downgrade to junk was inevitable. 'It would mean a dollar will suddenly cost R30. The consequences will be far-reaching.' His next comment was a direct appeal to Zuma: 'Yes, for the sake of our children's future, please resign!'

At the time, Ian Cruickshanks, then economist at the Institute of Race Relations, described Rupert's comments as 'weighty'. 'He is the first big businessman to say these things in public and on the record.'

Zuma, who later fired Gordhan on the basis of a suspicious so-called security report, found himself increasingly under pressure throughout 2017 as thousands of confidential emails were leaked to the media in the #GuptaLeaks scandal. At the ANC's decisive congress in December 2017, Zuma was replaced as ANC president by Cyril Ramaphosa, who narrowly defeated Zuma's ex-wife Nkosazana Dlamini-Zuma in the leadership race. A few weeks later, Ramaphosa became president of the country as well, after a still protesting Zuma finally resigned on Valentine's Day under pressure from his ANC comrades.

For the Guptas and Bell Pottinger, events took an equally disastrous turn.

In March 2017, a forensic analysis performed by the African Network of Centers for Investigative Reporting concluded that Bell Pottinger's campaign was created and overseen by employees and affiliates of the Guptas. Much of the campaign was run out of a Gupta-financed 'war room' at a marketing firm in India. The role of Bell Pottinger was to keep a close eye on social media platforms, which were inter alia fed with hundreds of tweets from fake Twitter accounts.

As racial animosity in South Africa deepened, angry groups

protested against Bell Pottinger both locally and in London. One demonstrator carried a photo of Victoria Geoghegan labelled 'Gupta's Girl', with blood dripping from her lips.

In April 2017, Bell Pottinger cancelled its contract with the Guptas because of 'increasingly strong social media attacks on our staff and our business'. In July 2017, the chief executive issued an 'unequivocal and absolute' apology – on the same day that Victoria Geoghegan was fired. The company was also expelled as a member of Britain's Public Relations and Communications Association.

The consequences were swift. Within days of Bell Pottinger's expulsion, one client after another jumped like fleas from the company's carcass. By September, all 250 employees were out of a job, and Bell Pottinger was declared insolvent.

The attacks on Rupert and 'white monopoly capital' had in any case not penetrated everywhere. In June 2017, on the eve of the ANC's national policy conference in Johannesburg that was set to discuss radical economic transformation as well as ways to overthrow white monopoly capital, the Progressive Business Forum, the ANC's fundraising vehicle, hosted a fancy gala dinner. A table reservation was rumoured to have cost R25 000 a piece. The reproach of 'white monopoly capital' had often been hurled derisively at the Ruperts – but at the dinner Anthonij Rupert wines accompanied the salmon roulade and other sumptuous dishes served to the ANC's big shots. The wine was produced on the L'Ormarins estate near Franschhoek, which had been taken over by Johann after the death of his younger brother.

The 'incomers'

After Rupert's return to the Cape in the 1980s, he decided he did not want to make Stellenbosch his home, preferring to settle in the neighbouring town of Somerset West. Rumour-mongering about the internationally renowned Rupert family was just too rife in the Town of Oaks, he felt, and he wanted to avoid conspicuous attention as far as possible.

He established his personal office on the outskirts of Somerset West, on the historic Groot Paardevlei estate with its Cape Dutch manor house. He and his wife Gaynor – a former University of

Pretoria rag queen – moved into their residence on the nearby Parel
Vallei estate.

Although no longer a resident, he regularly visited Stellenbosch.
He was chancellor of Stellenbosch University for ten years, until the
end of 2019. Remgro's corporate head office is located in the town,
and he also frequented the Volkskombuis restaurant. The people of
Stellenbosch came to know him as a man loyal towards his friends;
someone with strong views who tends to dominate table talk, but also
a South African business leader on first-name terms with influential
individuals in political and business circles around the world.

Rupert was always sceptical of Markus Jooste and the people of
Steinhoff, those he regarded as 'incomers' that had brought a 'different, newer culture' to Stellenbosch after his departure from the town
in 1975.

The first time Jooste aroused his suspicion was when he bought his
father's house in Hermanus and cut down five old Norfolk pines that
had been a landmark to fishermen at the Rupert house. Civilised people plant trees, they don't chop them down, he rebuked the 'incomer'.

Rupert's doubts were raised about Jooste's business practices when
his wife Gaynor, who breeds racehorses at her Drakenstein stud on
their farm L'Ormarins, asked him to look at the financial statements
of Cape Thoroughbred Sales. Jooste, the owner of hundreds of thoroughbred horses on the Klawervlei Stud Farm near Bonnievale, was a
director of Cape Thoroughbred Sales when Gaynor was asked to join
the board.

The company was established to promote the sport of horse racing
and the thoroughbred breeding industry. Cape Thoroughbred Sales
hosted the biggest horse-racing auctions in the country, Klawervlei was
the biggest vendor of horses, and Mayfair Speculators, which Jooste ran
together with his son-in-law Stefan Potgieter, was the biggest buyer. So
the same people were essentially behind all three entities.

Feeling uncomfortable about the situation, Gaynor Rupert
asked her husband for an independent opinion. Johann went
through the statements and thought: 'You can't do this!' He
requested PwC to examine the statements. When Jooste heard
about it, he 'threw his toys out of the cot'. Johann then advised his
wife to resign as a director.

She also told him that the bombastic Jooste bullied people when he didn't get his way, and that many in the horse-racing industry were afraid of him. What baffled Johann was where Jooste got all the money he spent on horses. The expenditure amounting to millions just did not seem possible when one looked at his statements and earnings as CEO of Steinhoff.

The last straw for Rupert was when, after a round of golf at the Seminole Golf Club in Florida, a prominent investor asked him who the 'damn morons' were that had bought Mattress Firm. After analysing Mattress Firm, the investor concluded that the company was worth between 20 per cent and 25 per cent of what Steinhoff had paid. When the investor shorted Steinhoff, Rupert knew it was curtains for Steinhoff.

At the end of 2017, shortly after the Steinhoff debacle erupted, Rupert phoned some of his Stellenbosch friends and reminded them that he had warned them. He tweeted as Cutmaker that it really irritated him 'that not one of the so-called "Stellenbosch Mafia" who are causing so much damage to the town's reputation was born or raised in Stellenbosch. All of them are "incomers".' He detested what had happened to his former hometown: 'People have chopped down trees and built palaces. I feel the culture has changed.'

On occasion, Rupert also used the fact that his home was in Somerset West to make fun of narratives portraying him as part of the 'Stellenbosch Mafia'. For instance, on receiving the *Sunday Times* Lifetime Achievement Award in 2017, he pointed out to the 'commander in chief' of the Economic Freedom Fighters (EFF), Julius Malema, in his acceptance speech: 'I don't know how I can be part of the Stellenbosch Mafia. We live in Somerset West.'

He also 'thanked' Malema for having made him relevant again with his claims that Rupert controlled the ANC, the Democratic Alliance (DA), the South African Revenue Service (SARS) and the Reserve Bank. Meanwhile people had distanced themselves from Malema and now it was said that he controlled Julius, Rupert quipped, although he had never met him. 'But I did send him a text message through a friend that if he doesn't stop lying about me, I'm going to tell the world that I actually do give him money!'

Rupert in the firing line

In December 2018, Rupert's criticism of political opponents provoked a storm of controversy when he made a rare public appearance in an interview with Given Mkhari, owner of the radio station PowerFM and chair of the MSG Afrika Group. He was the guest at the annual Chairman's Conversation event.

In response to a question by Mkhari about how Afrikaners' oppression by the English had contributed to the establishment and growth of the Rembrandt Group, Rupert said: 'That's the reason.' He explained how driven the post-Anglo-Boer War and depression-era generation of Afrikaners had been, how they had studied and saved 'like crazy'. 'They didn't go and buy BMWs and hang around at Taboo and The Sands [upmarket clubs] all the time.'

A member of the audience said Rupert's white privilege had helped enable his current level of wealth, and suggested that Rupert use some of it to help boost young black entrepreneurs in Mamelodi. 'I've tried my best,' he replied. 'My people who work with me are happy. They've all got homes. I look after their kids. I give them bursaries. But I am not Father Christmas. I can't look after the whole country.'

Challenging Rupert from the floor, the Power 98.7 presenter Iman Rappetti said she felt he suffered from 'cognitive dissonance': people listening to the interview on the radio and reacting on Twitter thought he was 'out of touch' with how South Africans experienced his message; that it was perceived as racist.

Rupert replied that those in his age group knew he was not a racist. 'It's that old thing, when you run out of arguments. In the old days, when you were against apartheid, you were called a communist.' Now that he was against corruption, he was accused of racism. 'How do you defend yourself against being called racist? You can call anybody a racist.' He said he took exception to that.

Responding to Rappetti's remark about expensive cars and clubs, he denied that he had said 'black people'. 'I said "people". Do you think white kids don't do the same? Do you think a whole generation of children don't do the same?' Previous generations did not spend as lavishly as young South Africans did, he pointed out. 'There is globally a sense of "consume now", and if people want to take it personally, they should really question what the parents gave up, what the grand-parents gave up. I'm talking in general, I'm not saying colour bias, race bias, sex bias. I'm sorry if it came across as racist. It's not racist. It's a philosophy, that you can't consume now and pay later.'

Andile Nomlala, president of the Black Management Forum (BMF), said from the floor that he had been 'offended' by Rupert's statements. 'We had the opportunity here to understand what our white counterparts think of us.' Young black professionals should deduce from the interview that they were now 'on their own', he said.

Rupert said he had endured attacks from the BMF for years without responding to them. He had come to the interview to tell people they should talk to each other in an open-minded way.

'Our country has got very serious problems, best illustrated by the clear division tonight. There's clear hatred, clear animosity, insults.

'Quite frankly, if that is the attitude, we are going to have serious problems. I've offered from my side ... [but] quite frankly, I am very happy not to get involved, to spend time with my friends and children and not to help. To be insulted like this ... instead of people debating facts, they get personal. They attack individuals and their children. If we carry on like this, the other side loses interest ... very quickly.'

From questions from the floor and subsequent commentary, and also the backlash on social media, it became clear that Rupert had probably underestimated the hypersensitivity of some black South Africans. Among other things, he was accused of being 'arrogant' and 'condescending', and the race card was played: he was branded a 'racist'.

Shortly afterwards, the journalist Ferial Haffajee wrote a column titled: 'So a really rich white guy said really dumb things, and you're surprised?' In her view, the fact that Rupert's interview 'so incensed people' showed that a pattern she had discerned 'of a black majority country placing the responsibility for its psychological wellbeing, and its self-understanding, in the hands of white capital' still existed. Black South Africa too often defined itself by whites.

But some other commentators, such as the News24 columnist Mpumulelo Mkhabela, a former station manager of Power 98.7, wrote that black people should rather take heed of the 'hard lessons' Rupert had spelled out.

Rupert subsequently revealed that the deputy president of the EFF, Floyd Shivambu, had advised him to do the interview while the latter was on a visit to Stellenbosch. This was after Rupert had told Shivambu of his opposition to apartheid and how he had met Steve Biko. On Rupert's return from New York he had opened a hair salon, Black Wave, in the Carlton Centre in Johannesburg as a joint venture with a black partner, Brian Gule. While in Johannesburg, he used to visit Soweto and regularly listened to jazz at the Pelican Jazz Club. It upset him that aspiring black businesspeople faced so many hurdles, which was why he persuaded his father to make funds available for the SBDC so that black entrepreneurs could build up business enterprises.

Shivambu denied that he had pushed Rupert to do the interview, but he did talk to Jannie Durand of Remgro and GT Ferreira as well. He did not deny that he had gone in search of money in the heart of Stellenbosch's so-called 'white monopoly capital', although the purpose was not necessarily to sustain the EFF leaders' Gucci lifestyle.

Rupert later elaborated further on his frustration, and for the first time mentioned openly that he was considering leaving the country. He had lost faith in the ANC; the country had 'already reached a point of no return', and the proximity of Deputy President David (DD) Mabuza to the top job was 'too close for comfort'. His phone was tapped; SARS 'sabotaged' him despite the fact that he had been by far the highest individual taxpayer in the country for the past twenty years.

His children lived in England, and he thought 'it's better that way. When they are here [in SA], we don't sleep. When they were here, they couldn't go out in public without being insulted. It affected my family.'

Rupert's warning has a bearing on the alarming exodus of wealth creators from South Africa, a phenomenon any government can only ignore to the great detriment of a country. The Knight Frank Wealth Report for 2018 showed that between 2012 and 2017 South Africa had lost almost a quarter of its super-rich (those individuals with a net worth of more than $5 million) – from 13 380 in 2012 to just 10 350 in 2017.

And in December 2018, executive recruitment specialists Jack

Hammer released the results of a survey showing that 86 per cent of top South African executives who were polled indicated they would be willing to emigrate – up from 47 per cent in 2016. Out of this group, hailing from 80 of the country's largest companies, half (49 per cent) were black professionals who indicated they were interested in relocating to 'greener pastures'.

Rupert's commitment to the country was reaffirmed when President Cyril Ramaphosa declared a state of disaster in South Africa in March 2020 during the Covid-19 crisis. Ramaphosa announced at the time that the Rupert and the Oppenheimer families had each donated R1 billion to help keep financially distressed small businesses afloat.

Rupert explained that the generous sum would be administered by Business Partners, the successor of the SBDC that had been established by his father on 3 March 1979 at Johann's insistence. The main aim of the donation was to pay the salaries of employees of SMEs and 'put money in their pockets' in the dire economic situation, Johann said.

Earlier he had pointed out that the SBDC was founded as a way of uplifting black entrepreneurs. The assistance made it possible for them to raise loans, also from banks. Full title ownership is one of the foundations of wealth creation and it secures property rights, he emphasised. He added that up to that point, he had sponsored more than 10 000 coloured and black households to obtain title deeds for their properties.

Rumours that Rupert intended to leave South Africa resurfaced when Remgro announced the unbundling of the company's 40 per cent stake in FirstRand at the end of 2019. Rupert himself quashed the rumours. He told Alec Hogg of Moneyweb that Jannie Durand had described the unbundling best by likening it to a grown-up child leaving home. He added: 'It's well known I'm the biggest taxpayer in South Africa. And that our companies have not taken a cent out of the country. My dogs live in Somerset West. And so do I.'

4

King of retail

Christo Wiese

A LONG-STANDING view that Afrikaners did not have it in them to excel as traders and industrialists was eventually dispelled by quite a few entrepreneurs. So much so that in 2016 one of their number, Christo Wiese, was named South Africa's richest businessman, with an estimated net worth of R81 billion. This was before the Steinhoff scandal wiped out a large chunk of his fortune after he had taken over the chairmanship of that company.

A close friend of Wiese's, Whitey Basson of Shoprite fame, likewise expanded so impressively that the duo would become known as the Kings of Retail. Basson grew the brand of the Shoprite/Checkers group on an unprecedented scale by setting up grocery stores beyond the national borders and across Africa, while Wiese's Pep stores sold affordably priced clothing to willing buyers all around the continent.

Wiese was the chair of both Pepkor Holdings and Shoprite Holdings, Africa's biggest clothing and food retailers respectively, with around 6 000 stores employing more than 150 000 people in 24 countries.

Christoffel Hendrik Wiese grew up in Upington where his parents, Stoffel and Kotie Wiese, farmed with sheep. His father also owned a garage in the town. Even as a schoolboy, Wiese, who was born on 10 September 1941, displayed the resoluteness that was to characterise his subsequent career. He went to school in Upington, but some of his friends attended Boland schools and told him about everything happening there. He was 15 years old and in standard 9 (grade 11) when he 'developed a strong desire to attend Boishaai' – the parallel-medium Paarl Boys' High that is rated as one of the top boys' schools in the country.

After the mid-year winter holidays he informed his teachers that he was leaving for Paarl, and they notified his father about this. Stoffel Wiese, who up to that point had only given Christo about six hidings – 'but they were hidings I remembered' – cut a cane from a peach tree and he had to bend over. After the tears, Wiese senior asked if Christo was now ready to apologise and return to school. But Wiese junior was adamant: he was going to Paarl. Eventually his mother intervened and a phone call was made to the principal of Paarl Boys' High, Gawie Pretorius. The principal was able to offer a private room outside the school premises, on condition that Christo fell under hostel rules and had his daily meals at the Imhoff school hostel.

After matriculating eighteen months later, Christo initially went to study at the University of Cape Town (UCT). His family were *Bloedsappe*, dyed-in-the-wool supporters of General Jan Smuts's United Party (UP). With his firmly held belief that UP children who studied at Stellenbosch 'turned into Nats', Stoffel Wiese was not in favour of his son attending that university. At UCT, however, Christo was a mediocre student and he left without completing his course. 'My less-than-illustrious academic record caused me to return to Upington with the strong conviction that I wasn't cut out for academic studies. I wanted to become a businessman.'

This time Stoffel Wiese concurred, and he bought a radiator repair business in the town. Soon the heat inside the little building in the already scorchingly hot Upington made Wiese think that it might not be a bad idea to resume his studies.

He was encouraged by Renier van Rooyen, who was related to the Wieses by marriage, to continue his studies in Stellenbosch. Van Rooyen was married to Christo's cousin Alice van Rooyen, the daughter of Stoffel Wiese's sister. With financial support from Van Rooyen,

Christo enrolled to study law at Stellenbosch University.

One of Christo's fellow residents in the men's residence Wilgen-hof was Whitey Basson, who would later head up the Shoprite food-store chain. Whitey also came from a *Bloedsap* family; his fa-ther, Captain Jack Basson, was a member of Parliament. Christo was Whitey's senior in Wilgenhof – he had arrived in Stellenbosch a year before Whitey, and at 21 he was older than most of the other students. The two were to become lifelong friends.

In his third year at university, Christo was at his parents' home during the holidays. At his father's garage, where he worked from time to time as a petrol attendant, he talked to Willie Gresse, a good buddy of Renier van Rooyen's. By that time, Renier had proved he was a successful businessman. He already had four or five stores – in Upington, De Aar and Postmasburg in the Karoo.

Willie Gresse told Christo about a plan Renier had. 'He wants to expand his business countrywide, but he's looking for partners. And he has an interesting philosophy: you can work at the business as a branch manager. You can only get a job if you're a shareholder, and you can only become a shareholder if you have a job at the company. That was the model – it was basically just branch managers and Renier. He was the buyer and the accountant and everything.'

That evening Christo told his father about the conversation and said he felt Van Rooyen was on to something. The family often had discussions about business; his mother had a shop in the town, and other relatives with Upington roots also had businesses. From their dinner-table conversations he learnt how business worked – the most basic principles: 'Knowing that the customer is king and that you should always be ready to deliver the best possible service.'

Stoffel Wiese then phoned Van Rooyen and he came to talk to them. Christo remembers the conversation well: 'It was decided my father would sell his business – by that time he had already sold the farm – he would invest in this new business, and he would be a direc-tor.' His father and his father's two brothers, he added, had grown up farmboys, but all three of them were entrepreneurs: 'shops, a garage and a farming operation on top of that'. Christo recalls that the two brothers came to see his father to express their concern about his new venture. It worried them, they said, 'because you've never worked for someone else in your life. Now you're going into a company in which you are not the boss, and Renier is a youngster, isn't he?'

Christo says: 'I still remember how well my father handled it. Because he was 60 years old; how much working life did he have left in him? The agreement we came to at the time was that once I had finished at university, I would join the business.'

The rise of Pep Stores

After obtaining his LLB in 1967, Wiese was admitted as an advocate, but he did not go on to practise law. His first job was alongside his father at Pep Stores in Upington – as the number two, he would always say. He was also the company secretary, but his main task was to find premises for new stores and recruit staff countrywide. With the Pep Stores head office and warehouse now in Cape Town, he spent most of his time in the Mother City.

By 1969, Pep Stores owned 27 stores. Out of the blue Sydney Press, the boss of the big listed company Edgars – and by far the largest clothing retailer in South Africa – approached Renier van Rooyen with a takeover bid. He said he had been watching Renier, he had an interesting business model; he would like to buy the business from him.

'Renier said: We've actually just started, but what kind of money are we talking about? And he said, well, give me your numbers. So Renier gave him the numbers, and he said, well, he thinks anything between three and four million rand,' Wiese recounts. 'In those days the richest man in Upington was Oom Abraham Liebenberg, and he was worth R200 000, according to my father. And here a man was talking about millions. So Renier pricked up his ears. He said, well, let's see.'

Press first wanted to have a due diligence investigation done, and then he wanted to negotiate. In Johannesburg, Van Rooyen, Wiese and an auditor sat down with Sydney Press's senior director, a certain Moffat, who frequently first wanted to discuss sticking points with his chairman. Van Rooyen eventually returned to Cape Town and left the negotiations up to Wiese, who in turn insisted on first discussing hitches with *his* chairman every now and again. Finally, after all the

toing-and-froing, they had moved to a purchase price of R4,5 million, which was almost acceptable to Van Rooyen and company,
except for R160 000. They wanted R4,66 million.

That was as far as he could go, Moffat said. They would now
have to speak to the chairman. Wiese had never met Sydney Press,
who was to him 'some kind of magical figure'. On their arrival at
the Edgars head office at the bottom end of Commissioner Street in
Johannesburg, Moffat first showed them Press's metallic blue Rolls
Royce in the basement.

'Once in his office, we presented our case about this R160 000.
He listens attentively, he is terribly polite, and he says: "No, I'm
afraid I cannot agree to that. Four and a half million is our absolute
maximum, and I just need to point out to you that I have already
identified 25 leases, premises, and if we don't do a deal I will open a
business like yours in direct competition. Within six months I'll have
25 to your 27 stores." In other words, war …'

They then had to weigh their options. On the one hand, they
faced a serious threat. On the other hand, if they accepted his offer,
'all of us would be two, three times as rich as Oom Abraham Liebenberg. So, what's to lose? My father was 63 at the time, and I was a
young, admitted advocate who now had a rich dad. And we said,
okay, we would return to Cape Town and then get back to him. To
cut a long story short, he said we had to finalise the contracts on a
Saturday because he wanted to announce on the Monday.

'Moffat phoned and said Edgars' attorneys weren't available on
the Saturday because they would be playing golf in George, but he
would find an attorney in Johannesburg who was prepared to work
on a Saturday. He obviously thought they had to strike while the iron
was hot.'

That Saturday evening they had a braai at Van Rooyen's house
where Stoffel Wiese was also present. They discussed the developments and the R4,5 million, and the younger men expressed their
doubts about the deal. Despite the tempting financial benefits they
believed they were building a substantial and successful business and
should continue with it.

'My father agreed with us. So, on the Sunday, Renier phoned
Sydney Press and said: 'Sorry, we're not accepting the offer.' And Press

was the moer in. What did he do then? He started the Jet Stores business. That was the beginning of Jet Stores.

'I'm telling this story so that people can understand this stuff; how things worked and what an emerging Afrikaner businessman was up against.'

By 1970, Pep Stores had 58 stores countrywide and credit of R500 000 had been obtained to acquire new cash registers. By the end of that financial year, sales had increased by 130 per cent to R6,6 million, and profits had surged by 268 per cent.

With their rapid expansion that necessitated more capital, Van Rooyen and his team decided to apply for a listing on the JSE in 1972. This was shortly after the 1969 crash that had made people very wary of the bourse. Pep would be the first significant listing at the time.

Wiese describes the situation as follows: 'In those days about 80 to 90 per cent of the bourse and the bourse committee were Jews and English speakers. Lafras van Rensburg and George Huysamer were the only Afrikaners. George was our broker. There was a spate of newspaper stories about our intentions because up to that stage there hadn't been a single big retail company owned and managed by Afrikaners that was a success. Not one. There was Uniewinkels, but all of them were weak in the knees.

'There was a conviction that Boere couldn't run a retail business. So naturally there was scepticism. Also about the extremely rapid expansion of this business that had grown from a small, rural three- or four-store operation to a listable company in the space of about five years. All of these were contributory factors.'

The JSE's listing day was always on a Wednesday. The bourse committee convened on the Monday before the Wednesday. By that time Stoffel Wiese had died, and Christo and his mother were preparing in Cape Town to travel to Johannesburg. Then he got a phone call from Renier van Rooyen; he had to fly up to Johannesburg at once, as the bourse committee had just informed Renier that they would not approve the listing.

Wiese was shocked at what Van Rooyen told him. 'According to their assessment our balance sheet wasn't strong enough – the amount of capital we had and the sales and the cash flow, *and* they compared Pep with the likes of Edgars and Truworths. Those were businesses of a different type, and they didn't seem to understand this. If a report had to go out that they refused the listing because the balance sheet wasn't strong enough – that would be fatal! I mean, a kiss of death.'

On their arrival in Johannesburg, the Pep team conferred with Harry Laurie, the managing director of Senbank, their merchant banker. He phoned the JSE chairman Richard Lurie to convene an urgent meeting of the bourse committee so that they could state their case. Van Rooyen and his team explained to the committee how their business model worked: that their balance sheet was absolutely sufficient to fund their business, that they were expanding, and that they were generating cash hand over fist.

'They listened, but you could see they weren't buying it,' Wiese continued. 'After an hour Harry Laurie stood up and said: It's clear that we can't convince you. So I'm giving you an undertaking on behalf of Senbank that – if the listing goes ahead and if within six months it turns out that the company is under strain, that it cannot meet its liabilities – Senbank will underwrite a rights issue of R3 million.

'Well, that was quite an argument stopper. Lurie and the rest just turned pale and said: "Well, if that's the case, I mean, we have no …" Harry Laurie then asked Richard Lurie: "Are you happy to confirm that in writing?" He replied: "You'll have your letter by this evening." Thereafter the listing went ahead. It was a huge success.'

In 1974, Christo started practising law as an advocate at the Cape Bar. He was not comfortable with remaining at Pep Stores in the number-two position, and he had wedding plans as well. But he retained his stake in Pep and stayed on as a board member.

By that time he had been in a relationship with Caro Basson, daughter of the politician Japie Basson, a founder member of the Progressive Federal Party (PFP), and his wife, Clarence, for a number of years. In 1975, Caro and Christo were married in the Three Anchor Bay Dutch Reformed church. They acquired a bungalow on Clifton's Fourth Beach where they would live for the next half-century.

Advocate and diamond trader

Wiese's business career was suddenly fast-tracked by an unexpected windfall in 1976. He acquired the Ochta diamond mine for a song.

Ochta, an alluvial diamond-mining operation, is situated on the banks of the Gariep River in the Kalahari, downstream from the famous Aussenkehr farm and about 80 kilometres from where the river flows into the Atlantic Ocean. The operation had initially been developed by a European adventurer in the 1930s, but after his death his son, Dr Otto Thaning, was not interested in such a substantial South African investment. Thaning became friends with a young articled clerk who did the mine's books, Johan de Villiers, to whom he said one day that he wanted to dispose of the mine.

Wiese was phoned by a friend who told him about two young men with a fantastic proposition: an option to buy a diamond mine. One of them was the 22-year-old Johan de Villiers, who had only R400. He reckoned the purchase price could be in the region of R2,5 million, but they had been unable to obtain a bank loan. The assets of the company, however, were worth about R10 million, at a conservative estimate. It sounded to Wiese like a fairy tale, but the young men wanted to fly to the mine at once as they only had three days left to clinch the option.

'At that stage I knew zilch about diamonds and even less about mining,' Wiese recounts. 'So we flew up to the mine and as the plane landed, I saw a fleet of cars come driving up from the mine village, with a white Jeep Cherokee in front. When the man behind the wheel climbed out, he turned out to be someone I'd known for a long time. He was a legend in alluvial diamond mining, but I hadn't seen him in years.

'Then I said, Blitz, let's take a walk around the hangar. We walked around it, and I said: "Blitz, why does the guy want to sell the mine? Look at all the assets here. Millions! There were 15 000 carats of diamonds in the safe. Why is he selling – have the diamonds run out?" And this man told me – those words still ring in my ears – Christo, there are enough diamonds here for you and your children.'

According to Wiese, this conversation was the full extent of his due diligence.

Johan de Villiers became a partner in the mine. As part of the bargain buy, they acquired the safe with the diamonds, the 100 000-hectare farm and a brand-new Learjet aircraft – at a time when there were only four private jets in South Africa. Additional assets included buildings in Springbok and Cape Town, plus a claim against the then state president Dr Nic Diederichs for a sum of R250 000 he had borrowed from the company.

'As a junior advocate, I had to make my way up to Tuynhuys from my chambers to tell Nic Diederichs he had to pay us. I had to say: Listen, I'm sorry to have to do this, but we've written you letters and whatever, we need the money – because I needed every penny. I'd borrowed money to buy the mine against the few assets I had at the time, so I had to go and ask him for the money.'

Wiese received and banked the presidential cheque.

He did his homework on diamonds and set out to learn from the experts in Antwerp, the European hub of the diamond industry where stones had been traded, cut and polished for centuries. He and De Villiers also set up offices in Antwerp and Zürich.

But the partnership was short-lived. 'The long and the short of it was that one day I told him: Johan, one of us must buy the other one out, because we are on two different planets. We're good friends, but I can't take on this race now. I'm married and I want to start a family, and this is where I have to draw the line. Anyway, in February 1980 I sold out to him.'

At the time the mine's annual production was R30 million, which was equal to $45 million. De Villiers battled to get the money together to pay Wiese for his stake. Then the mine's bulldozer fell into a hole; by a stroke of luck, the hole turned out to be one of the potholes in a paleo-channel in which alluvial diamonds had become trapped along with gravel. De Villiers was able to extract diamonds worth R30 million from the pothole in the space of a week.

'He is the only man I've ever met who'd gone to sleep bankrupt and literally woke up a multimillionaire,' Wiese said. 'I always tell my children this story in my own favour because I think they should learn something from it. I could have told him at the time: But Johan, you haven't yet fulfilled our contract, so I'm still the half-owner. Half of those diamonds belong to me because our transaction hasn't been completed. But I didn't do that. I told myself that for me, the luck lay in the fact that I got my money from him and because I had *that* money, I was able to buy out Renier van Rooyen.'

Two years later, Johan de Villiers was on his knees because the diamond market had changed. He had invested in other mines and cutting works, and his cash flow had dried up. Trans Hex bought out Ochta, and De Villiers settled in the United States.

Wiese's venture into the diamond industry in 1976 was followed soon afterwards by an excursion of a different kind, this time into politics. Although his wife Caro came from a political family, she was less than enthusiastic about a political career. She had even set conditions: 'There are two things you may never do. You're not allowed to go into politics, and you're not allowed to make movies.'

Nonetheless, Wiese decided in 1977 to stand for election as a candidate for the newly founded PFP. Van Zyl Slabbert had phoned him in London to ask him to stand in Stellenbosch. Caro immediately gave him her blessing as she knew there was no chance a Prog would win in that constituency. In the end, he stood in Simon's Town, where his opponent was John Wiley – the leader of the small South African Party who later became a minister in the National Party cabinet.

His foray into politics was not successful. Wiley was too solidly entrenched in the constituency he had represented on behalf of three different parties in the course of 21 years. The following year Caro's father Japie Basson was elected leader of the PFP's parliamentary caucus, but Wiese started moving out of party politics.

He still served on the PFP's federal council, but resigned from the party and joined the NP when PW Botha, who had succeeded John Vorster as prime minister, launched the President's Council. In Wiese's view, this body was the start of negotiation politics, but the PFP refused to participate in it because black people were excluded. He thought the PFP's stance was 'illogical and ill-considered' because the council 'was a step in the right direction', Wiese said after his resignation.

'Low prices you can trust'

Renier van Rooyen, who worked day and night to grow Pep Stores, had always intended to retire early, preferably at 50. After Wiese bought out his holdings in 1980, the young successor returned in 1981 and became increasingly more focused on Pep, which now had about 500 stores. These included Shoprite, of which Whitey Basson had taken over the control and of which Wiese would become chair of the board (see the next chapter).

Wiese was now number one and no longer number two at Pep, the modest, no-frills stores that targeted the mass market by selling good-quality clothing cheaply. Basic clothing – school uniforms, shirts and trousers, shoes and socks – attracted poor whites and the much larger black and coloured market. Wiese believed his business had basically been built on one slogan: 'Low prices you can trust.' Price was what really mattered to Pep customers.

'Wiese saw the opportunity faster than anybody else.' This was the opinion of Syd Vianello, a retail analyst from Johannesburg who had observed Wiese's business activities for many decades. 'He targeted the bottom end of the market, and nobody could argue his business had any element of waste. He cut out all the extravagance and gave people what they wanted at the lowest possible price,' he said in an interview with *Forbes* magazine.

Wiese was fanatical about curbing costs, which is crucial in low-margin retailing. To keep corporate expenses in check, Pep manufactured much of its clothing in a number of factories, one of which was situated next to the company's modest head office in the industrial area of Parow Industria. From the outset, Pep deviated from the pattern followed by most South African retailers of many deliveries from many suppliers to each shop, relying instead on a central distribution system with warehouses to store goods. As Basson explained: 'Getting one truckload to a store is substantially cheaper than getting 30 trucks to wait outside a store to offload 30 consignments.'

The Pep concept proved so popular that Wiese began expanding aggressively, sometimes opening as many as a hundred new stores a year. He focused on rural and poorer areas, while his rivals concentrated on the bigger towns and cities. His approach was that his customers should rather spend their money in his stores than spend it travelling long distances to reach them.

In 1986, Wiese spun off Shoprite and Pep into separate companies. The timing was good, because four years later the South African liberation movements were unbanned, Nelson Mandela was released and apartheid had come to an end. South African companies were no longer unwelcome in Africa. Pep and Shoprite's uncomplicated model was 'easily exportable', and they embarked on opening stores in the neighbouring countries and further north. Vianello summed it up succinctly: 'Wiese and Basson sat down and took a view that they could conquer Africa, and they went out and conquered Africa.'

Shoprite's size, the scale of the business, allowed it to move more quickly than local competitors. Vianello spelled out the challenges: 'How long does it take to clear a container in Angola or Nigeria? What bribes do you have to pay to get supplies in? Who on earth would finance them to put up stores? They had to build their own stores themselves. No one else would.' Wiese insisted that he had not spent one rand on bribery.

Elsewhere, growth through acquisitions increased. By the 1990s, Pep had expanded as far as Britain, and in 1990 Basson succeeded in making Checkers, which had been in the Sanlam stable, part of Shoprite.

Another much-discussed takeover followed in 1997: OK Bazaars. The purchase price has become legendary: R1. Basson would subsequently say with mock-seriousness that he had overpaid South African Breweries (SAB), who wanted to get the struggling chain off its hands. They should rather have paid *him* for taking it over.

Wiese and Basson had long discussions about the takeover of OK Bazaars, with its nearly 300 grocery and furniture stores, before they took the plunge. 'We bet the farm,' Wiese said. 'We paid a rand, but what people omit to mention: we scored R1 billion in assets. At that point Whitey's entire business was making R200 million profit a year, and OK Bazaars was losing R200 million a year. Whitey came to me and told me he was game for OK, but that it was a helluva risk.

'So I said to him: Whitey, I hear you, but number one – I have the confidence that you can fix it, you can turn OK Bazaars around, and then I'm going to compensate you. And that's where Whitey's shares came from, the ones there was such a hullabaloo about. [In 2005 Basson received a R59-million bonus from a share incentive scheme aimed at motivating him and other members of Shoprite to return the loss-making OK to profitability.]

'I told him I wanted him to think hard about this. Between him and Pick n Pay, he owns the bottom end of the market. There he is king, because Raymond Ackerman can't take him on there. But Ackerman owns the top end of the market; he won't get past him there.

'Now this is where your danger lies, I said: Sometimes you have to make a move that is defensive because eventually you want to take on Raymond Ackerman with your Checkers stores, and you'll be able to do it because you have your Shoprites pumping profits. Now if I were Raymond Ackerman, I would say: I already have the top end; Whitey is going to come for me there, but I'm far ahead of him. What I'm going to do is to cut off his gas at the bottom end. I'm going to buy OK Bazaars, then I'll squeeze him there at the bottom end, I'll put his profits under pressure there, and then he won't be able to get close to me.

'That evening we sat in the office for a long time and I spelled it out to him. The next morning he phoned and told me he was going to do it …

'Well, the rest is history. But at least Whitey always said he would give me the credit, since I told him to do things defensively. Because everyone criticised us, everyone said we were mad: You're buying a business that is losing R200 million a year – even if you are only paying one rand.'

Basson had praise for Wiese's strategy: 'Christo is a fantastic corporate-deal thinker. He always makes me think: What would the alternative be if I didn't make a deal? What happens if the opposition buys the company?'

Throughout his career Wiese has been known as a businessman who is prepared to take massive risks. To Syd Vianello, this is one of his key attributes. 'Africa is not a place for sissies,' Vianello said. 'You've got to have nerves of steel. In Africa they see him as a genius.'

Wiese himself says that his appetite for risk is 'a personality thing. I've never felt that the risks of business decisions caused me undue stress. People always have this question: Are you born with it, or does it come from your environment? If you had to ask me that question, I would say it's your environment – it's how you were raised, it's what you learn at your parents' dinner table.'

Wiese's visionary approach had an impact on the public sector as well. In 1993, he became chair of the Industrial Development Corporation (IDC) after President PW Botha had appointed him as a director in 1985.

As the first chair to occupy non-executive positions within the IDC, he could assist the post-1994 ANC government with an export-oriented industrial policy. In those days, there was inexpensive and abundant electricity that was supplied by Eskom as a world-class power utility. Under Wiese's chairmanship energy-intensive heavy industries were launched, such as the Hillside aluminium smelter in Richards Bay and the Columbus stainless steel plant in Middelburg.

An opportunity to beneficiate the country's raw materials beckoned in the Western Cape. Iron ore that was transported via the long railway line from Sishen to Saldanha was loaded onto ships, although part of it could be turned into steel for the export market. Under Wiese's leadership, the IDC embarked on the country's biggest industrial project since Sasol's plant at Secunda: Saldanha Steel, which could process the ore.

It took much convincing, inter alia because of environmental objections, before the right partners and suitable premises were found. During his tenure as chair, Wiese experienced the start of Saldanha Steel's production of hot-rolled carbon steel coil in 1998. He stepped down as IDC chair in 2000.

Two decades later, Saldanha Steel was taken over by the Indian steel group Mittal (later ArcelorMittal) along with Iscor. Towards the end of 2019, it was announced that the plant at Saldanha would be shut down, a step that entailed severe job losses for the West Coast region. Wiese's comment on the envisaged closure of Saldanha Steel was that steel factories worldwide had run into difficulties after China started exporting cheap steel. Even so, Saldanha Steel, like Highveld Steel in Middelburg, was a victim of the deindustrialisation and economic regression under the ANC government. High electricity and transport costs had also taken their toll.

A clash of two business titans

One of the instances where Wiese took a big risk resulted in a serious clash with Johann Rupert. It happened in 1999 when Trans Hex, the diamond company in which Remgro had a controlling interest, made a bid to take over the Namibian company Ocean Diamond Mining (ODM).

Some time earlier Wiese had received a tip-off that ODM, which supplied most of De Beers' marine diamonds, was hopelessly under-valued. As director of a consortium called Invicta, with Dave McKay and Mike Rose-Innes as co-directors and the business journalist Jeremy Woods as additional member, he began buying up ODM shares while they were still trading at R1,70. When Wiese heard of Trans Hex's takeover bid, he thought that at R3,09 Trans Hex's valu-ation of ODM was much too low. He then approached Thys Visser of Remgro about selling their shares to him, but Visser was not in favour of the idea.

A while later, Wiese was approached by Alastair Holberton, the chair of another diamond company, Namco, with a bid to buy ODM shares from him at R8 each because Holberton believed a merger could bring about 'critical mass' (hence control) in the industry. Wiese, who accepted that as minority shareholder he was in an un-favourable position, was not sure whether Holberton had sufficient capital at his disposal. Consequently, he approached Remgro's stock-broker and offered his shares to them at R8 – the price Holberton wanted to pay. Remgro again turned down the offer.

Holberton did not have enough money for the deal, but could se-cure a loan if he received an option from Wiese. Wiese was prepared to grant such an option premium on condition that the financing company, Investec, obtained clearance from the JSE that he was not in collusion with Holberton. The shares were sold to Holberton at R9,75 – the share price plus the option premium. ODM's shares had meanwhile risen to R10.

Namco then proceeded with its own takeover bid of Trans Hex's shares, since Remgro was not prepared to accept Holberton's offer of R8 per share. Remgro insisted on the same price he had paid Wiese and, furthermore, alleged that Wiese had colluded with Holberton. Johann Rupert accused Wiese of 'greenmailing'. Basically, this means the practice of buying enough shares in a company to threaten a hos-tile takeover in order to resell them to the company at a higher price.

By Wiese's account, he asked Johann Rupert what he was talking about. 'Yes, but you knew we were going to make a bid, he said. Then I said: How on earth should I have known that? I started buying my shares a year ago.'

Namco and Remgro kept buying up shares and eventually held 34 per cent each. This is the level at which buyers usually stop buying. If their interest goes beyond this, they have to make a mandatory offer to all the shareholders. In the meantime, Wiese had also started buying shares again and had built a significant 17 per cent stake, with which he could play the two groups off against each other and obtain control of the company. His comment about this was blunt: 'What does any man with half a brain do? He buys the 17 per cent and he says here's my phone number.'

The dispute intensified and culminated in a series of hearings before the Securities Regulation Panel. Though the hearings were held in camera, the *Financial Mail* and *Noseweek* published reports about the minutes. At the first hearing, the director of the panel, Richard Connellan, asked Rupert to state his case of alleged collusion between Wiese and Holberton. Rupert said he had been phoned by a very good friend of both his and Wiese's who had told him Christo and Holberton were acting 'in concert'. He was not prepared to disclose the name of the mutual friend.

He referred to a saying attributed to the British judge Lord Denning: if something looks like a dog, has hair like a dog, and barks like a dog, it must be a dog.

When Wiese started talking, he was interrupted by Rupert, whereupon Wiese said it was now his turn to speak, Rupert had to keep quiet. He continued by saying that those of them who had studied and practised law were familiar with more of Lord Denning's judgments, because that dog had ended up biting Rupert.

Connellan found that no facts had been advanced on which anything could be decided. Unless the identity of the person who had raised the issue of collusion was disclosed, he had no other option but to reject the charge.

Rupert appealed and won his case. Then Wiese appealed in turn to the highest authority, a five-man tribunal. The venue in Johannesburg was packed with advocates and attorneys, including Remgro's senior counsel, when Wiese, who represented himself, arrived. Rupert and Visser were not present.

During cross-examination Rupert's advocate confronted Wiese about the share price and the option. According to Wiese, the exchange between them went as follows: 'Mr Cohen, have you ever been to Upington? He said: Yes, I've been once. I said: Well, you can come as my guest to Upington. The people there are simple boere folk, but if you don't understand it, they will be able to explain to you what the difference is between an option and a sale.'

He thought the advocate would be angry. 'But he knew what a weak case he had. So he just laughed furtively. Because it was really just ridiculous.'

The tribunal's ruling was a four-to-one decision in Wiese's favour. He won the last round of the skirmishes, but his remarks about 'a classic case of Hamlet without the prince' did not go down well with Johann Rupert and Thys Visser. They held a grudge against him because they believed he had suggested they were liars. Wiese acknowledges that there was tension between them for years.

After Trans Hex's failed takeover bid, there was a further ironic twist. Namco had overpaid, and threw in the towel in 2003. Remgro later took over Trans Hex, but when it unbundled its shares in 2016, Wiese became the majority shareholder of the company. Wiese said that as a native of the Northern Cape, he had always been 'fascinated' by diamonds. 'Diamonds are wonderful things, things of beauty and everlasting value. It's just a very exciting business.'

But Trans Hex did not live up to his earlier expectations. The price of diamonds fell and, by October 2019, one of Trans Hex's subsidiaries, West Coast Resources, was placed in liquidation.

For a long time after the clash between Wiese and Rupert it was rumoured that he had said to Rupert: 'Just remember, I made my money myself.'

Wiese denies this emphatically. 'Look, people have said that to him in different words when he rubs them up the wrong way. I would never say that to a man. Because what is the truth? Can I honestly say that I went from a barefoot little boy to whatever? In Upington, my father had a new car every year because he owned a garage, and he had a farm too. To the children whose parents worked for the Railways, we were the rich people.

'If it hadn't been for my father and my mother – I mean, the whole Pep thing … I think what my father invested was R15 000, which was about his entire estate. It made him the second-largest shareholder in Pep. I subsequently pushed up the stake and, because of the money I made in the diamond mine, I could buy out Renier van Rooyen and thereby gain control of the company. So I could never tell a man: the difference between you and me is that I made my money myself,' Wiese said.

Businesspeople close to Rupert claim that the rift between them arose because Rupert, who had levelled similar criticism at Jannie Mouton, felt that 'Christo has always stepped on the little guy to get to where he is'. To which Wiese responds dismissively: 'My businesses haven't been built by stepping on anyone. We rather endeavour to build people up and provide jobs.'

The strained relations between the Ruperts and the Wieses did not improve after Markus Jooste arrived in Stellenbosch. Wiese made it clear where he stood in that he joined forces with Jooste and Steinhoff – the very 'incomers' Rupert disliked because they had imported a 'new culture' into Stellenbosch.

A suitcase stuffed with pounds, and other headaches

Wiese was caught up in controversy in 2009 over an incident that became known as the suitcase with £600 000. It was about a stash of banknotes he wanted to transport from London to Luxembourg that was seized by British customs officials, who suspected illicit origins. It took a three-year court battle before he finally got his money back.

On 27 April 2009, Wiese was detained at London City Airport as he was about to board a flight to Luxembourg. An amount of £120 000 in cash was found in his hand luggage, as well as £554 920 in two suitcases he had checked into the hold – the then rand value came to more than R12 million.

He explained that the money came from various diamond deals he had done over decades in the 1980s and 1990s. He had kept the banknotes in a safety deposit box in London's Ritz Hotel, as many other South Africans who held assets offshore did at the time. Keeping funds abroad took on such dimensions that the South African government eventually granted amnesty to people who declared their foreign-held assets. The 2003 tax amnesty programme alone revealed that R48 billion was held abroad illegally by more than 43 000 South Africans.

Wiese intended to transfer the money to a bank in Luxembourg. He had started moving his personal affairs to Luxembourg, inter alia because the main listing of Brait (a holding company in which Wiese's investment company, Titan, holds the controlling stake) was in Luxembourg, as well as the offices of one of his other companies, Tradehold. Board meetings were held there. 'So I asked my advisers, is there any problem with doing that? No problem. When you travel between EU countries you can carry as much money with you as you want. It's clearly not illegal,' he recounts.

But the British customs officials did not accept his explanations and refused to return the seized funds. Having had to cancel his flight and appointments, Wiese immediately resolved to fight the seizure. His barrister, Clare Montgomery QC, told him: 'Christo, they're not wrong, they are dead wrong.'

Newspapers had a field day when the case landed in court. *Rapport* published a drawing of Wiese standing next to a pile of banknotes. A report in London's *Daily Mail* had the gleeful headline 'It's just peanuts for me', with reference to Montgomery's remark that the amount represented less than two weeks' income for Wiese and 'a minute fraction of his assets'.

However, the judge in the magistrate's court ordered the forfeiture of the money, finding that on a balance of probabilities the cash came from criminal money laundering. 'Well, so naturally we appealed,' says Wiese. 'Then it took me three years to get them into the high court. They ducked and dived until I finally had to get a court order to compel them to come to court.'

The appeal case was over and done with within half an hour. Mr Justice Underhill said in his judgment: 'It is common knowledge and common experience that in countries with strict exchange control regulations citizens who need or wish to travel abroad frequently try to evade those controls; and exchange control is likely to be particularly irksome to very wealthy individuals who do not want to spend all their money at home, or in any event to be subject to restrictions as to how much of their money, and for what purpose, they can spend abroad.

'If such individuals succumb to the temptation to evade exchange controls, it will be important for them to leave no audit trail, certainly if the sums are, as here, very significant. By contrast, it is prima facie unlikely that a businessman of previous good character, already enormously rich from legitimate business, would become involved in money laundering.'

The judge, who did not award costs to Wiese, ordered that the money be returned to him, with interest. The judgment was handed down on a Friday afternoon, and Wiese requested his media representative Ben de Kock to notify the papers. But not a word about this positive outcome appeared in the weekend papers. An incensed Wiese phoned an old acquaintance, the journalist Jeremy Woods. 'He said: "But that's impossible, *none* of the papers!" He then called the editor of *Business Day*, and they carried a front-page report on the Tuesday. The only publicity!'

Wiese views the whole affair as a 'deadly catch-22 situation'. For a long time he did not want to speak about it publicly, for whatever he said would be misinterpreted. In business circles, however, it was rumoured that at times he sailed pretty close to the wind.

Nearly three decades earlier, Wiese had been equally sensitive about a newspaper report that had become an embarrassment to him. On that occasion, it was a report about a party in celebration of his fortieth birthday in 1981 that portrayed the event as an over-the-top, glitzy affair where the guests could hunt for diamonds in their dessert.

Renier van Rooyen had just retired at Pep Stores, and Wiese had taken over the chairmanship of the country's most dynamic retailer. His wife Caro wanted to arrange a surprise for his birthday celebration. She obtained four tiny cut diamonds from Wiese's partner in Ochta, Johan de Villiers, that would be hidden inside some of the doughnuts that would be served as dessert. According to De Villiers, the stones were only worth about R500, and he gave them to her as a gift. At the party, the master of ceremonies announced after the main course that all the guests should now eat their doughnuts and search for something inside them. Amid much laughter, only one guest, a judge, produced a minute diamond.

One Saturday about three months later, Wiese saw a report in *Die Burger* with the headline '*Miljoenêr laat gaste kou vir blinkes*'

('Millionaire makes guests chew for sparklers'). His initial thought was that the millionaire in question had stolen his wife's party trick, but then he saw to his great dismay that the story was about him. When he showed Caro the report, she immediately said he should sue the paper. 'I said: How can I sue *Die Burger*? It's the truth! There were diamonds in the cakes! Only one was found, but that's irrelevant now. But the tone of the article was that of French champagne flowing, the most expensive lobsters, and who knows what else, plus the diamonds. The image it created!'

Wiese decided that all he could do was to phone the deputy editor of *Die Burger*, Louis Louw. 'I said: Louis, you've known me for years, that's not who I am! I mean, I don't live like that. That's what a bunch of Johannesburg show-offs … I don't do things like that.'

The report had further repercussions. When Wiese bought Renier van Rooyen's stake in Pep, he needed to borrow R7 million. He could obtain the facility from Nedbank. But a week later he was approached by Senbank's managing director Eduan Pretorius – son of Gawie Pretorius, the Paarl Boys' High principal who had given Wiese a place at the school – who said Senbank could arrange the financing. Reluctant to offend Pretorius, he explained the circumstances to the people at Nedbank, who understood the situation and let their arrangement lapse.

Just before Christmas, however, a message came back from Senbank: his loan application had been declined. Wiese had to negotiate from scratch to restore the transaction with Nedbank. Meanwhile the bank rate had risen by 1 per cent, with the result that the cost for the 10-year term had increased by R1,4 million.

The next time he was at Senbank he bumped into Pretorius, who congratulated him on his birthday. Wiese responded that it had been his birthday three months earlier, in September, and then decided to take the bull by the horns. He asked Pretorius to tell him, as a friend, whether the loan application had been rejected by the board because of the newspaper story. Pretorius said yes and that the board had been reluctant to 'lend a 40-year-old guy who lives in the Cape R7 million to buy shares, but he puts diamonds in cakes at his party'.

Wiese said: 'Now you'll understand how sensitive I am about

anything that can give people a knife to stick into my ribs. I've sat on the boards of banks. I know how the guys talk. No, it cost me R1,4 million back then!'

Wiese's brushes with controversy were not limited to banknotes and diamonds. They also extended to the banking sector itself, and Boland Bank in particular. He had joined the board, but resigned as a director of Boland Bank in the eary 1990s when he served on the board of the Reserve Bank where he had succeeded Anton Rupert as director.

He resigned as a director of the Reserve Bank, however, when he again became involved in Boland Bank after new legislation required banks to hold more capital. He gradually acquired large blocks of shares in Boland Bank while there was also talk of a merger between the bank and the Board of Executors (BoE), which did happen eventually.

Wiese ultimately became the chair of Boland Bank, and he had big plans for expansion. He brought in a foreign partner, the Malaysian magnate Samsudin Abu Hassan, better known as Dato Samsudin, to recapitalise the bank and to realign the controlling structure. The new controlling structure, Samgro, was listed on the JSE.

Wiese also appointed the young Michiel le Roux of Distillers to take over the management of the bank. They parted ways with acrimony when Le Roux, who subsequently founded the highly successful Capitec Bank, resigned in 1998. He and Wiese had a serious falling-out about the final payout of a share incentive scheme that had been instituted on Le Roux's appointment.

Wiese soon bought out Samsudin's interests in Samgro. He then turned to another bank, the Natal Building Society (NBS). Thanks to complicated structures, Samgro – the pyramid company through which he controlled Boland Bank – managed to exercise control over the bank from KwaZulu-Natal. NBS Boland Bank was the fifth-largest bank in the country at the time.

Wiese built up a considerable debt burden in the many deals he entered into in the banking sector – according to the business journalist Deon Basson, 'a chain of debt … that would make any conservative banker shudder', which he estimated at R1 billion. In March 2000, Basson wrote in an article in *Finansies & Tegniek* that the chair of BoE, Bill McAdam, the chief executive, Phil Biden, and Wiese should resign from the board of BoE.

Wiese stated that he found Basson's articles 'quite incompetent'. In a conversation with Basson during which they disagreed sharply, he referred to Basson's 'idiotic' opinion.

A month after the conversation with Basson, Wiese resigned from all the BoE boards on which he served. He announced that he was selling all his shares in the banking group, which amounted to 150 million BoE shares valued at about R750 million. At the same time he repurchased BoE's shareholding in Pepgro for R450 million.

The Steinhoff bomb explodes

In the early 2000s, the economy was still growing briskly under the Thabo Mbeki administration. Mbeki's vision of an African renaissance served as encouragement to Pep and Shoprite to open numerous stores in the rest of Africa. Wiese also continued expanding internationally, using three vehicles for this purpose: Invicta, the holding company Brait, and Tradehold.

Invicta invested capital in industrial companies abroad, particularly companies with predictable, recurring revenue streams. Brait was more ambitious: majority stakes were acquired in the British discount retailer New Look and Richard Branson's gym chain Virgin Active, among others. Tradehold entered the British real estate market with investments in residential property, industrial structures and office buildings.

Pepkor's biggest deal was with Steinhoff, the furniture company founded by Bruno Steinhoff in Europe that had expanded globally under Markus Jooste as chief executive. In 2015, Steinhoff acquired Pepkor in a transaction valued at $5,7 billion (about R85 billion) that was settled in cash and with a share swap. The new company, Steinhoff International, which retained its head office in Stellenbosch, was registered in the Netherlands and would be listed on the Frankfurt Stock Exchange.

In May 2016, *Forbes* magazine sang Wiese's praises in a glossy article under the headline 'Africa's Sam Walton' (Walton was the founder of the biggest US retail chain, WalMart). He was described on the internet as 'The billionaire African behind the continent's greatest retail empire'. At the same time he was called 'a little Warren Buffett', which implied that he was as adept as the American investment guru when it came to amalgamating a portfolio of shares.

But in the eulogising article *Forbes* also mentioned a raid conducted by the German tax authorities at Steinhoff's offices in Westerstede on 30 November 2015. This happened a few days before Steinhoff International listed in Frankfurt on 7 December 2015. Steinhoff dismissed the German investigation into possible accounting fraud as 'baseless', but it 'spooked' the company's investors. The share price dropped about 15 per cent in a month, wiping away almost $600 million from Wiese's personal fortune.

Rob Rose writes in his book *Steinheist* that Wiese received an early warning about Steinhoff. In 2009, the portfolio manager Craig Butters made a 40-page presentation to Wiese. It was a scathing analysis of Steinhoff, a company Butters viewed with contempt – in his opinion, a rubbish business that had been cooking the books.

By that time, Wiese had met the Steinhoff people in that he had been invited to the announcement of their results at the Mount Nelson Hotel in Cape Town in 2006. He got on well with them and was invited along on hunting trips in England and Spain. Like Wiese, Bruno Steinhoff and Markus Jooste were fond of hunting, had retail in their blood and loved linking up businesses.

Three years later, Wiese was considering a merger between Shoprite and Steinhoff. In 2009, Steinhoff was a much smaller company than it would be at the time of Pepkor's deal with Jooste in 2014–15.

Wiese says he listened attentively to Butters, whom he found 'an extremely intelligent guy'. He then decided to back away, not as a result of Butters' analysis, but because he had looked at Steinhoff's balance sheet and thought there was too much debt. His companies had strong balance sheets. Both Pep and Shoprite had virtually no debt. In any case, he relates, at the time he could have given Butters 300 analyst reports that differed 100 per cent from *his* analysis because they were all in agreement that Steinhoff was a good buy.

Jooste approached Wiese again in 2012 when the latter wanted to sell Lanzerac. Jooste said he had a consortium who would buy the Stellenbosch farm from Wiese, but wouldn't he at the same time consider putting his PSG shares into Steinhoff? His plan, according to Wiese, was to make Steinhoff the single largest shareholder in PSG – 'and he had a very clever scheme for how he wanted to do it, a tax-efficient plan'.

By that time, Wiese had been on the PSG board for a few years, and he was the third- or fourth-largest shareholder. Jooste held 20 million PSG shares, just below those owned by the Moutons, as opposed to Wiese's 15,5 million. Jooste's 20 million, together with Wiese's 15,5 million and the shares of others such as GT Ferreira, whom Jooste also intended to approach, would get him to his goal of becoming the single largest shareholder in PSG.

The proposal set Wiese thinking. 'I then cast my mind back to Butters and co, and I said to myself: what man who knows that it's a total scam, if it should turn out to be some kind of Ponzi scheme, takes a billion of his own money and puts it into the pot? In today's terms: five billion. So I put in my shares because I'd analysed the thing and discussed it with my son Jacob. It was a more liquid share, and so on.

'A year later they invited me to join their board, and I told Jacob I'm now going to sit there and check things out, because I had received the warning – look at the balance sheet, the reports, how the market reacts, look at how the company is managed, what are its structures, how do they operate, who are the people.'

Regardless of the red flags raised by Butters, 'all the banks threw money at Steinhoff,' Wiese recounts. 'Now who should you believe? The lone voice in the wilderness, or the chorus that includes every regulator, the Reserve Bank, the PIC, the top fund managers in South Africa *and* overseas? Steinhoff is the only company in the world I know of whose statutory audit committee consisted of three people who each had a doctorate in accounting.'

Wiese took over the chairmanship of Steinhoff International in May 2016. Meanwhile, the German investigation into possible fraud at Steinhoff had apparently not made much headway. The investigation was completely below the radar until the German business magazine *Manager Magazin* reported on 27 August 2017 that Jooste and other Steinhoff employees were being investigated by German prosecutors in a 2015 case tied to possible accounting fraud. That evening, Wiese responded indignantly in an interview with Bruce Whitfield on the radio station 702: 'One would have to be an angel not to be angered by this sort of drivel that appeared in this magazine that I'm not familiar with.' The claims were 'devoid of truth'.

The rumours refused to die down. One of the Steinhoff directors who first suspected that something was wrong was Dr Steve Booysen, head of the audit committee. On 25 September, he received a letter from Deloitte in which the auditors raised their concerns about certain entries in Steinhoff's accounts. Deloitte were unable to get answers to their queries from the executive management. For the next two months the audit committee, comprising Booysen, Len Konar and Theunie Lategan, dealt with the process.

On 29 November, Wiese, as chair, was informed of the problems with the company's books that had caused the auditors to refuse to sign off the final annual financial statements. On the same day, the external auditors met with Wiese and Booysen to discuss a report they had compiled about the matter.

With the report in his hand, the one Dutch auditor, Jan Dalhuisen, asked Wiese if he knew that Steinhoff's management had been defrauding the company for years. He mentioned an amount of €6,1 billion and insisted on a forensic investigation. Wiese then pointed out to him that all these items appeared in the 2016 financial statements they had signed off.

Dalhuisen acknowledged that they as the auditors had a problem because they had signed off the statements. But he referred to suspicious entries regarding property transactions, cash and cash equivalents, among other things. The cash flow was affected by *Wechsels*, in other words, German bills of exchange that had to be reported as cash within 90 days of the closing of the books. Another problem was cash equivalents, in that secured debtors could be reported as cash equivalents in Germany but not in South Africa.

As chief executive, Jooste was called in to respond to the auditors' concerns. Following his explanations, the auditors decided to leave the forensic investigation in abeyance for the time being. The next day they made a U-turn and insisted on an independent forensic investigation. On being called in again, Jooste at first demanded that Deloitte be fired as the auditors, saying they were not independent because they acted for his estranged partner Andreas Seifert. Finally Jooste said he was flying to Germany that weekend, and undertook to bring back documentary evidence that would allay the concerns. Wiese phoned him there in the course of the weekend and requested that, as chief executive, he approve the appointment of Pricewater-houseCoopers (PwC) to conduct the forensic investigation so that it could be announced on the JSE's news service Sens.

The news about accounting irregularities had come 'like a bolt from the blue', Wiese said at the parliamentary inquiry that was held in January 2018. 'As chair, the first time I became aware that there was a serious problem was literally three working days before the accounts had to be finalised for the board meeting in December.'

On the morning of 4 December 2017, the Monday after the tense weekend, Wiese received a voice message from Jooste on his cellphone. His flight from Germany had just landed, he said. Dirk Schreiber, Steinhoff's head of finance in Europe, was with him, and they had all the documents the auditors had demanded. He asked that Wiese line up the two teams of auditors. He would be at the Steinhoff offices at 11 am for a meeting.

For Wiese, who according to other directors found it the hardest to believe up to the last minute that the doomsday tidings were true, there was at that point still a flicker of hope. 'And I sat there waiting … eleven o'clock, twelve o'clock, one o'clock. I didn't hear a word. That's where that cold feeling … then I knew, 50 years of my life were in their glory, because this man was definitely a fraudster.'

By late afternoon, the German lawyer Christian Droop, who had just been with Jooste, came to see Wiese. '"Jooste has now broken down," he told me. "He says he's done terrible things. He threatened suicide. He cried like a baby, and he said he can't look you in the eyes, but that I should tell you that he's tendering his resignation, you have to decide whether you want to accept it." I mean, this was now where the final curtain dropped.'

At the board meeting the following morning, Tuesday 5 December, Wiese brought the directors up to speed on the developments. 'You can imagine – the consternation! Everyone asking, yes, but what, how? What do I suggest? I said: Listen, I suggest that we don't accept his resignation. He has to come back. He's the only man who knows what's been going on and he has to come in to help sort out the mess, because it is now about saving the company.'

With the approval of the board, Wiese called Jooste that same morning to request that he come and help the Steinhoff people sort out the shambles. In April 2018, he said in a radio interview with Bruce Whitfield on *The Money Show*: 'He [Jooste] undertook to do so. But I was maybe naive. Clearly, he got other legal advice. He did not show up.'

That call was the last time he spoke to Jooste. He has neither seen him nor heard anything from him since. On one occasion, Wiese's son-in-law, Marco Wentzel, was eating at the La Perla restaurant in Sea Point when Jooste walked in. As soon as he spotted Marco, he turned around and walked out.

On Monday 4 December, two days before the results for the year ended September 2017 were due to be released, Steinhoff had announced that the group's consolidated statements would still be issued on 6 December as promised, but as unaudited statements. The supervisory board and the auditors had not yet completed their review of 'certain matters and circumstances raised by the criminal and tax investigations in Germany'.

In a supplementary Sens statement issued on Wednesday 6 December, Steinhoff announced that it was unable to release its statements because new information had come to light 'which relates to accounting irregularities requiring further investigation'. It was also announced that Jooste had resigned, and that a forensic investigation would be conducted. PwC had been appointed as external auditors to undertake the forensic investigation.

By that time, Steinhoff's share price had dropped by more than 96 per cent. From a peak of R95 in March 2016, it eventually fell to below R1.

The one question on everyone's lips that irked Wiese the most was whether he, as chair of Steinhoff's supervisory board, had known about the wrongdoing. 'Either people making these allegations are insane, or I'm insane,' he said in interviews. 'The questioner knows there are false statements, but what sane person would put his life's work into a company that is riddled with fraud? If the person asking the question is correct, I must be insane!

'I'm amazed that people ask that question. I was sitting with a business I'd built up over 50 years. I had many other options, yet I chose to invest the proceeds of that business in a place where the statements are not a true reflection? On top of that, a year later I put in another R25 million. We would have to be crazy!'

Why did Wiese, who emphasised that he had only been chair for 18 months, nevertheless keep believing for such a long time that Jooste was honourable, even against the warnings of friends such as Whitey Basson? Some people reckon it was hubris, that he had started to believe he was immune to the dangers of the risks he had been taking throughout his long career. Others are of the view that he was mesmerised by the slick explanations of the glib-tongued Jooste. After all, he was not the only one who'd had the wool pulled over his eyes; many other experienced people had also been duped.

Nine days after Jooste's resignation, Wiese, too, resigned as chair of the supervisory board of Steinhoff International. Booysen had pointed out to him that since he was the largest shareholder in the company, and also had the largest claims against it, it was advisable that he resign to avoid any conflicts of interest.

Heather Sonn took over as chair. Someone had to pick up the pieces, and she, Booysen and Johan van Zyl undertook the task. She likened them to people who had stayed behind in a burning building to help. PwC sent in sixty forensic auditors, divided into fourteen workstreams, to comb through everything: all the books, documents, statements and computer hard drives.

The Steinhoff debacle was a massive personal blow to Wiese, who had been inducted into the World Retail Hall of Fame in 2015. On being named the country's richest businessman by the *Sunday Times* the following year, he had quipped: 'They measure your assets, but not your liabilities!'

At that time he elaborated on his wealth in an interview: 'I don't like being flashy. In Upington, if you were a show-off, you became the butt of jokes. For instance, I rarely use a chauffeur – I drive myself.'

His office was still the Pepkor head office in the bleak Parow Industria, and he was never scared when driving home alone from there at night. 'My mother always used this beautiful Dutch saying: "*Een mens lijdt dikwijls 't meest door 't lijden dat hij vreest, doch dat nooit op komt dagen. Zo heeft hij meer te dragen dan God te dragen geeft.*'" (A person often suffers most because of the suffering he fears, yet which never arrives. Thereby he has to bear more than what God gives us to bear.)

He explained the Dutch as follows: 'It boils down to don't be anxious, but don't be reckless.'

At that stage Wiese, who has three honorary doctorates, had the largest shareholding in Steinhoff International Holdings as well as a controlling interest in Brait, Tradehold and Invicta Holdings, and a substantial interest in Pallinghurst. He owned 18 per cent of Shoprite Holdings.

In 2018, he was still ranked second (after Ivan Glasenberg) on the *City Press* Wealth Index, with a gross worth of R32 782 billion. This was almost 60 per cent less than the R81 billion of two years before. His Titan Group has lodged a R59-billion claim against Steinhoff, but of this enormous amount he would probably at best only be able to recover a few cents for every rand he lost.

Amid the adversity that had hit him, Wiese still felt up to a touch of wry humour. In March 2018, at a gala dinner held in celebration of the 150th anniversary of his old school Paarl Boys' High where he was the guest speaker, Wiese told an anecdote that people thought actually referred to himself.

The story in question was about a Karoo farmer who bought a number of farms at Loeriesfontein. But because the *oom* did not have a bank account, the bank manager went to see him. Yes, the *oom* said, they do have money, but they don't keep it in a bank. 'Our children know about a tiny bit, then there's another tiny bit only my wife and I know about, then there's another tiny bit only I know about.

'And then there's still another tiny bit.'

Wiese was absolved from blame for the Steinhoff scandal when a brief overview of PwC's long-awaited forensic report was finally released on 16 March 2019. The overview stated that, in general terms, the report found 'that the fictitious and/or irregular transactions had the effect of inflating the profits and/or asset values of the Steinhoff Group'. Pepkor and its segments were not accused of any offences.

The restated Steinhoff 2017 annual report that was released in

May 2019, however, made mention of a number of companies controlled by Wiese that had contracts with Steinhoff. Wiese stated that all of his business interests had been disclosed, and that the annual report complied with the requirements of Dutch law because Steinhoff had its headquarters in Amsterdam.

He said that under Dutch law, 'there is nothing like a related party. It doesn't exist.' He had invested R60 billion in Steinhoff, whereas his companies' contracts with Steinhoff only came to €1,7 million (about R25 million). 'See it in that context. How could that prevent me from seeing the accounting fraud? It now appears the fraud originated more than 10 years ago, before I had any connection with the company.'

He repeated that it had taken 18 months for PwC, with 100 forensic auditors, to unravel Steinhoff's affairs. Even the German forensic investigations firm FGS, which had been hired by the Steinhoff board to investigate the allegations, could find no trace of irregularities, he said.

After the Steinhoff debacle, Wiese suffered more blows. In the year ended March 2018, Brait's net asset value declined by about a third, particularly as a result of the write-off of its investment in the British fashion retailer New Look. The group posted a R9,7 billion annual loss. For the same financial year, Invicta reported an 81 per cent drop in its headline earnings per share after a tax provision of R400 million. Within a year, the value of Wiese's stakes in Brait and Invicta had fallen by 28 per cent each, and that of his holding in Tradehold by 30 per cent.

In Shoprite, sentiment turned against Wiese. The lead independent director, Professor Shirley Zinn, resigned abruptly after Wiese's re-election as chair at Shoprite's AGM in November 2019. No less than 72 per cent of the investors voted against his re-election, but thanks to the voting power of his controversial high-voting deferred shares he was able to retain his chairmanship.

Wiese's wife Caro and his children Jacob, Christina and Clare were solidly behind him throughout the Steinhoff crisis. According to him, his family's constant concern has been 'that I shouldn't mess up my health with this thing'.

The family have not made any drastic changes to their lifestyle. 'We've never lived like jetsetters. I use my planes for my businesses, among other things,' he said with reference to reports that he was selling two of his luxury private jets. 'I own a game reserve in the Kalahari which I need to visit regularly, and I have to fly around often to get to things.'

The business magnate, who will turn 80 in 2021, says unabashedly that these were without doubt the darkest times he had ever experienced. 'For the first time in my life I became depressed. It was certainly the most public, and financially the most damaging, disappointment.'

But life goes on. As far as his legacy is concerned, he hopes people will take a balanced view: 'Listen, this guy started with five stores, he worked for 53 years, he provided employment for 200 000 people, he helped create prosperity, and he made his contribution here and there. *That* is the whole picture; Steinhoff is really not the whole picture.'

Creditors are hovering like vultures over what Wiese calls the carcass of Steinhoff. More than 70 per cent of the value in Steinhoff lies in the businesses he put in, he says, including Pepco, which is now part of Steinhoff's European business, and Pepkor. 'All of it now belongs to hedge funds and banks thousands of kilometres away. People who have no understanding of the business and attach no sentimental value to it.'

He talks nostalgically about his visit in early 2020 to the premises of the original Pep store in Upington where staff members came to greet him one by one. To the banks and hedge funds, 'it's just pieces of paper. That's the really sad part. Money is one thing; you make it, you lose it, you make it again. But the business now belongs to a group of faceless financiers. And those who committed the fraud in Steinhoff over 20 years have nothing to show for it.'

In an earlier interview he said: 'If you sum up legacy in one word, I'd like them to say: "He was a fair guy."'

If he ever had to see Jooste again, there was only one question he would like to ask him: 'Why? Why? That's all. Why?'

He understood that people were angry. 'Of course, and they have every right to be. I get it. I'm angry too! Why would I be different from other people?'

When asked how he coped with the Steinhoff debacle on a personal level, the ageing, less assertive but ever-courteous, cool-headed businessman gave a considered reply: 'I looked in the mirror that week when these things came crashing down on me, and asked: How am I going to get through this? Then I decided I had to try and make three things clear to myself.

'Number one, I don't mourn the loss of money. You know, that would be another waste.

'Number two, I count my blessings. If Jooste had continued with his fraud for one more year, I would've lost everything. Then I literally would have had nothing, since it had been my declared plan to put all of my assets under the Steinhoff Group, and I was recruiting people who were on the verge of joining – top people. And the third thing, I resolved not to become bitter. Because, you know, no one has time for an embittered old man.'

Christo Wiese paused for a moment. Then he smiled faintly: 'Well, the first two I'm coping with. The third one I find more difficult.'

He referred to the Buddhist belief that life moves in cycles of fortune and misfortune. That is just the way it is: one needs to accept both the sweet and the sour.

5

A chicken in every pot

Whitey Basson

THE BIGGEST revolution in the retail food industry in South Africa since the heydays of Sam Cohen's OK Bazaars and Raymond Acker-man's Pick n Pay was brought about by a farmboy from Porterville.

Whitey Basson was the driving force behind the expansion of Shoprite/Checkers into Africa's largest food retailer. He is the kind of businessman who specialises in the bottom end of the mass market, striving to keep food prices as affordable and competitive as possible so that there may be a chicken in every pot.

Basson lives on the farm Klein Dasbosch outside Stellenbosch. The close proximity of his residence to the university town has been dragged into media reports and political rumour-mongers' narratives about supposed members of the so-called Stellenbosch Mafia. But he is also one of the high-profile Stellenbosch residents who escaped the carnage when Steinhoff's shares fell off a cliff.

Whitey, who was born on 8 January 1946 as James Wellwood Basson, grew up on Dasbosch – the farm in the district of Porterville owned by his father, Captain Jack Basson, who was, among other things, a United Party MP. He carries the names of the merchant JW Mushet, a Scottish immigrant who was a minister in the Smuts cabinet. Mushet and his wife, who were friends of the Bassons, had no children, and Whitey's parents named him after their Scottish friend. As 'Wellwood' was something of a tongue-twister to the schoolchildren in Porterville, the flaxen-haired boy was nicknamed 'Whitey'.

He matriculated at Rondebosch Boys' High School in Cape Town, and had planned on studying medicine at the University of Cape Town. But because the UCT course was due to start two weeks earlier than Stellenbosch University's year programme and a holiday romance was still in full swing, he promptly changed his mind about his choice of university, field of study, and future career.

At Stellenbosch, where he enrolled for a BCom course, he became acquainted with Christo Wiese in the men's residence Wilgenhof. They were both *Sappe*, supporters of the United Party, and they formed a fairly close-knit little group in the Nationalist-leaning university town. Their friendship was to last a lifetime.

After qualifying as a chartered accountant in 1970, Basson practised at the accounting firm Brink, Roos & Du Toit (later PwC) in Cape Town. He was living in Tamboerskloof at the time when Christo also started working at Pep Stores in Cape Town. The two of them would get together on Friday afternoons with other friends and play poker.

Pep Stores was one of Basson's clients, where he was appointed financial director in 1972. He started working closely with the Pep founder Renier van Rooyen who, by his own admission, had an 'enormous influence' on his life. 'He taught me how to paint, if I can put it like that. He taught me the art of retailing, how it works, and that probably helped me the best.'

Someone else he learnt from was his father, who was also a seasoned businessman. In his view, he was at least able to gain a better education in business than most children. Jack Basson ran a farm and owned liquor shops, and as a child Whitey 'grew up with buying and selling'. His father believed that Parliament should not pay members more than the cost of their accommodation. Another mentor was Professor Giel Loubser of Stellenbosch University, a trusted confidant of Basson's who later became the chair of PwC.

In 1974, Renier van Rooyen took early retirement and went overseas. Basson ascribes this to the fact that Van Rooyen's older friends were dying – 'and he had worked incredibly hard all his life, from poverty to what he had achieved, and I think he was simply exhausted'.

To Basson's disillusionment, however, Van Rooyen returned in full force in 1978. 'We didn't have a fight, but I told him: You know, it's not nice for me to run a business with you now wanting to disrupt everything I've put in place. It doesn't work for me. I'm not keen on this, so I'll resign and we will stay friends, but we're going to create bad blood if we carry on this way. Because I was like a child to him. Then he asked, what do you want to do? I said I'd like to go into food.'

The two of them visited Italy to study businesses that specialised in fast-moving consumer goods. Basson was on the verge of embarking on a joint venture with the company Pam Supermercati to bring a low-cost, limited-assortment business like Aldi or Lidl to South Africa. But then a friend phoned him about a golden opportunity: the possibility of purchasing a small eight-store Western Cape grocer called Shoprite. The company was owned by the Rogut family, and the partners had fallen out.

With Van Rooyen's support, Shoprite was acquired in 1979. This was the start of Basson's career in the group that would eventually dominate the South African retail food industry. He left his office at Pepkor with a car and a briefcase, and found a place in Lansdowne. There he sat on a chair that kept tilting because its previous owner had been obese, 'but I learnt a lot and worked hard'.

He concluded that if his company was to grow, its emphasis had to shift towards the largest segment of South Africa's economically active population, the middle-to-lower LSM market. Shoprite was restructured. Some of the old stores were closed, and new stores were opened. And he identified the potential inherent in acquisitions and turnarounds of ailing companies as a way of expanding the group.

Christo Wiese, who had been practising as an advocate in Cape Town in the meantime, returned to Pep in 1981 after Van Rooyen sold his controlling interest and retired. 'Well, Christo looked after the clothes and I looked after Shoprite, and he had more time on his hands to get many more shares for himself than what I owned. I had to do all the work, and he made all the money!' Basson recounts jokingly.

His first acquisition, that of six old Ackermans food stores, was the start of a process that saw Shoprite gradually expanding northwards. Shoprite listed on the JSE in 1986, and although still in the Pepkor stable, it operated as an independent concern. He had known from the start that Shoprite could not remain a small business: 'Our models were always based on growing very big, very quickly.'

In a TV interview with Theo Vorster on *Sakegesprek*, Basson related how he and his young colleagues approached the challenge of building an eight-store chain into a 'serious player'. He said 'playing' was exactly what it was. 'We really just played cat and mouse and bush war with our biggest opposition at that stage in the Western Cape.' He described it as an exciting time, the highlight being starting with something small and pitting yourself against the mighty Goliath. Each time you won something, you got 'that incredible adrenaline rush that told you, let's go for the next step'.

An initial bid to purchase the 27-store Grand Bazaars chain in the Western Cape was unsuccessful, but in 1990 Basson acquired the business at an even better price than the original deal.

The pattern repeated itself with Checkers. Basson's first bid to acquire the struggling Sanlam-controlled group failed. But, thanks to his personal relationship with Marinus Daling, the executive chair of Sanlam, a deal was struck on his second attempt, which saw Shoprite reversed into Checkers' holding company. Majority control was obtained of what was now the new Shoprite Checkers Group.

Checkers was in a financial predicament, with losses in its 169 stores almost equalling the turnover of Shoprite. The chain was in dire need of a turnaround. Wasting no time, Basson kicked off the makeover during the first lunch he enjoyed in Checkers' posh dining room where waiters with white gloves served them a three-course meal. 'It was very nice. I felt like one of those biblical aristocrats who got fed oranges and grapes,' Basson recalled.

Then he looked at his table companions and reminded them that Checkers was losing R45 million a year. This might not be their last supper, he said, but it was definitely their last lavish lunch. The dining room was locked the very next day. From then on lunch at Checkers meant 'that at five o'clock you discover you've missed lunch'.

Within nine months, the Checkers chain was turned around,

with 16 500 jobs being saved in the process, and Shoprite Checkers became a profitable company trading across all LSMs. The company operated under two brand names, with the different markets targeted by the stores in the Shoprite and the Checkers brands respectively. For the first time Shoprite was large enough to be offered the opportunity to compete in the modern shopping centres that were being developed.

Basson's major coup was the acquisiton of the widely known OK Bazaars in 1997 for a paltry R1. OK Bazaars, where Sam Cohen had wielded the sceptre for years, was mired in financial difficulties. The chain was losing more than the profits made by the Shoprite Checkers Group. In these circumstances, the sole shareholder, SA Breweries, was prepared to accept a nominal price to rid itself of the lossmaker.

Turning OK around was a mammoth task. More than 150 stores countrywide had to be converted and modernised. As in the case of Shoprite Checkers, the chain's brands were separated according to the specific areas and markets where the stores were located. OK's familiar brand name was retained. The furniture branches and House & Home were consolidated into the OK Furniture company, and the other branches fell under the OK Franchise Division. About 33 252 jobs were saved.

The new chain group steadily increased its market share, so much so that it has grown to above 30 per cent of the retail food market in South Africa.

Expansion in Africa

New opportunities arose for Basson to realise one of his most ambitious dreams in 1994: expansion beyond the country's borders from his relatively modest headquarters in Brackenfell in Cape Town.

Shoprite started opening stores in Africa. The first supermarket was in Lusaka in Zambia, from where they moved northwards up to Ghana and Nigeria. Shoprite became the first South African retailer in the Democratic Republic of the Congo when a supermarket was opened in Kinshasa in 2012. The group has become Africa's largest retail food chain, and that while the continent is strewn with the corpses of so many other businesses that failed. Basson's explanation for their success is brief: 'Our culture. How we do things.'

He tells the story of his very first store outside South Africa where an old gentleman with a grocery bag filled with apples came up to shake his hand: 'In this country,' he said, 'only the politicians could afford apples.' Now he was able to buy each of his grandchildren their very first apple. This is the kind of thing that delights Basson.

In Zambia, where old socialist legislation was still in force, people were not allowed to paint the outside of their houses. In Kitwe, the Shoprite team beautified the pavements. 'Within a year, the houses around us also started looking like that. We don't spend money on marble and stuff, we plant gardens at every shopping centre. It's about seeing something come into being. You not only get a business that provides a return, you influence an entire environment.'

By 2019, Shoprite operated about 2 900 stores in 15 African states. Despite success in these countries, there was one failed attempt. Restrictive legislation and red tape forced Basson to close his super-market in Egypt. 'In Egypt, we lost R40 million within six years,' he says with a wry smile . 'Before us, a similar British business lost in the region of R300 million within a year. Does that make us better than them, or worse?'

Basson believes that the infrastructure in African states, partic-ularly roads and ports, has improved considerably in recent years, notably as a result of Chinese involvement. Some countries are far ahead of South Africa when it comes to information and communica-tion technology, with internet speeds that are twenty times faster. Yet the approach of Africa's bureaucrats towards trade has not improved much. This is due to a plethora of laws that entangle businesses in lengthy and complicated processes.

South Africa, however, has even worse problems. He points out that in 2016 the then minister in the presidency said he wanted South African companies to do more cross-border trade with southern African countries. Basson then asked his head of logistics to compile a report on what this entailed.

The findings were shocking: 'We do 15 000 shipments to 14 African countries. For that we need 758 462 pages of documentation. That's 64 000 pages per shipment – 634 pages of documentation need to be completed to send one container out of South Africa.

Unless we fill in 758 462 forms, we won't get anything across the border. That's exports from South Africa. It's money that is supposed to keep the growth rate above 1 per cent.'

According to Basson, this kind of 'bureaucratic madness' is also stifling the development of the small business sector in South Africa. On the part of the government, 'all the talk is about supporting small entrepreneurial businesses. But it is just talk.'

The local regulatory requirements anger him. It frustrates him that red tape and unnecessary regulations are cutting the throats of small entrepreneurs – the fisherman at Langebaan who tried to supply harders to Shoprite, the aunties who were supposed to produce milk tarts and koeksisters with the free stoves provided by Shoprite. Because of the bureaucratic formalities they eventually throw in the towel. 'I have a thousand stories like that.'

Previously, he recounts, young people could work as tellers over weekends. Many youngsters could help pay off their study fees because of these casual jobs. Today, labour legislation has destroyed that possibility.

Also, the limits on working hours prevent people from earning more money. 'I have asked the trade unions in the past if we can't make exceptions for my staff. When workers want to work more hours, they should at least have the choice to do so.'

For all that, he has a good relationship with the trade unions. After his retirement, quite a number of trade union leaders personally phoned 'the richest boss in Africa', as they call him. 'I'm pro-trade union. I believe that there has to be a focused, central authority that represents the masses.'

In business, he believes, there is ultimately only one recipe for success, and that is 'the constant, constant energy you put into finishing off that thing you're busy with in the most perfect way possible and keeping it like that'. Maybe he was able to spot a mistake more quickly because of the years of experience he had under good guidance.

He is renowned for his strict requirements: stores must be clean and neat, with everything in its place, and service has to be fast and flawless. He kept his staff on their toes with his attention to detail: 'When I walked into a store through the back door, I knew that if the floor wasn't clean, there would be things wrong inside the store, etcetera. And when I receive a document, I try to wrap up the matter within a 24-hour cycle, not saying in six months' time, "bring me that file, leave it again for next month".' He regards himself as a 'terrible guy' who takes a decision today that has to be implemented tomorrow, 'and the day after tomorrow there must be action'.

Basson is a 'tremendous fan' of technology despite not being well trained in it himself. He believes that a different style of business is developing: another dimension where the machines teach one another and are smarter than people, and they learn faster. 'Even so, I think it will go through many metamorphoses. A more human element has to enter into technology, because I think you can't really solve a problem in that way.' But today it is impossible to tackle business problems, investigations and structures without technology, he says.

Shoprite is known for its massive distribution system from massive warehouses, some of the largest in southern Africa. Basson considers Amazon one of his favourite companies. And Amazon, contrary to popular belief, is basically just a good distribution company. 'They distribute information so fast to their distribution centres and follow it up so easily, their distribution method just simply beats everyone else's hands down.'

He expands on how Shoprite does cross-border trade: 'We buy in China in American dollars; we pay import duty in South Africa in rands; we calculate the foreign exchange rates; we then export the goods to Zambia against kwachas, and in the calculations we then still have to see what our profit margin is and what we would be able to charge before we conclude another buying transaction. Now imagine: a buyer with 5 000 different kinds of items, how much time would they have to spend to work out all of this on an adding machine? Today it is easier, and you can track everything. We know from the minute the ship is loaded what is inside the container, what progress the ship is making, when it is cleared by customs, what the import duty is. In most countries we ourselves print the documents we hand to the customs officials.'

With technology like that at one's disposal, distribution becomes very easy. 'Unless you can do that, you'll never build a big business. You can build small businesses, but you won't be able to become a big player,' he says.

Culture and business

Basson is outspoken about never doing business with Afrikaners merely because they are Afrikaners. 'We eat out together and we have nice conversations. So, if I want to find out about something, I can pick up the phone and say: Can you give me advice about this thing, I know nothing about it, or I'd like to do such and such, can you suggest a plan?

'But I don't think it makes any sense … here in Stellenbosch, in any case … that we go and sit round a table, close the door and say: Okay, we're now going to make a run on that thing. I've never been at a meeting like that.'

Talking about people he came to know, he says: 'I befriended Jewish people who could teach me. And it wasn't just about getting money from them or anything like that. My father told me the Jewish businessmen were much better than us Afrikaners. If you want to learn the best, you go and learn from them. That's why I bonded with them, and had many of them as friends. And a lot of them were old people.' His wife still accuses him of having been 'the stingiest in the world': when all her pals went to the beach with their boyfriends, he would be having afternoon tea with an old gentleman on Sea Point's beachfront, chatting to him about business or whatever.

'So, I am opposed to a white and a black business chamber, and so on. If I were a black guy, I would join the white business chamber if they were the dominant party, or vice versa. But it doesn't feel right to me to attach yourself to a group simply because you feel culturally at home there.'

It is of great importance to Basson that his businesses are involved in the community. In Shoprite, elderly clients are treated to a free cup of soup in stores at month's ends 'so that they can accept us as theirs. You have to gain acceptance, show that you're part of the community.'

The level of poverty in South Africa upsets him. 'I get depressed when I see poor people. I hate seeing people without food begging in the street.'

A voice against Steinhoff

Basson does not agree with the criticism that big conglomerates kill small businesses: 'I've worked in both, as you know. I was the business manager of Pep Stores where Renier van Rooyen put me in charge of a business at the age of 28. And I saw where we were better and where we were weaker, and big businesses *cannot* get the better of an efficient small business.

'No, the big businesses kill *clumsy* businesses, businesses that shouldn't really exist. Look, you're the master of your own destiny, aren't you? I mean, if you want to sell a diamond with a rand profit, there is no need for a corporate board telling you, no, you have to make 25 per cent to break even, because your expenditure profile is so much, and you have external audit committees, you name it. Remember, this corporate governance arose after Enron. I would really like to know what these things are costing us – supposedly to protect our shareholders between audit committees, corporate governances, etcetera, etcetera – and whether it wouldn't have been considerably cheaper to take out insurance and to say: Okay, you are protected against an Enron incident in the future.'

He is rather sceptical of Mervyn King's comprehensive guidelines on corporate governance, the reports up to King IV that have been revised three times since 2002. 'I think Judge King spends every day thinking of another thing he can add to make the book thicker. I can't really comprehend our annual statements – and I'm a CA. There are now so many formulas that have to be worked out ...'

Among shareholders and customers of Shoprite, hero worship awaited the outspoken and somewhat unconventional businessman when, prior to the eruption of the Steinhoff scandal, he dug in his heels and refused that Shoprite be merged into the Steinhoff empire.

Basson explains what happened in the case of the two takeover bids that were made for Shoprite during the Steinhoff drama. The first one was that all shares in Shoprite would be exchanged for shares in Steinhoff, which meant the transaction would be a carbon copy of the Steinhoff/Pep deal. The end result would have been that a Shoprite shareholder's shares would have been worth nothing unless they sold their Steinhoffs or had taken cash, if there had been any.

'I was strongly opposed to this type of transaction, and Christo and I said hard words to each other. I felt there were no synergistic benefits for Shoprite, and I was also not happy with what I'd seen of Steinhoff. On the contrary, I suppose I can say it today: I would have opposed the deal in public had it come to that point.'

The second bid was initiated quite a while later by the bankers and the people who would have liked to buy Wiese's shares. The share recovered to a reasonable price, which had not been the case with the first transaction, and the argument Wiese presented to Basson was that he basically still wanted to consolidate his interests in one channel, hence it would suit him to sell his Shoprites to Steinhoff.

'He also promised me that the listing of Shoprite would not be suspended, and then people would be able to decide which company they wanted to invest in. When these alternatives were put on the table, it would've been wrong of me to tell Christo what he should do with his shares because there was now really an opportunity for people to invest strictly in Shoprite.'

The second transaction entailed that Shoprite would be merged into Steinhoff Africa Retail (Star), a new, separate group comprising all of Steinhoff's African retailers and which was listed on the JSE in September 2017. Wiese and the PIC would exchange their interests in Shoprite for shares in Star, which confirmed on 30 November 2017 in a Sens announcement that the group had exercised the call options to acquire a controlling stake in Shoprite. A week later, on 5 December 2017, the Steinhoff bomb exploded.

The collapse of Steinhoff brought an end to the merger plans. The opposition of Basson and the other minority shareholders had safeguarded the interests of Shoprite's shareholders.

According to Shoprite's 2017 annual report, Basson held a total of 9 104 122 Shoprite shares, valued at about R2,3 billion at the time. Basson's 1,08 per cent stake was considerably smaller than the 16,89 per cent stake of Wiese with his 101 million Shoprite shares.

Basson has often been asked if the Steinhoff deal led to his resignation as CEO of Shoprite. 'The answer is no, because two years before that I already intended to start preparing to train people to take over from me. When someone asks whether I would have stayed on after my resignation, the answer is also no, since I'm not the type of person who felt like sitting in long debates in board meetings, and especially not with people who were in my opinion not on the Shoprite level of retailing.'

He refers to decision-making, which he deems more important than audit committees that hold lengthy discussions and want to know things like where certain documents are. 'I always say my greatest risk is, will I still have customers coming through my doors? A question like that doesn't occur to our audit committees.

'It's not that there was anything wrong with Steinhoff's people, but Shoprite towered above most of the retail companies, in terms of both financial success and training of excellent succession management.

'The de facto situation would have been that Shoprite would become a subsidiary of Steinhoff. Well, I've carried through two or three takeovers myself – you can't get away from the fact that the buyer who has that control can and will determine the direction, and it's never a comfortable situation because every guy has his own opinion about his competencies. So, it would've been hard for me to sit in such a Shoprite board meeting, particularly when from 1980 you've built up a business from eight stores to the few thousand it now had.

'It is just a fact that even from the time of Napoleon, when something is taken over, be it a castle or a house or a company, the front part is burnt down. I saw it at Checkers and at Shoprite and at OK, and I myself was responsible for taking drastic decisions because those companies were unsuccessful, unlike Shoprite. In the process I also lost a lot of good people, which I regret to this day.'

By virtue of his experience Basson was sceptical of some big conglomerates, especially where businesses with different cultures were lumped together in one stable. 'I'm very opposed to a business not being a focused entity, and I failed to understand how we could manage such a large group with numerous brands that trade in different countries in the world as a single business.

'That type of manager with a limited knowhow of [food] retail, a focused area where things happen quickly every day, must to my mind still be born. I don't know clever people like that who would've been capable of managing it.'

He stresses that there was nothing wrong with Shoprite Checkers, 'but it's a fact that culture can make or change a business'. He questioned what the culture would be of 'a company selling Gomma Gommas and mattresses, building materials and whatever you wish', and how food could be focused on in the same stable.

Many people have asked Basson whether the disagreements about Steinhoff resulted in a bad relationship with Wiese. 'The answer to that is no. We were very angry with each other, but what he decided was a personal choice and basically had nothing to do with me. Fortunately, I was in a win-win situation: if the business were to go belly-up, people would say Whitey Basson had been a smart guy, but his successor just couldn't cut it. If the business flourished, they would say, wow, that Whitey Basson really trained his people well. So, for me to have become involved in businesses that potentially had only a big losing side to them would have been wrong.'

Regarding his relationship with Markus Jooste, he does not beat about the bush. 'We didn't have a relationship, and we wouldn't have hit it off anyway. I can't really explain what the reasons were, but we just couldn't look each other in the eye … If I may be blatant: how do you sit at a boardroom table when you don't have respect for everyone there?'

He says he was never able to evaluate Steinhoff. 'I couldn't understand what they were investing in.'

Did Wiese say to him afterwards: you were right and I was wrong? Basson responds diplomatically to this question: 'Yes, but that's just between me and Christo, and I'm not cross with him or he with me about what happened. On the contrary, I feel sorry for him for having lost so much money that we all had worked so hard for. But he is very disciplined and doesn't have loose lips, and would never say that someone was crooked or not crooked.

'I believe that Christo, who was the biggest loser in the Steinhoff saga, didn't know about any irregularities that there might have been. The little I've known about him since our university days is that he really never acted dishonestly.'

But he does think that Wiese's reputation as business leader has suffered damage: 'A chair is associated with his chairmanship …'

Basson has never regarded Wiese as a great retailer, 'but he had a fantastic business brain that invested in retail, and mostly through good people. It beats me how this last one got past him, but we're going hunting one of these days, and maybe he'll tell me on the dunes what was going on in his mind in that final run-up to mergers.'

When asked if he had smelt a rat at an early stage of the unfolding Steinhoff debacle, in other words, before Jooste resigned, he replies laughingly: 'I'm not going to answer that question!'

After a career of nearly 45 years, virtually all of which was spent with Shoprite, Basson finally announced his resignation in October 2016. During that time the business grew from a small eight-store chain with a value of R1 million to a globally respected retailer with a market capitalisation of R114 billion and over 140 000 employees.

'I'm tired. The business is now so big and there is so much red tape and all sorts of stuff that take up so much time,' Basson said. He was succeeded as CEO by Pieter Engelbrecht.

The negative reaction to his salary-and-bonus cheque of R100 million was possibly a contributory factor in his decision to step down. 'Every year there's an argument about how much I earn, and I honestly have nothing to do with my salary. In 2004, I negotiated international standards for myself, and that's all.'

Expanding on this, he explains that he never asked for a pay rise. His stance was that he should get paid what people thought he was worth, and if they thought he was not worth it, he had to look for another job. When people asked: 'Why the hell are you paying Whitey so much money?' it was up to the chair to respond, in his view.

When Christo Wiese was asked questions like that, his reaction was that Basson had earned it. He'd created unprecedented value for Shoprite's customers and shareholders in the course of his career. Wiese responded emphatically to questions from critics by remarking that if he could find more Whitey Bassons, he would hire them all. Wiese told the *Financial Mail*: 'I would pay R1 billion in the middle of the night for another Whitey.'

In South Africa, a country with one of the highest inequality rates in the world, the debate about excessive CEO remuneration will undoubtedly continue to rage. The defence that South Africans are competing with international companies' highly paid CEOs is not an argument that is accepted in all quarters. This applies particularly to critics who hold the view that generous remuneration packages, bonuses and share options are in many cases paid out too soon, whereas it would be more appropriate after a long-term period of proven performance. Christo Wiese believes that this was precisely the case with Whitey.

Basson still regularly goes to his office in Church Street in Stellenbosch where he and other well-known residents of the town share offices in the Old College Building. He says jokingly that it prevents him from being a nuisance on the farm to his wife, Annelise. The couple have four children: two sons and two daughters.

People who wish to make appointments with him come to his office in town. His secretaries work flexi-time. Their sole mandate is that they may never be behind with anything. Their cellphones, which are linked to the office computer, have to be on hand 24/7 so that they can respond instantly to any query from him, regardless of their whereabouts.

After his retirement it was observed that throughout his career Basson's timing had been remarkable, and that he turned every favourable opportunity to his, and his company's, advantage. He successfully pioneered grocery stores outside South Africa, particularly in Africa, and developed a more impressive non-South African network than any other rival retailer.

Shoprite's share price reached a record high of R266 in March 2018. At that stage, it seemed as if Basson's timing had let him down somewhat because in September 2017, a few months after his retirement, he had sold his share option of 8,68 million shares back to the company at R201 a share. Since then Shoprite has run into headwinds, as happened to many other retailers as a result of the deteriorating economic conditions. By 2020, the share price had tumbled to below R120.

His successor faced the daunting task of successfully implementing and pursuing Basson's grand vision: growth in Africa, the construction of more massive distribution centres, and the expansion of high-speed digital systems.

6

Money in the bank

GT Ferreira and Laurie Dippenaar

A number of Afrikaners have made their mark in the South African banking industry since 1994. Two of them, GT Ferreira and Laurie Dippenaar, spearheaded expansions that resulted in their entry into the ranks of the major South African banks. Their bank, First National Bank (FNB), falls under the FirstRand Group, Africa's largest banking group by market value and one of the largest financial services groups in South Africa.

GT Ferreira

Gerrit Thomas Ferreira is the only child of a shopkeeper couple from Graaff-Reinet. His father was the general dealer, and his mother, who lived to the age of 101, was a fishmonger. All who knew him in his schooldays at Hoër Volkskool in Graaff-Reinet call him Gerrit, but

at the Army Gymnasium in Pretoria he acquired the moniker 'GT' because of the way his name was called out during roll call: Ferreira, GT.

When he started working in 1972 after completing his studies at Stellenbosch, Ferreira was persuaded by a friend from his student days, the later well-known stockbroker Mof Terreblanche, to go into banking. At the time when the duo were running the Cape Town Regional office of the Bank of Johannesburg, a newspaper published a photo of them and their assistant with a caption that read: 'You might go far to find an office in which every member is as highly qualified as at the Cape Town Regional Office of the Bank of Johannesburg. This office boasts more degrees than people. Pictured here are GT Ferreira MBA, liaison officer; Mof Terreblanche MCom, regional manager; Corrie Daniels BA.'

On Ferreira's return from a year overseas, Terreblanche, who had since been promoted to marketing manager at the Bank of Johannesburg, offered him a job in the capital market in Johannesburg. They borrowed money from insurance companies for leveraged leasing, with most of the contracts involving municipal projects. They enjoyed a tax benefit they could pass on to the client via lower interest rates that made the leases very attractive for the municipalities. Business was so brisk that eventually they had used up the complete tax base of the bank and had to approach other banks, until Ferreira realised they actually no longer needed the bank.

In the meantime, they had also started a company, Magnum Leasing, together with the businessman Martin Summerley. 'I then became a bit worried. Martin Summerley's business practices were not quite to my taste, and he also put all the money we made into planes. I was fed up, and so I walked over to the nearby Industrial Development Corporation (IDC).'

The person Ferreira went to see at the IDC was Pat Goss, an accountant who was not only a university friend but had also been with him at the Army Gymnasium. 'So I said: Pat, I have an idea, I want to start a business.'

Ferreira's proposal was to eliminate a bank as intermediary for such structured finance transactions. Goss immediately took to the idea. But they also needed someone who could work with numbers to explain the plan to clients. Goss suggested a friend of his, Laurie Dippenaar, a chartered accountant who workd with him at the IDC.

Dippenaar agreed to join them. With Goss as middleman, they put their heads together and by pooling their savings they were able to launch a start-up with R10 000 (in dollar value about R170 000 in 2020), with Ferreira as the biggest shareholder. They were well aware that it was a gamble, particularly in the tough economic conditions in South Africa in the wake of the 1976 Soweto youth uprising. But they chose an imposing name for their small financial structuring house, Rand Consolidated Investments, which they thought had sufficient gravitas to make up for the lack of pretty much everything else.

Rand Consolidated Investments and the quest for a banking licence

On 1 July 1978, Rand Consolidated Investments (RCI) came into being with only R10 000 capital, three partners and a secretary. By the end of 2018, the FirstRand Group that grew out of RCI would consist of 48 000 employees, with assets of R110 billion on the banking side, and a market capitalisation of R384 billion.

Paul Harris, a friend of Ferreira and Goss from their Stellenbosch days, joined the business a year later. All the founders were under the age of thirty. Goss and Harris were English speakers but had learnt to speak Afrikaans fluently at Stellenbosch.

Goss stepped down as founder member after three months, however, when his father died and he had to take over the family business in the Transkei. He remained a director, but his shares were bought out, although he could retain 5 per cent – an amount of R500 that would increase exponentially in value and help make him a multi-millionaire.

In the early days, RCI operated on a shoestring, as the business did not generate much cash. Ferreira quips that he married his wife Anne-Marie just in time for her to support him during the first nine months of RCI's existence.

Their office furniture was bought at an auction, on hire-purchase. For photocopying, they had to make use of the services of a copy shop on the ground floor of their office building. Ferreira became irritated with the hassle and the cost, and insisted that they buy their own photocopier. Dippenaar refused point-blank: 'When I told him we had no money, GT offered to buy a photocopier out of his own pocket and rent it to us on the same basis as what the shop charged for copies. I did the sums and realised GT would pay off his machine within three months.' So RCI bought its own photocopier.

Each of the three founders brought distinctive personal qualities to the partnership. Ferreira was regarded as the diplomat and the strategist; Dippenaar, the goalkeeper, the custodian of values and the number cruncher; and Harris the creative thinker who was prepared to take risks and who excelled as a dealmaker.

When talking about their history, all three of them are somewhat bemused by the success they achieved. 'If you had asked us when we started if we saw our future as running a company the size of Sanlam, we would have laughed. We were hustlers who saw an opportunity,' Harris related.

After a year or two, things started looking up for RCI. Bigger and bigger transactions were concluded with, among others, municipalities, Eskom and water boards. Then the tax legislation changed, and they had to venture into all kinds of other initiatives.

In the early 1980s, they tried to obtain a banking licence for their lending and financing business, but due to a moratorium on the issuing of new licences these items were as scarce as an honest politician. A new opportunity presented itself in 1984 as a consequence of Rand Bank having been declared bankrupt and placed in liquidation some years earlier.

Johann Rupert then bought the banking licence of Rand Merchant Bank, which was not in liquidation, and settled in Johannesburg. After a few years, however, his father, Anton Rupert, wanted Johann to return to the Rembrandt Group. Johann was looking for someone he could trust to take over from him, and he turned to RCI because Ferreira and his partners had helped the younger Rupert before by warning him against risky loans to Martin Summerley who operated a scam in the Magnum Group.

The outcome was a merger between the two companies. RCI, which was at that stage slightly more profitable than Rand Merchant Bank, obtained the controlling stake and swapped the name RCI for RMB. Johann Rupert stayed on as chair, but he felt he had to sell his shares in the bank to avoid a conflict of interests since Rembrandt had a stake in Volkskas. Ferreira was the first managing director.

As the bank grew, Ferreira as CEO became aware of a dynamic that did not make life easy for a leader: 'Especially in a merchant bank the egos are bigger than the building that houses them,' he said. 'The management principles and leadership skills for managing a bunch of merchant bankers are very different from managing clerks. You just have to work with these egos.'

During this period Ferreira adopted a saying that later became an axiom in the bank: 'There is nothing that we can't accomplish as long as we don't care who gets the credit.' Teamwork and a collaborative spirit improved the chances of winning. He compared it to a rugby metaphor: 'It doesn't matter who scores the try as long as you score the damn try.'

On the establishment of the holding company Rand Merchant Bank Holdings (RMBH) in 1987, Ferreira was appointed as the first chair, a position he occupied up to his retirement in 2018. He suspects that of all the chairs of companies listed on the JSE, his tenure was the longest.

A turning point and a new life in Stellenbosch

A shooting incident near Ferreira's home in Bryanston in 1992 changed his life. After an Allied board meeting, he was followed to his house and held up by robbers masquerading as police officials. He was shot in his torso through his tie, with the bullet just missing his heart. The tie with the bullethole ended up in Allied's museum as a souvenir of the incident.

'I spent two days in intensive care. Lying there, I started thinking about whether this was all one lived for and if there was a God and all kinds of things, and why this had to happen ... Actually, all I decided in the end was that I no longer wanted that hectic life. The point is just: you realise that you are mortal. You wonder if this is what you want to do for the rest of your life, because I've been working hard for so many years. I only got home by eight, nine o'clock at night. So I told Laurie: Listen, I'm sorry, but I'm out.'

This happened at a stage when the group was in the process of taking over Anglo American's interests in FNB and the insurer Southern Life. The merger of these assets with RMB and Momentum (which they had acquired earlier) resulted in the establishment of FirstRand, which listed on the JSE on 25 May 1998.

At first Ferreira's colleagues insisted that he only work in the mornings, but before long he was back to a full-day routine because Ferreira loved his work. He drew an analogy between a racehorse and a farm horse. 'When you put the racehorse on the racetrack, he can't trot. He wants to run. So my conclusion was: take the racehorse off the track and put him in a paddock on the farm, and he'll roll in the sand just as happily as the other horses. I needed to get off the track, and that's when I said: Okay, I'm done, I'm going to the Cape.'

He stayed on as chair of RMB Holdings, but only attended board meetings.

During the takeover of FNB it was initially decided in the negotiations with Anglo American that Laurie Dippenaar should be the CEO and Neil Chapman, the then head of Southern Life, the chair. Shortly before this was due to be announced, Anglo phoned Ferreira and told him Chapman's wife had cancer and he no longer felt up to assuming the chairmanship: would Ferreira please take on the role of chair?

'I was quite surprised by this, because I thought they wanted to maintain a balance between the two groups. So I went to talk to Laurie and said: Listen, they've asked me to serve as chair, but I don't feel like it. "What!" Laurie exclaimed. "You talk us into this massive deal and now you don't want to carry on? No, you need to roll up your sleeves!" So then I was back in the thing, but at least at a distance because I did it from Stellenbosch.'

Ferreira was in Johannesburg virtually every second week to attend board meetings. After a decade as chair of FirstRand he was succeeded by Dippenaar, who was replaced by Harris as CEO. The trio did not consciously divide roles among themselves, but they knew one another well enough to judge each partner according to his nature.

'I think we each had our strengths and our weaknesses, and each of us was at a certain point the right person to be CEO and so on. So each of us had his turn to run with the ball. Honestly speaking, I think all of us could do everything. But when you have one guy who can simply do it better than someone else, your ego shouldn't be so big that you don't realise it,' Ferreira recounted.

Besides his chairmanship of RMBH, Ferreira also became chair of Rand Merchant Insurance Holdings, the holding company for insurance brands that included Discovery, MMI (formerly Momentum) and OUTsurance, when it was established in December 2010.

After moving to Stellenbosch, Ferreira set up his own company with the playful name Best Little Company in the Whole Wide World. He runs this company and related interests such as his wine-and-olive farm Tokara from a building in Church Street in

Stellenbosch that used to house the old College. A few other well-known personalities have offices in the same building, including Jannie Mouton and his son Piet, Whitey Basson and Erna Meaker, daughter of the Rupert partner Dirk Hertzog.

Some economic lessons for politicians

On a few occasions during the Jacob Zuma administration, Ferreira came up against politicians who distrust businesspeople. One such encounter was with the then ANC treasurer-general Zwele Mkhize, who was included in the cabinet by President Cyril Ramaphosa and served as minister of health during the Covid-19 crisis. In their conversation, Mkhize asked Ferreira to explain to him who FirstRand was.

Ferreira outlined the company structure, with RMBH holding the largest stake in FirstRand. Mkhize drew lines on a piece of paper and asked, who sits above RMBH? 'When I said, well, the biggest individual shareholder is Remgro, you could see ... hmm, you know, Remgro is the big, white capitalist and all that. And then he said: Oh, okay, Mr Rupert.'

After they continued talking for a while, Ferreira remarked that Mkhize had not asked who sat above Remgro. '"But it's Rupert," he said. Then I said: "Well, interestingly enough, the Rupert family as a whole own about 7 per cent of Remgro's shares." "But it can't be," he said. Then I said: "Yes, well, the Public Investment Corporation (PIC) owns a 15 per cent stake in Remgro, so the PIC is twice as powerful as Rupert."'

Mkhize responded that it was interesting, he hadn't known that. Yet Rupert was still the chair of Remgro, hence he controlled RMBH. Ferreira pointed out to him, however, that there was more than one way of looking at the matter.

The PIC also had a 15 per cent stake in Remgro, Remgro in turn held 34 per cent of RMBH, and RMBH again held 34 per cent of FirstRand. 'So, if you work it all out, you arrive at a figure showing that Remgro actually owns a third of a third of FirstRand. Then I said: But now look at this, the same goes for the PIC, you can do the sums. The PIC has a stake here, plus it has a stake there. Here it has 12 per cent, and here also about 12 per cent. So if you take

12 per cent there, then you get another 12 per cent plus 3,6 per cent, and so on. And in a jiffy our findings show ... that the PIC owns 20 per cent of FirstRand,' Ferreira recounts.

'I could see he was flabbergasted. He said: "But it can't be." I said: "Well, you can go and study it. While Remgro now probably holds 5 per cent, the PIC is in fact our controlling shareholder. Then he just looked at me, he smiled and said: "Yes, but ..."'

Ferreira also expanded on one of the major problems of politicians: that they sometimes don't know what they don't know. 'When you know what you don't know, you can still fix it or appoint people, but if you don't even know ...' He referred to Jacob Zuma who had railed against banks: 'He said banks were monopolies and they controlled and they held everyone back and so on. And that I found interesting. Not the fact that he said it, but the fact that he believes it. *That* is frightening.

'Nothing can be further from the truth. Running a bank is *not* easy. Now Julius Malema, or whoever, accuses me of being a capitalist, white monopoly capital. Number one, I'm not a monopoly. What does a capitalist do? He tries to make money out of every possible guy. We'll lend money to anyone if we think that guy is able to repay us and we can make a bit of profit out of him. That's what a capitalist is. So, we are trying our level best to lend money to everybody.

'It's not as if we say: you are black or you are white or you are this or that. You are free to get the money. But that doesn't register. If I had to sit down with someone, even Malema, I would say: okay, you accuse me as a capitalist and so on, and blame me for the fact that there aren't black banks. Please, let them establish ten black banks, it would be wonderful. Then they are least part of the economy ...'

Politicans with that ideological bent claim that if the country had another black-owned bank, more money would be lent to black people. 'That's rubbish,' Ferreira said. They could certainly do so, but if the lending were done recklessly, 'that bank will go bankrupt'. His words came true with the collapse of the black-controlled VBS Mutual Bank in Limpopo.

On another occasion, Ferreira had to explain a few economic realities to the firebrand politician Floyd Shivambu, deputy leader of the EFF, in his office. 'He sat here and told me they had just come from Parliament, and that 10 per cent of the country's population owned 80 per cent of the assets. Or they owned more. The 10 big guys in the country owned 50 per cent more than the rest of the population. I said: yes, that's what the figures show and so on.'

Ferreira asked Shivambu whether he had a house, and a mortgage on the house. He also wanted to know what his assets amounted to. They worked out that his net assets came to about R1 million. Then Ferreira said: 'You, Floyd Shivambu, have more assets than 25 per cent of the population. "No, that's not true," he said. Then I said: "They have nothing, they have no net assets, they live on money they borrow, and they live from hand to mouth. So, if they have nothing and you have a million, I can tell you now that you own more.

'So, be careful about the figures you use. You'd be embarrassed if something like this gets into the papers. Then he just smiled and changed the subject. But these are the type of things one needs to get across.'

Ferreira and Dippenaar were two of the businesspeople who were spied on by the notorious Guptas, the brothers who were befriended by former president Zuma to facilitate state capture. This became known after the investigation by the former public protector Thuli Madonsela that led to the damning 'State of Capture' report.

The #GuptaLeaks investigation, during which emails and documents of the Guptas were obtained and analysed by investigative journalists, showed that the Guptas' business network also operated what was basically a spying network. The movements of prominent politicians and businesspeople were tracked, and sensitive information was sourced from well-placed 'moles' in state entities. Ferreira and Dippenaar's international travel arrangements, as well as their ID numbers, appeared in the leaked emails that #GuptaLeaks exposed.

According to evidence presented at the Zondo Commission of Inquiry into State Capture, which started its work towards the end of 2018, FNB and three other big South African banks – Standard Bank, Absa and Nedbank – were summoned in 2016 to meetings with both the ANC, at the party's headquarters Luthuli House, and an interministerial committee led by the discredited Mosebenzi Zwane, the then minister of mineral resources, to force them to re-open the Guptas' suspended bank accounts. FNB refused to attend any of the meetings.

The former FirstRand CEO Johan Burger testified that in his 32 years in banking, this was the first time he had received a request from a political party or ministers wanting to discuss banker–client relationships. Both the ANC and the interministerial committee – with Mzwanele (Jimmy) Manyi, a Gupta stooge who later took over the Guptas' *New Age* paper and their flailing TV channel, as 'adviser' – wanted to raise the closure of the Guptas' bank accounts with him after media reports had brought it to their attention. Burger notified the ministers that he could attend such a meeting only if the minister of finance, who controls, among other things, the legislative framework for financial institutions, was present. He was also not prepared to discuss confidential client matters with them.

Since the committee's acting secretary could not provide a specified agenda, Burger declined the invitation to the meeting. The meeting with the ANC was cancelled for the same reason. Absa's Maria Ramos, like the other bankers, did indeed meet with the ANC, but refused to talk to the ministers. (The ANC team was made up of the secretary-general Gwede Mantashe and his deputy, Jessie Duarte, as well as the ANC's head of economic transformation, Enoch Godongwana.)

Ferreira and his workers lose millions

At the end of 2017, Ferreira was dealt a heavy blow by the Steinhoff debacle. He and his farm workers on Tokara lost more than a billion rand when the value of their shareholding in Steinhoff dropped by 60 per cent in a single day and subsequently plummeted further. At the lowest point, the R1,1 billion shareholding was suddenly worth barely R20 million.

It was a traumatic experience for Ferreira. 'Shock. Disbelief. Disappointment. Rage. Self-reproach ...' were the words he used to describe his emotions. He learnt 101 lessons from this, with the key one being that you could not trust people.

'That hurt the most. When you think back, you start reproaching yourself and you ask: But why didn't I see it? Your self-confidence gets a knock, and you say: But I've always believed I am a good judge of character when it comes to selecting people to collaborate with. In Rand Merchant Bank, in FirstRand and so on we had fantastic partners. You knew you could rely on them. It never occurred to me that something like this could happen …

'It makes you sceptical about people, about humanity. You lose faith in your fellow human beings. But I also think it's not something you want to take to your grave. You have to learn to maybe just make better choices, because you can't go through life without trust. As I said before: when you give a person responsibility, then you have to give him the authority. You can't give one without the other, can you?'

He describes how he evaluated Steinhoff, which boasted six chartered accountants on its board: 'You look at the history of the company, then you look at the management, then at the board, and you look at the road ahead, and you say, okay … their numbers over the past years haven't been particularly wonderful, but they then suddenly started showing an upward curve and so on. Auditors … fantastic. There were no warning lights whatsoever as far as I was concerned.'

Ferreira had acquired the shares when Jooste, a former friend he'd come to know years before, proposed to him as well as to Coronation co-founder Thys du Toit and PSG co-founder Jaap du Toit in May 2015 that they exchange their shares in PSG, where Jooste was also a director, for Steinhoff shares. Jooste wanted to increase Steinhoff's 18 per cent stake in PSG to 25 per cent. Ferreira thought it 'had to do with negative control'.

Ferreira and his workers' trusts, Tokara BEE Trust and Tokara Employees Trust, owned a substantial block of shares in PSG: about five million each. It would be a share-swap deal, which meant in terms of tax legislation that capital gains tax only kicked in later. Steinhoff was also about five times bigger than PSG, therefore he regarded Jooste's offer as an investment from a smaller company into a bigger one that would give shareholders more local, as well as international, diversification.

On 18 June 2018, Ferreira and the two workers' trusts, represented by Geralt Simon Fortuin and Sharon Geraldine October, applied in the Cape High Court for the share-swap transaction between them and Steinhoff International to be declared null and void. In the court papers, in which they requested that either their PSG shares be returned to them or they receive compensation, Ferreira referred to Jooste's sudden resignation and the announcement that Steinhoff's annual financial statements had to be restated.

He declared that he felt aggrieved by the revelation that the very financial statements on which he had relied were false, unreliable and a misrepresentation of Steinhoff's financial position at the time the exchange transaction was concluded. Worse still, he felt aggrieved by the fact that Steinhoff 's management – who must have known that the company's financial position was not what the market had been led to believe – had proposed the exchange transaction without his having solicited it. In fact, he believed he had been 'duped out of' a valuable asset, the PSG shares, held by him and the two trusts.

Ferreira stated he had known the directors of Steinhoff personally and had had confidence in them. He referred to Jooste, Wiese and Ben la Grange, the former chief financial officer. He had also interrogated Jooste and La Grange about Steinhoff's strategy for the future. Both of them had spoken in detail about diversification and substantial growth potential. The discussions had often been 'informal', which was why he had no written confirmation of many of these conversations.

According to Ferreira, the two workers' trusts had been set up about 14 years ago and jointly had around 80 direct beneficiaries, while their families were indirect beneficiaries. 'These are working-class people.' The intention of the trusts was obviously to ensure that the workers and their families benefit from their contribution to Tokara's growth. 'The benefits that can (and will) flow from the trusts can influence the lives of generations.'

The trusts had built up substantial assets and had distributed R24 million to the beneficiaries in the previous eight years. The trusts had also purchased land for a housing project.

Though naturally upset about the calamity, Ferreira's workers said after the events that they had not lost faith in the man who had been looking after them for years. He spoke to them and explained what had happened. According to him there was still enough money available, albeit not as generously as before, to keep benefits such as allowances for housing, school fees and transport going.

He also told them that they knew what a *skebenga* was (a gangster or a conman in Xhosa). 'I said: "There are black *skebengas*, there are coloured *skebengas*, and there are white *skebengas*. Don't think there aren't any white *skebengas*."'

At the time of going to press, judgment had not yet been delivered in the case.

Notwithstanding the Steinhoff debacle, Ferreira was still 16th on the *City Press* Wealth Index in 2018, with a gross worth of R4,865 billion. Paradoxically, he says, the Steinhoff scandal proved one thing: that there is no such thing as the Stellenbosch Mafia.

'I can assure you that the Stellenbosch Mafia don't necessarily all dine out together. X doesn't like Y, and Y can't stand Z. There is so much resentment here. I think there are too many bulls in one kraal. One pushes the other one around and so on.

'The term "Stellenbosch Mafia" basically means that the guys conspire, that they plot together. And that's the last damn thing they do. They are in all likelihood too envious of each other, or jealous. I had a helluva problem when I held a birthday party. Who do you put at whose table?

'So, don't tell me about the Stellenbosch Mafia. Such a community doesn't exist.'

Laurie Dippenaar

Lauritz Lanser Dippenaar comes from a medical family. His father was an anaesthetist and his mother a general practitioner, and two of his children are also medical doctors. He matriculated at the Hoërskool Menlopark in Pretoria and obtained an MCom degree from the University of Pretoria before qualifying as a chartered accountant.

As a Tukkie student he attended lectures given by Dr Anton Rupert, who was the chancellor of the university, and his admiration for this global entrepreneur took root there.

His first job was at the Industrial Development Corporation where he started specialising in leveraged leases, a field of which he thought 'that these contracts have potential'. One of his friends at the IDC was Pat Goss, who told Dippenaar that GT Ferreira had exactly the same idea in mind for a business in the private sector. This led to the partnership of the Dippenaar, Ferreira and Harris triumvirate that would last for decades.

Although there was no shortage of contracts that could be concluded, their lending and financing business, RCI, was subject to legislation that compelled them to start hunting around for a banking licence. The opportunity to secure one was dropped into their lap by Johann Rupert, whose Rand Merchant Bank (RMB) they acquired by means of a reverse takeover: the one company was sold to the other in exchange for shares.

'We expanded this thing [RMB] nicely for eight years,' Dippenaar recounts, 'but a merchant bank's income can be fairly erratic because you start every day with a clean page.' Although they had to do nifty footwork and RMB was viewed by some as a cowboy bank, they managed it conservatively, particularly at a juncture that saw the failure of banks such as Saambou and BoE. 'We took fewer risks because it was our money,' Dippenaar said. 'We knew we didn't have a big daddy to bail us out in a banking crisis.'

Further diversification followed when the opportunity arose to buy Momentum, an insurance company that Remgro and Volkskas wanted to dispose of. RMB had been approached to facilitate the transaction, but instead of looking for a buyer they decided to buy the company themselves. It was again a reverse takeover.

While Momentum provided a far steadier income, it was a hierarchical company that was not very innovative. But according to Dippenaar the three partners asked stupid questions that required explanations, which stimulated the insurance people to reflect on these issues themselves. Questions such as: how do you guys make a profit?

To encourage a more relaxed company culture in which innovation could flourish, the hierarchical structure was disrupted by the introduction of various novelties. A graffiti wall was built on which employees could write any message they wanted to voice, comments such as: 'The chairman is clueless.' Everyone started calling each other by their first names, and ties were no longer obligatory unless one had to see a client. Job titles were changed, with 'head of technology' replacing 'assistant general manager'. Parking next to the lift was no longer reserved for the chair: it was now first come, first served. 'We dismantled the hierarchy and they started to become resourceful,' Dippenaar relates.

Shortly before the advent of a full-fledged democracy in 1994, Dippenaar and his partners identified the anticipated entry of foreign banks into South Africa as a threat to RMB. They knew competition from foreign banks was inevitable, and that such banks would mostly target their corporate clients: state entities and big companies. But because it would be much harder for foreign banks to make inroads into retail banking, they realised they needed a retail bank strategy. To this day there are not many foreign banks of this type in South Africa.

At long last an opportunity to acquire a retail bank arose in 1998 when Southern Life in Cape Town experienced problems. Momentum, the fourth-largest insurer at the time, decided it wanted to take over the Cape company. Southern Life was owned by Anglo American, whose bosses had recently decided they should concentrate on resources. Anglo was prepared to sell Southern Life, but only on condition that their bank, First National Bank (FNB), was bought at the same time.

'What frightened us about the deal was the size, the relative size,' Dippenaar recounts. 'We were, say, 4 000 people. The bank comprised 25 000 people, and these were two big companies we had to take over simultaneously. But we knew that, strategically, it was a wonderful opportunity; a retail bank that was not one of the Big Four was now on the market, and we wouldn't get another chance like that. So we just closed our eyes and decided to go for it.

'We used the same technique again: this time we sold RCI, Rand Merchant Bank and Momentum in the same thing, the reverse takeover. We needed R5 billion, which we then obtained in the market from shareholders in one day. This was the start of FirstRand.'

Ferreira commented afterwards that the sardine had swallowed the whale.

The three friends became retail bankers. Harris was appointed managing director of FNB, the oldest bank in South Africa, but he soon discovered that drive and oomph did not feature strongly at this veteran among the banks. 'At the first meetings, the guys from FNB saw this bunch of young merchant bankers who thought they knew all the answers. Not that I thought we did, but that was the perception. They told us: "You have to understand that most of the people here just want to come to work and collect a pay cheque at the end of the month."'

To Harris, such a mindset was the antithesis of everything he believed in. Turning FNB around required a metamorphosis: they had to get bankers to think like businesspeople. That approach created a culture in which a team had to develop a strategy, was given resources to implement it, and was then dispatched to execute it. FNB was transformed so successfully that it handles 80 per cent of FirstRand's business.

Today FirstRand as holding company incorporates the brand names RMB, FNB, Wesbank, the largest vehicle finance provider in the country, eBucks and Ashburton Investments. Dippenaar was the first chief executive of FirstRand, a position he occupied until 2005, when he became chair and Harris took over as CEO.

In 2018, Dippenaar was fifth on the *City Press* Wealth Index, with a gross worth of R15,629 billion. He retired as chair of FirstRand in the same year and was succeeded by Roger Jardine. Harris was at number 26 on the wealth index that year, with estimated assets of R1,716 billion.

Two new stars – Discovery and OUTsurance

Dippenaar points out that FirstRand has been one of the few large institutions to start something new from scratch. This applies in particular to two businesses on the South African scene: Discovery and OUTsurance. The concepts behind both these companies were conceived in the offices of FirstRand. Discovery was the first one.

In 1992, at the same time that RMB was engaged in acquiring Momentum, Adrian Gore, then a young actuary from Liberty, approached Dippenaar with a view to buying a dormant insurance licence from them. 'Then I asked: "What do you want to do with it?" He explained what he had in mind, and I said: "No, man, it's just another insurance company, we're not interested." I thought I'd never see him again.'

When Gore subsequently returned with the idea of a health insurer, Dippenaar asked him to describe this product to him. 'And he explained the idea of this new-generation product with a savings account and all those things, and I thought it would work. So I told him: Fine, resign from Liberty. I'll give you an office here and we'll pay you for three months, and then you draft a business plan. If we like it, we'll support you.'

According to Dippenaar, Gore displayed the necessary entrepreneurial daring. In 1992, FirstRand invested R10 million in Discovery, which consisted of one person at the time. By the end of 2018, Discovery's market capitalisation had increased to R108 billion. 'Adrian Gore has 12 000 employees, and he's in China and he's in England. And, funnily enough, he came from Liberty. This market capitalisation is twice the size of Liberty's,' Dippenaar said.

Discovery operates in 20 countries. In South Africa it provides health insurance through Discovery Health and Vitality; life insurance through Discovery Life; and financial services through Discovery Invest and DiscoveryCard. The group also owns the Dis-Chem pharmacy group.

Discovery announced at the end of 2018 that it was establishing its own bank and bought out FirstRand's 25,1 per cent stake for R1,85 billion. The new Discovery Bank could expect fierce competition from other new kids on the block. A prominent newcomer is Bank Zero of Michael Jordaan, a former CEO of FNB, while TymeBank – which has been taken over by Patrice Motsepe's African Rainbow Capital – was also launched in 2019. Two of the three new banks therefore have a previous association with FirstRand.

OUTsurance was founded after the actuary Willem Roos met the IT expert Howard Aron and the 25-year-old actuary René Otto in 1996 at Aegis, a company in the RMB Holdings group. They researched and developed the concept behind OUTsurance and presented it to the RMBH board. Laurie Dippenaar was impressed and requested them to draw up a business plan. The board approved funding for the concept within eight weeks.

OUTsurance was established in 1999 with capital of R25 million and two people. By 2016, the insurer had 4 000 employees, and its market capitalisation was R25 billion. The company has a simple business model that is based on superior risk management through innovative product design. The founders sought to develop a new company that was not only sophisticated and different but would also be fun for them and their clients.

Roos attributes their success largely to the fact that they underwrite risks accurately. 'To do that you need very good systems in place, as well as great actuarial skills. Because we deal directly with clients, we cannot rely on brokers to give good service – we therefore place a strong emphasis on our marketing strategy and our customer service standards.' Their actuarial rating and underwriting approach plus effective cost and claim management rest on the base of an efficient information technology platform.

In 2016, Discovery and OUTsurance were unbundled in Rand Merchant Investment Holdings (RMI). Roos stepped down at OUTsurance and settled in Stellenbosch to establish the 5G network Rain as chief executive. Rain's chair is Paul Harris and one of the directors is Michael Jordaan, who had been Harris's executive assistant and later became FNB's chief executive.

At the age of 46, Jordaan resigned from FNB, returned to his

Stellenbosch family farm Bartinney, and set up a venture capital firm, Montegray Capital. Montegray's investments in start-ups, particularly in data processing and the banking sector, and entrepreneurs such as Jordaan and Roos, have boosted the innovation that is flourishing in Stellenbosch and the Cape metropole to a greater extent than in any other environment in South Africa, or even in Africa.

A set of values for success

Dippenaar explains that the structure of FirstRand's group interests has been put together in such a way that it is jointly controlled by Remgro, which is the largest shareholder, Royal Bafokeng Holdings, and the three founder partners (Dippenaar, Ferreira and Harris).

'Together, we own 52 per cent of RMB Holdings, which in turn owns 34 per cent of FirstRand, which in turn owns 100 per cent of these banks. It is therefore a control consortium, informally. But if someone had to attempt a so-called hostile takeover to acquire control, they can't do it without that top structure agreeing to it collectively,' Dippenaar states.

'RMI holds our insurance interests. We own 25 per cent of Discovery, 25 per cent of Momentum [or now MMI] and 83 per cent of OUTsurance. We are the single largest shareholder in Discovery – even though it's only 25 per cent, *and* we behave like a 25 per cent shareholder. We're not the kind that attempts to exercise control when you don't own 51 per cent. I mean, we have representation on the board and so on, but they are a company you should actually leave alone to do their own thing, although with oversight at board level. But you shouldn't micromanage these people. They are entrepreneurs, and they are doing very well. So, that's the FirstRand story.'

All in all, Dippenaar believes, one can't really encapsulate the group's success strategy in a few words. The guiding principles are traditional values and innovative ideas. 'We have a strong values-driven culture, and when people ask me what I mean by traditional values, I say: it's exactly what your mother taught you.

'When you go to a restaurant with your mother, and a friend or a family member pays – do you order the most expensive dish on the menu? No. Then I say, fine, when the bank pays for your meal, please do the same. Did she teach you to respect people? Yes … The business was basically built on innovation, or inventive ideas, on continual renewal and so on.'

In addition to that, Harris believes that the secret of the three standard-bearers of capitalism is that they always trusted each other and left parts of the business to the one with the appropriate skills: 'It's like a sports field; we each have an area to cover. A team that runs around trying to cover each other's positions will not win the game.'

He adds that, as the years passed, the partners grew to value one another more – and worked at keeping their relationship healthy. Corporate politics never came into play. They adhered to a set of values: 'mutual respect, deal on a handshake, a win-win philosophy'.

Harris, too, stresses that through all the evolutionary stages of the business, innovation was always part of the group's DNA. 'Just about everything we did was based on innovation. We actually started the futures market. I named the SA Futures Exchange (Safex). We were the first in a lot of things. We took Safex and institutionalised it.'

RMB has a 'Book of Rules', which is required reading for every employee. On opening the thick blue book with its RMB logo, readers discover that it is completely empty except for a message that reads in part: 'At RMB we've always been guided by a strong set of values, and because we trust our people to live by those values, we've never needed a book of rules.'

Over the years the trio hired highly competent young people. 'You must understand that we have this fantastic team. We didn't do this on our own,' states Dippenaar's partner, GT Ferreira. Because they attracted the best talent, they had no fears that their clients would be worried about their successors. 'The lesson we've learnt is that the only assets you have are the people you appoint. The only difference between banks is the people, and the way they package and sell the money.'

Dippenaar has a deep understanding of the balance between entrepreneurship and risk acceptance on the one hand, and the social responsibilities of a bank on the other; a quality that is highly desirable in the leader of a banking group. He views banks as fundamental institutions in the economy, with huge responsibilities to maintain the integrity of the system. It is an outlook that was instrumental in the survival of South African banks during the 2008 global financial crisis.

Dippenaar has the knack of unravelling complex problems by posing simple questions. He is also renowned for his meticulous preparation for board meetings. He would take his simple questioning to the boardroom, cutting through highfalutin financial jargon and getting executives to explain their business plans in the most basic terms. 'He hates bullshit,' says one of his long-serving colleagues. 'He always makes people simplify things. He makes them go through that intellectual process. It can be humbling but it's very valuable.'

At times he would temper politicians' illusions in this way. On one such occasion, Gwede Mantashe, the future minister of mineral resources, who had at that point recently been elected ANC secretary-general, declared at an event that he believed the banks and mines should be at least 50 per cent state-owned.

Dippenaar was in the audience and put up his hand. 'Running a bank is hard,' he said. 'When things go wrong, you have to fund them. And finding ways to compete is hard work. If you're the government, why don't you just tax them instead? You'd get all of the upside but none of the headaches.'

But the common sense of a seasoned business leader such as Dippenaar would not easily drive out the ghost of Stalinist ideas that keeps floating around in the ruling ANC alliance. The desire for state control would remain a constant refrain, also in the pursuit of a developmental state that unfortunately depends on an efficient and effective public service.

FNB was the first bank to publicly state the reasons for terminating all accounts belonging to Oakbay Investments, the holding company for the notorious Gupta family's businesses. Dippenaar explained the reasoning behind the move in his chairman's report in FirstRand's 2016 annual report.

In light of 'an unbelievable amount of misinformation', he informed the group's stakeholders that because of 'strict client confidentiality requirements, which for banks are set down in law', he was only commenting on generic frameworks and principles. To highlight the potential risks banks run if they fail to 'do the right thing', he noted that global banks that had contravened regulations had paid fines to the value of about $290 billion over the past few years. This amount represented the total GDP of Angola, Morocco and Kenya combined. 'These fines decimated banks' profits, eroded their capital bases, permanently destroyed massive amounts of shareholder value and dramatically affected their reputations.'

He continued by pointing out that 'banks function on the back of customer trust and confidence'. South African banks operate in a globally integrated system and the Reserve Bank is a signatory to many international standard-setting bodies. If banks do not comply with local and global regulations and do not take principles regarding reputation risk management seriously, foreign investment flows will be significantly reduced. 'International investors run their own risk dashboards for South Africa and responsible banking conduct is a key input. The South African banking sector scores very highly on every international governance index and should never ever compromise on this,' Dippenaar stated.

On another occasion, Dippenaar voiced his disappointment with 'the number of large corporations that have been complicit' in state capture. 'I've been bitterly disappointed. We have expressed our disdain and disappointment [to these companies] and some of them will not get business from FirstRand again.' He was probably referring to KPMG, McKinsey, SAP and Hogan Lovells, companies that were identified as accessories to state capture during and after the collapse of Bell Pottinger.

He added that values are more important than rules. Ethical conduct demands more than merely ticking boxes on governance codes.

7

Revolutionising banking
for the poor

Michiel le Roux

MICHIEL LE ROUX is the founder of Capitec, which has been responsible for the biggest revolution in the South African banking sector
since Jan S Marais established Trust Bank in the previous century. The
rapidly expanding Capitec focuses on the millions of disadvantaged
and lower-income South Africans, the previously untapped market of
'the unbanked' into which the traditional banks had hardly dared to
venture in the past.

Capitec, with its 13 million clients, was ranked the best bank in
the world by the international banking advisory group Lafferty in
2016, the only bank out of hundreds to achieve a five-star rating.
Barclays, now known again as Absa, had four stars, and Nedbank,
Standard Bank and FirstRand each had three. Within a quarter
century, Le Roux has become a dollar billionaire: on the 2020 *Forbes*
Rich List for Africa he was number 18 among the richest people on
the continent, with a net worth of $1,3 billion.

Owing to his father's occupation as a mine ventilation engineer,
Michiel Scholtz du Pré le Roux attended schools in various mining

towns before matriculating in Alberton. After obtaining BCom (Law) and LLB degrees at Stellenbosch University, he started his career in the liquor industry, at Distillers. Le Roux was appointed managing director of Distillers, which became the largest wine and spirits company in South Africa, in 1979.

In 1994, he joined Boland Bank where the chair, Christo Wiese, appointed him managing director. When the bank subsequently merged with NBS Bank, he became MD of NBS Boland Bank. Following another merger – with BoE – he was appointed MD of BoE Bank.

Shortly after Le Roux's appointment at Boland Bank, Wiese entered into an agreement with him in terms of which Le Roux acquired a minority stake in the bank for an amount of R18 million, which Wiese advanced to him. To prevent Le Roux from becoming very rich overnight and leaving the bank, he was made a beneficiary in a share option scheme that came with 'golden handcuffs'. It was agreed that if Le Roux were to leave before a specified period, he would pay Wiese a portion of the 'calculated value' of Vensterberg Beleggings, the company that controlled Wiese's shareholding in Boland Bank.

On 2 May 1997 Le Roux, whose stake had increased to R88,3 million, concluded an adjusted agreement with Wiese whereby he paid R30 million of an amount due to Wiese. The remaining recalculated debt amounted to R14 million.

At the end of 1998, Le Roux resigned from BoE after a falling-out about the future direction of the bank. He claimed that Wiese and another director, Phil Biden, had made it impossible for him to do his job as managing director. This was disputed by Wiese. He sued Le Roux for R14 million in the Cape High Court. Le Roux maintained that, in the circumstances, he did not owe Wiese anything.

The lawsuit came to court in May 2001 and dragged on for close to a year. The court battle was a hotly debated topic in business circles. So much so that some Stellenbosch businesspeople felt mediators should intervene to help resolve the dispute. In the end, Gys Steyn, Le Roux's predecessor as MD at Distillers, phoned Jannie Mouton. Le Roux and Mouton's partner Chris Otto had been roommates at university, and Mouton had come to know Le Roux well through Otto. Since Mouton knew both Wiese and Le Roux, Steyn appealed to him to do something 'because it's not nice that people one knows are fighting in the courts'.

Mouton phoned both parties and inquired whether they were prepared to allow mediators to help settle the dispute. He also roped in GT Ferreira to assist him as a mediator. The foursome then met at Lanzerac. There Wiese told his side of the story to Mouton while Le Roux talked to Ferreira in a separate room. Thereafter the roles were reversed, and Mouton and Ferreira agreed on the outcome.

Both litigants accepted an out-of-court settlement. In a joint statement, the two former Maties announced that they would establish a bursary fund to the benefit of Afrikaans-speaking black students at Stellenbosch University. Le Roux paid R2,5 million and Wiese R1 million into the R3,5 million fund.

That evening, Mouton and Le Roux met socially. Mouton recounts that Le Roux was grateful 'the thing was off his back'. But since he was unemployed, PSG gave him an office in the Old College Building. It was there that the idea of Capitec Bank was born.

A revolutionary banking concept

Mouton had long believed that poverty could only be relieved by making capital available to people without collateral. Accordingly, PSG started buying up small microlending businesses in the 1990s. Mouton was also keen to acquire a banking licence.

A concept of a bank such as Capitec that operates in the microlending industry did not exist in the old South Africa. Apart from many regulatory problems, banking licences were also in short supply. In terms of the old Usury Act, the idea of microloans was simply forbidden. However, under Derek Keys, the minister of finance from 1992 to 1994, the microlending industry was one small window of deregulation that had been opened in that loans up to a certain amount were exempted.

In the late 1990s, a number of new banking licences were granted as well, but most of these banks folded quickly. PSG took over The Business Bank, which had been one of the casualties. It was this licence that enabled Le Roux and his colleagues to start the new bank. The initial base was the 300 or so small microlending businesses that were previously consolidated in FinAid and mostly conducted business in back streets.

After becoming more closely acquainted with the microlending industry, Le Roux recognised the possibilities. According to him, Mouton and Otto had asked him, after his departure from Boland Bank, to advise them on what they should do with PSG's microlending businesses. 'Look, we all thought it was a squalid business.' He was put off by what he had heard of unsavoury practices in the microlending industry, such as exorbitant interest rates of 30 per cent per month and lenders taking people's cards and PINs, and these were 'frightening concepts'.

'Then they said, no, man, come and see for yourself. So I went, and I became interested in spite of myself, and I visited all of their branches.

'And the branches were incredibly interesting places. You know, they were places where people were treated properly, whereas in a bank a client with a low income and a low salary just didn't get good service. And so I developed the idea … and said: but if one had to put this thing on an electronic base and you have that on a national base, and you provide people with banking services and a card and the ability to make payments, and not just a lending point, then this whole thing could cause a revolution. I suggested to Jannie that we consider something like that.'

Mouton recalls that Le Roux invited him and Chris Otto to dinner at his house one evening. 'He then introduced me to Riaan Stassen and Gerrie Fourie en André du Plessis, and he said: "This is the new team that will take over your microlending business." And they were wonderful appointments. It was Michiel's idea; Michiel got the management team together, and it was a huge success story.'

It took them a long time to come up with a name for the new bank, and various possibilities were considered. Eventually it was decided they did not want to be a 'people's bank' with the label of concentrating solely on the poor. On 1 March 2002, the name was changed to Capitec Bank, which suggests a combination of 'capital' and 'technology', and Le Roux became the first chief executive. In 2007, he was succeeded by Riaan Stassen, who is four years younger than Le Roux and had also previously worked in the liquor industry.

Stassen's successor as CEO was Gerrie Fourie, who had likewise started his career in the liquor industry. 'We always joke that we were a team of liquor people who knew the retail market well,' Fourie relates. Le Roux served as chair until Stassen took over from him in 2016, but he stayed on as non-executive director.

The major investor in the new venture was PSG, who had a strong backer of Capitec in the person of Jannie Mouton. PSG's shareholding varied as a result of the selling and repurchasing of shares, but has since risen to above 33 per cent. Le Roux and Stassen also bought up shares from the outset, which would turn out to be exceptionally profitable.

Capitec would in time become a great success, but initially the going was tough. In the early years, Le Roux feared they were on such thin ice that they would not be able to continue for much longer than another month or two before going under. In their first month they made a loss, and in the second month they ran out of money and had to put their own cash into the company. At one point, PSG had to assist to enable Capitec to pay its staff's salaries, Mouton recounts.

The timing of Capitec's launch was also problematic because it occurred in the same period that Saambou was declared bankrupt. The new ANC government showed considerably less patience for the Afrikaner-controlled bank than would later be the case when African Bank collapsed.

On Monday 18 February 2002, a week after Saambou closed its doors, Capitec Bank Holdings was listed on the JSE. It was 'a hard slog' to get the business off the ground, Le Roux recounts. 'That was a terrible time to list a bank and it also meant it was a terrible time to get finance whatsoever.

'I know I sound like an old man saying you learn from your mistakes, but it's true. Starting a business in good times is always very dangerous because you will think business is easy when the wind is blowing from behind and the sailing is smooth. When you start with the wind blowing from ahead, then you know business is tough and you grow.'

They thought big from the beginning. Le Roux and Stassen emphasise the management principles on which Capitec has been built, which they explain as affordability, accessibility, convenience and simplicity. 'We encapulated it by saying we want to be a financial friend to a guy who banks with us. We want to make things simple and transparent for him,' says Le Roux.

Le Roux has high praise for Stassen's role in building the new bank. 'Riaan is a very smart guy. I believe he built Capitec Bank. If I may claim some role, I would claim that I had a dream of creating a bank and Riaan made that a reality.'

'He actually created a different reality. My vision was that we should be a bank for low-income people; for instance, to my shame, I must admit that at that stage I said we should have books. Riaan laughed and said "you are crazy; we are in the electronic age". He said "we are going to build an electronic bank for the new age, and not for low-income people but for everyone", and that's what we have done.'

The Capitec philosophy – teamwork and hard work

Capitec does not have swanky offices, palms and pot plants, sofas and suchlike frills. For Le Roux, this was the intention from the outset: some people should not have better offices than others. The head office should not be luxurious while branches have to work in grotty conditions. 'Riaan also felt very strongly about that. When you have a big organisation of 12 000 people, as we are now – and we didn't know at the time we'd grow *so* big – you have to make your people part of your process.

'We both hate the idea of the CEO flying in a jet, the number two driving a big car, number three riding a bicycle, and number four having to walk. If we all work together, we can either all walk or all fly around. All our directors, all our chairs, fly economy class domestically. No one flies business class. In the case of overseas trips, we approach each trip on merit – and when we say "on merit", it doesn't apply to who you are; it applies to what you're going to do there, how long you'll be there. And we said everyone eats the same food. When you have to sleep over, you stay at a City Lodge, nothing fancier than that.'

Everyone at Capitec addresses each other by their first names. 'There is a woman here who used to serve tea when we started and she couldn't get herself to call me Michiel. So she called me Mr Michiel. But the rest of the staff call me by my first name', says Le Roux. 'I find it terribly embarrassing that if you become a senior in a company, some guys who used to call you by your first name are now basically forced to start calling you "sir".

'So it was a very conscious attempt to say you're trying to create a culture where people work hard, where everyone is treated equally, but that there is a big pay disparity because some guys make a much greater contribution to the success of the company than others. I mean, you can't get away from that.'

While Le Roux was still at Boland Bank, it puzzled him that banks had to close early in the afternoon. He just accepted that there was some or other legal or practical requirement, but could not really find an answer anywhere.

Later he concluded that in the earlier years tellers had to write down all the deposits they received throughout the day in one of the ledgers, and at the end of the day everything had to balance. And because this process took roughly one and a half hours, they closed at half past three. But once computers arrived, you don't need a minute or a second to wrap up everything. You only need to count the cash quickly, and nowadays even that is carted away quickly or dealt with in another way

'We said from the beginning: Capitec will be open for as long as its clients need it to be, hence all branches have instructions that they're not allowed to close if there are still clients inside or wanting to enter.'

The branches are open seven days a week, often for a few hours after five o'clock, and the doors are not closed because it is 'closing time' while there may still be clients waiting. Capitec opened 60 branches a year in the last few years, and the total has grown to nearly 800 branches countrywide.

The staff members are generally young people. They are hired in their early twenties and are trained very well in customer service. Many of Capitec's clients are uncomfortable with online banking, as they prefer personal interaction. Yet Le Roux does not believe this will be a lasting phenomenon since technology is changing banking so radically, as is proved by clients' uptake of the bank's digital app. On joining the bank, clients do have to have an in-depth conversation with the banking staff in order to obtain banking facilities, whereupon they receive a chip card that enables them to immediately withdraw cash from the ATM.

Capitec does not own any of their branch premises but leases them instead. This forms part of an inexpensive infrastructure. 'A bank branch is an expensive place because you have to protect cash. We said from day one that we don't want cash, so our tellers can't pay out cash; you have to use the ATM. As far as cash deposits are concerned, we are also in the process of switching to ATMs that can receive cash,' Le Roux says.

'Because we have personal interaction with a client, we find that a branch is a key point. Branches are also handy for security reasons, and for loans as well. But we can't see it as a permanent phenomenon. We've accepted that the cellphone is the key for the future, but as to how things are going to pan out ... for the moment we're just running hard to keep up. We don't know where we will end up, but it's very clear to us that a branch is not necessarily part of the future. It is highly unlikely that in 20 years' time banking will still look the way it does today.'

Le Roux and his team 'had to work very hard every step of the way in turning the business into a modern lending business'. Risk management was particularly important from the start. 'We wake up every morning knowing it's a massive problem. We don't think for a single day that we've now become smart and that we understand this market. So I believe that, in a strange way, it's actually a strength – that in a high-risk environment you never start thinking you don't have risk.'

When Capitec's closest rival, African Bank, collapsed in August 2014 and was placed under curatorship, Capitec wrong-footed doomsayers who predicted a similar fate for them on account of bad debts. Capitec sailed through the credit crisis, although Le Roux described it as a 'terrifying' experience: 'When they [African Bank] closed their doors it practically felt like a funeral. If they can sink, anyone can sink.'

Capitec did not go under, in part because it had a far more conservative approach to providing credit and set aside cash to cover bad debts. Le Roux admits that bad debts are high, but they are managed as well as possible and loans are not just rolled over. 'We do negotiate with a guy because we get a better performance if we grant him an extension, but we don't roll over his debt in the sense that we lend him more money to repay an existing loan. This only creates a false impression that you are successful while it is not the case. We are very conservative with regard to bad debts.'

Another advantage Capitec had as a fully fledged retail bank is that clients also deposit funds in bank accounts that can be used further on for other loans. African Bank, on the other hand, was a one-dimensional bank that only lent clients money that had been borrowed from other institutions. Over time, Capitec had also increasingly focused on attracting higher-income clients and achieved considerable success in building up a clientele with more capital assets. By 2019, the bank had 6 500 000 digital clients while about 6 million visited their branches monthly.

An unexpected attack was launched on Capitec from outside South Africa's borders at the end of 2017, hot on the heels of Steinhoff's collapse. Viceroy, a small group of self-confessed short sellers who had released a damning report on Steinhoff's alleged irregular practices two days after Markus Jooste's shock resignation, issued a report on Capitec shortly afterwards. The report raised questions about the bank's financial soundness. It also alleged that Capitec was effectively running a loan-shark operation and that it charged clients additional fees to refinance delinquent loans. Viceroy called for the Reserve Bank to intervene and immediately place Capitec under curatorship.

The bank's share price, which had reached a high of R1 100, fell by 25 per cent on that day, but started recovering when Capitec's management responded swiftly to refute the allegations. The Reserve Bank refused to place Capitec under curatorship and stated that Capitec 'is well capitalised, liquid and solvent, and meets all prudential requirements'. The Treasury concurred with this view, adding that Viceroy 'operated anonymously and opaquely' and that 'the reckless way in which it has released its report is clear proof that it is not acting in the public interest nor in the interest of financial stability in South Africa'.

In the meantime more details had come to light about the Viceroy founder Fraser Perring and his two 23-year-old Australian-based collaborators. Perring is a former social worker from Britain who was disbarred from practising his profession. Viceroy was also accused of plagiarism in that they used the work of other researchers in their reports, while in Capitec's case information was obtained from disgruntled ex-employees.

Above all, it was questioned whether such a small outfit was capable of thoroughly analysing big firms such as banks with thousands of clients. A serious ethical question kept nagging: how could a short seller with a vested interest in the decline of a share price issue speculative reports about that share? There was mounting suspicion that the purpose of Viceroy's 'research' seemed more like market manipulation and insider trading.

At the end of 2018, the Reserve Bank expressed praise for the report by the research company Intellidex on their investigation into the methods and agenda of the short sellers behind Viceroy. The Reserve Bank's report recommended inter alia that the media exercise caution when reporting on 'research'. Reserve Bank governor Lesetja Kganyago warned that Viceroy was a 'hit squad'.

By March 2018, only 1,4 million of Capitec's 9,9 million active clients had unsecured loans. This put into perspective the aspersions Viceroy had cast on the bank by suggesting that it was a reckless lender that was expanding at a breakneck pace.

Significant challenges would lie ahead for Capitec though, notably as a result of new entrants into the banking sector. Three new banks were envisaged in 2018: Michael Jordaan's Bank Zero, Discovery Bank, which was launched under the leadership of Adrian Gore, and Tyme Digital, which was started by Patrice Motsepe's African Rainbow Capital. It was expected that the digital newcomers would impact the profitability of all the existing banks, notwithstanding the substantial expansion of their use of advanced technology. From the side of the government, the idea of establishing a state-owned bank was mooted.

One of the most telling compliments Capitec received in mid 2019 came from a totally unexpected quarter. In the SACP's *Umsebenzi Online*, the communist Jeremy Cronin, who had served as a deputy minister in the ANC government, told the story of a certain Mrs N from Heideveld as part of an account of the disarray the ANC had fallen into.

This 60-year-old woman had to pay R10 for taxi fare on a rainy Thursday to travel to the offices of SASSA – the government's social security agency – in Gugulethu to apply for an old-age pension. There she stood waiting in a long line for three and a half hours, with no seating provided. When she finally got inside the building, a queue manager told her she had to come back the following week; new pension applications were only handled on Mondays. 'Welcome to the post-apartheid public sector and its interface with working-class citizens,' Cronin remarked.

Mrs N compared this experience with what happens in a private bank, which in her case was Capitec. As you enter, she told him, someone asks you what you need. The person checks whether you have all the required documents and then directs you to the right counter. 'Mrs N is savvy enough to know that the bank takes her money, while hopefully sometime soon she will receive a pension from SASSA. Still, she wonders why the public sector treats her, and probably millions of others, with such careless disdain.'

In 2019, Capitec – which was by then the biggest bank in the country by customer numbers (13 million) – was named the winner of the *Sunday Times* Top 100 Companies Award for the fourth time. On the same occasion, the new CEO, Gerrie Fourie, was named the paper's Business Leader of the Year. He attributed Capitec's success to four pillars: Focus, Confidence (in the bank's own team), Culture (valuing one another) and Strategy.

In 2018, Fourie – with a gross worth of R883 million – was in the 50th position on the *City Press* Wealth Index while his colleague André du Plessis, the chief financial officer, with a gross worth of R896 million, was at number 49.

Despite a bumbling government, Le Roux, who in 2018 was tenth on the *City Press* Wealth Index with a gross worth of R11,5 billion, feels strongly that South Africa is a country with incredible opportunities. 'We have good people, we have a big market, we have a sophisticated population, one that is surprisingly willing to try out new things. In Europe people are cautious and conservative; they don't easily change brands or banks. Someone once said the average European would more readily divorce his wife than change his bank account. In South Africa they also told us it is difficult, but in the end, if you come with a good value proposition, people are prepared to switch.'

8

Down and out and up again

Jannie Mouton

KNOCKED DOWN, got up – and went on to make a fortune. That is the story of Jannie Mouton, sometimes called the Boere Buffett because he has achieved some of the biggest successes in the financial services industry.

At the age of 49 he was fired by his partners from a stockbroking firm in Johannesburg. After moving to Stellenbosch, he not only built his PSG Group into a giant but was, ingenious entrepreneur that he is, also instrumental in the creation and rapid growth of Capitec Bank and the establishment of private schools by the educational group Curro. In 2018, he was the twelfth richest South African on the *City Press* Wealth Index, with a gross worth of R9,2 billion.

Johannes Mouton, known as Jannie since childhood, grew up in Carnarvon in the Karoo, where his father, Jan Mouton, was a shopkeeper. During their schooldays in the town, he and his sisters, Engela and Santie, used to carry out all kinds of tasks in their father's shop during the holidays, and he was able to observe at first hand how a business operated.

After his national service at the Navy Gymnasium, he enrolled at

Stellenbosch University where he and GT Ferreira were both residents of the men's residence Simonsberg. While studying towards an honours degree in economics, he also took a few BCom (Acc) subjects because, at that stage, he wanted to become an accountant. After completing his articles at the then Coopers Brothers (later PwC), he worked at Federale Volksbeleggings in Cape Town for a year before being transferred to Johannesburg in 1974. In 1980, he was transferred to the clothing manufacturer Veka before he worked at the meat company Kanhym for a year.

For much of his life he 'had a hankering to rather do something myself, but in the meantime, I did my duty and worked hard, as any Calvinistic farmboy would'. Hence he envied GT Ferreira, Paul Harris and Laurie Dippenaar when they started Rand Consolidated Investments (RCI), the precursor of Rand Merchant Bank. They were friends of his, and he was appointed as a director.

RCI would play a huge part in the formation of a broking firm of which Mouton was a founder member: Senekal, Mouton & Kitshoff (SMK). Mouton and the other two founders, Johan Senekal and Jannie Kitshoff, were friends.

RCI wanted to combine a capital market department with share broking, but at that stage a company was not allowed to have outside shareholding in a brokerage. Therefore, they had to start an independent firm with three partners, and Mouton and Kitshoff had to resign from the RCI board. The broking firm of Jean Sterianos was for sale, which presented them with the opportunity of acquiring a sponsorship and offices in one go. Mouton scraped together his third of the purchase price of R150 000 by borrowing R30 000 of his wife Dana's inherited money and the rest from his mother.

They started in October 1982, and by December of that year their profits already exceeded R1 million. According to Mouton, all of this was wiped out again in January 1983, which indicates that the new firm's business see-sawed at first. But they remained positive and were quite impetuous: 'We looked forward to the opportunities and never thought of the problems.'

They had thought that, as an Afrikaans firm, they could bank on gettting good business from the likes of Sanlam, 'but soon realised an Afrikaner begrudges others the air they breathe. Jewish businesses, the Liberties, gave us much better support.'

Mouton was on the share broking side while Senekal and Kitshoff looked after the government bonds. Bond trading was a novelty on the market, and before long this division of SMK, which handled bonds of large municipalities and state enterprises such as Eskom and Transnet, was the largest in South Africa.

SMK did extremely well. For their banker, Volkskas, SMK was a bigger client than Anglo American and General Mining. Some weeks their turnover in the bond division totalled R1 billion. Their client base grew in leaps and bounds, and up to 1987 they listed about forty companies, including M-Net, on the development capital board – one of the precursors of the current AltX.

The young aspirant tycoons were living the high life. 'We did amazing deals and the money was rolling in. Listings were a dime a dozen. We bought bigger houses and prettier cars,' Mouton recounts in his biography *And then they fired me*. He mentions that the later Steinhoff boss Markus Jooste, whom he got to know in Johannesburg, remembered how one year on Mouton's birthday they drove around the parking lot of the Linger Longer restaurant in Johannesburg in his brand-new Mercedes Benz convertible.

'I had grown too big for my boots. I remember phoning Kango Beachbuggies to ask in what colours they had the vehicle available, and then saying I would take one in each available colour – five altogether. Now I can only shake my head at the memory.'

To be that cocky, 'and with gearing to the point of bursting', was asking for trouble. All bubbles burst sooner or later, as this one did on 22 October 1987. 'A lot of us were cut down to size and got quite a kick in the teeth financially. Let me tell you, there was blood on the walls. It was the mother of all market carnages – the decline of about 30 per cent was the most significant in a single day in living memory.

'I was almost done for. And the partners who had got in with me also wept their hearts out. Just imagine: while things are upbeat, you're the hero, but when the market tumbled, I was a big thug ... One day we were the kings of the development capital market, the next day humble servants.'

The market recovered eventually, and the tempers cooled down as their egos and wallets began to look better. At that time, Kitshoff left them to rejoin RCI when the group acquired control of Rand Merchant Bank, and Senekal went to farm at Prince Albert. Mouton, the only remaining founder member of SMK, became managing director and there were nineteen partners, 'all smart guys'.

'We had gigantic successes and made excellent profits,' Mouton recounts. Highlights were major listings such as Rand Merchant Bank, Richemont, Mediclinic and Naspers. From the 42nd largest firm, SMK had grown to the fifth or sixth largest. Mouton thought the foundations had been laid for a financial giant.

Then the bombshell was dropped.

One day in August 1995, he was in a daily morning meeting with his colleague Jean du Plessis when they were called to the conference room at the front. To Mouton's surprise, Mof Terreblanche, the Cape partner of SMK, was present. He and the economist Louis Geldenhuys, Pierre Brink from the bond department, James Bredenkamp and Henk Klopper from the shares department, and Jannie Grobbelaar from corporate finance were sitting there, waiting for them. According to Mouton, Terreblanche started off by saying he was the oldest and would do the talking. He said that the seven partners represented the majority of the firm, and that it had been decided Mouton had to resign with immediate effect.

Mouton was completely stunned. In his bewildered state he was unable to take in Terreblanche's explanation of the reasons behind their decision: 'Even today I can't for the life of me remember the reasons given.'

Mof Terreblanche, who had known Mouton for a long time by then, says it has often been written that *he* was the one who fired Mouton – and that while the title of Mouton's much-discussed biography by Carié Maas is specifically *And then they fired me*. The real story is that, as the senior partner, he was ordered to bell the cat. He had a mandate from all nineteen partners to break the news to Mouton.

Some of the staff had started complaining about Jannie's management style at SMK. 'The guys said Jannie was becoming impossible, a dictator. It caused much tension in the firm,' Terreblanche explains. Staff members threatened the partners that unless they fired Jannie, they would resign en masse. 'It was almost like a pistol to our heads.'

The partners also felt that Jannie, who had to decide on matters such as the share percentages of partners, had become too high-handed and domineering. 'Sometimes that happens: when things are going too well, then the pawpaw hits the fan.'

Looking back, Terreblanche, who has since restored his relationship with Mouton to a tolerable level in Stellenbosch, observes: 'Jannie turned the setbacks around to his advantage, with exceptional success ... and built a financial empire.' He even later remarked jokingly to Mouton that he thought Mouton should give him a million or so because they had fired him, seeing that he was much more successful afterwards.

For Mouton, however, his dismissal was a devastating blow. A period of self-examination followed for a man who himself acknowledged that he had a short fuse: 'I don't enjoy admitting it, but I have some contrariness, some obstinacy, some call me a hard-ass. I don't like not getting what I want.' His former partner Johan Senekal also reminded him from his farm: 'Jannie, you can be a little contrary and aggressive when you choose to.'

The start-up years and growth of PSG

A Chinese saying Anton Rupert liked to quote, that every disaster is also an opportunity, was to prove true over and over for Mouton. He set up an office in his house in Northcliff and realised that wallowing in resentment and despair would not be of much use. A former colleague at SMK, François Gouws, brought him a book by Warren Buffett. He had not been in the habit of reading business books, but the American investment guru turned him into a convert – maybe one of the reasons why he was later called the Boere Buffett.

He started reading other business books and summarised them in Afrikaans to order his thoughts. Honest introspection impelled him to decide what his mission statement, his dream, was. The eventual plan he wrote down to direct the dream included that he wanted to develop a new company successfully, and also wanted to be free and not work for others.

Months of agonising came to an end thanks to an opportunity that presented itself when Jannie Kitshoff sent his brother-in-law,

Piet de Jongh, to Mouton with a proposal. A personnel agency was for sale: Professional Assignment Group (PAG) – a listed company in the financial services sector whose shareholders were in trouble. But the company, with its 32 offices, was still making a profit. The liquidators were keen to find a buyer. Mouton managed to arrange financing for the bid process at Rand Merchant, and he, Chris Otto and the top management of PAG acquired shares at 36c. The stockbroker for the share transaction was SMK.

De Jongh, the son of the former Reserve Bank governor Theunis de Jongh, was appointed chair of the board and Mouton and Otto became directors. In 1996, Mouton moved to Stellenbosch and set up an office in the Old College Building in Church Street, the building that would become PSG's head office.

PAG's shares started rising. Later Louis de Waal, a former Democratic Party politician with good people skills, was appointed managing director. He reconciled warring factions in the company and knew how to motivate the salespeople.

Mouton and his colleagues also started a separate stockbroking firm in Cape Town. His former colleague Jaap du Toit came to mind as one of the SMK people with whom he would most like to collaborate in such a venture. He raised the idea with Du Toit, who told him that he and 'a few other Cape guys' were also thinking of portfolio management for wealthy clients, and asset management, beyond SMK's narrow scope of only stockbroking. The discussions with Jaap and his companions led to their signing a handwritten contract in Du Toit's flat.

Du Toit suggested the name Professional Securities Group, derived from the PAG name, for the new firm that soon became widely known as PSG. Mouton with his self-acknowledged 'hellish temper' had found an ideal counterweight in the more mild-mannered Du Toit. He had 'infinite respect' for Du Toit – who did not want to sit close to him in the office – because he had such good manners and was so talented.

At that stage, there was a flurry of personnel agency takeovers, and PAG was sold. Mouton and his colleagues could not believe their luck when they received a bid of R107 million from Educor for the company they had bought eighteen months earlier for about R7 million.

PSG grew rapidly from their small beginnings. The stockbroking company developed into three parts: PSG Online is the stockbroking business that only trades shares and provides an online trading platform for this purpose; wealth management for private clients falls under PSG Konsult; and the asset manager became PSG Fund Management. The prefix 'PSG' was valuable in that it could easily be linked to a variety of business names.

PSG Konsult developed from an idea that originated with Willem Theron, an auditor who had realised in the late 1970s in the Eastern Cape town of Middelburg that affluent people such as farmers and doctors not only wanted their books done, they also needed financial advice. He started off with short-term insurance and over time expanded to life insurance and investments.

Theron's business had grown to such an extent, with 13 partners in 10 offices in the Eastern and Western Cape, that he reckoned his model for high-net-worth individuals could be taken further. In 1998, he joined forces with PSG, after which PSG Konsult established offices countrywide.

Mouton regards PSG Konsult, which operates 'like a well-oiled machine', as a living monument to his model of ultimate empowerment. PSG owns 70 per cent of the shares while the remaining 30 per cent is in the hands of the people who manage the branch offices, and the field workers. Since they share in the profits, they are much more motivated to increase growth and retain satisfied clients.

Mouton constantly strove to lure competent and talented people to his businesses, especially because he believed there were too many young men at institutions like banks; Afrikaners in particular, who despite their success, too seldom shared in the profits. He offered incentives to people who joined PSG – his catchword was ultimate empowerment.

For the most part, he would only interfere in subsidiaries' activities when things went wrong. This meant they were afforded the freedom to use their own initiative in growing their businesses. He referred jokingly to the benefit he derived from having given the right people a stake in the enterprise: the more they earned, the more would be left over for him. 'When you have a stake in a company,' he said, 'your heart is also in it.'

PSG has produced several millionaires in the process.

PSG Konsult and PSG Fund Management were consolidated in 2011, with Willem Theron as the chief executive and Jaap du Toit as non-executive chair. By 2019, there were about 250 Konsult offices in South Africa, Namibia and Botswana, and PSG Konsult's total assets under management had increased to R222 billion.

Capitec: A bank card for all

One of the biggest success stories that flowed from PSG's offices is Capitec, the microlending bank that developed into a giant in the South African banking industry.

From early on, Mouton had the idea that PSG should also acquire a banking licence. In 1998, R1,2 billion was raised through a share issue to list PSG Noble Capital on the JSE. The following year it merged with PSG Investment Bank, which listed on the JSE as the seventh-largest bank in the country, with share capital of R400 million. In the same year, Mouton became chair of Specialised Lending, the predecessor of Capitec.

PSG entered the microlending industry as a result of Mouton's conviction that the only way to relieve poverty in South Africa was to make capital available to people who had no collateral and could therefore not be assisted by traditional banks.

PSG's first enterprises that granted such microloans were started as a trial run, a cash-store experiment in what was then considered a fairly disreputable terrain of the national economy. Offices that extended credit to poor people were mostly situated on the wrong side of the tracks, the regulators constantly threatened to shut them down, their money was stolen and robbers shot at them.

For all that, by 1998 three microfinancing enterprises were operating under the PSG umbrella: Werner du Plessis's PSG Smartfin Financial Services, Jacques Fischer's Anchor Finance, and the former clergyman Neels Borstlap's FinAid. Business was humming, but as entrepreneurs they needed to be 'rehabilitated' to master concepts such as risk management, cost control and accurate management information.

During this time, Mouton and PSG came in for a lot of flak. Johann Rupert told him in front of the entire Remgro board: 'Yes,

Jannie, you guys who are exploiting the poor.' He felt: Your own people detest you. 'At a point, my wife didn't want to speak to me because we were seen as the biggest loan shark in South Africa,' he said.

They had to make microloans respectable, and quickly. Mouton decided to draw in Michiel le Roux as a consultant. Le Roux, previously a banker at Boland Bank, had resigned from BoE some months earlier after a run-in with Christo Wiese. He had reservations initially: 'I was quite surprised that PSG was involved in such strange, almost sordid, businesses.'

In spite of his misgivings, he accepted the offer. He investigated closer cooperation among the three groups and advised them separately. Le Roux found that cash-loan stores had a much better relationship with their clients than the way they would have been treated at traditional banks. Sophisticated electronic pay systems were of little use to them, as they had to get to a pay point on foot only to wait in long queues. Therefore a countrywide network had to be created by buying a cash-loan store in every town.

'We believed in Michiel, so we provided the financial backing because PSG had a bit more money than Michiel and his team, but the idea was at least born here with us. It was true that the image of the industry was not right for PSG, but Michiel turned it around,' says Mouton.

PSG became the biggest investor in Capitec, which opened hundreds of branches after struggling at first. Capitec is hands down PSG's biggest asset – its 31 per cent stake constitutes about two-thirds of PSG's assets. Le Roux, with a gross worth of R11,5 billion, also overtook Mouton on the 2018 *City Press* Wealth Index. He was number 10 on the list, and Mouton at number 12 with a gross worth of R9,2 billion.

Curro: An answer to the decline at government schools

Mouton's passion for education, which he sees as the key building block of a society, was decisive in PSG's support for Curro, the company that would grow into a countrywide chain of private schools.

Mouton and his colleagues were told about a former deputy principal from Cape Town who had started a small school in the vestry of the Bergsig Dutch Reformed church in Durbanville. They became acquainted with Dr Chris van der Merwe, who had obtained a doctorate in curriculum studies from Stellenbosch University in 1997 after starting off his career as a primary school teacher.

Van der Merwe had applied for a position in curriculum development at the Western Cape edcuation department but failed to get the job due to the transformation process in the public service. He and his wife Stephnie, both deputy principals at schools in the Tygerberg area at the time, then decided to start their own school in collaboration with the prominent educationalist Boetie Ungerer, who spearheaded gifted education in the Western Cape.

With his severance package of R240 000, the 34-year-old Van der Merwe paid off the R160 000 mortgage bond debt on his home and R5 000 he still owed on his rusty Datsun. On 15 July 1998, Curro kicked off with 28 learners in the vestry of the church. 'We simply taught up a storm!' Van der Merwe says with a laugh.

The success they achieved over time with smaller class sizes, excellent teaching and outstanding exam results was contagious. Jannie Mouton was impressed by Van der Merwe and described him as 'an inspiring man with entrepreneurial blood in his veins'.

More schools were constructed and acquired, and the concept spread countrywide in response to the growing demand for quality education. Owing to the deterioration of many government schools, more and more parents resorted to private schools. By 2019, Curro was the biggest private education group in the country, with more than 57 000 learners in 164 schools on 68 campuses. In the same year, Curro's teacher:learner ratio was 18 learners per teacher, compared with the department of basic education's target of 30 learners per teacher for government schools.

Curro's success led to inquiries from parents about the possibility of the institution offering tertiary education as well. This resulted in the establishment of Stadio, a private university with campuses in the country's biggest cities and which is therefore better described as a 'multiversity'. The company was listed on the JSE in 2017.

Stadio, which has 14 campuses in various cities, offers more than eighty accredited programmes, from higher certificates to master's degrees and doctorates, to more than 30 000 students. After an initial focus on teacher education, their offering has expanded to commerce and management courses, as well as fields of study such as the internet and creative economies, fashion design, and the film and TV industry. Plans are already afoot to offer training in medical science and engineering.

PSG and black empowerment

Shortly after the founding of PSG, Mouton's concept of ultimate empowerment was extended to black economic empowerment (BEE). He had a few bruising experiences in the process.

PSG's first such deal was in 1998, when many were still only paying lip service to BEE. Siphumelele obtained an 11,5 per cent stake in PSG to become involved in the takeover of Servgro. This was wangled through the issue of 10 million PSG shares at R9 each to the empowerment group, at a time when the market was at a high. Share prices fell, however, and Siphumelele was unable to pay off its debt. Since the shares had been the security, Old Mutual took them back and wrote off the debt. Two years after the empowerment deal fell through, the shares were resold to PSG.

Another hot potato was the interest the ANC politician Desmond Lockey obtained in Arch Equity Investment Holdings (AEIH). Lockey, a son-in-law of the Reverend Allan Hendrickse, who was a party leader in the days of the tricameral Parliament, was unhappy about the distribution of the 51 per cent shareholding among the black shareholders. He insisted that his grouping (of which he owned 85 per cent) get the lion's share. According to Mouton, he also 'had an obsession with cashing in his shares'.

The situation became so stressful that eventually Mouton could not even speak to Lockey any more. Finally, after a fierce dispute about the future strategy, Lockey threatened to resign for the umpteenth time. This time his resignation was accepted. Thanks to his partnership with PSG, his initial investment of R6 million had increased to R120 million. Mouton, who regards Lockey as 'an out-and-out opportunist who hit the jackpot', reckons that if he stayed longer he could have walked away with R400 million. Episodes like that caused him to start wondering whether those who had to be empowered actually wanted to remain empowered.

But over time he 'realised what a huge opportunity BEE was: if a white person wants a stake, he pays the market price; a black person pays less than the market price and also gets financing. To help a black guy solve his problem makes a lot of sense business-wise. You help to level the playing field in South Africa instead of being politically incorrect due to sheer obstinacy …'

In November 2006, however, an empowerment partner appeared with whom a long and mutually beneficial partnership was forged. Zitulele Combi, who was a businessman in his own right, would in time occupy some of the highest positions in the PSG Group.

Combi is commonly known as KK, a nickname given to him on account of his autocratic manner while he was part of his school's debating team, with reference to former Zambian president Kenneth Kaunda. Born in Retreat in Cape Town, he experienced his family's forced removal to Gugulethu as a child. He completed a course in public relations at Damelin College and worked at Old Mutual for a year, where he was named salesman of the year.

His first business venture was a self-service café in Gugulethu, and in 1989 he opened the first service station in that area. Two big developments followed a few years later: the R45 million Nyanga Junction in 1994, and the Ultra City Engen One Stop in King William's Town in 1995. That same year, he founded Master Currency, a joint venture with Rennies Foreign Exchange, which expanded forex outlets from banking halls to shopping centres.

When KK joined AEIH, his stake in Master Currency, where he was the executive chair, was swapped for a block of shares. The former Arch Equity started flourishing under his leadership and was renamed Thembeka. As a black-owned investment holding company focusing on BEE deals and private equity investments, Thembeka fell under Paladin Capital, PSG's preferred investment vehicle outside the financial services and agricultural sectors.

Mouton and the KWV drama

PSG also made considerable investments in agriculture, a sector of the economy that had interested Mouton since his schooldays in

Carnarvon when he cultivated a patch in the school garden during agriculture classes. He took the lead in consolidating the group's interests in agribusinesses under the tradename Zeder. Zeder Investments was listed on the JSE in 2006 with what the group described as 'a colourful basket of holdings in agribusinesses across southern Africa'. They mainly acquired non-controlling interests in a wide spectrum of agribusinesses.

By 2019, these included Kaap Agri, Pioneer Foods and Quantum Foods, while Zeder held a controlling interest in Zaad Holdings, Capespan and The Logistics Group. In 2019, the multinational company PepsiCo, which operates in 200 countries and territories, made an offer of R24 billion to buy out Pioneer. It was at that stage one of the few large investments made in South Africa by a foreign company.

Mouton was appointed a director of Remgro in 2005, but it did not take long before he resigned from the board in October 2006. This happened after he had made an investment in KWV, which created a conflict of interest due to Remgro's stake in Distell and PSG's growing stake in KWV via its agribusiness subsidiary Zeder. It was also said that the Remgro chair, Johann Rupert, was unhappy about the appointment of Christo Wiese, with whom he had clashed in the past, as a director of PSG.

Mouton recounted that he and Rupert have bumped into one another a few times since then. When GT Ferreira had an evening function for his birthday, he and Rupert were both present, but were seated far apart. A waiter came up to him and said 'that gentleman', meaning Rupert, would like Mouton to join him outside for a smoke. 'So we bonded over a cigarette, and now we're good pals again.'

Mouton's entry into the wine industry via KWV was highly controversial and caused a bout of *broedertwis* (Afrikaner infighting) that was at times more reminiscent of a clay-stick fight among schoolboys. He was accused of being an 'asset stripper' and an 'opportunist'.

His involvement in KWV had started in 2004. In his capacity as PSG Capital's adviser to the KWV, Mouton was standing in the office of the KWV chair, Danie de Wet, when Christo Wiese phoned De Wet with an offer to buy the so-called Group of Five's interest. This group consisted of a consortium called Anglo African Trading, a company headed by JP du Plessis that had acquired 11 per cent of KWV. People who fell under the Group of Five included GT Ferreira, Pug Roux, Paul Meaker, Hansie van Niekerk, Lambert Retief and Thys du Toit.

Mouton advised De Wet to accept Wiese's offer. 'He's a friendlier shareholder,' he said, meaning that Wiese did not have plans with the board. He thought KWV was an 'iconic asset'. In a twist of irony, PSG acquired Wiese's block of shares in KWV a while later when he swapped it for a 5 per cent stake in PSG. Wiese had been unable to get his way with plans he had presented to the KWV board.

Afterwards Mouton could kick himself: 'It was the worst deal I've ever done in my life for a listed company like PSG. Just after the deal with Christo I happened to bump into Whitey Basson, who said to me: "Jannie, don't you know that you never buy a bargain from Christo?"'

At the end of 2006, PSG consolidated its interests in unlisted agribusinesses under the investment company Zeder, which was listed on the JSE. Zeder gradually bought up more KWV shares and, in 2007, Mouton was elected as a director of KWV after he had resigned at Remgro. By 2010, the stake in KWV had grown to 35,3 per cent. In the meantime, however, Mouton had become increasingly disillusioned with the way KWV was run. He describes how he pressured them to obtain proper financial statements, which they were unwilling and unable to give him. Meanwhile, they had these wasteful formal board meetings that involved sleeping over and partying. And he and Danie de Wet were at loggerheads because the votes for the chairmanship had been 'cooked'.

With regard to the dividend policy, Mouton describes in his biography how he proposed to the board that the KWV Investments (or Distell) dividend be passed on directly to shareholders. He maintained that the greatest value of the KWV share was that Distell was listed and that the Distell stake represented the most value. KWV's own activities had always been propped up that way.

'The comparison [between KWV and Distell] showed how KWV's own operations were, after 91 years – and despite pricey lekgotlas and sky-high directors' fees – making a loss of R42 million. Splendid farewell parties with sit-down dinners in dark suits and waiters, long-winded political discussions on the board and newspaper advertisements for financial statements, instead of a focus on the affairs of the business, are luxuries a very successful company with a gigantic turnover can afford, not a small, unlisted one making losses. I detest the waste of shareholders' money as if it's a company's personal account.'

It was no wonder, according to Mouton, that PSG was constantly subjected to accusations of seeking to slaughter a holy cow and of not understanding how the wine industry worked. In response, he said that the KWV's story 'is a proud, thick scroll' and that the company 'has fulfilled its original role thoroughly and with dignity. However, its modern profit history is a crying shame.'

Further dramas followed, as Mouton relates in his biography. Eventually he got Thys du Toit involved as director at KWV, where he chaired the board from 2009 to 2011. 'Thys is a terribly correct person ... he reads his board documents. Thys also has the gift of knowing what is a good investment and what is not.'

Both Mouton and Thys du Toit regarded KWV as a relatively small company compared to much larger investments. Du Toit noted that KWV's turnover had remained stagnant for ten years. He pointed out that KWV had a fairly narrow range of products that were predominantly dependent on grape alcohol; it had a very small market share in South Africa (2,5 per cent of the high-price market for bottled wine and 7 per cent of the local brandy market) and a few big international clients that exposed it to a strong rand.

The upshot of the tug of war – which also brought an end to PSG's intentions to buy up more KWV shares – was that the former trade unionists Johnny Copeland and Marcel Golding of Hosken Consolidated Investments bought the 31,8 per cent interest from PSG at R11,80 a share. It was close enough to the R12 that PSG believed KWV was worth.

To Mouton and his PSG colleagues, the sale of their stake in KWV was 'a deal like any other in the normal course of our business'. They were 'quite happy' with the selling price of R285 million and return of R126 million on PSG's investment. 'By ploughing that in with our business we can probably earn five or six times more than at KWV,' Mouton stated.

PSG caught in the crossfire

Nevertheless, it was not all moonlight and roses for PSG over the years. They experienced their fair share of setbacks and failures.

One such setback, which became a hot topic in the media and in business circles, concerned Pioneer Foods. The food company was found guilty of colluding to fix bread and flour prices together with Tiger Brands, Foodcorp and Premier Foods, which had been the first to confess to cartel activities. With Pioneer facing astronomical fines, protracted court battles and settlement attempts followed. At one stage Jannie Mouton suggested that he and all the other directors on the Pioneer board resign.

Eventually KK Combi of Thembeka fame took over the chairmanship and the former KWV chair Thys du Toit became one of the non-executive directors on a reconstituted Pioneer board. Combi and PSG Capital's Johan Holtzhausen negotiated with the Competition Commission about a settlement until the authorities agreed to let reason prevail. Pioneer was fined R500 million. It had to commit itself to lowering its profit margin by R160 million, and it had to undertake to spend an additional R150 million on capital projects that could result in the creation of jobs.

The settlement agreement was hailed as groundbreaking since it was the first time fines were returned to the consumer instead of going to the Treasury. Combi was quoted approvingly: 'With the lowering of the profit margin we extend a hand of apology to consumers.' From Mouton's perspective, it proved the truth of an old saying: sometimes it's better to settle than to win a good battle.

According to Mouton, a failure that PSG 'won't and can't hide' was mCubed, a company that was suspended from trading on the JSE in July 2007. This happened after a merger between mCubed and Escher Investment Solutions, an entrepreneurial venture under the wing of PSG. Escher had been the brainchild of Philip Croeser, whom Mouton considers the country's pioneer of multimanagement. Multimanagers select funds on macro level and put them together in order to, with their joint brain-power, ensure the best returns for clients, while the analysis of shares is left to fund managers.

Before long, Escher took off like a rocket. The money started rolling in, and the company was listed on the JSE. Management problems began to arise, however, and the stock market collapsed. Croeser had to look for a partner, and in April 2001 Escher merged with its biggest multimanager rival, mCubed. The managing director was John Storey, a chartered accountant with an MBA. Mouton was especially impressed by Storey because of the high regard he had for his father, the Methodist minister Peter Storey, who together with fellow clerics such as the Reverend Allan Boesak and Archbishop Desmond Tutu was a leading figure against apartheid.

But it soon became evident that the merger had been a huge mistake. Mouton and his colleagues started thinking that rather than being well spoken, Storey was 'just a glib talker who ducked questions'. The money collected from policies was invested badly, among other things in unlisted companies and even in 'Ponzi-type fly-by-night investments', while regulations were flouted. Mouton resigned from the board within a year.

The Reserve Bank had also smelled a rat. PSG got rid of Storey in 2005. Fines had to be paid to the Reserve Bank and the SA Revenue Service. The remaining money was paid out to the shareholders, and the cash shell was sold.

Mouton, who had learnt a 'sad, but valuable lesson', acknowledged that he had allowed himself to be blinded by what psychologists call the halo effect – 'you think someone is a saint on the basis of a single trait'.

When a strong shareholder becomes a weak shareholder

In his biography, published in 2011, Mouton refers more than once to 'my friend Markus Jooste'. He writes there that he would be 'eternally grateful' to Jooste for having jumped in 'when a hostile takeover from within the Absa stable threatened PSG in 2002'. Jooste said: 'But it's not simply there for the taking!' He then 'started buying shares like mad together with some other friendly parties'. Thus the takeover was averted.

Mouton's friendship with Jooste, whom he got to know in Johannesburg, dated back to the 1980s when Jooste worked at the furniture company Gomma Gomma in Ga-Rankuwa, near Pretoria. PSG also handled Steinhoff's listing in 1998. In 2002, Mouton, then 56, became a director of Steinhoff, while the 41-year-old Jooste was in turn appointed to the board of PSG. Jooste was managing director of Steinhoff at the time.

Jooste gradually started buying more PSG shares. In 2005, Bruno Steinhoff, who had invested in Gomma Gomma earlier, was also appointed as a director of PSG and held shares in the company as well, but he resigned in April 2008.

Jooste had increased his shareholding to 20 million by 2008 – thus 11,8 per cent of PSG. In the same year Christo Wiese, who had been appointed as a director in July 2007, doubled his shareholding in PSG to 15,5 million shares thanks to a share swap deal with KWV shares.

In 2012, Jooste and Wiese swapped their PSG shares for Steinhoff shares. In this way, Steinhoff, with its 37,2 million shares obtained 20 per cent of PSG. Wiese then resigned as a director of PSG.

GT Ferreira and two other directors of PSG, Thys du Toit en Jaap du Toit, swapped their shareholding in PSG for Steinhoff shares in 2015. As a result, Steinhoff's stake in PSG increased to 25,5 per cent. Mouton was reportedly furious about the deal that had occurred without his knowledge. In the same year, Steinhoff moved its primary listing to Frankfurt.

Up to that point, Mouton had for years been particularly kindly disposed towards Steinhoff. Unlike some businesspeople, for whom it is almost a hobby to serve on various boards, he states in his biography, he preferred to stick to the PSG trade.

'The only exception I've been making for years is the Steinhoff board, due to my respect for Bruno Steinhoff and Markus Jooste. Bruno, who is so successful globally and knows his company so well, epitomises humility and is gentle, someone for whom I have immense respect.

'Markus is a workhorse, resolute and intelligent. Whatever he tackles is a success. "Crystal clear" is a term he often uses when he understands a plan and appreciates how it can benefit shareholders. Our minds work in a similar way, and time and again, as with Remgro earlier, attending meetings is very stimulating. Despite our age difference we are friends, we cultivate wine together and trust each other in much more than business deals,' he stated.

It therefore came as a surprise when in May 2016 Mouton unexpectedly resigned as a non-executive director of Steinhoff, a position he had occupied since 2002, and sold his Steinhoff shares in July of that year. He stated at the time that he had sold the shares with the aim of putting the Jannie Mouton Foundation, a charitable trust, on a solid footing.

Regarding his resignation and the sale of his shares, it was rumoured that Mouton kept a little black book on hand in which he made notes at board meetings for future reference. If a question he had asked three times remained unanswered, or still had question marks hanging over it, he would say: 'Goodbye, guys.'

Asked after the Steinhoff collapse whether this story was true, Mouton replied: 'Well, let me tell you this quickly. My friends and my colleagues here came together and told me: Jannie, don't talk to the press at all. They got me a lawyer who is highly respected, and he also phoned me while I was in Plettenberg Bay. He said: Jannie, don't comment at all. Just say you resigned in 2016 and sold your shares. So, unfortunately that's all I can say at the moment.'

But he did refer to a long article on Steinhoff in the German business magazine *Capital* in 2018 in which he was quoted as follows. '"For most South Africans, the name Jooste is toxic today. Markus was my friend, as everyone knows," says Jannie Mouton, an ex-Steinhoff board member. "But I have decided: if you are dishonest or do something irregular, you are no longer my friend. He is doing something different. Bruno [Steinhoff], such a wonderful person – I feel very, very sorry for him."'

In his biography, Mouton elaborates on honesty under the heading 'Short cuts are for crooks'. He refers to Jon M Huntsman's book *Winners Never Cheat: Everyday Lessons We Learned as Children (But May Have Forgotten)*, noting that Huntsman wrote 'if the ethical boundaries are moved or removed, the addiction to wealth becomes engulfing'.

Jannie Mouton's son Piet, who took over from him as chief executive of PSG in 2010, recalls that 'things [with Markus Jooste] started turning sour' when GT Ferreira, Thys du Toit and Jaap du Toit swapped their PSG shares for Steinhoff shares in 2015. They were all good friends of Jannie's and wanted to tell him about the transaction. Jooste had said no, he would talk to Jannie. But that only happened once the deal was almost finalised.

'We had quite an argument about this thing. But what can you do? Steinhoff is a 25 per cent shareholder in your group, so you just end up saying: no, it's fine, and you carry on with your life,' Piet says.

Still, that was not the reason for Jannie's resignation. 'I think they then made peace again, but there was always this little thing that niggled,' Piet said.

A bigger motive was rather the decision in 2015 to list Steinhoff overseas. Jannie had supported the decision, but he had never been very fond of travelling. 'So Jannie told them that in that case, he would resign. He didn't feel like going overseas four or five times a year to attend board meetings. He turned 70 at the time,' Piet recounts.

By the end of February 2017, Steinhoff owned 55,5 million shares, or 25,5 per cent of PSG. But on the the evening of Tuesday 5 December 2017, Steinhoff International announced at 20:44 that an investigation would be conducted into 'accounting irregularities', and that Jooste had resigned as CEO. The next day, there was a bloodbath on the stock exchange. Steinhoff shares immediately plummeted by 60 per cent, and were eventually 96 per cent down.

On the same day that Jooste beat a retreat at Steinhoff, he tendered his resignation as a director of PSG where he had been a board member since 2002. It was accepted. Steinhoff had to hurriedly start selling assets to raise cash for its operations.

For PSG, Steinhoff had become a huge embarrassment. 'The day after the bomb exploded we said we now have a weak shareholder, plus we're going to have a reputation problem because we're associated with Steinhoff, so we have to deal with it carefully,' Mouton stated.

After consultation with Steinhoff chair Christo Wiese, who also resigned shortly afterwards, a portion of the shares were placed in that first week. 'Then we went off on holiday and when we came back, we placed the rest. Because you have a weak shareholder, and that's not a nice thing to have,' according to Mouton.

The impact elsewhere in Stellenbosch was similarly disastrous. Many residents of the town, including Steinhoff officials, suffered huge losses. Mouton and Jooste lived across the road from each other and used to visit each other, but after the scandal broke in December Mouton never saw him again.

Piet Mouton, who believes Steinhoff got a satisfactory price of R236 per share for the PSG shares they sold, has also not seen Jooste since that episode. He had initially thought highly of Jooste.

Admittedly, he says, Jooste was 'self-confident and a bit ego-centric. But when you talked to him, he knew what he wanted in terms of where he wanted to drive the company. I think he was a very good non-executive director at PSG. He didn't force us to do business with Steinhoff. He always read his documents very carefully and offered good comments. That's exactly what you want from a non-executive director.

'And then, what he had in addition – he saw these things in inter-national terms, so his comments would set you thinking. He wouldn't say 'no' or 'yes', things like that. He'd only say: just think about it, take this into consideration if you want to do that. His commentary was very helpful.

'I think in his own group he was much more of a driving force. Steve Jobs, who changed the world incredibly, was just as headstrong, if not more so. People were fired here and tantrums were thrown there, upsetting everyone in the process, but he made some of the greatest technological advances and built one of the biggest compa-nies the world has ever seen. So, that in itself is not a sign that there is a problem in the company.'

In Piet's view, Markus's personality is that of someone who is driven. 'The main thing I can perhaps say … [the line between] the company's money and personal money became very blurred. All com-panies have parties and some corporate entertainment. But I believe there are limits. You have to know when you're dealing with your own money, and when you're dealing with the company's money.'

With all PSG's Steinhoff shares sold, Steinhoff was out of PSG's life, evidently to the great relief of Jannie, who had distanced him-self from Jooste in the meantime. But when the octogenarian Bruno Steinhoff visited Stellenbosch a while later and invited Mouton to go hunting with him, Mouton accepted the invitation: 'Shame, he's such a lovely person and I want to do it to give him some support. How bad must it be for him? He's a good person.'

The Carnarvon streak

As a result of PSG's growth and expansion since its establishment, the group comprised more or less three main parts by 2020. The financial giants such as Capitec and PSG Konsult fall under PSG. The agricultural companies such as Pioneer Foods have been consolidated under the tradename Zeder. Paladin is the umbrella name for smaller private equity investments such as Thembeka.

Although PSG started off with financial services, it is no longer limited to this sector. Instead, Mouton views the group as an investment company. Value has been created for shareholders in two ways: either by starting new businesses or by acquiring strategic stakes in existing businesses such as manufacturers.

As an investment company, PSG invests in different sectors, and Mouton has been able to live out his passion in the world of investment. It suits him, he writes in his biography, because the group's head office is small and he has 'immense expertise' around him. The head office is financed by the related companies that they provide with advice – they levy fees from them for managerial assistance. 'I suppose it's quite opportunistic that a head office makes a profit, but it's a fantastic position to be in,' he says.

When PSG celebrated its twentieth birthday in 2015, it was calculated that the group had generated an extraordinary annual compound growth in earnings of 50 per cent.

In his biography, Mouton admits that he is extremely proud of what PSG has accomplished. Even that 'the kick in the backside' SMK gave him was probably something for which he should be grateful: 'It gave me a chance in life.' Since that time, he writes, he has had quite a lot of contact with his former colleagues at SMK. 'Things have also turned out well for them and we have long ago buried the hatchet.'

Jannie has never sold a single PSG share. He sees PSG as the basket in which he keeps all his eggs. He has even gone against the conventional advice that one should never buy shares with borrowed money by often acquiring PSG shares in this way. His son Piet, too, is a multimillionaire. On the 2018 *City Press* Wealth Index he was listed as number 35, with a gross worth of R1,27 billion. He was just ahead of long-standing Mouton partner Chris Otto, who was in 36th place with a gross worth of R1,24 billion.

Piet has calculated that if one had bought R100 000's worth of PSG shares in 1995, they would have been worth about R500 million in 2019.

His father used to have reservations about family businesses, but changed his tune over time when he realised his children had the appetite and the ability to tackle things with him. His sons Jan, the elder of the two, and Piet both became directors of PSG. Before standing back as executive chair in 2010 Mouton had recused himself from the executive board, and Chris Otto and the other executive members appointed Piet as chief executive. No one said a word, according to Mouton, because if his children started abusing their position, nobody would respect them.

Mouton, in his capacity as non-executive chair, still played a big part. He continued going to the office in Church Street every day as usual.

Looking back on his career, Mouton says he accepts that he is not very popular on a board. He was fired at SMK, but he subsequently resigned from other boards as well. Colleagues would come to see him and ask: 'Jannie, won't you rather resign, because you're too aggressive, you know, and so on. So, I wasn't fired only at SMK ... I was fired at Capitec, I was fired at PSG Konsult, also at Pioneer. It's probably the Carnarvon streak in us.'

In May 2018, he disclosed that he had been diagnosed with an early form of dementia. In a surprising public statement in the form of a letter to shareholders, the 72-year-old Mouton announced that his short-term memory 'does not always function as it should,' with the result that he sometimes forgets people's names, repeats himself or may appear disoriented.

'PSG is my life and I have dedicated myself to the company for the past 22 years. I am incredibly proud of the businesses we have created over the years,' he stated. He referred further queries to his son Piet and his executive team, but announced that after consultations with senior colleagues he would be staying on as non-executive chair.

Piet said the letter was issued in order to 'nip ugly gossiping in the bud'. Rumours had been going around that his father had brain cancer. He added that the condition was not very serious. 'Here and there he forgets a name and he repeats himself occasionally, but then you would eat out with him and not detect anything. He can still carry on functioning like this for a long time. And he has medication that helps.'

In early 2019, Mouton was succeeded by KK Combi as independent non-executive chair. Combi leads a board that controls a group with a market capitalisation of R55 billion and with further influence over companies with a combined market capitalisation of close to R200 billion, of which Capitec alone contributes roughly R150 billion. The nearly twenty companies also have further subsidiaries; PSG Konsult, for instance, has about thirty.

Mouton, who'd still been going to the office every day, was lauded for his frank and transparent statement. He remained positive, with an outlook on the country that some found controversial, but which he regularly expressed: 'Focus on being the expert in finding opportunities, not the expert in what is wrong with South Africa.'

9

Family office for the treasure chest

Thys du Toit

ANOTHER STELLENBOSCH investment expert who has achieved exceptional success in the financial services industry is Thys du Toit, the former head of Coronation. He became a trendsetter with the concept of family offices for wealthy families.

As managing director of Coronation, he built the company into the second largest of its kind in South Africa. After stepping down at Coronation, he opted for Stellenbosch as the location to establish a family office – the concept of managing the assets and interests of wealthy families that has increasingly taken root worldwide.

Matthys Michielse du Toit, a farmboy, grew up in Bonnievale and matriculated at the local high school. He graduated with a BSc in agriculture and an MBA (cum laude) from Stellenbosch University. After completing his national service as lecturer at the Military Academy in Saldanha, he joined George Huysamer & Partners in 1985 as a stockbroker on the Johannesburg Stock Exchange.

There he learnt an early business lesson from Jannie Mouton that has stood him in good stead in his career. They were sharing a lift in the JSE building in Diagonal Street when Mouton, who did not know him at the time, remarked that he had noticed Du Toit was a newcomer at George Huysamer's firm. Mouton, who according to Du Toit brimmed over with confidence, immediately dished out free advice: 'Make sure you get shares in the business!'

In 1990, Du Toit relocated to Cape Town and worked as portfolio manager at Syfrets Managed Assets before he and four colleagues broke away and started Coronation Asset Management in 1993. The four other co-founders were his boss Leon Campher, Tony Gibson, Matt Brenzel and Hugh Broadhurst. Du Toit recalls that it was a very good time to start a new firm: 'In the early 1990s an environment was created where fantastic new businesses were started: Investec and RMB, Discovery, PSG, Capitec ... a whole bunch, because it was a friendly environment where rainmakers, entrepreneurs, felt they could build businesses. And these are the people who ultimately succeed in creating jobs, in taking the economy by the scruff of the neck and picking it up.

'There are undoubtedly still such people in South Africa,' he says a quarter century later, 'but rather than them wanting to take their money offshore, it should be attractive for them to invest it in South Africa. This is not the case at present. But one should guard against pessimism, because pessimists don't build companies. Companies are built through optimism, or by optimists – of whom there are few at the moment.'

He was appointed managing director in 1996. Coronation Fund Managers was listed on the JSE in 2003. Under his leadership, Coronation grew from a small fund management business to the second-largest independent fund manager in South Africa. Du Toit occupied the position of MD of Coronation Fund Managers for more than ten years (April 1997 to November 2007). During this period a unit trust business was launched, a life insurance licence was obtained, and international offices were established in Dublin and London.

He was also instrumental in the establishment of the Association for Savings and Investment South Africa (ASISA). His former predecessor and colleague Leon Campher is currently the CEO of this industry body.

Du Toit has served on various boards, including those of Coronation, ZCI, KWV, PSG and Pioneer Foods. He serves on Stellenbosch

University's investment committee and is the chair of Stellenbosch Trust.

In 2009, after his retirement from Coronation, Du Toit started Rootstock Investment Management, which is an investment management business for family offices and select individuals. In South Africa, but also elsewhere in the world, family offices have gained in popularity as a way of managing wealthy people's liquid assets and investments. It is actually an old concept that dates back to the organisations that controlled the fortunes of 19th-century American robber barons such as JP Morgan and John D Rockefeller.

The phenomenon has grown since then, with several hundreds of family offices in various countries that have already been in operation for at least three generations, some with a few hundred members – an indication of an acceleration in the number of billionaires worldwide. In the Global Family Office Report for 2018, produced by UBS and Campden Wealth, over half of the 311 family offices that took part in the survey were serving the first generation of wealth.

Du Toit points out that in South Africa in particular, more and more corporate entities got rid of their CEOs or they were pressured to resign, while others carried through very profitable deals. As an example, he refers to the owner of a transport company whose business is bought out. 'They hand you a cheque for R100 million … You knew how to manage trucks worth R100 million, but you don't know how to manage R100 million in cash. This is where the concept started that a person in that position should establish his family office with his money assets.'

Single-family offices serve the needs of one family only, whereas multi-family offices support multiple families to manage their wealth. The management role of some family offices has expanded from that of a trusted adviser on anything from investment problems and succession planning to a range of other services, including assistance with sensitive family matters such as antenuptial contracts, divorces and advice regarding the black sheep of wealthy families, the payment of bills and even travel arrangements.

Rootstock, which also has an office in Malta, is a multi-family office in which the Du Toit family's assets are invested along with those of 40 other families, with the Du Toit investment being the largest.

Since Rootstock only has a share mandate from the other families, he solely manages the buying and selling of shares on behalf of them all. 'So I'm basically just an investment person that manages my own money and that of other people, people similar to me.'

Like some other Stellenbosch residents, Du Toit also had a brush with Steinhoff. In June 2015, he and another PSG director, Jaap du Toit, swapped their PSG shares for Steinhoff shares. The combined value of the transaction was about R1,8 billion. The deal also pushed up Steinhoff's stake in PSG.

A few months later, in December 2015, Steinhoff listed in Frankfurt. The share swap deal was sharply criticised by Magda Wierzycka, CEO of the asset manager Sygnia. She referred to 'the cynical move by shareholders in PSG to, in a sleight of hand, swap their shareholding in PSG for a sudddenly-Frankfurt-listed Steinhoff, thereby externalising their wealth without the need for foreign exchange control approvals'.

Du Toit responds emphatically to her claim: 'That was never the case. My shares were, and still are after the Frankfurt listing, part of the South African share register, not the German one. The value of the shares was therefore never taken out of South Africa.' This is confirmed by a statement from the transfer agency Computershare Investor Services.

Mouton was 'furious and disappointed' about the share swap, as it was the first time members of PSG's inner circle had sold PSG shares. But Du Toit says he was given the mistaken impression that Mouton had approved the proposed exchange transaction. 'I only found out later that he hadn't done so. In spite of that, we're still friends today.'

Du Toit confirms that some of his own family structures suffered losses as a result of the Steinhoff debacle. The net asset value of Du Toit's company RCapital fell by 18 per cent. It was possible to limit the decline, however, because he reached a settlement with Steinhoff due to a safeguarding mechanism of his share transaction. By contrast, Rootstock Investment Management as third-party fund manager had no exposure to Steinhoff and none of the Rootstock clients suffered damage as a result of the debacle, according to Du Toit.

Another well-known family office headed by a former Stellen-bosch resident is Stonehage, which was renamed Stonehage Fleming in 2014 as an amalgamation of British and South African families. Stonehage Fleming's former CEO and now managing partner is Giuseppe Ciucci, the son of an Italian prisoner of war, who matric-ulated at Paul Roos Gymnasium and who speaks fluent Afrikaans. Prior to the merger, Stonehage had served a number of overseas-based and locally resident South African families. One of the members of the British Fleming family was Ian Fleming, author of the best-selling novels about the fictional character James Bond.

Stonehage Fleming, which looks after over 250 families globally, has its headquarters in London and South African offices in Cape Town and Johannesburg. For quite a while the company had an office in Stellenbosch, which was headed by Mof Terreblanche prior to his retirement.

Ciucci, who graduated with a BCom LLB from Stellenbosch University and worked at Deloitte & Touche before joining Stone-hage in 1991, says the aim of family offices is 'to offer the families whatever they need, whenever they need it'.

Stonehage Fleming South Africa's CEO Johan van Zyl (not to be confused with his namesake from Sanlam and African Rainbow Capital) says the group has learnt many lessons from the complex needs of the Flemings that can be applied in less complex cases. Each member of their team focuses on a specific area of expertise, whether investments, accounting or legal matters.

A British cultural critic, Peter York, has described the role of fam-ily offices as 'super-help for the super-rich'. *The Economist* anticipates that 'the family office is entering a Gilded Age', with more and more family offices that follow a do-it-yourself policy in managing their wealth. If this approach mainly produces the kind of capital growth that ensures greater wealth for only a tiny elite group, however, it will likely help fuel the inequality the French economist Thomas Pikkety warned against in his book *Capital in the Twenty-First Century*.

10

Adventure in insurance

Johan van Zyl

TWO AFRIKAANS-SPEAKING trendsetters in the insurance industry, Johan van Zyl and Douw Steyn, have strongly divergent personalities. Both of them, however, forged a special connection with a prominent black leader: Van Zyl with the richest black South African, Patrice Motsepe, and Steyn with the statesman Nelson Mandela.

Van Zyl, under whose leadership Sanlam was revitalised, is an agricultural economist who was vice-chancellor of the University of Pretoria (UP) before he exchanged academia for the business world. He was CEO of both Santam and Sanlam, which is where he became more closely acquainted with Motsepe, the founder of African Rainbow Capital. In time, he joined Motsepe in an executive capacity to help expand the latter's business empire.

As a young man, Johan van Zyl, who started his school career at a small farm school called De Grootboom near Lydenburg in Mpumalanga, intended to go into farming like his father – a fruit farmer who exported citrus fruit and also kept cattle. But his mother, who had to leave school after standard 6 in the depression years to start working, persuaded him to go to university first. At UP, the head of the department of agricultural economics, Professor Jan Groenewald, admitted him to the course with the concession that he could take mathematics and geology as subjects.

After obtaining his honours and master's degrees in agricultural economics cum laude, he worked at the department of agriculture in Pretoria for two years. He subsequently obtained two doctorates: the first in agricultural economics at UP, and the second in macro- and micro-economics at Vista University.

He was appointed as professor at the age of thirty and became vice-chancellor and principal of UP in 1997. Besides having been a visiting professor at Michigan State University in the United States during a sabbatical, he also served a stint at the World Bank in Washington. The international experience broadened his horizons.

Professor Groenewald was one of two people who had a huge influence on his life. Groenewald impressed Van Zyl, who came from a typical National Party background, 'because he wasn't a typical Afrikaner. He asked questions, and the way he thought about things [was different].'

The other person was Anton Rupert, who was the chancellor of UP at the time that Van Zyl was vice-chancellor. Van Zyl's wife, Cristelle, is also distantly related to Rupert. According to Van Zyl, Rupert would invite him down to Stellenbosch every month or two. 'Then we would sit at the Fleur du Cap estate, or at his home, or at the Decameron restaurant,' Van Zyl recounted.

'We would spend about three or four hours discussing the university, the country, the things that needed to be done, difficult things. He had an incredible influence on me as a young guy … I was barely 40. As a sounding board, his ideas were incredibly helpful to me in terms of providing guidance. I never really had a mentor, except for that time. He was chancellor for four of the five years that I was there, and we had a very good relationship.'

As vice-chancellor of UP, Van Zyl spearheaded the transformation of the university. Marinus Daling, the executive chair of Sanlam, was impressed by his performance. When Van Zyl's term as vice-chancellor came to an end in 2001, Daling persuaded him to join the short-term insurer Santam, where the CEO Leon Vermaak was due to move to Sanlam. This happened because Daling, who was both Sanlam's executive chair and managing director, fell ill and was consequently forced to split his position in two. Van Zyl was appointed in Vermaak's position at Santam.

But within four months Daling, who had to unbundle Sanlam after he had been instrumental in expanding the company into a giant business conglomerate, died unexpectedly from cancer. Ton Vosloo, who had been appointed to the Sanlam board in 1989, took over the position of non-executive chair.

The 40-year-old Vermaak, although expert in the short-term insurance market, struggled to make headway in the life-insurance market. Market share dropped, investors lost confidence, and Sanlam's share price, listed as R6 at the time of demutualisation, fell back to R5,80. At a board meeting in December 2002, during which Vermaak put the blame for Sanlam's sluggish performance on their shareholding in Absa with which he wanted Sanlam to merge, senior directors objected and sharply criticised 'the destruction of value'. It was Vosloo's task to ask Vermaak to leave the boardroom. Vermaak did not return.

Van Zyl, who wanted to avoid being called an April Fool, was appointed with effect from 31 March 2003 (at one day's extra pay!) as the new chief executive of South Africa's second-largest life insurer. According to Sanlam's centenary book, published in 2018, he 'hit the lacklustre organisation like a thousand volts and provided the much-needed leadership and vision in abundance'.

Van Zyl's academic and international experience stood him in good stead when he entered the South African business world. In the late 1980s, he had taught at Vista where he had to explain different economic systems, from communism and socialism to capitalism, to the students. But the black students would have none of capitalism. They all said he could talk until he was blue in the face, they would never vote for it, everyone should get the same, and so on. After they had written their first test, he handed them their marks: everyone had scored 51 per cent, which was the class average. Amid general muttering, the brightest student put up his hand and said there was a problem: he had asked around, and the whole class got 51 per cent.

'I said: Yes, but that's what you voted for, isn't it?' Van Zyl recounts. 'You declared that you all wanted to get the same, so why wait until we're a communist or socialist state? We're starting today.'

When Van Zyl continued with his lecture, the bright student's hand shot up again: 'Professor, but I think I did better than that.' Van Zyl replied: 'Of course you did, you scored in the eighties. But your friend next to you got in the twenties, so he received a portion of your marks. What's more, the next time you won't study because no matter how hard you work, you'll only get the class average. Your friend, who attended one lecture, won't bother about coming to class in future. He'll always get a free ride on the backs of others. Next time the class average won't be 51 per cent either; because no one will work, there's no incentive to work, so the average will drop to 30 per cent.'

The student spoke again: 'Professor, you've proved your point. I'm a capitalist.'

Van Zyl subsequently repeated the anecdote in the business environment to illustrate the inherent shortcomings of communism and socialism. Sanlam's directors were in stitches about the students' about-turn, until he asked: Why do we do the same in Sanlam?

'We pay everyone the same bonus, irrespective of their personal contribution and performance. Let's change it,' he told his colleagues. He regards this mind shift, this moving away from socialism, as one of the key contributing factors to the success Sanlam achieved under his leadership.

'We instituted incentives. Only those people who were really performing well and taking us forward were rewarded properly and more than others, and we put the focus on the business. That's the biggest change I introduced in Sanlam. How can I tell a guy in Johannesburg whether he needs two secretaries, or that the one he has is sufficient? We only need to hold him accountable for what he does. If he doesn't do it right, there should be disadvantages, like some or other punishment, and if he does it right, there should be compensation of some kind. It's just the basics … it's not complicated.'

Patrice Motsepe and black empowerment at Sanlam

Under Van Zyl's leadership, Sanlam embarked on black empowerment after their 1993 sale of Metropolitan Life (previously known as African Homes Trust) to a company with an 85 per cent black shareholding consortium.

Van Zyl's initiative to gain a much bigger foothold for Sanlam in the growing black market was the start of a long alliance with the black business leader Patrice Motsepe, the first black South African to feature on the *Forbes* list of the super-rich. In 2004, a year after Van Zyl became CEO, Motsepe was appointed to the board as the first black deputy chair of Sanlam.

After his undergraduate studies at the University of Swaziland, Motsepe graduated with an LLB degree from the University of the Witwatersrand. In 1994, he was appointed the first black partner of the Johannesburg law firm Bowman Gilfillan. His wife, Dr Precious Moloi-Motsepe, who completed her medical studies with the assistance of a study loan from the Helpmekaar Study Fund, is a fashion entrepreneur who started the organisation African Fashion International to encourage young South African fashion designers.

Motsepe entered the mining industry by starting to mine worked-out mine shafts. Through contract work for established mining companies he eventually expanded his business to such an extent that he acquired operating mines and founded the company African Rainbow Minerals. The company has interests in gold, platinum, coal, iron ore and copper.

Motsepe, who has been adamant that he wouldn't touch a deal involving people who are linked to state capture, picked up considerable knowledge about both business and mining in his early years. He got to know mineworkers, and helped with various tasks in his father's shops and restaurants and his mother's bottle store. He points out that many South Africans are unaware that there were already great black entrepreneurs in the apartheid days: 'We had people like Dr Sam Motsuenyane, Richard Maponya, Habakuk Shikwane … In many ways, they defied the apartheid laws that restricted them and set up successful businesses.'

Motsepe's exposure to Afrikaans in his youth played an important part in his decision to partner with Sanlam. His father, Augustine Butana Chaane Motsepe, a chief of the Bakgatla ba Mmakau community who ran businesses in Hammanskraal, sent him to an Afrikaans-language Catholic boarding school in Aliwal

North. According to Van Zyl, Motsepe believes that Afrikaners have deep roots in the country and will stay here, and there is a very close affinity between the two of them. He never speaks English to Van Zyl and other Afrikaans-speaking businesspeople, only Afrikaans. When he gets angry, Van Zyl says, he speaks only Afrikaans, even when English and other board members are present.

At the stage when Motsepe became a director, Sanlam was facing headwinds. Because of a lack of leadership there was no clarity of vision or agreed business model. Motsepe had a choice of financial services groups to partner with, and was in the process of negotiating with Old Mutual as well. 'He partnered with us because he believed he could get further with the Afrikaners and Afrikaans-speaking people; because of our history of empowerment and the fact that we don't have other places. So, it's actually a very beautiful story,' Van Zyl says. 'Besides, this was at the very time that Old Mutual went to England, and Anglo American and SA Breweries moved their primary listings to London. Especially the ANC and the black people found this quite hard to accept. They felt, now that *we* are in control, the English are running away to England.'

Former president Nelson Mandela was instrumental in convincing Motsepe to partner with Sanlam. The ANC's pension fund was already with Sanlam, and Mandela maintained that what Sanlam had achieved with Afrikaner money could also be done with the money of black South Africans.

A broad-based empowerment transaction was concluded with the Motsepe company Sizanani-Thusanang-Helpmekaar (Pty) Ltd, and in April 2004 Ubuntu-Botho Investments (Pty) Ltd came into existence. The name of the company gives expression to Motsepe's commitment to ubuntu, the African concept of giving and caring for your neighbour and other members of your community – the same concept the Helpmekaar movement promoted among Afrikaners a century earlier. And this relates the compound term 'ubuntu-helpmekaar', one of Motsepe's favourite expressions, to his conviction that black and white South Africans form one nation and are interdependent.

The new company's black partners were not handed anything on a plate: the transaction was based on sound business principles. Trade unions, traditional leaders, and religious and community organisations were made part of the broad-based empowerment group. The group, which acquired 8 per cent of Sanlam's shares at R6 a share with debt financing of R1,2 billion, rapidly started growing and expanding, so much so that Ubuntu-Botho is viewed as a model for black empowerment. By 2006, the first dividend of R50 million was paid out to over 700 shareholders and the Ubuntu-Botho Community Development Trust. The trust supports community upliftment and development projects in mainly rural areas with a structured development plan.

During the state of disaster due to the Covid-19 pandemic in 2020, Motsepe, who also owns the football club Mamelodi Sundowns, pledged R1 billion for emergency relief shortly after it was announced that the Rupert and Oppenheimer families had donated R1 billion each.

Motsepe only ever missed one Sanlam board meeting, Van Zyl said in 2018, and that was because he'd been overseas at the time. Although it was 4 am in the United States, he had phoned in from there. 'This is the kind of approach that can be expected from a director.'

Motsepe's entry into Sanlam in 2004 coincided with the termination of an agreement that had resulted in the insurance company staying out of the emerging black market for a decade. This was partly the consequence of an empowerment transaction with Metropolitan Life that Marinus Daling had entered into ten years earlier. Sanlam had undertaken not to compete with Metropolitan for a period of ten years. In so doing, Sanlam 'basically sold its future', as Van Zyl subsequently put it. Many of Sanlam's clients switched to Metropolitan, while other rivals also exploited an advantage they had over Sanlam.

Sanlam unbundles and innovates

While the unbundling of conglomerates became more common after 1994, Van Zyl believes that with hindsight, Sanlam under Daling's leadership probably unbundled too early. 'Worldwide, it was a fashion that firms started focusing. In South Africa it was of course a bigger trend, because we hadn't been able to invest outside the country, everyone had to reinvest in South Africa. The moment the world opened for South African companies, SAB sold off businesses and focused on beer. They became the second largest in the world, fairly quickly, having put some of the money to good use.

'What Marinus and his colleagues did was to sell off all those companies, at a slightly lower price and too soon. They didn't sell after 1994, when the prices tripled; they sold them before 1994. So, those businesses were all sold at half-price.'

Van Zyl accepted that the whole world had changed after the transition of 1994 and that Sanlam's old recipe no longer worked. 'The vultures were circling,' he recalls. Stronger concentration on the growing black market was imperative as part of a more streamlined and business-oriented strategy. At the same time, he declared publicly: Sanlam is a South African business, they had no intention of running away and listing in England.

Van Zyl explained that the business model he would implement required optimal management of capital. He reintroduced an executive committee at group level that would be in control of a variety of business clusters with decentralised decision-making powers. In June 2004, Roy Andersen became the new chair of Sanlam.

In Van Zyl's view, one notable advantage Sanlam enjoyed was that it had the best people, especially academically speaking. In addition, leadership and managerial strengths from diverse backgrounds were brought in to get the strategy right, and Sanlam's investment capabilities were expanded.

Whereas in the past management meetings had been mostly dominated by speakers who did not concentrate on the essential business of the four main clusters, Sanlam's focus was now returned to business. Four chief executives to whom the rest had to report on what was happening in their businesses were promoted to a higher level. The head office consisted of 500 people. 'We brought it down to 100, merely by saying: if you're important to the business, the business will give you a job, but you're not going to sit in the head office to stop the business. Businesses aren't postboxes – because that's what they did,' Van Zyl recounted.

He remarks jokingly about this turnaround: 'Sanlam developed from a company where one boss knew everything to the current situation where the one in charge knows nothing.'

He also insisted that the marketing of products had to be understandable and simple. 'If I can't understand what people (such as smart actuaries) say in three minutes about a product, how will we be able to sell the thing to a guy with no training? It should be simple, everyone should be able to see it, everyone should know what you're working towards, and then you're just like an evangelist: you talk about us, what we're going to do, and you set an example. If you want the people to start work earlier, you have to make sure you're the first to arrive. If you want them to stay later, you have to stay later.'

Furthermore, Sanlam had to learn how to cut costs. Companies that had become a millstone around their neck had to go as soon as possible. Van Zyl undertook to effect a R250 million cost reduction per year at Sanlam Life.

Van Zyl's insistence on ethical behaviour, even if it meant losses, is one of his traits on which seniors at Sanlam agree. One of his executives put it like this: 'You know that suspicious transactions will never be swept under the carpet.'

Perhaps the most significant step, a transaction Van Zyl sees as the turning point in Sanlam's recovery, was the sale of Sanlam's stake in Absa to Barclays, which had disinvested in 1986 but wanted to return to South Africa. Following 'tortuous negotiations', Sanlam got a capital inflow of R10,3 billion from the transaction. The group's capital shortfall was wiped out. Sanlam could buy back some of its own shares and was now in a position to acquire businesses that were able to grow its life business.

Above all, it was now possible for Sanlam to enter formerly unexplored markets. Expansion outside South Africa was an important part of the growth strategy, especially after the Ubuntu-Botho empowerment deal enabled the company to achieve the diversity Van Zyl strove for. The company started offering financial services in emerging markets elsewhere in Africa and in Asia, as well as in specific developed markets. When Sanlam celebrated its centenary in 2018, Van Zyl stated that Sanlam had been transformed into a multinational organisation with a footprint spanning across 36 countries in Africa, Britain, India and Malaysia.

In the decade that followed Van Zyl's assumption of the leadership in 2003, his strategy bore fruit. By 2013, Sanlam served all levels of the market, and 30 per cent of its shareholders were black. There was a new commitment to the ideal of working for the advancement of South African society as a whole. 'Sanlam's history has been a key driver of empowerment, economic advancement, wealth creation and protection. This is a legacy and responsibility that we take very seriously,' Van Zyl declared.

Van Zyl stepped down as chief executive in 2015 and was replaced by the chartered accountant Ian Kirk, but stayed on as director. In September 2019, Stephen Cranston wrote in *Business Day*: 'Sanlam's secret, after Van Zyl was appointed CEO in 2003, was to accept that managing capital is a serious fiduciary responsibility.' This was a far cry from the Sanlam of the 1980s 'which followed National Party instructions and was used as the buyer of last resort for failed businesses' such as Checkers and Nissan. At the time of its demutualisation in 1998, Cranston wrote, 'nobody would have said Sanlam would ever have a market capitalisation 50 per cent higher than its historic rival Old Mutual'.

'This bunch of crooks'

A decision Van Zyl made shortly after stepping down as CEO, but one he would rue afterwards, was the acceptance of a directorship of Steinhoff International in May 2016, about a year and half before the company's share price collapsed in South Africa's biggest corporate scandal.

It was not Markus Jooste who approached him to serve on the board, but Christo Wiese, who was not yet chair of Steinhoff at the time, and who argued that Steinhoff needed more independence on its board. 'Markus and I are actually not friends at all. I've never been at his home or anything. On the contrary, we had quite a serious row in 2004 about funding Sanlam gave them,' Van Zyl says.

Van Zyl declined the offer since he was too busy, but after his resignation he said he might consider it, on condition that he served on no committees and that a few nagging questions about Steinhoff were answered. The issues that bothered him related to the raid that had been conducted on Steinhoff's premises in Germany by the German Central Crime Inspectorate in Oldenburg in November 2015. Fraud was suspected, and the inspectors seized documents and data. The public prosecuting authority in Oldenburg launched investigations against several Steinhoff executives and their private homes were searched. This happened two weeks before Steinhoff's listing on the Frankfurt Stock Exchange.

Van Zyl says Wiese explained to him 'what they do and why and how he understood it, but of course he got his information from Markus, didn't he? That's how a company works. The board members sit there and ask questions, and then they tell the CEO: You now have to go and find out this and that. So, the wolf is in charge of guarding the sheep.'

He also met with the company's auditors, Deloitte, and with RMB, the bank that handled the listing. Both institutions assured him they had investigated all the allegations and could not find anything wrong. He then declared himself willing to serve as director for a three-year term. 'So I told Christo: Fine, then we'll proceed on that basis. And a year later, the bomb exploded.'

Van Zyl's first instinct had been to resign at once, as he wanted nothing further to do with 'this bunch of crooks'. 'And then some major shareholders – they held probably 50/60 per cent of the shares – implored me to stay on until we had a new board in place, and that's what I did.'

With an executive team without Jooste and a leaderless board after Wiese's resignation, Heather Sonn was appointed acting chair of Steinhoff's supervisory board. PwC was instructed to conduct a forensic investigation into the suspected large-scale fraud in the international firm. Van Zyl became chair of an independent committee that had to pull the chestnuts out of the fire in an attempt to save something of Steinhoff's remains. The two other members were Sonn and Van Zyl's friend Steve Booysen, who had suspected at an earlier stage that something was fishy.

According to Van Zyl, the board members raised many questions. 'Facts had been misrepresented. When we queried them, we didn't get proper answers. Consequently, we brought in several experts – forensic lawyers and accountants – to investigate the misrepresentation.'

Booysen had told him about a month before Jooste's resignation that there was a big problem: a number of things warranted serious scrutiny. 'He went overseas, even went to speak to that investigator from Oldenburg. Markus insisted on going along.' Van Zyl relates that they decided Booysen should go a day earlier so that he could first meet with the investigator on his own, with Markus seeing him after that. This process was then followed. 'And the investigator from Oldenburg had a lot of allegations, but he was unable to substantiate them. By then they had been investigating for almost a year and a half, with a team of 80 people! So, this thing isn't simple. It's not just a matter of saying: in this instance money was stolen or so. This is something that was set up a long time beforehand.'

On his return, Booysen put questions to Deloitte regarding the additional information in the Oldenburg report he had brought with him. Deloitte had done many investigations in the past, and they then checked the details again. Van Zyl relates that at first their auditors said they could not sign off the financial statements, but they did an about-turn after Jooste gave them an explanation. Finally, their forensic investigator in the Netherlands told them: 'No, no, no, when you look at these items individually, they all make sense, but when you look at it from here to there, connecting all four steps, it amounts to fraud.'

That was when Deloitte refused to sign off the results. This was more or less a week before the scandal broke.

Van Zyl explains that the audit committee was the place where the irregularities should have been picked up, but Steinhoff's international composition across multiple jurisdictions was an enormously complicated construction of money that was shifted around, as well as intercompany transactions, some legal, others suspicious. 'But Steve had done a great deal of investigative work, and basically pressured the auditors to come to a point where they had sufficient information to say "no". Of course they would now say that they were the ones to pull the plug, but in the end it was actually Steve.'

The three members of the independent committee under Van Zyl's chairmanship soon found themselves in hot water when it was announced that they would receive an additional remuneration of at least €100 000 (about R1,6 million) for their services. The news was met with a wave of public outrage, as it was pointed out that Steinhoff had already lost R300 billion due to the collapse of the share price.

Van Zyl said that if shareholders understood what was going on, they would have realised Steinhoff would have gone 'belly-up' unless they had stepped in to provide leadership during the initial liquidity crisis. PwC had been asked to look at the remuneration structure of the directors and committee members, and they were the ones who made the recommendation about the additional payment that was referred to shareholders. 'From the start, my own position was that I won't take additional money, despite having put in additional time. But meanwhile this issue caused such a stir that we changed that entire decision, on my recommendation. And, you know, that's not what it was about. The whole thing was about trying to save Steinhoff.'

The management team and the board had to be bolstered. 'You can imagine what a business it was to find directors. I had to ask more than 40 people to eventually find five who could be added to the board.'

For him, it was a question of 'about 10 per cent of my life that has now gone awry. I just have to see to it that we get other directors who can continue with the work and then I can step aside.'

In the course of attending to the crisis at Steinhoff he encountered considerable schadenfreude, particularly from the ranks of government. 'People couldn't wait to start telling you the story. It was almost as if they were gloating.' Those who had been involved in, or had kept quiet about, state capture and billions of rands' corruption under the Zuma regime were able to claim that 'the Afrikaners are no different from us, that type of thing'.

Van Zyl said in response to this: 'Yes, well, I think that's true, of course. There are rotten apples in every basket.' He stressed the old adage about the need for eternal vigilance: 'But always! Everywhere! It's absolutely true. And these things aren't over, Steinhoff wasn't an isolated case. There are quite a few others, and some of them are big companies.'

He referred to the parliamentary inquiry into Steinhoff that did not make much headway. 'They have no idea. There are going to be court cases, people are going to be wrangling about this till kingdom come, and they [the parliamentarians] want answers right away. But nobody knows.'

Three days before Steinhoff's annual general meeting in April 2018, Van Zyl resigned as a member of the supervisory board. He said in a statement: 'I have thus completed my assignment on the board and fulfilled my commitment to major shareholders of the company.' He initially wanted to resign in December 2017 but had stayed to provide continuation on the board, according to a statement published on Sens.

Scathing criticism was directed at Van Zyl and the other directors. It was said that they must have been aware of what was going on and had neglected their fiduciary duties. The Democratic Alliance's shadow minister of finance, David Maynier, issued a statement in which he welcomed Van Zyl's resignation but accused him of not accepting responsibility and showing no remorse.

It subsequently emerged, however, that while DA MPs were hauling Markus Jooste over the coals about fraud at Steinhoff in Parliament in 2018, their leader Mmusi Maimane was using a vehicle Jooste had donated to the party. Maimane denied a report claiming he had still used the Toyota Fortuner for another four months after it had been decided to return it. The DA's finance committee cleared him of wrongdoing after an internal probe.

Van Zyl maintained that a board operated on a basis of trust between the management and the board. But when you are a part-time member of a board and someone else spends 24 hours a day on scheming in order to deceive you, they would likely get away with it. 'So, when you discover that there is a completely different "inner circle" of people concluding transactions you don't see, and that there were structures to mislead the board, shareholders, analysts and auditors, you don't stand a chance.' He explained that these were 'off-balance-sheet entities set up deliberately to bamboozle the governance structures, including the supervisory board and the auditors'.

The forensic report PwC issued after their investigations, which had lasted for over a year, confirmed what Van Zyl had to discover to his disillusionment: that there had been lie upon lie. 'The initial summary is that there has been fraud on a grand scale, focused around a small group of individuals.' He added that one should focus on 'getting those people behind bars'.

He also referred to the many reported cases of corruption and state capture in South Africa where no action had been taken against those implicated. The lack of consequences for wrongdoing has not set a good precedent, with the result that people think they can do what they want to and get away with it. 'Let's focus on the few things we can prove and that are fairly obvious.'

In Van Zyl's view, charging people on a hundred counts was counterproductive; they should rather be charged with three major offences and be convicted.

The growing success of African Rainbow Capital

Prior to the disruption of Van Zyl's life caused by the revelation of the Steinhoff scandal, he had become more closely involved in Motsepe's growing operations in a new chief executive position. Motsepe is not only the heavyweight among black businesspeople in South Africa; he also has weighty political connections. His one sister, Tshepo, is the wife of President Cyril Ramaphosa, and his other sister, Bridgette Radebe, is the country's richest and most powerful black woman. She is married to Jeff Radebe, a leading member of the Communist Party, who has headed some of the most important ministries in the ANC government.

Motsepe, who in 2018 was in third place on the *City Press* Wealth Index, founded African Rainbow Capital (ARC) in 2016. It is an investment holding company that makes investments in South African and African businesses. As founder chair, he appointed Van Zyl and his Sanlam colleague Johan van der Merwe as the co-CEOs and executive directors of ARC. The alliance between the two groups, with ARC as Sanlam's empowerment partner, expanded further.

By this time Ubuntu-Botho had largely achieved the objective of the first phase of its development: to accumulate sufficient capital in partnership with Sanlam to become the country's premier black-owned and black-controlled financial services entity. By 2019, the empowerment group had become the largest shareholder in Sanlam with a shareholding of 18,5 per cent, compared with the Public Investment Corporation as the second-largest shareholder at 12 per cent. With Ubuntu-Botho's shareholding, which is valued at about R17 billion, the second development phase has been about partially investing this capital in ARC.

Investments have been made in a broad range of businesses, from new technological developments such as data processing, to the digital banking sector, as well as in mining, agriculture, property development and financial services. ARC's business philosophy has two distinct focus areas: to create value for shareholders, and to plough money back into communities in order to make a difference in the lives of ordinary South Africans.

One of the property investments is a 20 per cent stake in the Val de Vie estate between Paarl and Franschhoek. Among other associations ARC has entered into are businesses such as the mobile operator Rain and the exclusively digital retail bank TymeBank. Rain, a mobile data-only network, in which ARC holds a 20 per cent stake, is headed by the OUTsurance co-founder Willem Roos.

ARC has entered the digital banking sector with TymeBank, which aims to provide a service to people who have virtually no access to banks. ARC has a 66 per cent stake in Tyme Digital, which has set up self-service kiosks in Pick n Pay and Boxer branches that enable people to transfer money. TymeBank is in competition with two other new digital banks: Bank Zero and Discovery Bank.

Of the three new banks, TymeBank has been first off the blocks, with a million clients in 2020.

Van Zyl feels strongly about data usage, including 5G, the fifth generation of cellular technology that offers much faster connection speeds: 'It's the thing that's going to make South Africa competitive. It will drive everything – communication, cellphones, data downloads. Currently this is driven by cable, but it's much cheaper and much faster to be able to do it wirelessly. We want to make data 50 times cheaper.'

ARC also seeks to make it easier and cheaper for ordinary investors to trade shares. Accordingly, it has acquired a 'modest' interest in A2X, a low-cost competitor for the JSE. 'Our Bourse is very good, the JSE is among the best in the world, but it is expensive to trade on; two, three times more expensive than the others,' Van Zyl stated. 'It doesn't make ordinary share trading accessible to ordinary people, and we make it cheaper. So, we take a bit of the money we make and capitalise it and people invest in us.'

Van Zyl has remained closely involved in transformation projects. Education tops the list of the issues he emphasises. Alongside it is land reform, on which the Vumelana Advisory Fund focuses under his chairmanship. He puts his experience to good use by assisting communities in the Land Reform Programme to develop their land.

Motsepe was instrumental in the decision that Van Zyl should succeed Desmond Smith, who had been the Sanlam chair since 2010, in 2017. Motsepe turned down the chairmanship to which he had been elected and instead proposed Van Zyl, while he retained his position as deputy chair.

In March 2019, Sanlam announced that Van Zyl would be stepping down as non-executive director at the annual general meeting on 3 June 2020. CEO Ian Kirk stated that while Sanlam endeavoured to stay at the forefront of the latest corporate governance practices, the game had changed and 'ex-post Steinhoff' everyone now saw it slightly differently. According to Kirk, Van Zyl was not considered completely independent due to his relationship with Sanlam's empowerment partner (ARC).

Van Zyl explains the situation: 'Sanlam said we can deal with the conflict of interest, we'll get a lead independent director. But I said I didn't want to continue, I've basically had my turn at Sanlam. I can assist from the side as a consultant if they need me. Because I also have a fair number of businesses and sizeable farming interests to attend to. It just takes up a lot of time. That's what I don't have.'

11

Meerkat takes the gap

Douw Steyn

DOUW STEYN, an entrepreneurial insurer who disrupted the South African insurance industry with the innovations he introduced, built up an international insurance conglomerate that has made him one of the wealthiest South Africans. He also became a close friend of Nelson Mandela.

Steyn is descended from one of the oldest and most prominent Afrikaner families. His ancestor was Douwe Geerbrants Steyn, a master mason who came to the Cape around 1669 and was involved in the construction of the Castle in Cape Town. He was married to Maria Lozee, a slave woman from the Cape. She had a two-year-old son, Jacobus, who adopted the Steyn surname. Jacobus was the progenitor of that branch of the Steyn family from whom both President MT Steyn of the Orange Free State and President Paul Kruger of the Zuid-Afrikaansche Republiek (Transvaal) were descended. The two presidents' respective grandfathers were second cousins.

Douw Steyn, who was born in Brits in 1952, was given the family names Douw Gerbrand. He matriculated at the Hoërskool Linden in Johannesburg where, as a schoolboy, he began to display the resourcefulness of a true entrepreneur. His parents were not well off and he devoted much time to magic tricks, with which he made money. As a student he used to present magic shows at the school on Friday and Saturday evenings. Half of the proceeds was for the school fund, the other half for petrol money for when he started studying.

According to a schoolfriend and later business partner Stephen Klinkert, even at school Steyn had been someone who had dedicated himself to being the best at what he chose to do. In his case it was not schoolwork but magic, and he would spend hours practising to perfect his tricks. In later years, he would entertain business acquaintances and friends with conjuring tricks such as making coins, playing cards, balls and other objects appear and disappear. The actor Kevin Spacey related how Steyn did a rope trick that astounded him. 'You saw the little boy in him, you saw the kid on the street who had to make money by doing magic tricks when he was first beginning his life,' Spacey said. 'And he's really good at it! You know, David Copperfield, look out!'

Though Steyn was a student at the then Rand Afrikaans University and at Potchefstroom, he did not complete his studies and obtain a degree. During university holidays he worked as a conductor on the trains to Soweto. He had heard that the overtime was calculated incorrectly, and by working 24 hours a day he could earn more than a lawyer, he later recounted. He became used to sleeping on a train bench.

When Steyn did not graduate, he heard about a study programme Siemens offered in Germany. He applied for the programme and received a study bursary. On his return after completing the two-year course in business administration, he started working at his father's estate agency in Melville in Johannesburg. It was here that his ideas for bigger things originated.

As estate agent, he was interested in a new insurance product and began selling policies as an insurance broker by going from door to door, as was customary at the time. But he was unable to obtain a licence for insurance broking, as the registrar believed there were too many insurance companies. Consequently, he left the country and started working in California where he founded an insurance company called Calamerica.

There he heard that a South African company called Crusader was for sale because it was bankrupt, with debts amounting to

R300 million. He returned to South Africa and persuaded the registrar that he would save the company provided he obtained the necessary licence. Friday 13 December 1984 was his lucky day: he finally received his insurance licence.

He entered into negotiations with the creditors and made them a full and final settlement offer. The claims were settled, and with a personal investment of R50 he took over the company. He changed the name to Auto & General, merged the broking businesses into it, and started recapitalising the company.

Steyn could now stop selling insurance from door to door and, typical of an entrepreneur, came up with exceptional innovations. He introduced the concept of telemarketing in the country and became the pioneer of paperless insurance in South Africa. Auto & General was also the first company in the country to replace stop orders with debit orders.

Steyn explained to the banks that stop orders were impractical for car insurance since they had to be signed every time the premium changed, for instance when a car was sold or a new one purchased. He proposed to the banks that the premiums be changed with a debit order when a client gave an instruction to that effect. He persuaded the banks that this could be done by offering them an amount as security and providing them with a statement of the monthly premium payments.

Steyn's innovation with regard to telemarketing was equally radical. He thought the application form for insurance was too long and complicated, and there were constant complaints and misunderstandings. 'So I said there must be a better way: we're going to do it by telephone,' he related. 'Well, a few of my directors resigned. They said: "It will never work; you've now lost your marbles." They argued that insurance was "a confidence thing: if you don't go with a pinstripe suit, you'll never sell anybody insurance."'

Steyn, however, maintained that doing it telephonically was possible and much more efficient. The telephone calls would be recorded and all the data stored on a sophisticated computer system.

Klinkert, who would in time become the deputy chair of Auto & General, started working at Steyn's company during his university holidays. Steyn eventually approached him in 1978 to set up a computer facility. Auto & General, which handled tens of thousands of calls every day, kept the records for a period of five years. Before long, the company became a market leader in short-term insurance in South Africa.

Another innovation saw Auto & General becoming the first insurance company in the country to run its own panel-beating service. The project failed in the end, but not before Steyn had built the largest panel-beating shop in the southern hemisphere. He had spotted a gap when general sales tax, the predecessor of value-added tax (VAT), was introduced. When an insurance company used a client's panel beater, 13 per cent tax was payable, but not when the company had the work done themselves. To Steyn, it was obvious that they could achieve an immediate saving of 13 per cent on turnover.

Soon 400 to 600 cars a month were sent to his 'massive' panel-beating business. It did not work, however, since 'a panel beater works because it's a small place ... it's a little bit like a restaurant. If you make it too large, you lose control. The thefts and bad workmanship outweighed the savings, so we closed it up and sold it,' he explained.

Auto & General's new head office building, a 60-metre-high glass-and-concrete structure in Johannesburg that extends over 5 700 square metres, was officially opened in 1990 by President FW de Klerk. De Klerk lauded Steyn as 'an entrepreneur par excellence' and a good role model for young South Africans.

When starting up Auto & General, Steyn had been backed financially by Dick Enthoven, a member of the family that owns the Hollard insurance group and the global fast-food chain Nando's, both of which originated in South Africa. Shortly after 1990, Steyn expanded overseas. At Steyn's 50th birthday party in 2002, Enthoven declared that the highly successful business was poised to become a world-class firm. 'I don't think I can thank you enough for what you did for me. You made my wildest dreams come true,' Enthoven said.

A haven for Madiba

For years, Steyn had not been interested in politics at all. 'I had my head down and I was making money,' he recounted. But circumstances began to change in the 1980s after both the National Party government and the ANC had long been opposed to talking to each other. Feelers were put out and there was secret contact between the warring groups, which subsequently became generally known as 'talks about talks'.

Other businessmen who took part in covert meetings with the ANC outside South Africa added Steyn's name to their list because they knew he had a jet. In 1987, he flew to Dakar and Lusaka.

In Lusaka, where the ANC's headquarters in Africa was based after the movement had been declared a banned organisation, he met Thabo Mbeki, Alfred Nzo, Steve Tshwete and other leading ANC members. He enjoyed the experience of becoming involved in politics, and many of the meetings were held in his hotel suite in Lusaka.

One evening only he and Mbeki were left after a meeting was over and everyone else had gone. Mbeki said he had recognised everyone in the room, but he had never seen Steyn or heard of him before: who was he? According to Steyn, he replied: 'Well, you know, I have the jet ... So Mbeki said: oh, so you're the transport. I think he still calls me the transport.'

They became good friends. On a subsequent visit, he and Mbeki sat drinking KWV brandy one night – which was in short supply in Lusaka – until the sun came up. 'Now Thabo has this wonderful ability to go right through the night, sleep a few hours, and be as bright as anything the next day. I obviously have to sleep till midday before I can join the meeting. But, anyway, as the sun rose in Lusaka, he said: "You know, I presume, that Mandela was one of the first black lawyers, and he wasn't allowed to practise in Johannesburg, because it's white. So what do you think about that?"

'And I must say, I hadn't given it much thought until then. He said: "Don't you think it's immoral? Don't you think apartheid is a sin?" And I thought about it, and I said: "You're right, I'm behind you now ... whatever you need." And so began a long involvement.'

On their return from Lusaka, *The Star* published a photo of Steyn with Mbeki and Kenneth Kaunda on its front page. Auto & General lost 3 000 policies that first day because, in the eyes of these angry policyholders, Steyn had joined 'the enemy'. After about a month, the cancellations had still not subsided. 'We were facing destruction, we were going to go out of business. And then, thank heavens, it stopped, after we had lost about a third of the policyholders.'

Nick Mew, who later became the chief executive of Telesure Investment Holdings, recounted that they decided to simply continue with their business, offer an excellent service, keep the price right and allow market forces to play their part. The approach worked.

Steyn maintained his friendship with prominent ANC members. He met Mandela shortly after the ANC leader was released from prison in 1990. Following the first direct talks with the NP government in Cape Town, the ANC's top structure returned to Johannesburg. Mbeki asked Steyn if they could use his boardroom for a meeting, and he was invited to attend it as a non-ANC member. After the meeting Mbeki introduced him to Mandela.

The ANC had bought a house for Mandela in Houghton, but it first had to be fixed up. Mbeki then asked if Steyn would put the ANC leader up for a while since he had said that his mansion, the luxury residence in Sandhurst in Johannesburg that would later be converted into the Saxon Hotel, was open. 'I said it would be an honour for me. So then Madiba moved in, and it was a wonderful time. In those days, I had lunch and dinner with him almost every day, and you become so used to that, you don't appreciate how valuable times like that are. But then we became very good friends as well. And the ANC used the house for meetings, and I'm very glad that I was a part of that.'

After his divorce from Winnie Mandela, Mandela stayed with Steyn at his house for six months and worked on his autobiography, *Long Walk to Freedom*. Many ANC meetings were also held there.

Mandela, who was usually protected by three or four bodyguards, was walking in the garden one day when a new Rolls-Royce of Steyn's was delivered at the house. He took a great interest in the luxury car and suggested that Steyn take him for a spin. Steyn decided that instead of just driving around inside the grounds, they should also go outside. The top of the convertible was down and drivers of passing cars recognised Mandela, who waved at them. According to Steyn, one or two were so surprised at seeing Mandela in person that they almost collided with a tree.

Meanwhile the security detail had discovered that Mandela was missing. Reinforcements were summoned, and cars sped out of the gate to look for him. Steyn had only driven around the block, and on their return one of the bodyguards charged at him and gave him a tongue-lashing. They nearly came to blows when Steyn retorted: 'You don't talk like that to me.'

Steyn had high praise for Mandela and De Klerk: 'For De Klerk to take his own people across the divide, and for Madiba to come across the divide … the two best leaders at the right time, at the right place. Magic. No blood. Without that, it would have been devastation.'

When asked whether these experiences had changed him, Steyn replied: 'No, I don't think so. I've been the same arrogant, aggressive person I've always been.'

Activities in the United Kingdom and the Meerkat campaign

Steyn relocated to England in 1992 and got divorced there from his first wife, Liz. Their two sons, Louis and Tjaart (also known as TJ), grew up in the UK, but later chose to study in South Africa.

Steyn established his head office in Peterborough in Cambridgeshire where he bought an estate with a manor house, Thornhaugh Hall. His new business in the United Kingdom, Budget Insurance, was initially an underwriter, but struggled to make headway. Finally, Steyn summoned the whole board of directors to his estate for a brainstorming session.

Without beating about the bush, he told the directors: 'Well, we need to take a decision this weekend: do we carry on in the UK, or do we stop?' He told those who wanted to get their money back and jump off the bandwagon that they were free to do so. The other directors were ordered to call their wives and girlfriends, as they would all be staying there until they had a solution to the problems. The majority chose to stay, and they spent the entire weekend analysing where they had made mistakes, where they could improve, and so on.

After that meeting, a new approach was adopted. Steyn believed that instead of replicating the South African model, they should rather exploit the terrain of insurance brokers. Budget Insurance Services, which was founded in 1997, ceased underwriting the following year and became an intermediary business that marketed policies for a panel of insurers. Following its transformation from underwriter to insurance distributor, the business went from strength to strength.

Telesure Investment Holdings – which would eventually also become the South African holding company – was established in 1998 to house Budget Holdings Limited (SA) on the island Guernsey. In 1999, the brokerage Arnott Century was acquired and BHL's future chief executive officer Matthew Donaldson joined the group. He sensed 'a lot of South Africa' in the business: 'I think the bullishness, the bravery, the creativity, the innovation – the times I've been in South Africa absolutely speaks to the culture of our organisation. Then Douw himself, and indeed many others, including Stephen Klinkert, are great South Africans in their own right, and they've clearly brought a lot of that into the business.'

Among Budget's acquisitions on its growth journey were Dial Direct and the motorbike insurer Bennetts in 2001. In 2002, Junction was launched, a major contributor to Budget's growth through partners such as the British Post Office, M & S Money, Bradford & Bingley and Yes Insurance. Within a few years, Budget Insurance was noted as the institution that provided the cheapest car insurance cover and the most competitive home insurance in the UK. A contact centre was established in Cape Town as well. Budget changed its name to BGL Group in 2007.

Even greater success followed as the result of a television advertising campaign featuring a talkative meerkat that enchanted the British population. The ingenious Meerkat publicity campaign, which was launched in 2009, was associated with Comparethemarket.com, a price comparison website. In the adverts, a fictional meerkat named Aleksandr Orlov, who spoke with a fake Russian accent, promoted insurance products together with his meerkat sidekick Sergei. Orlov was portrayed as an aristocratic billionaire from Moscow who owned a mansion in London.

Steyn, who has a passion for African wildlife, liked the name Meerkat very much. It also served as a play on the word 'market' and was specifically chosen to convey Comparethemarket's message. Donaldson says that with this campaign they gave themselves a 'brand essence' which he thinks is very South African in its own right: 'dare to be different'. The concept was fun and turned out to be a hit: within about twelve weeks, the group's market share increased from 5 per cent to 20 per cent .

Aleksandr Orlov's catchphrase 'Simples', indicating how simple it is to insure, became a national phenomenon in the UK, and eventually 'simples' was included in the Oxford English Dictionary in 2019. Over time, more family members were added to the meerkat cast. The furry characters were sold as cuddly toys, and movies were made about the meerkat characters and their promotional campaigns. Parts of the advertising campaign were filmed at Steyn's game reserve Shambala in Limpopo.

The *Daily Mail* wrote that Steyn owed much of his success and wealth to Aleksandr Orlov. When the meerkats first appeared on British television screens in 2009, Steyn was worth about £200 million, according to the *Sunday Times* Rich List. As the Meerkat campaign grew, his income 'soared' to an estimated £420 million within three years, the *Daily Mail* noted. In 2014, he was number 172 on the *Sunday Times* Rich List of the wealthiest people resident in the United Kingdom, ahead of Queen Elizabeth at number 285. In that year, her fortune was estimated at £330 million, almost half of Steyn's £600 million (about R10 billion at the time).

Besides other innovations of the Telesure group such as Dial Direct, there is 1st for Women, the first female-focused South African insurer. Auto & General also owns the insurer Virseker, which targets the Afrikaans-speaking market. Auto & General has entered into an agreement with the trade union Solidarity, which markets Virseker's products to its members and the civil rights group AfriForum. Premium income is also donated to the Virseker Trust for projects such as the private university Akademia and the technical training centre Soltech.

In 2016, BGL returned to life insurance with the launch of Budget Life. The group's market share in the UK increased to more than 40 per cent. They also embarked on expansions to other countries, including Australia, Singapore, the Netherlands, Turkey and France. By this time, the group was offering comprehensive services, inter alia life, vehicle and home insurance, together with an array of supplementary broking and related services, as well as legal services, hotel management and property development.

Steyn divided his time between South Africa and the UK. At one point, he was a visiting professor at the University of the Free State, where he gave lectures to the students in the faculty of economic and management sciences. He cautioned students against overplanning: 'When you have an idea, you should run with it. If something doesn't work, rather fix it as you go along than delay the implementation of your idea. When someone talks to me in terms of five years, I lose interest. My mind works in terms of six weeks, six months, and one year maximum.'

Steyn continued tackling major projects in South Africa, over and above the attention he gave to his business empire. His private residence was converted into the Saxon Hotel, and Shambala, one of the biggest private nature reserves in the country, was established on more than a dozen farms he had purchased near Vaalwater in the Waterberg. He also embarked on the development of one of the biggest private luxury estates in the country, Steyn City, which is situated between the Diepkloof informal settlement and the up-market Dainfern golf and residential estate in Johannesburg.

In an effort to help combat the country's crime wave, Steyn more than once made the ANC government a generous offer. In 2006, he sent the then president Thabo Mbeki a document he had compiled on crime in South Africa and pledged R1 billion to support the police. His initiative had been prompted by the emigration of his sister Elsa due to the high crime levels.

Unless Mbeki took action with regard to crime, Steyn wrote, neither he nor anyone else would invest in the country. He proposed a three-point plan that would involve 'a whole new approach to fighting crime', which included the use of hi-tech facilities such as satellite equipment and computers as well as helicopters that would be on regular patrol and available to police units all over the country to boost visible policing.

'Mbeki told me that I had got it wrong,' Steyn recounted. 'He said: "We don't have a problem with crime in this country. The problem is, we have a perception of crime." Of course, I knew Thabo from years ago. But by the time he got to be president, he seemed to have lost complete touch with reality.'

He could not forgive Mbeki for his reaction, and the two of them became estranged.

Shambala and Steyn City – sanctuaries from the stresses of urban life

Shambala is the Tibetan word for Paradise on Earth. The private game reserve is one of only three game farms in South Africa large enough to hold half-yearly or annual auctions of trophy game. Steyn, who reintroduced the Big Five on the farm along with other species, invested, among other things, in an expensive buffalo herd. In 2010, he owned 21 disease-free buffalo valued at close to R30 million. In that year, he bought a buffalo bull called Bill for R6 million, the highest price fetched up to that point for a wild animal in South Africa. One of the buyers of Shambala's trophy game has been President Cyril Ramaphosa, who owns a wildlife farm near Bela-Bela.

Mandela's private assistant, Zelda la Grange, relates in her book *Good Morning, Mr Mandela* that Steyn invited Madiba and his third wife, Graça Machel, to the farm. 'It was a relaxed luncheon that was planned with just Douw, his wife Carolyn and his staff on the farm. When Madiba and Mrs Machel returned they told me that Douw had offered to build a house on the farm for Madiba and Mrs Machel's use, where they could relax and go to as no one would be able to disturb them there because of the privacy of the farm. Madiba and Mum (as we started calling Mrs Machel, imitating Madiba) knew not to refuse the offer as Douw didn't take lightly to being refused. In no time he built the most beautiful house on the farm, before even completing his own.'

The first visitors to sign the guest book at the Mandela residence were the former US president Bill Clinton and Thabo Mbeki. Oprah Winfrey visited Mandela there on a few occasions, while the actors Morgan Freeman and Matt Damon dropped in during the filming of *Invictus*. Other celebrity visitors included movie stars such as Whoopi Goldberg, Arnold Schwarzenegger, Kevin Spacey and Will Smith.

La Grange remarks that Mandela always valued the time he spent with Steyn. The lavish lifestyle of the rich and famous fascinated him. 'Douw would tell Madiba about his extravagant deals and it would intrigue Madiba that one person could have so much wealth.'

Mandela also attended the official launch of Steyn City in 2007 and sowed the first bush willow seeds for the forest that would be planted on the enormous housing estate. Steyn declared at the event: 'I am so unbelievably happy that Madiba, the greatest man, can open what we considered to be the greatest project. We're going to try and make this the best suburban place to live in the country.'

On the website for the Steyn City project, Steyn stated that he could have chosen to invest in a luxury residence in the United States or Europe, but he chose South Africa instead because he had confidence in the country. He said people always asked him why Steyn City was called after him. 'Did anyone ever ask Donald Trump why he called his building in New York Trump Tower?'

Steyn embarked on developing the 800-hectare housing estate together with his partner Giuseppe Plumari, a property developer who had started buying unused land in the area in the 1980s, to which Steyn added further tracts. Steyn's private mansion in Steyn City, known as Palazzo Steyn, was said to be the most expensive private residence built in South Africa up to that stage. The 3 000-square-metre, Tuscan-style villa, which is the size of a convenience shopping centre, has seven bedroom suites and a wine cellar. The basement also serves as a garage with enough space to display his car collection of 33 sport and vintage models.

Steyn has always loved the atmosphere of European cities. Discussing the design of the envisaged self-contained 'lifestyle resort', Plumari remarked that the oldest cities were the most popular. The reason for their appeal was their human scale: they were designed with community living in mind and were largely pedestrian-focused. 'The old European cities are the polar opposite of South African cities where motorised roads have promoted insulated lifestyles,' Plumari said. Traffic is therefore kept to a minimum in Steyn City. An arterial ring road feeds into villages with crescents and cul-de-sacs, while the residential hubs are connected to each other with a network of footpaths through green park-like belts. The design is 'an antidote to big cities dominated by cars, highways and high walls'.

'Giuseppe and I share the same vision – to create a lifestyle estate unlike any other in South Africa, built on the foundation of quality of life. A country estate offering country living, but with all amenities conveniently within reach,' Steyn declared. 'Too much time is wasted in cities sitting in traffic and commuting between home, work, schools and the shops.'

He envisaged that 12 000 houses, a school, a heliport, a gymnasium and a five-star hotel would be built, as well as an 18-hole golf course designed by the US golf legend Jack Nicklaus. In 2019, amid the constrained economic situation in the country, Steyn City launched the next phase of its development vision, a new R5,5-billion flagship development. Known as City Centre, it offered over 700 luxury apartments and 17 penthouse suites. Additional attractions were a 300-metre clearwater lagoon that created an inland beach setting, and a heliport that enabled residents to escape traffic jams by means of helicopter flights.

Steyn City, which has provided employment for 10 000 people, caught the attention of envious politicians. The Economic Freedom Fighters' so-called commander-in-chief, Julius Malema, who constantly threatens to seize white people's land without compensation, ran into an unexpected hurdle when he wanted to 'occupy' the estate in 2017. Instead of concurring with his plan, the shack dwellers from the nearby Diepsloot prevented him from causing havoc in Steyn City.

'I had to make a retreat because the masses said "not this man",' Malema explained. When the EFF said the land owned by this white man should be 'returned to rightful owners', the 'rightful owners' said 'no, he is part of us and we can work with him'. The people of Diepsloot told Malema that Steyn was involved in their community, and was creating employment and investing in schools.

What money can't buy

No fewer than three former presidents attended Steyn's 50th birthday party in 2002: Mandela, De Klerk and Clinton. Mandela stated that he was much indebted to Steyn for everything he had done for him after his divorce: 'From the moment I left Orlando you took me into your house, and I lived there happily until I was able to find alternative accommodation. Men and women like yourself are rendering a wonderful service to South Africa.'

In his tribute to Steyn, Clinton said that he could identify with some parts of 'Douw's truly extraordinary life'. Both of them had had a boyhood dream to be just like Elvis Presley, and both of them gave it up. As a young man Douw travelled and studied before finally deciding 'he did not want to play second fiddle to corporate bureaucracy. He went home to South Africa with much bigger goals in mind. By the time he was 27 he'd made his first million. Today he employs more than 3 500 people on three continents.'

The reference to Elvis was not just plucked out of thin air. When Steyn appeared in public he indeed looked mostly like Presley, for whom he has great admiration. He would usually wear a black shirt, black trousers, black shoes and matching designer sunglasses.

By this time Steyn was a very wealthy man. The publicity-shy tycoon kept a low profile, but in 2006 he granted the journalist Hanlie Retief from *Rapport* a rare interview in his private suite in the Saxon. When she asked why his name did not appear on the list of South Africa's twenty richest people, he replied: 'I don't live here, lady, I live in London.'

Then he added with regard to his wealth: 'R10 billion strong.' He laughed at Retief's initial guesstimate of R500 million – that was what the farm and the hotel alone were worth. Then there were still his house in England, his cars (three or four Rolls-Royces), boats and helicopters. 'No, I'm very rich, lady. You can just say I'm a multibillionaire.'

Steyn remarried in 2003, but his marriage to the South African actress Carolyn Steyn lasted a mere five months. A tumultuous period in Steyn's private life followed after their divorce. By 2006, Steyn had been drawn into a court case that involved his former fiancée Donné Botha, a personal trainer, and a former girlfriend Bianca Ferrante, a nail technician. Botha had allegedly assaulted Ferrante with a champagne bottle after having caught her in bed with Steyn in his suite in the Saxon Hotel.

Steyn, who had to testify as a witness, raised eyebrows with his strange behaviour in court. Among other antics, he had cut off his trouser legs with a knife outside the court building and walked barefoot through the corridors of the court because he felt hot.

Botha was eventually sentenced to a R3 000 fine or 12 months' imprisonment, suspended for three years. In a separate lawsuit, Ferrante sued Steyn and Botha for R1,2 million in damages, while Botha in turn instituted a private prosecution against Steyn. Botha claimed that Steyn had married her in a ceremony in London. But he argued that it had been merely a 'blessing ceremony' and that there was no legal marriage, as well as that she had completed blank spaces on a pro forma prenuptial contract which she had coerced him into signing while he was intoxicated. He rejected all monetary and other claims she had lodged against him.

Steyn spoke openly about the unsavoury publicity generated by the lawsuit: 'I'm a private person, and I've managed to stay out of the limelight for twenty years. But now my life is hell. I've lost many of my friends. My legal costs are far more than double the amount that Ferrante wants from me.'

In February 2013, Douw and Carolyn married for a second time. Reflecting on her marriage, Carolyn said that while Douw was 'a very difficult man', there was an umbilical cord between them that could never be cut. 'I could never get him out of my system, and I tried so hard! But he's a fascinating man, he's a visionary. He's amazing. He's an incredible man,' she said.

Steyn has suffered from diabetes for years and needs regular insulin injections. After Palazzo Steyn was completed, he has spent most of his time in his villa in Steyn City, with carers looking after him while he receives medical treatment for symptoms of dementia. In 2020, his companies donated R320 million to support the South African fight against the Covid-19 pandemic. Though the donation was structured across a range of initiatives to bolster health and humanitarian responses, the bulk of the money – R200 million – was allocated to feeding schemes in Diepsloot and other areas adjacent to Steyn City.

12
Daring to dare
Roelof Botha

AT A RELATIVELY young age, Roelof Botha, who works in Silicon Valley in California, was named by *Forbes* magazine as one of the leading venture capital investors in the world. This was after he had been appointed by Elon Musk, eventually the richest person on earth, in his first job in the United States and became a member of the so-called Paypal Mafia.

Botha is regarded as one of the pioneers in the field of internet technology and venture capital, which has globally created the most wealth over the past decade. He is one of the three stewards heading the partners of Sequoia Capital, one of the largest venture capital firms in the United States.

Roelof is the son of the economist Dr Roelof Botha and grandson of South Africa's longest-serving minister of foreign affairs, Pik Botha. The young Botha, who has the family names Roelof Frederik like his father and grandfather, was born in Pretoria in 1973. His parents later divorced amicably, and both married again and had more children. According to his father, the young Roelof was an excellent carer for his half-brothers, Dawid and Frederik Botha and Michael Scheibe. 'He has been very responsible since his childhood. I can't recall ever reprimanding him. If I told him what the rule was, he kept to it,' Roelof senior relates.

He was an exceptionally bright learner at Hoërskool Jan van Riebeeck and topped the merit list in the Cape Province in his matric year in 1990, with distinctions in all six his subjects. His science teacher, Trevor Robertson, described him in 1990 as 'an extremely intelligent, first-class student and human being who always delivered the very best when it came to his academic work as well as sport'. A far-sighted Robertson noted in a testimonial: 'Roelof is the kind of man our country sorely needs to help build a modern civilisation in a highly technological age where demands of the highest order will be made on our potential and brain power for survival.'

During his studies at the University of Cape Town, Botha stayed with his grandfather, then still a cabinet minister, in his official residence. At UCT he once overheard someone accrediting his academic success to his grandfather's influence. This served as further motivation for him to prove that he could stand on his own feet.

He obtained a BSc degree in actuarial science, economics and statistics in 1996, with the highest average marks in the history of the business school. Eighteen months later, he became the youngest actuary in South Africa's history. After a stint at McKinsey in Johannesburg as a business analyst, he left for California in 1998 to study at the Stanford University Graduate School of Business.

It had always been Botha's ambition to study abroad because he wondered whether he would be able to compete against the best in the world. He explains that during the mid 1990s, when the internet boomed, he 'had a feeling that something interesting was about to happen in Silicon Valley. There was something dynamic, people were creating new businesses and were busy changing the world.' He had a desire to get into that environment and considers himself lucky to have been accepted at Stanford, the kind of luck that in his view played a big part in his career.

At Stanford, one of America's most prestigious universities, he obtained his MBA degree and was again the top student in his class. In his last semester at Stanford in 2000, he was affected by the emerging markets currency crisis. The money he had saved up in South Africa to attend the business school lost 40 per cent of its value overnight. Unable to pay his next month's rent, he had to borrow money from family and friends.

Prior to his graduation he had already declined two job offers, but a third offer was decisive. None other than the world-renowned Elon Musk recruited Botha for a job at X.com, the company that was to develop into the online payment giant PayPal. He was appointed director of corporate development as part of a group of entrepreneurial young businessmen who soon became known as the PayPal Mafia.

The rise of PayPal

Botha's first desk at the company was next to Musk's, and he still has his original recruitment letter signed by Musk himself. Musk, himself a former South African, would eventually become one of the most famous entrepreneurs in the United States. Among his other innovations are his SpaceX rockets and envisaged space flights to the planet Mars, the much-discussed Tesla electric car with driverless technology, and the Hyperloop, a proposed ground transportation system that would reduce travel times from hours to minutes by means of capsules racing through low-pressure tunnels at subsonic speeds.

Musk, who thought traditional banks were outdated and had failed to keep pace with rapidly developing technology, founded X.com to focus on online financial services and email payments. In the same building in Palo Alto, a rival company called Confinity had developed their own online money-transfer service called PayPal under the leadership of Max Levchin and Peter Thiel. The competitors spent millions of dollars on marketing and promotions 'while millions more were lost battling hackers who seized upon the services as new playgrounds for fraud'. Finally the two groups decided in 1999 to merge before they ruined each other.

From the outset, Botha was responsible for X.com's financial and risk management. Among other things, he developed a risk model to deal with the challenges of corporate fraud. Among the new stars of cyberspace, however, he found himself in a rather unconventional environment. In 2007, *Fortune* magazine published a photo of former PayPal employees that led to the moniker 'PayPal Mafia'. Musk does not appear on the photo, but Botha is among the thirteen members of the group in 'faux gangster attire', posing in seated and standing positions around tables filled with glasses and bottles. They looked like 'some of the most poorly dressed men of the 2000s. Behold the outsized sportswear, the leather blazers, the silky shirts.' But by that time they could afford to laugh off any criticism because, between them, they were worth billions of dollars.

According to Botha, when he started at the company PayPal was already an excellent service with a large – and growing – number of consumers, but there was nobody to take control of building a business model and to figure out how the company should grow into a big business. 'I took the initiative to build a model and to start a conversation with the management team to help them make decisions to turn it into a company,' he said.

But soon after joining the company he found himself in the midst of a palace revolution. The different cultures of the merged companies did not mesh well with each other. Confinity had the ownership rights with regard to PayPal, but was financially not as strong as X.com. Musk, a whizz at coding and a hard worker who would sometimes toil through nights on end, had secured venture capital financing after the famed Michael Moritz of Sequoia Capital decided to back him.

Musk, however, kept championing the X.com brand while most of his co-workers preferred PayPal. Further fights broke out about the design of the company's technology infrastructure, with the result that Thiel resigned two months after the merger.

Botha said afterwards that he did not think Musk had provided the board with a true picture of X.com's problems. Under the pressure of thousands of new clients, computers crashed almost weekly and fraud had increased. New competitors had appeared on the scene, and X.com lacked a cohesive business model to turn the situation around.

Resistance to Musk's management style intensified to such an extent that a coup was staged while he was on his honeymoon. In a night-time conspiracy hatched in a bar, a small group of employees of X.com decided to persuade the board to oust Musk as CEO by bringing back Peter Thiel. On Musk's return to Palo Alto, he was confronted with a fait accompli: he'd been replaced as CEO, and in June 2001 Thiel rebranded X.com as PayPal.

In September 2001, Botha was appointed the new group's chief financial officer at the age of 28. In his view, Musk had made mistakes and had learned from them, but indeed should not have stayed on as chief executive. 'I think it would have have killed the company if Elon had stayed on as CEO for six more months,' said Botha. 'The mistakes Elon was making at the time were amplifying the risk of the business.'

What impressed him immensely, Botha recounted later, was how well Musk handled the situation after Peter Thiel became CEO. 'You would expect someone in Elon's position to be bitter and vindictive, but he wasn't,' Botha said. 'He supported Peter. He was a prince.'

Musk kept investing in the company and became the largest shareholder in PayPal. 'He actually had a lot of confidence in the team. Everyone is still friends with him after all these years and after what happened,' Botha related.

At the age of 29, at a time when the dotcom bubble of the late 1990s had burst, Botha was in charge of the financial affairs of a billion-dollar company. 'I don't think I was ready for it and I had to work hard to earn my turn, but people were prepared to take a chance on me and my future.'

He managed PayPal's accounting system, financial planning and analysis, as well as corporate development, while at the same time being responsible for public relations and investor relations. He developed the group's business model further by bringing about integration between the financial and strategic management systems.

Botha reckons the combination of his background as actuary – which trained him how to solve complex problems – and his MBA was decisive in the success he achieved at a young age, especially when it came to building a business model which meant PayPal became a convenient and secure online payment system. He sums up his contribution as follows: 'An actuary is basically a financial manager for insurance products, pension products and so on. It's very mathematical and it's very analytical, because unlike an accountant who has to think one year in arrears, an actuary has to think 25 years into the future. You need to think very carefully, because when you're an actuary you make decisions about this very long-term period when it comes to pricing the product … where do you set the premiums, what are your assumptions about deaths, or if it's about health insurance, what is the morbidity? So, I think that long-term thinking helped a lot, and a part of what the MBA helped me with was self-confidence.'

I Ie admits that one easily feels intimidated when one comes from a small country such as South Africa. 'In America there are many people who attended one of the top high schools in the world and who've studied at one of the top universities, and there is always this question mark at the back of your mind: Can I compete with these people? But immigrants have a lot to prove, and of course there's the fact that the immigrants had to overcome many things just to be here in the first place. How many of the South Africans who apply are accepted at Stanford? It's a small percentage. So the people who come here are already a tiny fraction of the population of their home countries.

'And then, because you don't have this established network, you have to work hard. It's not just a given that you're going to be successful, it's not through your family connections or friends that you will get a job or something. You have to roll up your sleeves and get to work.'

Botha also led PayPal through its initial public offering (IPO) in February 2002. Soon afterwards Paypal was sold to the well-known online auction and shopping platform eBay for the astronomical sum of $1,5 billion, a transaction that injected new life into the depressed technology markets. Botha, who led the due diligence investigation, was one of the members of the PayPal Mafia who became dollar millionaires.

During the acquisition, Botha received an attractive offer to stay on at PayPal, but Michael Moritz phoned him to ask whether he would like to join Sequoia from the beginning of 2003. Although Botha's background did not match the role they were seeking to fill, Moritz served on the board of PayPal. He knew, therefore, that Botha had developed PayPal's model, and he'd sat in at the board meeting where Botha presented PayPal to the directors shortly before the IPO.

A talent for spotting potential

Sequoia Capital, where Botha has been working ever since, is a giant among venture capital firms in the United States. The firm was founded in 1972 by Don Valentine – the man 'blessed with an eye for mavericks who could launch great companies'. It was he who took a bet on Steve Jobs in 1978 by backing the Apple founder, despite thinking that he smelled odd and 'looked like Ho Chi Minh'. In 1999, Valentine handed over the managerial reins of Sequoia to Moritz (the later Sir Michael) and Doug Leone, an Italian immigrant.

The firm mainly focuses on the technology industry and specialises in identifying the potential of new companies, as well as in providing financing to start-ups they choose to invest in and helping to guide entrepreneurs through their companies' establishment, development and growth stages. As Sequoia puts it: 'We help the daring build legendary companies, from idea to IPO and beyond.'

Since its founding, Sequoia has invested in more than 250 start-ups, including Apple, Google, Oracle, YouTube, Instagram, Yahoo!, Airbnb, PayPal, Stripe, Dropbox, FireEye, Palo Alto Networks, Square and WhatsApp. In 2017, the combined stock market value of these companies came to about $1,5 trillion, equivalent to 22 per cent of Nasdaq.

By 2020, there were seven technology companies that were ranked among the ten most valuable publicly traded companies on the planet: five from the US, namely Microsoft, Apple, Amazon, Alphabet (with Google) and Facebook, and two from China – Alibaba and Tencent. In August 2018, Apple made history by becoming the world's first publicly traded company to reach a market capitalisation of $1 trillion.

Botha gradually became one of Sequoia's stalwarts, and in February 2017 he was promoted to the position of one of three stewards that make up the leadership triumvirate of the global partnership. The other two stewards are Doug Leone and Neil Shen. Botha explains that the stewards occupy a special position in the firm's complex but fluid and adaptable structure – they are, as it were, the first among equals on Sequoia's managing board.

'There is no sense in us being islands that only share a name, because then there would be no need for us to have the same name or the same emblem. So, we've created this central thing we call a board, and the board has representatives of each of the businesses that meet every few months. Their mandate is to look at what is in the best interest of everyone, as a whole, therefore only to provide the central management oversight.

'On this board there are three people who are stewards. They have more reponsibilities for our firm globally: there is a senior steward, Doug Leone, who has been with Sequoia for 30 years; Neil Shen, who runs our China business; and then me, who has assumed more responsibility for our US operations.

'We're a partnership, so in a daily investment decision in our venture capital business, I'm only one of six partners. Since I have a leadership responsibility in that business, I take more on my shoulders in terms of: do we have the right team, can we persuade other people to join our team, are there certain others I think should leave the team because they're simply not doing well enough?

'But when we take a decision about an investment, I'm one of six votes for that investment decision. It's a very strange concept, you know. My power is soft. It's sort of having to manage through influence, not power – if that makes sense,' Botha says.

The influence he is able to exert is also in keeping with his passion to act as a mentor for young people. When he sees young people with talent, he says, he is willing to give them a chance because he tries to give back by doing for others what he experienced in his own life: that people gave him opportunities and took a chance on him. In addition, he stresses that empathy, the ability to put yourself in someone else's shoes, is an 'underappreciated skill'.

In 2018, the trio of stewards all featured on the Midas List, *Forbes*'s list of the world's top venture capital investors. The then 44-year-old Botha was at number 14. His most notable transaction was listed as Square, a payment service with more than two million small businesses in the US as clients, but he himself rates the earlier one with YouTube as his most successful.

The two other stewards, Shen and Leone, were above him on the list. Shen was in the top spot after having led the US IPO of the Chinese internet conglomerate Alibaba, and Leone was ninth on the list. All three are dollar billionaires, since according to *Forbes* there were twenty such super-rich individuals on the Midas List.

Over time, the top management of Sequoia decided their firm should be a truly global business, not just an American firm with a Silicon Valley focus. 'Before most other people did it, we opened offices in India and China, and in Israel, and we also set up a few other businesses in the United States. And then, as we expanded, we decided the best way to recruit very good people was to empower them by giving them the freedom to make decisions. That's the only way to get excellent people to work for us in China or India. They have their own decision-making process and can recruit their own personnel,' Botha explains.

The way in which Sequoia works is to start by launching a venture capital fund. The money comes largely from what they call limited partners. The general partners are the people who run the fund and make investments out of it, while the limited partners are the investors. The majority of these investors are foundations, endowments (especially from private universities) and nonprofits.

'Organisations such as the Wellcome Trust [a research charity], or the Howard Hughes Medical Foundation, invest in us and use the gains to fund basic medical research. Or we have an investor like a foundation that, say, helps to distribute malaria nets, or that invests in equality and justice, and that type of thing. The Ford Foundation is one of our long-standing investors, and they invest massively in the developing world to help advance human rights and so on.

'So, we are capitalists, but what we *can* do is to decide who invests in us. We want the returns we produce to go towards what we consider great and good causes, and we are not motivated to work in order to make a bunch of rich people even richer. If you tell me that from tomorrow I have to work at Sequoia to invest some or other Russian oligarch's money so that he can grow even richer, I would resign, because the people who are here are not interested in doing that type of thing. We really care about our returns going towards these wonderful goals,' Botha says.

Sequoia gets a percentage of the profits. When a fund of, for example, $400 million grows to $2 billion, Sequoia gets a percentage of the $1,6-billion profits. At the same time, the firm's partners can also invest, say, $40 million of their own capital alongside the limited partners, who are the primary investors.

'My compensation comes from those profits, and part of my compensation comes from investing my own capital in these companies. When the company is sold or goes public, and we then own a certain quantum of shares thanks to our previous investments, we have an opportunity to either get cash or receive shares in the company,' Botha explains. Examples of this are Google, which acquired YouTube for $1,65 billion, and WhatsApp, which was sold to Facebook for the enormous sum of $19 billion in the largest ever deal of its kind.

Besides his responsibilities in Sequoia Capital, Botha sits on several boards as part of the firm's business-building support they provide to the companies they partner with, including those of Jawbone, Eventbrite, Evernote, Mahalo, Square, Tokbox, Tumblr, Weebly, Unity, Whisper and Xoom.

Sequoia did not invest in any of Musk's projects. Botha readily admits that this was a mistake. 'I mean, SpaceX is now worth $15 billion. Tesla is now a listed company, so it's too late for us. We don't get all the investments right; it's part of what keeps one humble in this business. We make mistakes.'

Another success story they missed out on was Twitter. Since this was an oversight for which Botha accepts personal responsibility, he has often reflected on that misstep.

In the spartan head office of Sequoia's US operations in Menlo Park where he works on a daily basis, there are four lines of business.

Firstly, there is the venture capital business that invests seed-stage or early-stage venture capital in start-ups. Sometimes two or three people would serve in this team, sometimes ten. When Sequoia invested in YouTube, Botha was one of the six partners, who included the three founders of the company. He helped them build the business.

Part of Sequoia's strategy, and in Botha's view the reason why they do so well, is their investments in companies in which they also become directors. They work alongside the entrepreneurs as their business-building partner, using their experience to help guide the companies they partner with to become much larger businesses. In this regard, he likes to use a quote from the business world: a good board member acts as a shock absorber, not an amplifier. As a result of Sequoia's success, they receive numerous requests daily from people who try to persuade them to look at their companies, probably up to 10 000 companies a year. Of these, about 1 000 are given a half-hour hearing to pitch their ideas, of which they would typically fund about 15 to 20.

Secondly, Sequoia has growth capital in a growth fund with a capital outlay of $4 to $5 billion, and here, too, Botha is one of the six partners. Besides these, there are two other businesses in the US. One is a hedge fund that invests in public utilities and listed companies. It falls under a separate team in which Botha does not serve. Lastly, there is a heritage fund that chiefly manages the capital of the Sequoia partners, but also the capital of some of the founders of their portfolio companies. Botha is an investor in that team, but not a partner. This fund manages about $3 to $3,5 billion globally in one account.

Sequoia was drawn into a gender-diversity controversy in 2015 when Moritz, in response to a question about the firm's lack of female partners, replied by saying that they had looked very hard for women to hire, but were not prepared 'to lower our standards'. He was heavily criticised for having implied that there were no bright and competent women who wanted to work in technology. Moritz subsequently issued a statement that read: 'I know there are many remarkable women who would flourish in the venture business. We're working hard to find them and would be ecstatic if more joined Sequoia or other firms.' In October 2016, Sequoia hired the CEO of Polyvore, Jess Lee, as investing partner, and she became the first female investing partner in the group's 44-year history.

Botha refers to Lee and another newcomer who has joined Sequoia, Mike Vernal – previously one of the top executives at Mark Zuckerberg's Facebook – as examples of the firm's modus operandi and approach. 'We won't persuade people like that to join us as partners if they feel I'm their boss, and I don't want to be their boss. I think they're excelllent, and I have to give them as much autonomy as possible to do interesting work. My responsibility is to help them be successful, to advise them, to teach them the business as a mentor, but *not* to be their boss.'

Future thinking plays a key role in the firm, all the more because of the accelerating rate of change Alvin Toffler described decades ago in his book *Future Shock*. Because of it, Botha says, the world is going to look very different, partly as a result of the exponential curve technology is experiencing as well as its growth. 'Our brains aren't developed to grow exponentially. It's not intuitive for us.' Botha mentions as an example that we find it hard to believe that in ten years' time a $1 000 computer will have the same brain power as one human brain, and that in thirty years' time such a computer will have the same brain power as all the people in the world combined.

'These types of things are hard for us to accept. If I told you ten years ago self-driving cars would drive around Silicon Valley for hundreds of miles, you wouldn't have believed me. I wouldn't have believed it. But it's just a small glimpse into the pace of change we'll be seeing.'

Because software is infiltrating so many parts of the world, computer science is becoming a foundational subject in the same manner that maths was decades ago. Botha points out that when he joined PayPal, there were some 250 million people in the world with an internet connection. Thirteen years later, that number had increased tenfold to more than a third of humanity. Smartphones have become personal computers, and 'there is an abundance of consumer service innovation taking place because of the accumulation of technology and the ubiquity of computing devices in consumers' hands'.

What scares him the most does not necessarily have anything to do with Sequoia's business; it is rather what humanity is doing to the Earth and to nature. If you look at history and our changing climate, he says, it can sometimes change very suddenly, such as in the case of meteorites and their impact on Earth in the course of history. 'The pace at which we're changing our world with its seven billion people, that's what scares me the most. Some people are worried about things like artificial intelligence, but I don't think Silicon Valley and its innovations are a threat to our lives. It's nature that will be a threat to us.'

In 2012, Stellenbosch University awarded Botha an honorary DComm degree for 'his inspiring and pioneering leadership in the development of a safe and convenient payment system for the Internet, as well as for his imaginative and visionary entrepreneurial spirit in recognising, and developing through venture capital, the potential of new companies'.

Botha's wife, Huifen Chan, whom he met at Stanford, comes from Singapore. Since she speaks Chinese and her second language, like his, is English, it is hard to teach their children Afrikaans. The two of them, Saskia and Bosman, do know a couple of words, with 'stoutgat' (a naughty child) being one they know really well, he says with a laugh. His son is crazy about rugby – like his father, who watches rugby every weekend.

Botha's nostalgia is shared by many other South African expats who are part of the brain drain that has intensified under successive ANC governments since the Mandela administration. He still has very strong ties to South Africa, which he visits fairly regularly. But under the circumstances he has no intention of returning to the country of his birth.

13

The world is your oyster

Hendrik du Toit

THE PROMINENT asset manager Hendrik du Toit, founder of Investec Asset Management, plies his trade on the opposite side of the Atlantic Ocean from Roelof Botha. He spends most of his time in London, where he lives, and in planes, crisscrossing the globe. In 2012 the British *Financial News* named him Chief Executive of the Year at the paper's prestigious annual Awards for Excellence in European Institutional Asset Management.

Du Toit distinguished himself as an asset manager of note after joining Investec in 1991. At the time he founded Investec Asset Management as a start-up, he managed assets of only R200 million. By 2019, the company managed about R2,1 trillion in assets globally.

Du Toit regards his mother, Hermien, as the person who had the biggest influence on his life. His father, Thys, a parliamentary official, died when he was 14 years old. He was the couple's only child. 'My mother had to raise me on her own for the last bit. Right was right and wrong was wrong. She taught me to compete with myself rather than with others. She taught me one should always do one's best. "Good enough" was never good enough for her. She encouraged me to be ambitious, but to always maintain a balance. My parents taught

261

me never to look down on people and to treat everyone with dignity, regardless of social status.'

These were guidelines that would stay with him throughout his career.

They lived in central Cape Town close to Hoërskool Jan van Riebeeck, where he matriculated. As a schoolboy, he would regularly read the share prices in the paper for an elderly family friend whose eyesight was not very good. This gentleman was the father of the winemaker Graham Beck, and Du Toit considers him one of the most successful businesspeople of his day. Consequently, his interest in the share market was already kindled in his teenage years.

After obtaining an MCom in economics with distinction at Stellenbosch University, he departed for Cambridge University where he earned an MPhil in economics and politics of development.

Du Toit's first job was as an analyst at Old Mutual in Cape Town. In 1990, the year in which the ANC and other prohibited organisations were unbanned and Nelson Mandela was released, Du Toit became increasingly disillusioned with what he regarded as Old Mutual's inability to adapt to the new political realities. The last straw was a statement Old Mutual released in November 1990 about the political situation in South Africa. In Du Toit's view, it showed how out of touch the industry was with the situation on the ground.

By that time, Du Toit had already crossed paths with Investec. A schoolfriend who worked there told him Investec was an interesting place to work at. And in an interview in his capacity as analyst with Investec's CEO Stephen Koseff and Bernard Kantor, a director, Du Toit asked them such piercing questions that they considered hiring him.

Investec was started by Larry Nestadt, Errol Grolman and Ian Kantor in Johannesburg in 1974 as a small finance company. It expanded through growth and acquisitions. They secured a banking licence in 1980, and in 1986 the group listed on the Johannesburg Stock Exchange after a merger with Metboard, a trust company. In 1990, Investec bought the property management company I Kuper & Company, Corporate Merchant Bank, and the trade finance company Reichmans.

Bernard Kantor approached Du Toit a few times with a job offer to start up Investec's asset management company after they had launched a limited range of unit trust products subsequent to the acquisition of Metboard. Du Toit, however, did not show much interest. Kantor would even waylay him on the beach in the evenings when he emerged from the sea with his surfboard at Fishhoek or Muizenberg. This lasted for almost a year.

The day after the Old Mutual statement that upset Du Toit so much, Kantor phoned him again and spoke bluntly: 'I've now taken you to lunch twelve times. It's time for you to make a decision.' Finally Du Toit agreed, though he did not relish the prospect of moving to Johannesburg. In hindsight, he believes that for him, who did not come from a commercial family, it was the ideal leap to escape from the very structured corporate environment.

When Du Toit resigned at Old Mutual, he thought he was joining a big firm. But Investec managed less than R200 million in assets. In Johannesburg, there was no one from human resources to welcome him. He was shown to an empty desk without a computer. 'But that was life at Investec, and it was fantastic. It was a "can-do" place built from scratch by people who were given opportunities, and I think that philosophy is so important.'

According to Du Toit, the corporate team at the time did not understand that asset management differed from corporate financing and trade activities. He had to explain what managing other people's money involved. Moreover, 'the toughest thing in any business is getting through the first five years. That's when you have to bed things down.' In these 'chaotic times', they nonetheless 'had this idea that there was space for another competitor, even though it was an industry dominated by the big incumbents', particularly insurance companies and the recently founded Allan Gray. 'We believed we could do things differently and maybe even better.'

Du Toit reckons that what set them apart in the beginning was their mindset. In the early 1990s, there was a general air of despondency in South Africa. The managers saw only doom and gloom and clung to bonds; they did not want to touch any shares other than those of the big companies. Du Toit advocated a different strategy: shares of medium-sized companies with an eye on the next decade and multiple expansions. In that way, he believed, they could establish a performance track record and serve clients wherever they were located.

'What drove us is that we believed in risk. We had a risk-driven set of products while many others avoided risk. If you panicked every time emerging markets caught a slight cold, you would've lost a lot of money, whereas if you invested over the longer term and embraced risk, you would've done well,' Du Toit explained

There was also the need for independence, which provided a reason for setting up the business in Cape Town. Du Toit thought about the fact that Sir John Templeton, the American-born British fund manager who has been described as 'arguably the greatest global stock picker of the [20th] century', managed his billions from the Bahamas. 'I asked myself, if Templeton could run money from an island, why can't we run it from Cape Town? It has a better airport, it's a nicer place and the coffee is better, so why not build the business from here and eventually internationalise.'

After struggling initially until 1993, the business grew rapidly, thanks to the loyal client base they had built up in South Africa. In the late 1990s, it was decided to expand Investec Asset Management to the United Kingdom when a small asset manager was acquired.

From 1998 to 2004, Du Toit worked one week in Cape Town and one week in London, flying home to his family on weekends. By 2005, when his children were older, the family relocated to the UK. Du Toit says his wife, Lorette, a former financial journalist, was incredibly tolerant in putting up with him, and she kept the family together. 'When I was young I used to work 24/7, but now weekends became family time. My children understood that I had to work very hard, but my daughter Inge's school concert and my son Matthys's rugby match took priority over the most important board meeting.'

Lorette was the first journalist who wrote about Jannie Mouton when he started PSG. She convinced Hendrik to invest in PSG because she told him about her interesting conversations with Mouton and how motivated he was. 'When the share price had increased five-fold, I decided that was enough and sold the shares without phoning Jannie. Every time I see Jannie, I tell him it was the biggest mistake I ever made.'

He regards London, and particularly the City, the financial hub with its many international head offices, as a 'fantastic melting pot'.

According to Du Toit, the access he has there to people not only in his own field but also to others who are the best in their respective fields is an incredible privilege. The international expansion enlarged Investec Asset Management's playing field.

Yet a larger and more varied market requires that 'you have to be much clearer about who you are, and you need to select your niches very well'.

It sharpened up their business: 'You're not one out of five or ten choices, but one out of a 100 or 300. You have to differentiate yourself from the rest of the pack.' They worked hard, thought carefully about the products they wanted to offer, and gradually put down deep roots. In his view, this has turned Investec into a global player that can compete anywhere in the world.

Kantor had high praise for the way in which Du Toit had built Investec Asset Management from a start-up into a business that by 2016 managed £75 billion. 'We've never told Hendrik what to do. Again, the culture kicks in,' Kantor said. 'Give him the parameters. Hendrik, go and build your business. To this day, Hendrik runs the business as he sees fit. We meet with him in board meetings, or if he has an issue, he'll come and talk to us. After so long with these individuals, it's like going to war with the same generals. Why would I second-guess them?'

In 1992, Investec also entered the UK banking market by acquiring Allied Trust Bank in London, its first international acquisition. Further acquisitions in London were those of the merchant banks Guinness Mahon and Hambros in 1998. In the same year, President Nelson Mandela opened the new Investec building in Johannesburg. He stated in his speech: 'Here is a company which stands head and shoulders above its peers – not merely because of its phenomenal growth or its sound management of assets, but because it is a trendsetter.'

The group has a South African head office in Sandton as well as an international head office in London. In 2002, Investec listed on the London Stock Exchange as well. In a BEE transaction in 2003, empowerment partners acquired a 25,1 per cent stake in the South African-listed branch. Further international acquisitions followed, including the full acquisition of Rensburg Sheppards, which was re-branded as Investec Wealth & Investment. The Irish brokerage firm

NCB was acquired in 2012, with the result that Investec employs 240 specialists in Ireland.

After Du Toit settled in London, Investec Bank in South Africa was implicated in the Brett Kebble scandal. This arose from a non-performing loan the bank granted in 2005 to JCI and Western Areas, which along with Randgold were under Kebble's control. Kebble's business empire had crumbled after he illegally spent and stole millions of rands, in order to, among other things, line the pockets of ANC politicians. He was shot dead in 2005 in what turned out to be a contract killing.

Investec Bank's loan, which had been advanced with the consent of JCI's major shareholder, Allan Gray, to prevent the liquidation of the Kebble businesses, enabled JCI, Randgold and Western Areas to stay afloat. Various settlements were also concluded with different parties.

Several damaging allegations made against Investec, including that the bank had colluded with Kebble's crooked dealings, were refuted by the bank in a detailed statement. In 2011, minority shareholders instituted a claim of R1,3 billion against the bank for what they deemed oppression of their minority rights when a settlement amount for their shares was agreed upon. Investec opposed the application with the defence that in terms of applicable legislation, the shareholders were not 'members' of the company and therefore had no legal standing to bring the case. The case dragged on for years in the courts. In 2017, the Supreme Court of Appeal dismissed the appeal of seven shareholders, but allowed other registered shareholders to join the case. A trial about the merits of their case was expected to be heard by 2020.

Investec also burnt its fingers as a result of the Steinhoff fraud. In May 2018, the company announced that losses incurred in respect of exposures to Steinhoff Africa's subsidiaries amounted to R220 million in that financial year. Investec stated that its exposure to Steinhoff International had been negligible. Its loss amounted to less than 3 per cent of its after-tax operating profit.

The group stated that its performance had been satisfactory against the backdrop of challenging economic conditions in the UK and South Africa. The annual results were presented by Stephen Koseff, who stepped down as CEO in October 2018 and who was replaced by Du Toit and Fani Titi as joint chief executives of the Investec Group. As CEO of Investec Asset Management, Du Toit received a paycheque of £6,088 million (R109,9 million), which included a bonus of £5,637 million.

Open-mindedness and looking beyond the numbers

In this period the Investec Group embarked on the unbundling and separate listing of its asset management group.

Du Toit had anticipated that Investec Asset Management, the group's most profitable subsidiary, would eventually change its name. This occurred in March 2020, when the company was listed as Ninety One in the midst of the global financial crisis caused by the Covid-19 pandemic. The new name was a nod to their heritage in that it referred to the company's founding year, but the company also regarded 1991 as the year that saw the beginning of the end of apartheid (though by that time a great many apartheid measures had already been scrapped).

'We believe a brand is much more than a name. We will be sad about the loss of the zebra [the group's emblem], which we helped to build. But the core proposition it stands for, the freshness, the willingness to serve and the focus on the client, that will always be with us,' Du Toit stated as Ninety One's chief executive.

By that stage, Investec had grown into a global bank and asset management group that managed more than £166 billion in client assets. The group employs more than 10 000 people and provides a diverse range of financial products and services to a niche client base in three principal markets – the UK, South Africa and Australia, as well as certain other countries.

Ninety One's operations are spread across more regions globally, with investment offices in London, Cape Town, Singapore, Hong Kong and New York and further operational and client-service offices in, inter alia, Namibia, Botswana and Italy.

The Investec Group is organised as a network made up of different entities: the asset management subsidiary (Ninety One), the specialist bank (Investec Investment Banking Private Banking and Corporate and Institutional Banking), Property, and Wealth & Investment.

In response to a question about how to achieve success in his business, Du Toit summed up his recipe as follows: 'People, organisational culture and values are the key to everything. This is especially important in enterprises that rely more on human than financial capital. Clients like working with happy people and organisations they have confidence in. As head of an investment company that invests our clients' capital in other businesses, I've learnt to look beyond the numbers.

'Businesses with strong, sound value systems and a culture that is accepted and respected by employees across the organisation usually have good leadership at all levels. Such businesses are well equipped to maintain the right balance between risk management and dynamism.'

He elaborated on what he considered the key requirements for constructive business leadership in today's world: 'Afrikaans has the expression '*oopkop*' (open-minded). Successful business leaders are *oopkop*! They are alert, take an interest, and always look ahead. They inspire, but they listen as well. They learn continuously.'

He considers it a privilege to serve on the board of Naspers, where he was appointed the lead director in 2020. 'It's not only South Africa's biggest company in terms of market capitalisation; it's also a business that innovates and changes on a daily basis. Koos Bekker never stops learning, and the executive team under Bob van Dijk implements strategy at the speed of white light.'

Besides being receptive to new ideas, business leaders should also develop and nurture their own ideas – original thinking, along with the capacity to implement, to inspire. 'But that's not enough. Today, in the world of social media, business leaders should also have a grasp of the broad issues of the day and be able to read the tea leaves. After all, we do business with the "approval" of society. Business leadership involves much more than the pursuit of profit because today big businesses are also social institutions, whether they like it or not. The era of stakeholder capitalism has replaced the era of shareholder sovereignty.'

In his view, one should not overestimate the role businesspeople can play to influence politics and society at large. 'Businesspeople aren't your most profound thinkers. They're focused on making a living every day. They may be building a company, but there's not always a lot of vision involved. They're not necessarily equipped to command the kind of respect and provide the kind of leadership communities expect of them. So, don't expect too much of businesspeople. But the business sector does have a responsibility to make a success of the country. We have a responsibility to participate, as in Dr Anton Rupert's concept of co-partnership: "I can't sleep peacefully if my neighbour is hungry."'

According to Du Toit, political considerations, both national and international, play an increasingly significant part in decision-making. Such issues will gain in importance 'now that capitalism as we know it is even being questioned in the United States by young people. No business will be sustainably successful without a "social licence to operate". Hence business leaders need to exert themselves to understand the political context within which they do business. At the same time, however, they should keep their eye on the proverbial ball and not become distracted by the political "noise" that dominates the media on a daily basis.'

Furthermore, he says, humanity is currently experiencing a period of unparalleled technological and societal change. Our world is being radically transformed as a result of the combination of factors such as urbanisation, connectivity (3,5 billion smartphones for seven billion people), developments in artificial intelligence, the imperative of sustainability in the context of harmful climate change and environmental destruction, and unprecedented technological and scientific advances.

'The nature of work and our way of life are changing rapidly. Though these changes hold the promise of massive business opportunities, they can also create much anxiety among communities. The price of the progress is the loss of many of the old certainties. Unless we help those who are left behind to stay on board, the "progress" will lead to great instability. Business leaders need to know that they don't operate in a vacuum.'

Du Toit served on the Business and Sustainable Development Commission, a United Nations initiative, as part of a select group of international business, labour and civil society leaders. It was established to draw the attention of business enterprises in particular to the global efforts required for achieving the Sustainable Development Goals (SDGs), but also to highlight the massive opportunities for businesses in the coming transition to a cleaner, better economy. The commission has since been dissolved, but it stimulated various new initiatives.

Having grown up in Africa, he says, he has seen how climate change affects communities: depletion of fish stocks, deforestation, pollution of rivers. 'We know that we – seven billion people – have a disproportionate impact on the Earth. We also know we can't turn the whole world into a game reserve or a museum. We need to reconcile socioeconomic development and job creation with the protection of natural resources. If we don't do that, we'll be in trouble.'

Accordingly, he strongly believes there should be a non-executive director on the board of every public company to oversee the drive for sustainability and hold management to account on its sustainability agenda. Such a director should be an expert in the field of ESG – the environmental, social and governance criteria that together establish a long-term framework that has increasingly gained recognition globally to ensure a future for posterity.

As a businessman who believes in the free market, Du Toit is still optimistic about capitalism's capacity for self-correction. He reckons people are too inclined to drive themselves into a depression because 0,1 per cent of humanity has amassed so much wealth. These are the businesspeople who arrive at Davos in jets, he says, 'not the guys like us who come by train'. 'They own everything. What's wrong with that, by the way? They've provided something which was bought by people around the world, which benefited consumers, and most of them give that money away when they die and invest in good causes.'

At Investec, it took them years to properly define the purpose that drives their business. Du Toit says with conviction: 'We want to build a better firm, we want to invest better, and by doing that, contribute to a better world – very simple.'

Asked what advice he would give the South African government on achieving sustainable economic growth and turning the country into something like the Singapore of Africa, he replied: 'Let's kill corruption. That's the easy part. By simply stopping the looting we can raise GDP growth by a few percentage points. But that's not enough. The answer lies in education and training. Put discipline back in schools. It starts with the teachers' unions. Confront them and put them in their place.

'Then, strive for excellence. Make that South Africa's national project. The people in South Africa are paying a high price because they don't know how ruthlessly competitive the world is today. Asia waits for no one. Unless Africa wakes up fast, it will only be left further and further behind. It's time for our national leaders to start being straight with the people.'

Du Toit 'devours' biographies and has been motivated through the years by 'stories of incredibly remarkable people'. Alan Paton's *Cry, the Beloved Country* touched him deeply, as did *The Diary of a Young Girl* by Anne Frank and Nelson Mandela's *Long Walk to Freedom*. William Shakespeare's *Macbeth* taught him that conspiracies and intrigue are not a good formula for life.

Still, he says, even though he reads voraciously, the Investec co-founder Ian Kantor always said knowledge is to be found on the streets, not in books. He therefore gets his best perspectives and ideas from his travels and conversations with 'people in the know'.

'I've also been extremely privileged to have learnt much from a variety of people and leaders in our community thanks to my direct interaction with them. It started with amazingly dedicated teachers at Jan van Riebeeck, people such as Professor Sampie Terreblanche at Stellenbosch, Dominee Kobus van der Westhuyzen [Dutch Reformed minister of the Groote Kerk in Cape Town], Dr Zach de Beer and many others who made time to help shape my outlook on life. Later on, people such as Vusi Khanyile, Popo Molefe, Frank Chikane and others taught me how powerful the combination of the right idea and the willingness to sacrifice can be.'

His advice to young people of South Africa? 'Our country faces enormous challenges, but for every challenge there is also an opportunity. For those who strive after excellence and don't try to sponge on a system, the world of today offers incredible opportunities. Get yourself into a position where you can use the chances. Gain knowledge and expertise, and work as hard as you can. The world doesn't owe you anything and the competition is merciless, but the opportunities exist. That's the way one can contribute towards a better South Africa.'

14

Master of the universe

Markus Jooste

ONE OF Anton Rupert's best-known sayings was that money can sometimes be a dangerous thing. Money is also like a rope. You can throw the rope to someone as a lifeline, or you can use it as a gallows rope.

Undoubtedly the super-rich are always subject to the temptation of flying too high. Some may succumb to the delusion of invincibility and fancy themselves a master of the universe. Perhaps that is what happened when Markus Jooste gave himself too much rope.

In his satirical novel *The Bonfire of the Vanities*, the American writer Tom Wolfe coined the term 'master of the universe' to describe Wall Street's money-grubbing hotshots of the 1980s. It applied to a bunch of bond traders on the New York Stock Exchange, people who shift dollars and shares around and are often criticised because they mostly create nothing substantial of their own and, with their opulent but essentially meaningless lifestyles, contribute little to society.

Among present-day Afrikaner businesspeople, Markus Jooste is the prime example of how the seduction of wealth may cause high flyers to believe they can do whatever they want to and get away with it. Jooste was the mastermind behind the complex conglomerate Steinhoff International, the global holding company with investments in diverse retailers, whose convoluted structure was conceived and run from South Africa before it collapsed in what has become the country's biggest corporate scandal.

Jooste was the only high-profile businessman who declined to respond to questions for the purposes of this book. In the past, his activities attracted widespread attention and he granted several interviews to the media. But a few months before the Steinhoff scandal erupted, he started retiring into his shell. In response to a request for a personal interview, he replied on 5 April 2017 by email: 'Thank you very much for having thought of me for your book. However, I try to maintain a very private life for the sake of my children and do not participate in any media/press or private profile articles/books.'

This was eight months before the sensational collapse of Steinhoff's shares in December 2017. At the beginning of that year, Jooste's reputation as money-maker was still at its zenith, but he was probably already prepared for what might go wrong. In hindsight, there could be little doubt that Jooste's reluctance to talk about himself and Steinhoff was wholly due to the fact that he already knew by then how hollow the Steinhoff shell was.

He had come a long way from his schooldays in Pretoria, the little Markus Jooste who was a runner between bookmakers during horse races. In his heyday, he was the country's biggest owner of racehorses – champions that won prestigious races with the highest prize money. He was the chief executive of a global furniture retailer that aspired to dethrone Europe's famous Ikea from its top spot. He flew to and fro between South Africa and foreign destinations to attend board meetings and high-level management conferences – and to meet his own victorious horse and its jockey, beaming before the eyes of international VIPs, at various race courses.

His parents were not well off. His father, a Post Office employee who 'liked a flutter on the ponies', worked in Bosman Street in Pretoria next to a Tattersalls betting shop. Markus's interest in horse racing was already whetted as a schoolboy when he would accompany his father to Tattersalls on race days where they listened to commentary on races via radio. As a twelve-year-old, he 'ran between bookmakers with tickets laying off their bets with each other'. It was not the betting as such that attracted him – he would later proclaim that he never bet on horses himself. His dream was rather to emulate the racehorse owners he looked up to, people like Harry Oppenheimer and Laurie Jaffie.

Markus, who was born in 1961, matriculated at the Afrikaanse Hoër Seunskool in Pretoria. His father, who couldn't afford many other things, devoted much time to helping him with his homework and instilled in him a drive to become successful.

After matric, Markus went to study accounting at Stellenbosch University with a scholarship and stayed in Wilgenhof, a residence mockingly nicknamed 'Bekfluitjie' (mouth organ) by others on the campus on account of its architectural style. After returning to Stellenbosch as a businessman years later, he donated a black Jaguar with the personalised number plate Willows-WP to the residence. He thereby followed the example of one of Wilgenhof's best-known housemasters, the rugby legend Dr Danie Craven, who had left his old green Jaguar to Wilgenhof.

Johann van Rooyen, the son of the Pep founder Renier van Rooyen, became a Wilgenhof resident in the same year as Jooste. He says Jooste had his own clique, mostly consisting of fellow students from Pretoria, and remembers him as 'the sort of person who aspired to be popular and part of the in-crowd'. Jooste did not care much for extra-curricular activities, but apparently relished initiating first-year students or 'punishing' passing students who had tauntingly shouted 'Bekfluitjie!' with a customary cold shower. Another former Wilgenhof resident, Thys du Toit, recounts that they used to call Jooste 'a *sluiper* [an unobtrusive person], and then he became the big shot after that and he duped all of us, including me'. Also among Jooste's contemporaries at Wilgenhof was Rian du Plessis, a long-time friend who would later become CEO of the racing group Phumelela.

According to Jooste, he left university with a student loan debt of about R100 000. He started working as an articled clerk at the law firm Greenwoods in Cape Town, and in the evenings he studied for his honours degree in accounting through the University of Cape Town. He shared a house with two friends who would later become colleagues at Steinhoff: Frikkie Nel and Jan (Krommetjie) van der Merwe.

On the first day of his articles at Greenwoods, Jooste was part of an audit team assigned to Christo Wiese's company Ochta Diamonds.

The offices of both Ochta and Greenwoods were in the old Trust Bank building in Adderley Street, but at that stage Wiese had not yet taken control of Pepkor. Nonetheless, according to Rob Rose in his book *Steinheist*, Wiese made an instant impression on Jooste: 'Christo … built things, put deals together. I thought, I wanted to be like him.'

Wiese, for his part, remembers noticing Jooste 'as a bright young guy'. He had also been told that Jooste got the highest mark in the country in his board exam. Then Wiese moved to Pepkor's head office in Parow's industrial area when he bought control of the group. He lost touch with Jooste and did not meet him again for years.

The tax expert and furniture manufacturer

Jooste, who firmly believed that you couldn't get rich by earning a salary, finished his articles and resigned from the auditing firm at the age of 24. In 1985, however, he and his former housemate Van der Merwe were conscripted for their mandatory national service in the Defence Force. Owing to his accounting qualifications, Jooste was appointed as a deputy director at the Receiver of Revenue during his army years.

He specialised in tax, and the expert knowledge he gained during this period he would later harness with great skill. His knowledge of tax legislation was considered one of his key strengths; he made sure that Steinhoff paid the least possible tax. In the five years up to 2015, for instance, Steinhoff's average effective tax rate was 11,2 per cent – compared with South Africa's corporate tax rate of 28 per cent.

After completing his national service, Jooste started working as an accountant for a businessman named Michael Delport. Delport ran various companies from Ga-Rankuwa, an area outside Brits that had been declared part of the so-called independent homeland of Bophuthatswana. At the time, companies that set up their businesses in homelands such as Bophuthatswana were given generous tax breaks.

Delport and Jooste had just sold their business to the canning company Gants when they saw a sign across the street from their canning factory in Ga-Rankuwa saying that a building would be auctioned off. They attended the auction and bought the building, in which the furniture company Gomma Gomma was a tenant. When the owner,

Rafie Steel, experienced cash-flow problems a few months later, they recapitalised Gomma Gomma and took control of the company. This was the start of Jooste's entry into the furniture business.

He soon roped in his former Cape Town housemates, Nel and Van der Merwe, to help him run the new enterprise. Nel was the financial director and Van der Merwe was 'busy in the factory planning and loading trucks and doing the buying', while Markus ran the company and handled the sales. For the most part, the furniture Gomma Gomma manufactured consisted of upholstered lounge suites, of which they would produce as many as 150 on some days, as well as a range of coffee tables.

They worked hard; Markus harder than anyone and regularly putting in more than sixteen hours a day. He'd often still be at the factory till 1 am, drinking brandy and whisky with his staff. He could get by with little sleep and would be back in the office early in the morning, none the worse for wear. A business acquaintance who was once on the same flight to London as Markus related that he worked the entire time, going through documents and balance sheets and making notes. Asked after the flight whether he had slept, Markus replied: ' I took an hour or so.'

For Terence Craig, an analyst from Allan Gray who visited the factory in Ga-Rankuwa, there was an incident that stood out. The visit took place just after the transition of 1994, and Craig inquired whether Gomma Gomma would still be profitable if the apartheid-era tax breaks were to fall away now that the Mandela government had taken over. 'Markus's answer stuck with me until today,' he says. '"No, we wouldn't be profitable in that case," he said, "but we'll always find a tax break somewhere."'

More than twenty years later, Craig said he had thought about Jooste's answer plenty of times since the relevations of the Steinhoff chicanery first emerged.

Jooste's expertise with regard to tax issues became legendary in the business world. Among other things, he testified in tax cases before a judge who is a tax expert. The judge, Dennis Davis, once told the former DA leader Tony Leon that Jooste was the most intelligent witness that had ever appeared in front of him.

A leap ahead opened up for Jooste when Claas Daun acquired

an interest in Gomma Gomma in 1995. Daun, a German tax lawyer who specialised in turning around ailing companies, had recognised new investment opportunities in South Africa under the ANC government. He was introduced to Jooste by Jannie Mouton, who in his Johannesburg days was constantly on the lookout for opportunities.

In 1993, Daun & Co. had already bought a controlling interest in the struggling furniture company Victoria Lewis. One of the first acquisitions after Daun acquired an interest in Gomma Gomma was Bakker & Steyger, a Cape Town company that specialised in upper-end household furniture.

Daun was a good friend of Bruno Steinhoff, who had by that time already built up a big furniture company in Germany. Daun, who lived 40 kilometres from Steinhoff, recounted that 'if it wasn't for our friendship, Bruno would never have come to South Africa'. He introduced Steinhoff to Jooste, and these two also became good friends and business partners. Both Daun and Steinhoff later served on the board of Steinhoff International.

From his head office in the German city of Westerstede, Steinhoff built up an international furniture network and became so successful that in Europe he was only overshadowed by Ikea. In 1966, Steinhoff had registered Bruno Steinhoff Möbelvertretungen und -Vertrieb, the company that would later become Steinhoff Europe. Soon after, he built a new factory and head office in Westerstede, and later a giant warehouse that used a fully automated system to control the furniture receiving, packing, storing, retrieving and dispatching processes.

The company gained a reputation for providing high-quality, low-cost furniture. By 1993, Steinhoff was employing 3 000 people, and the company operated in several countries in Eastern and Western Europe.

In 1997, Bruno Steinhoff acquired a 35 per cent stake in Gomma Gomma thanks to his friendship with Daun. In the same year, Jooste and Daun made an unsuccessful bid to purchase Afcol, a large furniture manufacturer under the wing of South African Breweries, which wanted to unbundle some of its interests. The winning bid came from Pat Cornick, with an offer of R17,50 against Jooste and Daun's R17,25 a share.

Jooste and Daun, however, were still intent on expanding by, among other things, consolidating their interests. In 1998, with a view to listing on the JSE, Gomma Gomma merged with Bakker & Steyger and Victoria Lewis. The new company, Steinhoff Africa, and Steinhoff Europe consolidated their operations, and Steinhoff International listed on the JSE.

The new group, with 13 000 employees in 18 countries, kicked off with a listing price of R4 a share. A few months later, the company managed to acquire the struggling Cornick's interest in Afcol, at a price that was considerably lower than their initial bid a year before: R3,82 a share as opposed to the R17,50 Cornick had paid.

The acquisition of the Cornick group meant that Steinhoff International became the largest furniture manufacturer in South Africa. The 38-year-old Jooste was the executive chair of Steinhoff Africa, with Daun on his board, while Bruno Steinhoff was the executive chair of Steinhoff International. Further expansions would follow. Steinhoff also acquired a stake in Daun's KAP International, and Jooste was a non-executive director of KAP.

Prior to Jooste's departure for Stellenbosch in 2011, he and his wife, Ingrid, had lived in the upmarket suburb of Waterkloof Ridge in Pretoria. His daughter Andréa later married Stefan Potgieter, his son-in-law who served with him on the board of their controversial company Mayfair Speculators. He has another daughter, Milanje, and a son, Michael.

In Stellenbosch, Jooste again forged close ties with his old friend Jannie Mouton, the founder of the PSG Group, who appointed Jooste to his board. Mouton and PSG were the power behind the throne of Capitec, the bank Michiel le Roux had founded and built into one of the South African banking giants.

Christo Wiese made a sensational revelation about this banking interest. In May 2019, to the surprise of all, he turned up at the Cape Town launch of an unauthorised biography of him, *Christo Wiese: Risk and Riches* by TJ Strydom. At the event, he personally answered questions in the course of the discussion. Among other things, he disclosed the real reason behind Jooste's interest in PSG: he had set his sights on acquiring a bank.

'One of Jooste's big plans with Steinhoff was that Steinhoff would become the controlling shareholder of PSG, which was in turn the largest shareholder in Capitec. It would have completed the circle.' Asked about this story, Wiese said: 'This is the interesting little aspect the journalists haven't yet cottoned on to. Here is one of the enigmas of Mr Jooste.'

Jooste owned 20 million PSG shares, which made him the largest shareholder after the Mouton family. Wiese recounted that with his own approximately 15,5 million shares, he was the third-largest shareholder in the group. 'Then Jooste came to me and said: "I want Steinhoff to become the largest shareholder in PSG." He had a number of reasons. One of them related to tax, but I don't want to go into too much detail about this,' Wiese said amid giggling from the audience.

If Jooste had succeeded, he would have owned the controlling interest in the fastest-growing bank in South Africa.

Other aspects of the way in which Jooste operated had come under the spotlight at an earlier stage. In front of other businesspeople he usually came across as suave and polite, and he was seen as a 'charming, easy-going ladies' man'. But in his interaction with employees and subordinates he displayed a bullying, callous management style.

Christopher Rutledge, a former Steinhoff employee, wrote in an article in *Huffington Post* that behind his back, those who worked with Jooste called him 'The Seagull'. It was a nickname Jooste 'had earned, not by virtue of his free-flying nature, but instead, as a result of his uncompromising, hard-nosed executive style. Markus was the seagull because he would fly in, shit all over his executives and then fly out.'

According to Rutledge, Jooste once ordered the management team of one of his companies to be at the factory at eight o'clock on a Saturday morning. He made the management team walk through the factory and pointed out all kinds of deficiencies. After subjecting the managing director to 'a humiliating tirade', he summarily fired the man by telling him: 'Get out of my fucking factory!'

Jooste would frequently remind his executives: 'We can't get rich by earning a salary.' That was why shares were Jooste's 'preferred currency', Rutledge wrote. By feeding his subordinates with a constant stream of shares through shares schemes, he kept them 'docile and unquestioning'.

Wiese concurs that Jooste was a male chauvinist; uncompromising and inclined to intimidate people. In Wiese's view, an 'assertive style' such as Jooste's is not necessarily a disadvantage in business. 'I can say I'm not aware of any of the CEOs of my companies, bar maybe one or two, who don't have that sort of streak. It's their way or the highway.' It was because he knew how Jooste could intimidate people, Wiese said, that he had some sympathy for the executives who were now being blamed for not having detected Jooste's accounting shenanigans.

Horse breeder and 'a man among the rugby *manne'*

Jooste brought the flashiness of new money to Stellenbosch. He had a swanky residence built in a contemporary Cape-Dutch style, complete with a jacuzzi, sauna and indoor swimming pool. The house is on the farm Bengale, which was renamed Jonkersdrift after he had bought it jointly with Frikkie Nel and Danie van der Merwe, who later became CEO of Steinhoff.

He gained renown in racing circles as the owner of some of the best racehorses in the country, such as The Conglomerate that won the Durban July in 2016. His interest in the racing industry grew as he achieved financial success. The first racehorse he bought, National Emblem, had cost R100 000, but ended up winning R1,9 million in prize money.

This champion horse became a successful stallion. Jooste reinvested all profits from National Emblem's stud career and developed the horses into a big business in his private family affairs and Mayfair Speculators.

Together with his partner in the racing industry, Bernard Kantor, he entered into a partnership with the Irish magnate John Magnier from Coolmore Stud, which allowed him to participate in races all over the world. His horses were able to compete in France, England, Hong Kong and Dubai.

At his peak, Jooste was regarded by experts in the racing industry as the world's second-biggest racehorse owner after Sheikh Mohammed bin Rashid Al Maktoum, the ruler of Dubai. In South Africa he was a partner in the country's largest stud farm, Klawervlei, in the Bonnievale district.

Jooste, who occupied various management positions in the South African racing industry, stated in an interview with the magazine

Sporting Post: 'I make the chain of activity a complete cycle. At Stein-hoff we grow the trees, cut the wood, make the furniture and sell the furniture. My racing business is modelled on the same lines.'

He was appointed to the board of the licensed horseracing operator Phumulela, where his student friend Rian du Plessis was the CEO. He was also a director of the Racing Association and a trustee of the Horseracing Trust. His tentacles were everywhere. As *Sporting Post* put it: 'We have never experienced dominance of the magnitude displayed by Markus Jooste.'

Wiese was concerned about Jooste's large interests in racehorses, but Jooste assured him that he never bet a cent on horses himself. 'Everything Markus did, he did correctly. What he said he would do, he did, and there was never a hint of dishonesty,' Wiese said.

In the rugby-mad Stellenbosch, Jooste evidently wanted to bark with the top dogs, because Steinhoff started sponsoring rugby on a large scale. The company's involvement had started as far back as 2006, before Jooste relocated to Stellenbosch in 2011, with a sponsorship for residence rugby. Every Friday, teams from the university residences would take to the field with the brands of Steinhoff subsidiaries on their jerseys.

In early 2008, Steinhoff expanded its sponsorship. The Varsity Cup was launched as a tournament between rugby teams from the top South African universities that played against each other on Mondays. From the Cape to Limpopo, Steinhoff's branding appeared on students' rugby jerseys, on rugby fans' T-shirts, on playing surfaces and on rugby posts.

The decision to sponsor rugby surprised the Stellenbosch clique, because Steinhoff International was not exactly a household name in the university town. Piet Mouton, CEO of PSG, quizzed Jooste and Steinhoff's chief financial officer Ben la Grange about it. 'I mean, there's no product called "Steinhoff", so what is the point? They said they wanted to market Steinhoff as the employer of choice for young graduates. I thought the answer was flimsy and unbelievable. I would have thought Hi-Fi Corp, Unitrans or any of the other brands would be better to promote.'

He added: 'It was perhaps more about their egos than anything else.'

In the end, it was probably more about Jooste's ego than anyone else's. From the time he moved to Stellenbosch, he wanted to become part of the Stellenbosch set. Rugby was the passport to influence among the elite: a man among the rugby *manne*.

At the Danie Craven Stadium, large advertising boards were erected, bearing the words: Steinhoff, Main sponsor of Maties Rugby. Jooste succeeded in elbowing Remgro out of involvement with the Stellenbosch Rugby Football Club, the largest of its kind in the world and one of the most famous. The Remgro CEO Jannie Durand related that Steinhoff literally kept Remgro away from the club: '[T]hey were scared of our involvement. It wasn't out in the open, but everyone knew we didn't like each other.'

In December 2015, Steinhoff pulled off another coup when the South African Rugby Union announced that the company would be the main sponsor of the Blitzbokke. The name 'Steinhoff' was emblazoned on the Sevens players' jerseys.

Jooste's focus on rugby gave a new dimension to corporate extravagance in 2015 when the Springboks advanced to the semi-final stage of the Rugby World Cup and lost 18-20 to the All Blacks at Twickenham. Steinhoff, which had acquired executive boxes at the famous rugby stadium, brought about sixty people, including Jooste's children and friends, to London for a three-week stay. They were given five-star treatment in The May Fair, a posh hotel in the heart of London, and were royally entertained.

Every day, the guests, who included Steinhoff bigwigs as well as hangers-on who had little to do with the company, received a printed programme of the day's activities. They could go hunting on hunting farms or go on angling trips. They had a helicopter at their disposal to move in and out of the bustling city. Among the guests spotted in the popular bar was Malcolm King, Jooste's shadowy British business partner under whose name the Lanzerac wine estate was purchased from Wiese. Jooste himself was reportedly in his element in the rugby boxes during games, regaling guests and friends with tales about his exploits.

Durand described the pleasure excursion to the rugby tournament on which money was lavished as a prime example of the prevailing company culture at Steinhoff: 'Nearly everyone in the town received invitations to accompany them to England. We at Remgro said, no, we don't go on sponsored trips because we don't want to compromise ourselves … I attended the tournament, but I bought six tickets, including one for my wife, and paid for them myself.'

Johann Rupert confirmed that Durand had acquired tickets via him from the London rugby club Saracens in which Remgro has an interest. 'We paid for our tickets,' he said.

Two years later, Steinhoff's rugby extravangences came to an ignominious end. In Stellenbosch, the ubiquitous advertising boards that blazoned forth Steinhoff's corporate logo in the same maroon colour as that of the Maties' sports teams disappeared one after another, some overnight. The sponsorship of the Maties rugby club was terminated, as were the sponsorships of the cricket and hockey teams. The Blitzbokke, former Sevens world champions, lost their sponsorship, while the Varsity Cup rugby competition suffered the same fate.

The 'Ikea of Africa'

By the time Wiese joined the board of Steinhoff International in 2013, the group had increasingly expanded internationally and had full control over the entire supply chain. It rested on a low-cost manufacturing base with factories that had mostly relocated to Eastern European countries such as Hungary and Poland. Self-sourcing of raw materials was boosted by the purchase of the particleboard manufacturer PG Bison. The distribution network was bolstered by the acquisition of Unitrans.

Retail sales grew as the group acquired companies in Australia, New Zealand (Freedom Group) and Britain (Homestyle). Their retail footprint in Europe was expanded through the acquisitions of the German furniture chain Poco and Conforama (Europe's second-largest furniture retail chain with 200 shops in various countries). Well-known brands such as the JD Group, Incredible Connection, Hi-Fi Corporation and Timbercity fell under Steinhoff's umbrella in Africa.

One of Steinhoff's largest transactions was the acquisition of the Pepkor Group in 2015. The purchase price was roughly R60 billion: R15 billion in cash and the remainder in Steinhoff shares. Wiese's

839 million shares made him one of Steinhoff's largest shareholders.

In the same year it was decided to list Steinhoff International overseas. The listing would be on the Frankfurt Stock Exchange as well as the JSE, but the company was registered in Amsterdam because of the more favourable tax environment of the Netherlands.

The company was often referred to as the 'Ikea of Africa'. By 2016, according to Steinhoff's annual report for that year, it was selling household goods and general merchandise, straddling more than 40 different brands, in more than 32 countries across four continents. Globally, the group had 26 manufacturing facilities and more than 12 000 retail outlets, and owned property that extended over 4 million square metres. Steinhoff employed 130 000 people.

In 2016, the company posted revenue of €8,645 million and a net profit of €1,510 million, representing a year-on-year growth rate of 11,8 per cent. On 23 May 2017, from an earlier high of R95, the share price on the JSE was valued at R50,25, which equated to a market capitalisation of R240,5 billion.

At this stage, before he became increasingly tight-lipped about Steinhoff, Jooste was still quite willing to talk to the media. In an interview with Alec Hogg from Biznews in June 2016, Jooste expanded on how he enjoyed establishing the new international company. Steinhoff's listing on the Frankfurt Stock Exchange was 'a dream come true and the start of a new episode in our lives', he said.

He explained how advantageous it was for South African shareholders that the company was registered in Amsterdam. (Compared with South Africa's corporate tax rate of 28 per cent, partnership tax in the Netherlands is only 20–25 per cent.) The double tax agreement between the Netherlands and South Africa was also a very favourable and fair way of distributing tax between the two countries, according to Jooste. Shareholders who swapped their shares from a South African company to a Dutch company received 'rollover relief on capital gains', otherwise the listing would not have been possible.

He acknowledged that luck had played a role in his decisions. But the lucky breaks had also been game changers for him: opportunities that put his rise in the business world on a new trajectory. One of these was meeeting Daun as a young man, and another was his purchase of Steinhoff's business. The big game changer in Europe was the acquisition of Conforama in France in 2011, and then there was the merger with Pepkor in 2015.

He described in detail how Steinhoff's 'worldwide exco' met 'religiously' once a month. It included the CEO of every country, and Wiese and Steinhoff joined them as well. The meeting would start at two o'clock and continue for as long as necessary, sometimes late into the night. Every potential corporate transaction, after it had passed the operational report stage, would be on the agenda. This was followed by a due diligence, and the report would be discussed at the monthly meeting and either be approved or disapproved.

'Every CEO around the world on that video conference that day gets a chance to say what he thinks – it's a fantastic forum of highly qualified, very diverse operational people. Add in Christo's deal-making capabilities, and it's like a bank's credit committee. It's not "the Markus Jooste show", as the media might sometimes suggest.'

Jooste emphasised that this was obviously the area he enjoyed the most. 'My life has always been about relationships. All these things happen because of relationships – trust each other and eventually you will do something together.'

It was these very relationships of trust, which had been built up so laboriously, that collapsed in December 2017.

In the wake of the scandal, all kinds of other stories were spread about Jooste, such as that he had a secret mistress. *Huisgenoot* published an article with photos of the 35-year-old Berdine Odendaal. Steinhoff managers were quoted as saying that Steinhoff chauffeurs regularly drove the polo-playing socialite around, and that many people in the group knew about the affair.

When the story leaked out, Wiese said he had not been aware of the relationship. In his time as chair of the Pepkor Group, he fired three executives because they had cheated on their wives: 'If a man can lie to his wife, he will lie to me too. Whitey sometimes had the same issue at Shoprite. He always said he could forgive a footprint, but not a footpath.' Wiese confronted Jooste when he first heard the story in 2016 or 2017. 'I said, people tell me you have a girlfriend. He looked me in the eye and said: "Christo, you of all people should know I don't have the time to keep a girlfriend." Straight in the eye.'

Steinhoff's governance structure consisted of two boards, the two-tier model that is favoured in Germany, the Netherlands and a few other countries in the European Union. One is a management board (made up of executives of the company), and the other a supervisory board (consisting of non-executive independent directors). The model that mostly applies in South Africa is that of a single board on which all the directors sit together, with two or three executive directors who are directly involved in the company's activities. The other directors are usually non-executive and independent, hence from outside institutions.

The disadvantage of a single board is that the independence of directors can be compromised more easily, which can dilute their oversight role. The risk in the case of the two-tier structure, in turn, is the possibility that the management board does not report properly to the supervisory board and basically hijacks the company. In both cases the wry joke may apply that 'strong' CEOs treat the board members like 'mushrooms': you keep them in the dark and feed them manure.

By 2016, three directors served on the management board of Steinhoff International: Markus Jooste (chief executive), Ben la Grange (chief financial officer) and Danie van der Merwe (chief operating officer). None of the three served on the supervisory board.

The following people were the directors of the supervisory board in 2016: Wiese (chair), Dr Len Konar (deputy chair), Dr Steve Booysen (chair of the audit committee), Daun, Dr Johan van Zyl, former CEO of Sanlam, Thierry Guibert, former auditor at KPMG, Steinhoff and his daughter, Angela Krüger-Steinhoff, Dr Theunie Lategan, Heather Sonn, who had succeeded her father Franklin Sonn as director and would eventually take over as chair in the midst of the crisis, and Jacob Wiese (Christo Wiese's son).

The two boards of Steinhoff abounded in chartered accountants. There were six in all, including Jooste himself, Daun and La Grange. Three directors with doctorates in accounting served in the audit committee: Booysen, a former CEO of Absa; Konar, a member of the King Committee on Corporate Governance and former chair of the external audit committee of the International Monetary Fund, and Dr Theunie Lategan, former CEO of FirstRand.

The directors' remuneration was considerable for their four quarterly board meetings: each earned about $100 000 a year (roughly

R1,5 million), while the chair earned three times that amount.

For years these heavyweights in the financial industry and the corporate sector saw no hint of trouble.

Steinhoff lists in Frankfurt

Towards the end of 2015, a few days before the listing in Frankfurt, the first storm clouds appeared on the horizon. Steinhoff confirmed that the German authorities had raided its offices in Westerstede on 26 November. The German newspaper *Handelsblatt* reported that the management had allegedly falsified balance sheets.

The German Central Crime Inspectorate in Oldenburg seized documents and data from Steinhoff. Fraud was suspected; there were 'suspicions that sales were overstated' and they were looking into the 'balance sheet treatment of certain transactions', the prosecuting authority stated. A week later, on Friday 4 December 2015, Steinhoff announced that the search by these authorities had found no evidence of any contravention of German commercial law.

The dust settled for the time being, and the following Monday, 7 December, Steinhoff International was listed on the Frankfurt Stock Exchange. Jooste was not present at the joyous event, supposedly because of an old neck injury that prevented him from travelling. The listing on the DAX was the biggest that year on the Frankfurt bourse. At that stage, Steinhoff International's market capitalisation was €19 billion, a rand value of close to R300 billion.

For a while after the listing there was silence about possible fraud. Steinhoff continued its acquisition drive after the company had already been expanding aggressively for the previous seven years. A joint venture was entered into with Cofel in July 2016, and the acquisition of Poundland was carried through. In the same year there were indirect expansions via Pepkor, which acquired GHM! and Tekkie Town. Tekkie Town, a distinctive South African institution with 320 branches countrywide, had a turnover of R1,3 billion in 2016 (when it became part of Steinhoff).

The biggest deal, however, was the merger with Mattress Firm, a company that had created the world's largest retail network for the distribution of mattresses from its head office in Houston, Texas.

Steinhoff hereby gained access to the large American market. But analysts were astonished at the purchase price of $3,8 billion, in which debt of $1,4 billion was included. Steinhoff paid $64 a share for Mattress Firm, more than double the closing price of $29 a few days before.

Apart from the fact that the share price was overvalued, Mattress Firm had been engaged in its own acquisition race and had added 1 500 stores within a few years. By September 2016, the number had grown to 3 500 branches across 48 states in the US, with more than one outlet within a few street blocks from each other in some cities. Eventually it would emerge that some of the property transactions had been highly suspicious and had benefited outside interests. In November 2018, Mattress Firm escaped bankruptcy by closing 660 stores.

In South Africa, Wiese wanted Shoprite to be merged into Steinhoff, but his friend Whitey Basson was vehemently opposed to Shoprite shares being swapped for Steinhoff shares. After it was finally decided that Steinhoff could combine all its retailers in a new company, Steinhoff Africa Retail (Star), Star was listed separately on the JSE on 20 September 2017. Ackermans, Bradlows, Pep and Hi-Fi Corporation moved in under Star's umbrella. Shareholders of Shoprite could decide which company they wanted to invest in. This was the compromise that satisfied Basson.

Star's chair was the former trade unionist Jayendra Naidoo, a director of Steinhoff. The CEO was La Grange, the financial head of the Steinhoff Group. There was strong interest from investors in the listing, and the opening price of R20,50 quickly jumped to R22,50. This increased Star's value to more than R75 billion at close of business.

Steinhoff had meanwhile been steaming ahead. Until 24 August 2017. On that date, an article appeared in the German business magazine *Manager Magazin* that turned a highly critical spotlight on Steinhoff.

The article alleged that losses were being concealed in off-balance-sheet entities and an overview was given of Steinhoff's history of frenzied acquisitions. Mention was also made of an ongoing legal dispute between Steinhoff and Andreas Seifert, the mysterious owner of XXXLutz, an Austrian furniture group, a former joint-venture partner of Jooste. The dispute was about the ownership of some of their European retail operations, inter alia Poco, in which each had a 50 per cent stake. Steinhoff's half was later sold back to Seifert after court battles.

Steinhoff issued a statement in which the allegations in *Manager Magazin* were denied and Seifert was indicated as their source.

The course of events in the unfolding drama during which Jooste resigned as CEO and Steinhoff's shares collapsed has been set out in two books: Rob Rose's *Steinheist* and James-Brent Styan's *Steinhoff: Inside SA's biggest corporate crash*.

The director of Steinhoff who was apparently the first to suspect that something was wrong with the company's accounts was Steve Booysen, chair of the audit committee. He gave a brief outline of the drama at a hearing of the parliamentary inquiry into Steinhoff in January 2018 during which Wiese said that to him as chair, the news had come 'like a bolt out of the blue'.

Booysen had informed Wiese about the problems only three working days before the annual financial statements had to be finalised for the board meeting. 'Normally when you're in a business – and you're responsible – you can see the problems coming, you're aware of them. The sales go down, the liquidity dries up, people start leaving the sinking ship, and you can take corrective action – but this came like a bolt out of the blue,' Wiese testified.

Booysen told the parliamentarians that a magazine article in Germany led to their being informed on 20 September 2017 of certain issues the management had to resolve. They then liaised with the external auditors about these matters. 'And the bolt to which Christo referred hit me on 14 November.'

Booysen subsequently worked flat out at the company to investigate the allegations. Confirmation of the irregularities was only obtained on the evening of Monday 4 December 2017. He said Jooste had been summoned at 09:45 that day to provide the audit committee with explanations. 'We waited the whole day for him. He didn't turn up. And then he resigned that evening at 19:45.'

An SMS he received from Jooste was to him corroboration that there was indeed something wrong with Steinhoff's books. It confirmed Booysen's greatest fear: that, at best, there had been accounting irregularities, and, at worst, fraud.

That evening at 19:45 a German lawyer went to Wiese as board chair and said Jooste was tendering his resignation. On the same evening, Jooste sent a letter via email to Steinhoff's employees in which he acknowledged that he had made 'big mistakes'. A direct translation of the letter, which was written in Afrikaans, reads as follows:

Hi there,

Firstly I would like to apologise for all the bad publicity I caused the Steinhoff company the last couple of months. Now I have caused the company further damage by not being able to finalise the year-end audited numbers and I made some big mistakes and have now caused financial loss to many innocent people. It is time for me to move on and take the consequences of my behaviour like a man.

Sorry that I have disappointed all of you and I never meant to cause any of you any harm.

Please continue to live the Steinhoff dream and I must make it very clear none of Van der Merwe [Danie, the COO], La Grange [Ben, the CFO], Stehan [Grobler, Executive Group Treasury and Financing] and Mariza [Nel, Corporate Services, IT and HR] had anything to do with any of my mistakes.

I enjoyed working with you and wish you all the best for the future.

Best regards
Markus

On the Monday, Steinhoff's long-time auditors Deloitte refused to sign off Steinhoff's final annual financial statements for the 2017 financial year when they did not receive the information they had asked for. In a statement, the supervisory board confirmed that the group's consolidated statements would be issued on 6 December 2017 as promised, but as unaudited statements.

Steinhoff added in the Sens announcement that no additional information had been obtained to change the group's earlier views on the investigation. 'The Company expects to publish the audited 2017 consolidated statements before 31 January 2018.'

On the Tuesday morning, Wiese phoned Jooste to come and help sort out the mess, but he failed to arrive. On Wednesday 6 December Steinhoff had to issue another Sens statement. 'New information has come to light today which relates to accounting irregularities requiring further investigation,' the supervisory board announced.

This board announced that, in conjunction with the group's auditors, it had approached another audit firm, PwC, to conduct an independent investigation. Jooste had tendered his resignation with immediate effect, and the board had accepted his resignation. Wiese had been appointed as Steinhoff's interim executive chair.

As the shockwaves of the announcement reverberated through the business community, the market was hit by even more disturbing news when a research report by the relatively unknown American investor group Viceroy Research was issued on 6 December. The damning report revealed various irregularities in Steinhoff's financial statements.

Among other things, Viceroy claimed that there were three companies that were used to do business with Steinhoff that did not appear on the group's balance sheet. These companies – Campion, Southern View and Genesis – were in turn controlled by existing and former Steinhoff executives, including a former chief financial officer of the group. According to the report, most of Steinhoff's investments and loans were 'used to finance the companies to take over Steinhoff subsidiaries that suffered losses'. These companies were therefore used to obscure losses and inflate earnings.

Fraser Perring and his two colleagues at Viceroy described themselves as 'protectors of shareholders', but they were in fact short sellers who bought shares in the expectation that the price would drop. Viceroy acknowledged, however, that their focus was to research companies where 'signs of accounting irregularities and possible fraud are found'.

Viceroy initially considered the US company Mattress Firm as a share to short and was therefore shocked to see Steinhoff's bid price. 'Either the market was undervaluing it by 100%, or Steinhoff was overpaying by 100%. And if it's too good to be true, something is up,' they stated.

Steinhoff had not been on their radar at all until Steinhoff decided to acquire Mattress Firm at $64 a share – more than double the closing price on the day the transaction was announced. They had started looking into Steinhoff from about mid 2017, Viceroy told *Business Day*. 'It was a bit like *War and Peace*. This was like a big novel, there were a lot of names, there were related-party transactions ... There were many signs that something was wrong.'

Viceroy shared its report on social media within a few hours of Jooste's resignation. The share price subsequently plummeted further. It had dropped from R55,81 on Friday 1 December to R6,00 by Friday 8 December.

'A blot on the reputation of Afrikaner businesspeople'

In South Africa, commentators reacted with anger to the Steinhoff revelations. The economist Iraj Abedian stated that morality and ethics were seriously lacking in corporate governance. Among the scathing criticism that elicited the most discussion was that expressed by Magda Wierzycka, the CEO of Sygnia Asset Managers, who emerged as a campaigner for justice in 2017. On the morning after Jooste's resignation, she pointed out on CapeTalk's breakfast programme that the Government Employees Pension Fund (GEPF) had lost R14 billion.

On 7 December she wrote in an article on Fin24 that the serious question to ask was how asset managers, who prided themselves on meticulous research and interviews with management, missed 'what was obvious from the beginning: that this was as close to a corporate-structured Ponzi scheme as one can get'. When she analysed the financials of Steinhoff, she wrote, it took her only half an hour to figure out that the structure was 'obfuscated', that financial items made no sense, that the acquisition spree was not underpinned by any logic, and that debt levels were out of control.

'I firmly believe that the blind faith in the Midas touch of Christo Wiese made many oblivious to the obvious,' she added. Taking a swipe at asset managers, an industry in which she herself operates, she said she did not believe 'that active asset management adds value commensurate with what is being charged to investors'. She shares this 'core belief' with Warren Buffett.

If Jooste had received advice elsewhere about his conglomerate, it could not have come from Buffett. The American investment guru's company, Berkshire Hathaway, owns 63 companies, and he usually writes only one annual letter to the CEOs in which he sets out the objectives for the year. He lays down only two rules for them: 'Rule No 1: Never lose any of your shareholders' money. Rule No. 2: Never forget Rule No. 1.'

By that time Buffett had been living in the same three-bedroom house in Omaha in Nebraska for fifty years because he has everything there that he needs. He drives his own car and buys a hamburger and a Coke on the way to his office. His frugal lifestyle differs markedly from the flashiness that in Jooste's neck of the woods has become known as the 'Mostertsdrift syndrome'. In the Stellenbosch suburb of Mostertsdrift, once the refuge of academics whose remuneration remained relatively static over the years, the new super-rich have torn down old family homes and erected ostentatious new mansions.

It is in this suburb that Anton Rupert lived for half a century in the same house in Thibault Street. His son Johann reacted to the Steinhoff debacle with disgust. With reference to the town of his birth, he tweeted under his Twitter handle Cutmaker: 'Although I left Stellenbosch in 1975, it really irritates me that not one of the so-called "Stellenbosch Mafia" who are causing so much damage to the town's reputation was born or raised in Stellenbosch. They are all "incomers".'

The fall of Steinhoff caused great consternation in Stellenbosch, where many people lost a lot of money as a result of the collapse of the share price. Apart from the fact that some among the business elite in the town who had interests in the share know each other well, several employees of Steinhoff have family and friends who live there. One of the victims was Danie van der Merwe, who saw a fortune evaporating. As one of the largest shareholders in the group, his 6,1 million shares were worth about R550 million at their peak. A year after he had been appointed CEO in December 2017 to help save Steinhoff, the value had shrunk to barely R15 million.

The property market in Stellenbosch suffered the effects of the fallout. A large number of properties suddenly came onto the market –

notably residences of people who had financed their purchases with Steinhoff shares. Dismayed architects and builders were informed that huge projects had been summarily cancelled. Stockbrokers and financial services groups sensed that clients started looking at them sceptically on being told they could trust them with their money.

The financial shockwave was felt around the globe and dented international confidence in the country. A view held by foreign investors and businesspeople that while South Africa had a corrupt government the top business leaders had a solid reputation, turned negative as a result of the Steinhoff scandal.

The rating agency Moody's downgraded Steinhoff's credit rating to junk status. In America, four of the largest banks – JP Morgan Chase & Co., Bank of America, Citigroup and Goldman Sachs – announced that they jointly had more than $1 billion of loans linked to Steinhoff. Steinhoff owed a total of $22 billion to international banks.

Among the biggest losers in South Africa were millions of investors in pension funds, including government employees. The names of companies that suffered huge losses appeared on Moneyweb when the financial news website published the shareholder register of Steinhoff on 6 December 2017. Based on a share price of R16,50, Coronation's investment amounted to R3,55 billion, Foord's was R2,68 billion, Sanlam's R1,95 billion, Investec's R1,51 billion, Nedgroup's R1,17 billion, Old Mutual's R530 million, Allan Gray's R370 million and Discovery's R310 million.

Thys du Toit noted that Steinhoff did business with about 180 banks worldwide. 'Therefore it passed through 180 banks' credit committees. Deloitte, one of the big five, audited its books. The investment community – and there are a few exceptions – all swallowed his story to a large extent, and when Christo Wiese brought in Pep, there was the conviction that it had now really become a company of substance. And that, I think, is the point where I also made a mistake, because I, too, thought Pep Stores was a good asset with all its affiliates ... So, he's a master con man.'

Jooste *had* to keep up the pretence, Du Toit says, which was why he had to make more and more and bigger deals whereby companies that did have substance were added. 'I mean, from 2009 onwards that company made no profits, yet it paid dividends during that time. In other words, it paid dividends with money it didn't have, or profits it hadn't made. It might have had the cash.

'So, it's a shameful blot. It's a blot on the reputation of Afrikaner businesspeople. We – the auditing profession, the financial services profession in South Africa – were regarded as very clean. Afrikaner businesspeople were seen as people with integrity. And suddenly there's the biggest of crooks, the adder in our midst.'

For politicians, especially those who had merrily taken part in state capture and continually defended Zuma although he had been a fugitive from justice since the day he was sworn in as head of state, the Steinhoff scandal was a lightning conductor par excellence. They seized on it as proof that the private sector was just as corrupt as the state. Johan van Zyl recounted that politicians were basically gloating.

In the circles of the commentariat, the former newspaper editor Peter Bruce wrote with schadenfreude that Steinhoff had 'exploded the myth' of Afrikaner business; that Afrikaner capitalism supposedly 'represents a uniquely productive form of wealth creation because it recognises the power of ethnic bonds'. Moreover, opponents of both capitalism and white business were having a field day because to them Steinhoff proved that white business was no less corrupt than black government. 'That's inaccurate – corrupt government steals from everyone,' he added. 'Corrupt businesses steal from their investors and customers.'

Wiese said 'part of the great sadness is that the business world in general has been tarnished by the Steinhoff disaster. My only request is that people shouldn't take a one-sided view. One rotten apple doesn't mean that everyone is rotten.'

He added that the scandal was not only bad for corporate South Africa, but particularly 'for segments that have been knocked by it, such as the so-called "Stellenbosch Mafia" and Afrikaners. Many people who are innocent are being tarred with the same brush, not least of all myself.'

All forms of corruption ultimately harm the poorest section of a population the most. Yet a strong case can be made that in fulfilling a social contract with the citizenry, the state and government officials bear a heavier responsibility to deal with integrity with the money taxpayers entrust to them. Because taxpayers have no choice; they *have* to pay tax. If they fail to do so, the state can claim it from them, and even take it from their bank accounts. In the private sector they can still choose whether to invest with a particular private operator or not.

Du Toit has calculated that Steinhoff's loss of value is ten times more than was the case with African Bank in 2012. The write-off of the debt of African Bank, which was fined R20 million for reckless lending in 2013, amounted to R32 billion. The ANC government, however, was more willing to bail out African Bank than had been the case a few years earlier with Saambou.

'Just to put it into perspective,' Du Toit says, 'the extent of the accounting fraud in Steinhoff in round figures is $7 billion. Now if you multiply that at the current exchange rate it is fraud of plus-minus R100 billion, but the value that was destroyed from when the share traded at its high to its low is R300 billion. The fraud is therefore almost a third of the loss of value ... ten times bigger than African Bank.'

A giant Ponzi scheme exposed

As the ripples from the Steinhoff shock continued to spread, one director after the other resigned, eventually 11 out of the 14 directors. Among these were Wiese and his son Jacob, Konar, Van Zyl, Lategan, Naidoo, Daun and Steinhoff himself. At the annual meeting of 20 April 2018 in the Sheraton Hotel at the Schiphol airport outside Amsterdam, there were three left: Heather Sonn (chair), Steve Booysen and Angela Krüger-Steinhoff. Six new independent directors were added to the board.

In January 2018, La Grange resigned as financial director and at the same time Danie van der Merwe took over as acting CEO. He was replaced in Jooste's former position in November 2018 by Louis du Preez, who was at that stage Steinhoff's commercial director. His big task would be to endeavour to reach settlements with the group's creditors.

PwC's long-awaited forensic report was finally released on 16 March 2019. More than 100 auditors had combed through the labyrinth of companies and documents. The full report was more than 3 000 pages long, with over 4 000 documents as annexures, but it was kept confidential because it implicated people in different jurisdictions and was subject to legal privilege. Only an 11-page overview was released into the public domain.

The extent of the apparent fraud that had taken place over about seven years, hence over a far longer period than was initially suspected, was astounding. According to PwC, between 2009 and 2016, Steinhoff apparently created fictitious profit-boosting schemes totalling R106 billion. This was just under three times the net profit of the company over that period.

The seasoned investor Karin Richards captured the full impact of the report in a concise tweet: 'Steinhoff was in effect just a giant Ponzi scheme. Fictitious receivables were "settled", in a merry-go-round, by increasing property valuations, trademarks & goodwill. These inflated values were then supported by intergroup rentals/royalties & orchestrated intergroup "payments".'

The summary of the report spelled out, albeit not in full detail, that a small group of the Steinhoff Group's former executives and other non-Steinhoff executives, led by a senior management executive, structured and implemented various transactions over a number of years that had the result of substantially inflating the profit and asset values of Steinhoff over an extended period.

Apparently this small group of individuals 'created fictitious and/or irregular income at an intermediary Steinhoff Group Holding company level' that was allocated to underperforming Steinhoff operating entities. These entities then received 'contributions' from other Steinhoff companies or from supposed external companies which, it turned out, were actually funded by Steinhoff.

This resulted in a web of intercompany loans and 'receivables' within the group. The cash and 'contributions' that were shifted around made Steinhoff appear more profitable and valuable than it actually was. The flow of money between entities, with the sole purpose of shifting debt burdens off the company's balance sheet, was difficult to trace. Although the Steinhoff manoeuvres seemed to be another classic Enron case of fraud, there was, however, a difference because unlike Enron, which was an energy trader dealing in financial instruments, Steinhoff is a retail company.

In Steinhoff's complicated construction, property valuations were manipulated and inflated values were assigned to intangible assets such as brands and goodwill. According to the summarised overview, 'the transactions identified as being irregular were complex, involved many entities over a number of years, and were supported by legal documents and other professional opinions that, in many instances, were created after the fact and backdated'. In other words, documents had been forged.

The PwC report named a number of the suspicious companies, in particular the Talgarth Group, which was registered in the British Virgin Islands and through which a total of €4,2 billion flowed from at least 2009 to 2016. From then on, large sums started flowing to another company, TG Trademarks.

In a complex scheme, Talgarth was seemingly used by Steinhoff under the pretext of promoting brands. Talgarth would carry the costs and provide the revenue to Steinhoff. Some brands did not exist, while Steinhoff lent money to Talgarth which Talgarth would then drip-feed back to Steinhoff as 'interest repayments'.

Since Talgarth was a 'debtor' that owed money to Steinhoff, Steinhoff provided a *Wechsel* (a German acknowledgment of debt) to Talgarth, which acted as a 'guarantee' for this debt. In other words, Steinhoff was in fact guaranteeing its own debt, but the company would classify the debt as a 'cash equivalent'. This artificially boosted Steinhoff's cash flow, but the 'income' from the repayments was fake because Talgarth was never going to repay the debt.

One group that was specifically absolved from blame in the PwC report was Pepkor and its affiliates. According to the report, no evidence was found that either Wiese, the largest shareholder in Steinhoff, or his group had participated in fraud. The finding could strengthen his case in the claim for damages of R59 billion he had instituted against Steinhoff and Jooste. In the summarised report, Steinhoff indicated that they intended to delve deeper into the alleged offences because there were still unanswered questions with regard to 'the identification of the true nature of the counterparties or the ultimate beneficiaries to various transactions'.

Steinhoff did not identify the main suspect, who was surely named in the PwC report. The company did state that its two boards 'believe that the facts identified in the PwC Report raise serious allegations, against the senior executive in particular'. This suspect was obviously Jooste who, even in Parliament, denied any responsibility for the fraud. He maintained that he was 'unaware of an accounting black hole' in Steinhoff's accounts when the share price crashed.

Louis du Preez, who took over the unenviable job of Steinhoff's CEO, said after the release of the overview of the PwC report that there were two questions he was most pressed about: can we see the full forensic report, and when will Jooste be arrested? According to him, the full report had to remain confidential because of Steinhoff's own court cases, including a claim of R850 million against Jooste, as well as possible litigation in foreign jurisdictions. As for Jooste, it was not the company's job to prosecute him, Du Preez added, but Steinhoff was cooperating with the authorities and had almost daily contact with them.

The scope of the PwC report was strikingly described by a member of Steinhoff's supervisory board, Alex Watson, a former professor of accounting at the University of Cape Town. Steinhoff's accounts were 'the most complex financial statements you could ever imagine preparing,' she said. 'It was the longest audit opinion ever seen. Students will be studying this for years.'

According to the PwC report, all the executives concerned had left the company, except for one individual who was assisting with the investigations. This pointed to a whistle-blower, presumably La Grange, who testified in Parliament that Jooste had influenced a number of transactions that contributed to the accounting irregularities.

Jooste refused to testify at the first parliamentary hearing in January 2018, as well as the second one on 31 March 2018. Wiese and Heather Sonn, who had succeeded him as chair, did appear at the first hearing. Sonn informed the joint parliamentary committee that the company had reported Jooste to the Hawks, on suspicion that he had committed offences under the Prevention and Combating of Corrupt Activities Act. A top National Treasury Official, Ismail Momoniat, said that up to R200 billion in shareholder value was lost due to the decrease in Steinhoff's share price.

Jooste was eventually summoned to testify at the parliamentary inquiry about the events that had led to the collapse of Steinhoff's share price. On 5 September 2018 he turned up at the third hearing, flanked by four lawyers, after it had been agreed that MPs were only allowed to question him within certain parameters.

Jooste put the blame for the Steinhoff fiasco on his former partner Andreas Seifert. He also claimed that Seifert was the person who went to the German tax authorities with information about their business activities over a period of eight years and convinced them to investigate Steinhoff for alleged mismanagement of taxes and other accounting irregularities.

According to Jooste's version, his biggest mistake was that he had started a joint venture with Seifert to form a strategic partnership. They bought Conforama in 2011, but Seifert was unable to pay his 50 per cent. Jooste then assisted him with a loan. When Seifert pushed for the acquisition of Kika/Leiner, his biggest competitor in Austria, in 2013, the 'red lights went on' for Jooste. He claimed that Seifert had again been unable to pay his share. They had a falling-out in November 2014 and the partnership was terminated in January 2015, on legal advice.

Jooste, who insisted in Parliament that he was unaware of any accounting irregularities in Steinhoff's accounts, stated that he had been opposed to delaying the release of Steinhoff's annual results on 6 December 2017. In his view, another delay after an investigation that had lasted nearly two years would have had a 'devastating effect' on investor confidence, credit lines and the share price. He had recommended that new auditors be appointed and that unaudited results be announced in the meantime. The board disagreed with him, however, and the consequent delay in the issuing of financial results had caused the fall of the share price, he claimed.

He said he felt sorry for the people who had lost money. His family trust, which controlled his investment vehicle Mayfair, had owned 68 million shares. On the day the share price collapsed, he lost R3 billion. Mayfair had since sold all its Steinhoff shares as part of the collateral security for bank loans. He stated emphatically: 'I would like to say that I never lied about the activities of the company.'

When pressured to do so in Parliament, Louis du Preez named eight suspects: Jooste, La Grange, Siegmar Schmidt, former CEO of Steinhoff Europe, Dirk Schreiber, a German citizen who was the former CFO of Steinhoff Europe, Stéhan Grobler, South African company secrectary, and three forcigncrs, namely Alan Evans, Jean-Noel Pasquier and Davide Romano. This cabal around Jooste could expect to appear in court in future on multiple charges, unless one or two of them turned state witness.

The MPs from the four committees that heard the testimony were lambasted for having mostly been ill-equipped for their task. With the exception of Alf Lees (DA) and Floyd Shivambu (EFF), they failed to pose incisive questions, and the hearing was rather an embarrassment to those who were itching to see justice done. *Business Day* accused the MPs of 'bluster, faux indignation and grandstanding at an egregious level'. The presentations of the National Prosecuting Authority and the Hawks gave little comfort that Jooste would be prosecuted expeditiously.

Jooste's day of reckoning

Eighteen months too late, Steinhoff's long-awaited restated and audited financial results for 2017 were finally released – at midnight on Tuesday 7 May 2019, on the eve of the country's general election. The delayed report was replete with revelations about questionable business practices, such as suspicious transactions with an array of related companies, conflicts of interest, unauthorised bonuses, and corporate gifts and extravagance. As was uncovered earlier in the PwC report, 'fictitious and irregular transactions' from 2009 onwards totalled R106 billion.

One of the revelations was that a property in Portugal had been bought from the Steinhoff subsidiary Conforama in order to obtain 'golden visas' for directors and top executives. In terms of the Portuguese golden visa programme, a €500 000 investment in property and a two-week stay per year guaranteed residency permits for a family, including dependent children. The transaction had not been approved by the supervisory board, even though the Dutch corporate governance code stipulated that an executive director was not allowed to benefit from a business opportunity to which the company was entitled.

Other properties were used as hunting farms. In the 2017 financial year, Steinhoff sold a subsidiary called Delta Properties, which owned numerous properties, mainly used for hunting purposes, to Steinhoff Familienholding GmbH, which belongs to the family of Bruno Steinhoff and his daughter Angela Krüger-Steinhoff. According to the annual report, Jooste and Dirk Schreiber, another executive, had approached Steinhoff with the request to buy Delta Properties. Judging by the minutes, the conflict of interest was neither declared nor approved by the supervisory board.

A loan to Jooste's investment company was revealed in the 2017 annual statements. In December 2016 the Dutch company Hachmer Beheer BV – a subsidiary of the company Habufa until 29 December 2016 – had granted a loan of R934,6 million to Mayfair Holdings. At that stage Steinhoff held 50 per cent of Habufa. The ultimate shareholder of Mayfair is a family trust of Jooste's. The loan was also in conflict with the Dutch corporate governance code and should first have been approved by the supervisory board. Moreover, according to the report, Jooste received a €500 000 bonus without the requisite approval.

Compared with half a page on related-party transactions in the previous financial year, the restated annual statements contained a five-page list of such related groups. Seven entities that belonged to Jooste or close relatives of his were named by Steinhoff as 'materially related parties' with whom transactions had been entered into. Among these were the Mayfair companies in which Jooste had a large interest, as well as a company that was indirectly controlled by him, Lodestone Brands, a manufacturer of sweets and soft drinks that sold its products in Pepkor's stores. Other entities with which Jooste and his close relatives had a direct or indirect or special relationship included Upington Investments (which was controlled by Wiese), Kluh Investments, a subsidiary of Fihag Finanz und Handels Aktiengesellschaft, Erfvest Properties and The Brood.

Many of the more serious transactions led to huge write-offs, such as those with the Talgarth Group in the British Virgin Islands and Campion. This company posted a loss of €4,3 billion for the financial year.

The suspicious shifting around of money, the shadowy related-party transactions and the vast personal enrichment at the expense of shareholders totalled about R256 billion, which made it 'one of the most audacious frauds ever committed'. Peter Armitage, the founder of Anchor Capital, wrote in a note to clients: 'The financials give further details of the extent of irregular transactions, false profits and manipulated accounts. It is hard to believe it is so big. Remember the world's biggest fraud, Enron, was R650 billion.'

He doubted whether Steinhoff could continue as a going concern: 'Sadly, in my opinion, there's no value left.'

In the 2018 annual report it was announced that Steinhoff still suffered a huge loss of €1,2 billion (close to R20 billion) in the financial year, but that it was profitable at operating level. According to the report, Jooste did not receive a severance package after his resignation, and he also lost bonuses and share rights. During the two months of the 2018 financial year that he was still in Steinhoff's employ he did receive a salary of €326 000, equating to a princely sum of about R2,5 million a month.

Months after the Steinhoff scandal erupted, it was still doubtful whether the state would be able to prosecute Jooste and his cronies successfully. The criminal justice system had been hollowed out by inefficiency and corruption, notably as a result of pliant cadres Zuma had appointed in key positions during his tenure in his efforts to stay out of jail.

Advocate Shamila Batohi, the head of the National Prosecuting Authority, stated at a press conference in November 2019 that the NPA was understaffed by 800 prosecutors. Apart from misgivings as to whether prosecutors possessed the necessary expertise, the police service's specialist unit, the Hawks, also did not inspire confidence that their forensic abilities could unravel the complex Steinhoff web sufficiently to ensure a successful prosecution. They seemed to have relied mostly on the PwC report instead of conducting their own investigations.

In its 2018 annual report, Steinhoff announced plans to 'claw back' large sums from Markus Jooste. Between 2009 and 2017 Jooste had extracted salaries and bonuses to the amount of R448 million from the shareholders he had plundered. The bonuses that were supposed to reward his vigilance and proficiency as chief executive amounted to more than R205 million. Among these were bonuses in the 2017 financial year that had neither been proposed by the human resources and remuneration committee nor approved by the supervisory board.

Steinhoff's intention to recover such remuneration from Jooste 'where applicable' was seen as an important step by market analysts. It would create a precedent worth following for other companies faced with similar problems.

The Financial Sector Conduct Authority (FSCA) also intimated that the main figures in the Steinhoff scandal could expect heavy fines. In September 2019, the FSCA imposed a fine of R1,5 billion on Steinhoff for 'misleading financial statements', but reduced it by 96 per cent to R53 million due to several mitigating circumstances.

The FSCA's new head of investigation and enforcement, Brandon Topham, explained in an interview with the *Financial Mail* that a heavy fine would not affect the true culprits – they had all left the company. The real issue was to get at the perpetrators who had been responsible for the misleading financial statements. According to Topham, he had about ten individuals on his radar – and 'these guys won't get away with a R53 million fine'.

He also promised 'decisions and fines' with regard to possible insider trading on Steinhoff shares. This was a reference to an SMS Jooste had sent on Thursday 30 November 2017 – a few days prior to his resignation the following week – to his friend Jaap du Toit. A translation of the message, which was revealed in a claim the trustees of Le Toit Trust launched against Steinhoff, reads as follows: 'You always ask my opinion … it will take Steinhoff a long time to work through all the bad news and America. So there are better places to invest your money. Take the current price immediately. Delete this SMS and don't mention it to anyone.'

The Le Toit Trust claimed R740 million for PSG shares that had been swapped for Steinhoff shares in 2015. If Du Toit, a trustee, had acted on Jooste's advice, he would have saved a fortune. He did not sell any shares, however, and was not found guilty of insider trading.

Besides the R59 billion claimed by Wiese, Steinhoff faced various other legal claims, including a class action suit in the Netherlands. The combined claims against Steinhoff could come to as much as

$10 billion (about R170 billion). Lengthy and tough negotiations and lawsuits that lay ahead would also put further pressure on Steinhoff's shrinking resources.

In October 2020, the JSE imposed a fine of R13,5 million on Steinhoff for breaching listing requirements, which included the maximum permissible fine for having published incorrect, false and misleading financial statements in financial years up to 2016. Shortly afterwards, Jooste as an individual was fined R122 927 366 by the FSCA for insider trading. He could also be held liable for further fines of R38,6 million levied on three other individuals, including his friend Ockie Oosthuizen, the former Springbok. The SMS he had sent them turned out to be an expensive message: it could ultimately cost as much as R161 million.

The University of Stellenbosch Business School undertook a comprehensive analysis of the rise and fall of Steinhoff that is likely to serve as a case study for students in the future. The academics found in their report that Jooste was evidently a charismatic leader who had developed a strong and devoted following within the company and among his many professional and social networks. They invested him with superhuman status because they saw him as a retail star who had reached the pinnacle of success.

But he operated in the rarefied atmosphere of the super-rich who often think they are above the law. 'Driven by his own self-confidence, entrepreneurial talents and adulation from people around him, Jooste became a larger-than-life CEO who took great liberties with Steinhoff's money and seemingly crossed all sorts of ethical boundaries,' the business school's report read.

In their book *Snakes in Suits*, the psychologists Paul Babiak and Robert Hare analysed interviews they had conducted with 200 high-potential executives. The authors classified 3,5 per cent of them as fitting the psychopathic profile, which was three times what one would expect in the wider population. 'All had the traits of the manipulative psychopath: superficial, grandiose, deceitful, impulsive, irresponsible, not taking responsibility for their actions, and lacking goals, remorse and empathy.'

According to Babiak and Hare, such 'corporate psychopaths' lie with impunity, have a sense of entitlement, and have clear dictatorial tendencies that often manifest in bullying.

But all superstars who consider themselves above the law and ethical norms can ultimately expect a day of reckoning. This was the case with other super-rich overreachers, including the Enron scandal's Kenneth Lay and 'wolves of Wall Street' such as Bernie Madoff, the New York financier who ran the largest Ponzi scheme in history before ending up in jail as a result of fraud totalling $65 billion. For years, Jooste managed to keep saucersful of money in the air like a juggler. But when the fall started, the many saucers came crashing to the floor. Like in a classical Greek tragedy, Jooste had been overtaken by hubris: ruin and humiliation because overweening ambition, excessive pride and too much arrogance had predominated.

He was forced to start selling assets on a large scale to raise funds. Shares and properties were disposed of. A few hundred racehorses had to change hands. Mayfair Speculators sold the expensive racehorses under pressure from the banks. In 2019, it was the turn of Pierneef paintings. Art experts pointed out at the time that the mass sale of works by the famous Henk Pierneef that could directly or indirectly be traced back to Jooste was responsible for an oversupply in the market that triggered a sudden slump in the auction prices of Pierneef paintings.

By this time Jooste's reputation had long since reached its nadir. Yet, despite being for the most part a prisoner in his own home, he was able to move around freely. People would see him walking around at Lanzerac as if he still owned the place. Indeed, though, he was waiting for that ominous knock on the door: the law in search of the master of con men.

15

The mega-farmer as ultrapreneur I

Dutoit Group, ZZ2, Karsten Group,
Schoeman Boerdery, Wildeklawer

– by Jacques Dommisse

The political changes in South Africa towards the end of the previous century enabled, virtually overnight, entrepreneurial farmers to sell their produce directly to an end consumer worldwide. The changed environment also gave them access on a larger scale to state-of-the-art international farming practices, technology, equipment and implements – which have been instrumental in assuring food security domestically.

Now when, particularly for political reasons, the land question had become a highly contentious issue in our national politics, it is striking that some of the most successful farmers in South Africa farm on a large scale. They have become known among some as mega-farmers.

Although some of these farmers did not exactly like the name, *Megaboere* was also the title of a popular series on the Afrikaans television channel kykNET. The series depicted their exceptional achievements in this challenging agricultural country, with its relative lack of fertile soil, scarce water resources and periodic droughts, plagues and pests. The group of ten whose activities are described in this chapter and the next one make up a significant part of the less than 20 per cent (about 6 000) of the country's commercial farmers who produce roughly 80 per cent of the country's food.

The director of the first television series, Wynand Dreyer, also covered a number of them in his book *Megaboere*. He never asked the farmers what they earned or what their profit and turnover were. In his view, these farming enterprises are not really farms any more: they are businesses, industries – and they are immensely impressive. 'We did discover that there were common denominators: they are all

307

exporters and their products meet export requirements, each one is a proven market leader in his product, there are identifiable innovative actions in each case, they all diversify; they also have leadership qualities, they are visionary, and they are creative businesspeople to boot,' he recounts.

The neologism 'mega-farmer' applies to the ten leading agricultural groups that have continued to set the trend as farming enterprises owned and managed by families. Over and above aspects such as turnover, profit, herd size, hectares under irrigation and service provision, these farmers are characterised by an urge to innovate, by tenacity, and by a shift away from monoculture (a single crop or livestock species). It is their mindset in particular that is an additional defining trait.

The ten can be classified as ultrapreneurs, because apart from the abovementioned skills the ultrapreneurs still run family businesses – where decision-making usually happens much faster than in the case of corporate groups. They are people who can even make provision for water and electricity if need be, because a 'boer maak 'n plan'. Their attunement to their environment, entrepreneurial mindset, forward thinking, sound judgement and pursuit of improvement all play a role. They are also negotiators, counsellors, educators and philanthropists.

They want to make a difference and ensure prosperity. Moreover, for years they have been at the cutting edge of another new era, the fourth industrial revolution, where they are already leaders in genetics, agricultural science and technology.

Pieter and Gys du Toit: Dutoit Group

At the time of the political transition of 1994, a new day also dawned for the Dutoit Group of Ceres when the family farming enterprise's previous practice of cooperating separately was replaced by that of farming together. 'Mine is mine and yours is yours' became 'everything is ours'.

Family farms have a long tradition worldwide – many of which end in tears or sometimes in the courts. But where families in South Africa work together, their farming businesses have become unprecedented success stories. As leaders in the fresh produce industry, the Dutoit Group is at the forefront of the country's so-called mega-farmers.

The group exports to some 42 countries across the world. Their major trading partners are Britain (although the British market is shrinking while the African market is increasing) and Europe, as well as the Middle East and the Far East. In 1991, it produced 80 000 tons of fresh produce (high-quality fruit and vegetables), which had increased to 200 000 tons by 2011 and will soon reach 300 000 tons. The group's produced tonnage has therefore grown at an average rate of about 10 per cent annually.

When Gysbertus du Toit decided to settle on the farm Kromfontein in the Koue Bokkeveld area in 1893, the Du Toit farming enterprise, in which the family names Gys and Gysbertus abound, started in earnest. Today his grandson, Pieter du Toit (above left) is the managing director of the group. Together with their late uncle Jan-Linde du Toit, Pieter and his elder brother, Gys (above right), were responsible for the business going from strength to strength. The seed of the success was planted when the concept of 'ours' was adopted, bringing an end to the yours–mine dispensation.

Nine family members are currently involved in the business, and Pieter mentions that at one point thirteen relatives named Gys were involved. Another family name is Petrus Stefanus François, although only two Pieters are at present part of the 'Seven cousins', as they refer to the family members in the business.

In 1998, the Du Toits restructured the company and divided the management responsibilities between the two brothers: Gys manages the agri-business and looks after new business, genetics, production and marketing, while Pieter, as managing director, is in charge of the day-to-day affairs.

The two brothers' father, also called Gys du Toit, considered water the most important element of farming. If you don't have water, you can't farm. He was already in his nineties when he told Wynand Dreyer, the author of *Megaboere*: 'I soon realised we have to build dams. Every year.'

Kromfontein, where Oom Gys lived for almost 60 years, is not far from the well-known Boplaas. Boplaas in the Koue Bokkeveld was the birthplace of the Afrikaans poet Boerneef (Izak van der Merwe, 1897–1967), who immortalised the farm in his poems.

It is said jokingly that the original settlers in the Koue Bokke-veld should have received a hardship allowance because it can get so cold there. Oom Gys went to settle in the area after the family had originally been sheep farmers at Franschhoek. They'd had grazing rights in the Bokkeveld since 1746. Trekking around with flocks of sheep between grazing areas happens to be an activity that his son Gys (Gysbertus the fourth) still misses most of all in a business which is by now such a large-scale operation that it has probably become one of the biggest on the continent. He recalls how, as a young boy, he would trek up into the Karoo with the livestock herds when his family went in search of grazing in the cold months. Each annual 'trek' was a new life experience of perseverance and persistence, for both humans and animals.

The two brothers have great respect for their ancestors. Although their grandfather farmed on a more modest scale, he did have an auditor who kept an eye on the finances. He founded one of the first private agricultural companies in the country and started exporting to Angola, which was a strong trading partner at the time. As far back as 1946, the farming activities were structured into a company, some-thing which only later became a craze among other farmers.

Pieter says it was of great significance in his life that the grand-children had to visit their grandfather in the town as often as possible, because he transferred important values to them. Key among these were probably his positive attitude and unshakeable faith in the future.

Although Pieter as the managing director no longer fulfils the role of farmer on a daily basis, he reckons that if you have grown up as a farmer interacting with nature, you develop a certain disposition. 'You know, a farmer is by nature someone who is cautious, because we harvest only once a year. As a result, a certain kind of conservatism becomes part of your character.'

The core focus of the Du Toit farming operation used to be apples, but today they also produce a variety of other crops. The resultant diversity ensures that they are not dependent on a single product line. It also allows them flexibility with regard to water. When they plant vegetables, they first do a calculation to determine whether there is enough water for the fruit, and then scale the vegetables up or down in accordance with the water resource.

Over the years, the Du Toits have built dozens of dams, in the Ceres area and more recently in the Langkloof area, to meet the farming operation's needs. Their late Oupa Gys and his brother Jan-Linde agreed that their ability to fully utilise the available water on the farm was the key to their success. Both of them believed the breakthrough in their farming business came when dams were built in the mountains. The Ceres district is in a winter-rainfall area, and they had to come up with a plan to store water. In summer they took advantage of the hot climate to plant vegetables. They were able to irrigate the vegetables by means of gravitation furrows. They devised plans to channel stormwater. Every drop counted.

Their Oupa Gys always said the second most important component of a successful farming operation is the workforce. If you looked after your workers, it was half the battle won. This tradition has been continued through the generations, and the Dutoit Group makes sure that their workers on all their farms have good housing and are happy. There are also crèches, schools, clinics, sports facilities and after-school centres with trained personnel on their respective farms.

In a labour-intensive environment such as theirs there are, however, a number of challenges that other industries do not have to contend with. The Du Toit brothers say research shows that productivity can be improved by about 30 per cent if one had to bring in mechanised processes. Trade unions are active among seasonal workers in particular, and the packhouse environment is pertinently affected by this. According to Gys, some trade unions do grasp the benefits of a growing industry, and negotiations with them about new management systems have been going more smoothly.

The Dutoit Group has partnerships in several companies across a wide spectrum in the fresh produce industry. Many of the enterprises are successful empowerment businesses. Among the benefits they derive from the partnership are market access, technical support, financial support and mentorships. A whole array of joint ventures have been established in conjunction with black empowerment companies, as well as with farmworkers and workers at packing facilities.

Pieter recounts that after careful consideration the Dutoit trademark was changed from the 'Du Toit' spelling to the new 'Dutoit', and the brand was already strong and established by the time he joined the company. When the industry was deregulated in 1997, they could market their brand to the rest of the world. While this gave a whole new dimension to the business, it also brought various new challenges to the fore, because any business enterprise ultimately has only one boss: 'the client'.

Innovation is part of the Du Toits' DNA. Pieter believes the base was established correctly, but a business enterprise dare not stagnate. Various innovative projects to the value of hundreds of millions of rand were launched particularly in the Ceres and Langkloof areas, whether investments in packing and processing facilities, new land or larger interests in distribution networks. In this way, the group strongly expanded its interests in various wholesalers, particularly in Europe.

To spread risks, Pieter and Gys diversified. They did this by buying land in other parts of the country or by entering into partnerships, for example. The diversification enabled them to manage the risks of nature better, but also the market risks with regard to product lines. They are constantly investigating new possibilities and product lines. For instance, as a result of Gys's great passion for the genetics of new plant varieties – something that in itself has become a large part of the expanded business – they started investing in blueberries, a crop that was not previously suitable for large sections of their production areas.

A revolution with regard to plant material is under way because the period within which product types can be grown can be shortened considerably by means of new technology. The Dutoit Group is at the forefront of this revolution. The science involves the cultivation of plant material that brings together the optimal traits of a product for specific climatic conditions, but also takes customer preferences into account, such as the colour of a specific fruit. The Du Toits have acquired the rights to produce a red-fleshed apple, for instance. Because consumers nowadays look at a variety of factors when they buy fruit, the Du Toits make sure that they keep abreast of technological advances. This is why Gys says he 'will never retire, because it's just too interesting'.

The Dutoit Group's interests in the Western Cape include 11 farms (mostly near Ceres, but also around Worcester and in the Sandveld), two empowerment projects and three packing plants and coolstores. In the Eastern Cape (Langkloof), they farm on 12 farms where they also have four packhouses or coolstores, and two farms that are in a workers' trust.

According to Gys, farming rests on five legs: soil, water, climate, labour and management. By means of genetic research and new technology, all five those legs can be strengthened where necessary. Today products not only have to taste good; they must also have an attractive appearance, offer health-promoting properties, have the ability to retain their quality, and contain extra antioxidants. To be profitable, you need to have product lines that are unique and for which the consumer is prepared to pay more. The Du Toits already have about 100 different product lines and cultivars.

The group's business philosophy is quite simple: they want to get a high-quality product to the consumer as quickly and as efficiently as possible.

It was much harder to do business before 1994, Gys and Pieter explain. They were unable to sell their fruit in Africa or take it into the world with confidence. Since then it has been possible to do business with virtually anyone. The political change in the mid 1990s also enabled them to gain access to the best technology from across the world.

Pieter and Gys note that you always need to keep your eye on your competition: if your organisation can do better than them, you will survive. The single biggest risk is managing input costs, they say, because on the consumer side there is sometimes virtually no inflation in the markets in which they compete. They therefore have to keep the cost-increase side as low as possible to protect margins. There are of course other risks, such as exchange rates, over which they have no control, but that applies to everyone in the industry.

A family-owned farming business has its own challenges and needs. The family eventually developed a model in terms of which a family forum determines the rules of the game and the inclusion of family members in the company. Communication in a family differs from communication lines within a corporate structure. Every family member is free to choose whether or not he wants to join the company.

'We put him in a position in the business where in our view he can best exercise his talents,' says Gys du Toit. But the company has grown beyond the family, and they won't hesitate to 'import' specialists where necessary. 'Our family wants to remain in agriculture, which we love. It's what we know and it's the terrain in which we have confidence. It's in our blood and we understand agriculture.'

On the Dutoit Agri side, the family recently put their new policy into action by taking the unusual step of appointing an 'outsider' instead of a family member as managing director. Willem Coetzee, former managing director of Kromco, was appointed as the new CEO of Dutoit Agri with effect from 2018.

As part of professionalising the governance structures, the family also in recent years appointed a board with strong independent directors, such as the chair, George Steyn – previously from Pepkor – the empowerment strategist Dr Ernest Messina, and Dr Sizeka Magwentshu-Rensburg, who is, inter alia, a director of Old Mutual and the Industrial Development Corporation (IDC).

The Du Toits of Ceres have transformed their farming enterprise into a multinational business. Their interests extend deep into the export markets where they are involved. Yet they insist that they prefer to stay under the radar. For instance, Gys provided inputs to President Cyril Ramaphosa's land reform panel and committees 'from behind the scenes'.

Though reluctant to talk about politics and land reform, Gys does mention that there are aspects that stand out for him. For one, in his experience, there has been less investment taking place in commercial farming since the land issue has again taken centre stage. And, secondly, that goodwill and the willingness of the country's commercial farmers to assist emerging and established black farmers on a large scale and enter into partnership with them, are being totally understated. 'Someone should record all the things that are being done by the [white] farmers,' he reckons.

The success of the Du Toits can certainly be summed up by saying that in their sphere of farming, they realised that you need to have an interest in every facet of the value chain: in other words, right from the start, before the seed or seedling is even planted, all the way through to the hands (and mouth) of the end consumer. And to do it on a large scale as well.

Tommie van Zyl: ZZ2

In 1702, a charge of 'insubordination' – often a distress call on the part of a weak leader to get rid of enterprising subordinates – resulted in an ancestor of the Van Zyls of the large farming group ZZ2 being fired as an employee of the Dutch East India Company (VOC) at the Cape.

As a gardener based at the Rustenburg nursery in what is now the suburb of Rondebosch, Willem van Zyl was responsible for planting thousands of trees in avenues in and around Cape Town – he would also have planted many of the oak trees in Stellenbosch by hand, Louis Changuion maintains in his book *A Farm Called ZZ2*.

After losing his job with the VOC, Van Zyl bought a farm at Simondium in the fertile Franschhoek valley where he farmed with fruit, vegetables, wine and livestock. His wife, Christina van Loveren, who had accompanied him to the Cape from the Netherlands in 1699 in the hope of making a fresh start, unwittingly gave her name to the renowned Van Loveren wine estate outside Robertson in the Boland. The Retief family, considered by many to be the largest family-owned wine producer in the country with their Four Cousins brand, are descendants of Willem and Christina. Christina's bridal 'trousseau' chest is still displayed in the Van Loveren tasting room.

Around 1836, Van Zyl's descendants left the Cape and migrated northwards as trekboers during the time of the Great Trek. In about 1880, some of the Van Zyls eventually settled in the region to the east of Pietersburg (today Polokwane), but the need for independence and a passion for farming have always been part of their history.

Yet the Van Zyls' great trek did not end in Mooketsi between Louis Trichardt and Tzaneen. While ZZ2's farms are primarily in the Limpopo province, where they mainly cultivate tomatoes and avocados, the group also operates in the Western Cape, Eastern Cape, Gauteng, North West, Mpumalanga and Namibia. In large parts of the country they also grow mangoes, onions, dates, cherries, apples, pears, stone fruit, almonds and blueberries, besides farming with cattle and game.

The group regards the ZZ2 brand as 'a well-known icon in South Africa with a proud history backed by a great customer value offering and superior economic value for all our stakeholders'. The name 'ZZ2' stems from new regulations that were issued after the Anglo-Boer War whereby farmers received a registered number with which to brand their livestock. In 1903, the code ZZ2 was awarded to Burt van Zyl, grandfather of the famous Bertie van Zyl, the actual founder of the ZZ2 farming enterprise. At the time, four Van Zyls received the codes ZZ1 to ZZ4. At some stage the ZZ2 branding irons were used to stamp potato bags in red paint before they were sent to the market. The mark migrated over time from a branding mark for livestock to a trademark for all products of the ZZ2 Group that today enjoys international recognition.

Bertie van Zyl was born on 16 November 1932 on the farm Boekenhoutbult in the Mooketsi valley. He left school at the age of 16 to take over the farming responsibilities from his ailing father. At the time the farming activities centred on a mixed crop, but the main focus was on potatoes. Life was hard and the family barely survived. The enterprising Bertie soon realised that his neighbour made more money planting tomatoes than potatoes. The climate in the fertile Mooketsi valley made it possible to plant tomato crops all year round.

He had to battle to convince his father of the viability of tomatoes, but his first successful tomato crop was harvested in 1953. It was grown on only one hectare of land, which was all that his father had allowed him. Because market prices were high, Bertie doubled his plantings. The price fell, however, and he had neither the infrastructure nor the labour force to deal with the expanded operation. He recounted that he nearly lost all his money at the time. But since then, ZZ2 has been regarded as the biggest tomato-farming operation in the southern hemisphere.

Tenacity, an eye for a business opportunity, a knack for communicating with employees in their own language and an unwavering self-belief stood Bertie in good stead over the years. In 1966, the ZZ2 Group was registered as a private company and by the time of Bertie's death in 2005, he had built up ZZ2 into a multimillion-rand farming conglomerate. He had also made his mark on public life, not only in the agricultural community but also at provincial and national level. Thousands of his workers, along with various cabinet ministers – including the then minister of agriculture Thoko Didiza – paid tribute to him at his funeral; inter alia for what the Van Zyls had done for emerging farmers and in the country.

Over the years, the Van Zyls have systematically diversified their product lines to avocados, onions, stone fruit and livestock. It is probably only the massive Westfalia Group, which was started by the philanthropist, geologist and scientist Hans Merensky (1871–1952) on his farm Westfalia near Duiwelskloof, that will trump ZZ2 when it comes to avocado production. But Westfalia, which is controlled by Hans Merensky Holdings, is rather a corporate group while the ZZ2 Group is still a family-owned and -run business.

ZZ2 also has farms at Musina in Limpopo. They grow apples and pears at Ceres and Riebeek West and in the Langkloof area, with some of their business done in cooperation with the Dutoit Group. The group has also started expanding to eSwatini. Dates, a new crop, are farmed in the Karas district of Namibia.

Tommie van Zyl, managing director of ZZ2, who together with his brother Philé took over the business interests from their father, says that as far as business growth is concerned, ZZ2 is constantly looking at how they should adapt their business. 'We benchmark ourselves against the best in the world and we will adapt our system to be optimally suited to the environment we're in. We're firmly established in South Africa, but also, where it makes economic sense, in neighbouring countries.'

ZZ2 was at first a conventional commercial farming operation, but they have moved to an environmentally senstive approach to commercial farming by aiming to farm in harmony with nature. 'The ZZ2 philosophy is to create an ecosystem and to bring this know-how together,' Tommie explains. 'Systematic thinking is necessary. We were industrial farmers but, due to repeated incidences of pests, we went organic and developed the concept of nature farming. We found that the mealie bug pest was almost impossible to get rid of with chemicals. ZZ2 began an insectary in 1997 to raise insects to combat predators and parasites. We've also created bio-reservoirs on all our farms.'

For Tommie, it was a long and challenging road to becoming chief executive officer of a multibillion-rand business. He did not get the job because he was Bertie van Zyl's son, he says openly. As a child, he had already tried to teach himself what farming and doing business successfully required. 'My father was a very strict man and he didn't want us to go to school.' Bertie wanted him to leave school after grade 8 to start working, but with the help of neighbours and uncles, Tommie persuaded his father to allow him to study.

After school he obtained a BCom degree in economics and agricultural economics at Stellenbosch University. Following the completion of a postgraduate honours degree, he was awarded a Fulbright scholarship to complete a master's degree in food and re-source economics at the University of Florida. While he was in the United States, he was awarded membership to Gamma Sigma Delta, an international honour society dedicated to recognising accom-plishments of leaders in agricultural and related sciences. In 1986, Tommie returned to the family farm where he started working as a buying clerk, which was in keeping with his father's philosophy that everyone had to start at the bottom.

In 1992, at the age of 27, he began performing certain managerial tasks. 'But we had a very interesting managing system. I had the title and the responsibility, but not necessarily, at that time, the authority.' It was only in 2001, when they established proper governance structures, that Tommie started gaining full authority as chief executive officer and reported to their board of directors. The father of four took over the reins of the conglomerate in full in 2005. His son, Burtie, followed the family tradition by starting off as a junior project manager before being promoted through the ranks to his current position of general manager for the avocado plantations.

The ZZ2 operations at Mooketsi are so extensive that Tommie and some of his managers fly to the orchards in a helicopter or light aircraft. The group's total production of tomatoes, of which there are five main varieties, is now close to 200 000 tons while avocados are picked on 1 000 hectares. The ZZ2 Afrikado nursery (the brand is a combination of the words 'avocado' and 'Africa') has the capacity to deliver 300 000 avocado trees per annum. ZZ2 has 27 different production lines of apples, pears and stone fruit. Cherries, almonds, dates, blueberries and tomato juice are also marketed on a large scale. In addition, the Van Zyls farm with game and cattle with the Pinzgauer and the PinZ²yl studs. The PinZ²yl is a new breed ZZ2 developed by cross-breeding the Nguni breed from Africa with the best production qualities (meat and milk) of the Pinzgauer, a breed of Austrian origin. It offers Africa an economical and low-maintenance breed. ZZ2 has built several small villages for their workers and their families closer to the farms. Each farm has its own clinic, as they are far away from the nearest hospital. ZZ2 also provides bus services for workers' school-going children and has dozens of crèches. At the beginning of 2019, ZZ2 employed 25 000 people and had an annual turnover of R24 billion.

'Money doesn't really impress us,' says Tommie. 'When you think you're a king, you're a pawpaw, when you think you're a pawpaw, you're a king. I'm very intrigued by value in a broad sense. We're impressed by the value of the things we produce and the meaning that we're creating for many people.'

He believes agriculture has a bright future in South Africa, but because the economy remains under pressure, the group has also diversified into superfruits in order to counteract an economic slow-down.

Piet Karsten: Karsten Group

'Excellence is the result of caring more than others think is wise, risking more than others think is safe, dreaming more than others think is practical, and expecting more than others think is possible.'

This is the motto of Piet Karsten, who began farming on an island and became one of the country's biggest farmers. In 1968, Piet and his late wife, Babsie, started their family farming enterprise on Kanoneiland west of Upington on the banks of the Orange River. Twelve years later, in 1980, they bought the farm Roepersfontein, which now serves as the headquarters of the Karsten Group.

When they initially built a shed, they lived inside the shed in a caravan while they grew rotation crops and farmed with raisins. Babsie, who had been born and bred on Kanoneiland, had trained as a teacher in Stellenbosch and was able to pay the farmworkers' wages with the R85 she earned in her teaching job.

Piet says his big breakthrough came when he realised the future of table grapes lay in seedless. On 2 February 1990, he was in Germany 'hawking some grapes to small corner shops', because at that stage South Africa was totally excluded at the big retail groups. The day after former president FW de Klerk's speech in 1990, 'it was as if a new door had opened for us in the world'.

In 2000, the Karsten Group acquired a deciduous fruit and vegetable farm in the Ceres region where the focus is mainly on apples, pears and cherries. New Vision Fruit was established in 2004 as the export and logistics arm of the group. More recently, together with two other shareholders, Horizon Fruits was established to take care of the logistical services, in addition to sharing some of the marketing functions of New Vision Fruit.

Karsten UK was established in 2005 as the distribution service provider of the group in the United Kingdom and Europe. In 2012, as part of its strategy to broaden its marketing footprint, the group purchased several table grape farms in the Western Cape. The following year, New Vision Fruit BV was established in Rotterdam to deliver products in Europe. In partnership with other South African companies, the Karsten Group established a marketing structure, Hydix, to market its products in both the Middle and the Far East.

The Karsten Group has a strong logistics and international marketing structure with enterprises and offices in London, Rotterdam and Cape Town, backed by companies in the Northern and Western Cape. The group exports to various parts of the world, and besides grapes, it farms with sweet melons, apples, cherries, citrus, dates, pears, pecan nuts, plums, watermelons, boer goats, cattle and game.

In 2015, Piet Karsten was named the Agricultural Writers of SA's Farmer of the Year. He had followed a somewhat different route to the one his 'wise grandmother' had in mind for him when she sent this youngster from Namibia to the Cape to learn how to speak English and to become a clergyman. Neither of these wishes was realised, he says. But his grandmother nonetheless has reason to be proud.

One would imagine a farmer of his calibre to be a third- or fourth-generation family farmer. But when he joined the family's farming operations on Kanoneiland in the Northern Cape after his Air Force years in Pretoria, there was less success. 'I wanted to be part of the family business, but it was made clear to me that I should rather go and work elsewhere,' Piet recounts.

'So Babsie and I then bought a piece of land of our own, about 6 hectares on Kanoneiland, from an old lady, for R15 000. The women lent me R10 000 over five years, and for the rest I had to gather R5 000. That's where we started.'

Piet's father died in 1974, but prior to this event he had managed to buy a further 16 hectares on Kanoneiland with the help of his father and that of the bank. In between, he lent a hand at the family's operations and eventually expanded his own little patch on Kanoneiland to 36 hectares; besides a small quantity of grapes to produce raisins, he grew rotation crops.

'In 1974 we ran ahead of the flood. We couldn't stay there any longer. We couldn't develop. It was small, it was limited, and we didn't have accommodation … then a piece of land on the eastern side of the river outside of Kanoneiland came out on tender – about six kilometres away from us on outside land. We got it. This land had water rights for about 60 hectares.

'Remember, we only got Eskom power in 1977. That's where our breakthrough came. After that, we planted as much as 10 hectares of vines at a time – still raisins. In the mid 1980s the European market started moving away from seeded table grapes. The Chileans had come in with a considerable quantity of seedless grapes in Britain, which stimulated the market.'

Entrepreneurs spotted the gap, he says. 'Locally, things were still regulated by the Deciduous Fruit Board in those days. You weren't allowed to do anything on your own. And then they also saw the potential, provided a bit of assistance and encouraged farmers to export seedless grapes.'

The advantage of raisin grapes was that Piet could switch them over easily and quickly to table grapes by using different means of production. 'South Africa had by that time been exporting table grapes for years, but it was primarily from the Hex River Valley and Paarl. We could get into the market earlier, however, thanks to our warmer conditions. We had the seedless variety, and in the Western Cape there was nothing. Everything was seeded. We were absolutely at the right place at the right time.'

Today the Karsten Group has tentacles stretching from the Northern and the Western Cape into China, Russia, the United Kingdom, the Netherlands and South America.

It was partly thanks to dates that the Karsten Group was able to move its activities into fifth gear. In the mid 1990s, Piet was approached by the Industrial Development Corporation (IDC). The IDC owned the Pella date farm in partnership with the legendary Oom Gertjie Niemoller. 'Oom Gertjie had retired. His sons didn't want to continue farming, and they then approached me to manage the date farm. After six months we decided to take a stake in the business. We negotiated with the IDC, and they put in the date farm and cash to acquire an interest in our group.

'With expertise from Israel, among others, the dried-date

production was switched to fresh dates, because it's a more profitable business. There's a greater demand for the fresh product. This cash injection, too, enabled us to expand faster.

'We established vineyards as if there was no tomorrow – as much as 120 hectares annually. We started planting across the entire area, and this helped us enormously to put the farming operations on a faster trajectory,' Piet recounts.

By the early 1990s, the Karsten Group had a solid and diversified footprint, as well as favourable financial support. 'When the interest rates fell, the rand was strong again, and this hurt the export industry. A lot of guys lost their appetite for business, but we managed to stick it out and keep going. It was the right decision.'

The new South Africa of 1994 had a significant influence on agriculture in the country in all kinds of ways. Piet Karsten relates: 'It was as if heaven had opened for us, and before 1994 we'd already thought we were in heaven. We were well protected, but the system never encouraged personal initiative. We saw afterwards that it hadn't actually been a good system. There was no reason for entrepreneurship. After 1994, regulation was abolished; and when the free market was introduced, we realised we'd have to take control of our product.'

It was then that the Karsten Group embarked on doing business directly in foreign countries, and not only from home soil as a producer. 'We started talking directly to our clients, and our target was the ten largest retailers in the world. It was through that that we changed the market, because at that stage the traditional producer–exporter–importer–client system was in use. Everyone in the system took their cut. We then cut out the middleman. We persuaded the chain stores to deal directly with us. It changed marketing in the world – and we take pride in the fact that we were part of that change.'

This change brought along great pressure and expectations. 'We had to deliver the goods. But we knew it would be difficult to succeed if we operated only from South Africa. So, about 15 years ago we opened an office in Spalding in Britain. This is where our chilled storage and packing facilities are located.

'We do the picking ourselves. We transport the product to the port. We have a logistics company – we do all the shipping ourselves. We never lose control over the product until it's on the shelf. And we put it on the client's shelf within hours. Our whole secret with the thing is speed, speed, speed. It's a perishable product. When other guys are partying on Christmas Eve or New Year's Eve, our people are standing on the bow of the ship, making sure that the ship departs.'

The Spalding model was replicated in Rotterdam. In addition, the group acquired an interest in various marketing companies in the Netherlands, China and Russia.

One often hears South African farmers talking about the competition they experience on the world markets from South America, for instance. Piet says that 'out of every embarrassment, an opportunity arises'. In this regard, the Karsten Group has turned a potential enemy into a partner by getting involved in cooperation and partnerships in, inter alia, Chile, Brazil and Peru.

'We work with big clients. We cooperate technically. We aren't importers and we don't work on commissions. We agree on a cost. We also don't come between a producer and a client. They negotiate with each other about a price ... and we make sure that the product gets to the right place in the world at the right time. It works for us because in the industry as a whole, cargo is king. If you have cargo all over the world, you can bargain with the shipping companies.'

The Karsten Group retains control over their product at all times – from the time it is planted to the time it ends up on a fresh produce shelf elsewhere in the world.

Without being asked about the reasons behind his success, Piet Karsten changes the topic from cargo ships to 'it'. 'It is a whole lot of grace from God and wind from behind. And everything we're talking about here comes down to people – this is a people business,' he says.

Up to this point, it has been the businessman speaking. Now he speaks as the founding father of the enterprise. 'We decided very early on as a family that we'd struggle to make it on our own. But sharing is in our genes. That's why we could bring the IDC into a family business with a stake of about 30 per cent. Furthermore, management also has a 10 per cent interest in the Karsten Group.

'Today we have about 6 000 people working with us and it's harder to reach every guy individually, but that's why the top layer of people in the business are so important; they need to have walked with you for a number of years. Together, the top five people in our group have more than 150 years' experience in the business. They understand the culture and the work ethic. They roll it out to the next guy and the next guy, and in that way you have to spread the seed so that you can reach your people, all 6 000 of them – everywhere. Whether it's a Pole or a Russian or a Czechoslovakian or a Dutchman. Whether it's a brown, white, black, pink or purple guy. They're people. And we are each other's people.'

Several members of the Karsten family are involved in the business. Piet's son Pieter (Pieta), who will succeed his father as head of the group, is the managing director of the export company New Vision Fruit as well as head of marketing of the group, and his wife, Riana, is in the marketing division. Belia Karsten is involved in finance at Durbanville and Jannetje Slabbert works in the Northern Cape, also in finance (her husband, Rudi, is involved in production). Piet's daughter Elizca Kies is involved in finance in the Northern Cape, while her husband Cobus is also in production.

Babsie Karsten, Piet's wife who died of pancreatic cancer in 2014, played a major role in the growth of the enterprise, particularly with regard to the social development of their employees. Sandra Karsten (née Botha) is now at Piet's side.

In Piet's view, the country's two biggest problems are illiteracy and poverty. And farmers are the very people who are close enough to the land and its people to make a difference in that regard. 'Talking alone doesn't help. We have, for example, a very big training and social development department in our business. We have foreign clients who support us so that we can develop the people. To us, training is of cardinal importance.

'It doesn't help us as farmers to whine every day about Jacob Zuma's plane and how much money they've now stolen again and invested for themselves. That doesn't get us anywhere. It's the job of the media and the opposition to give attention to that. We as farmers have to ensure that people talk agriculture. You have to reach out to the community, and many farmers have already been doing that for donkey's years,' reckons Piet.

He says he uses the old-school system: 'Empower, support, train people and check whether the people understand what's going on. It's about instilling confidence in a person, it's empowerment. And out of that comes the beautiful stories, such as that of One-boy Maleko who started off as a general worker but is today a full-fledged production manager. That's how he's been empowered.

'We have a woman with us who's studying to become an accountant. She's the chair of one of our trusts, and she has come through the system. The same system has also produced electricians, motor mechanics, plumbers. Agriculture is about much more than hoeing with a spade and having to drip with sweat.'

He has no time for farmers who do nothing to uplift their employees and at the same time only complain. 'The bad impression of agriculture that exists here and there is the fault of those guys.'

The joys and sorrows of his fellow human beings are also his, because their well-being affects him personally. To him, this, too, is an area where he can make a contribution to progress and improvement. And for that reason he believes in what agriculture can mean to South Africa. 'There's for instance this view about the importance of mining, and that agriculture by comparison makes a small contribution to the gross domestic product. That agriculture is therefore less important. But does anyone think about sustainability and *where* agriculture has a lasting impact?'

'There's this thing people need to understand about agriculture: farming is practised countrywide in the most remote areas where there's often not even a proper café. The farmer is *there*. And he has a large number of people for whom he's a vital artery. And without those people, this country is also sunk.'

Piet says the importance of agriculture and farmers has nothing to do with what percentage the sector contributes to the GDP. 'What does matter, is the sustainability of agriculture to house people and to provide them with a livelihood,' he says.

Piet gestures with his hand towards the open plains he is seeing in his mind's eye. 'Agriculture carries entire communities, and it drives us. For years, we as a family, along with our shareholder, didn't take a cent of dividend; not a cent. Because we're 6 000 people who are together in this thing. We can forget about just criticising. It won't work. The country is going through an evolution – that's for sure. It's tough. But we will have to make our contribution, because we have a role to play.

'If farmers had no role to play, I'd also want to get rid of them. But the reality is that there's a very, very big role to play. It's a mindset. The big commercial farmer is an entrepreneur. He wants to progress and he wants to grow for a thousand and ten reasons. He needs to apply his mind. He doesn't have time to think of negative things because that drags you down mentally. He doesn't want to be dragged down. He wants to stay motivated. *That* is the difference.'

Hendrick Schoeman: Schoeman Boerdery

Schoeman Boerdery celebrated its centenary in 2019 – a hundred years of development characterised by the right leader at the right time for each generation of this family-owned farming business. The visionary leader Karel Schoeman – a man who looked far into the future – started Schoeman Boerdery near the modern-day Delmas. He was followed by the expansionist, Hendrik, who greatly expanded the farming operations. Next in line was the consolidator, Kallie, who implemented specialisation.

Today it is the turn of Hendrik junior to ensure Schoeman Boerdery's long-term future by pursuing sustainability. Hendrik, Brent Parrot and Jacques Roos, his cousins' husbands who are also involved in the business, make up a formidable team.

Good leadership over the years has enabled the farming business to introduce timely developments and adaptations, to consolidate when it was necessary, and to focus on long-term sustainability today. And to keep expanding. Kallie Schoeman and his family partners recently bought the irrigation farm Granary Normandien (1 700 hectares), downstream from Hopetown, from Harvard University's alumni fund. The farm was renamed Zoetwater. Pecan trees have been planted on about 170 hectares, while they also farm with winter wheat and, in summer, with maize and soya beans by means of 70 centre pivots.

Kallie, managing director of Schoeman Boerdery, relates that in 1918 his grandfather Karel Schoeman (1892–1966) started farming with his father-in-law, Andries Neethling, at Delmas and on the farm Moosrivier at Marble Hall. They primarily farmed with cattle on the Highveld, and would trek down to the Bushveld in the winter for grazing. Karel, one of 18 children, grew up where the Hartbeespoortdam is situated (Schoemansville). The state bought out Schoeman's land, 'so Oupa Karel married a woman with land,' Kallie quips.

Karel and his wife Annie set up camp at Moosrivier because there was no housing on the farm. He realised that the climate near the river mouth was similar to that at Hartbeespoort, where there had been a grapevine with grapes that ripened earlier than those in the Cape Province. His father-in-law agreed that he could clear a patch of land where he planted grapes with great success. It eventually earned him the title of 'Father of deciduous fruit in the Transvaal'.

Schoeman Boerdery's humble beginnings date back to 1919 when Karel bought this farm from his father-in-law. Since the Olifants River flows through Moosrivier, he decided to irrigate his crops from the river and imported a ram pump from England (this type of pump uses the kinetic energy of flowing water). It was a revolutionary move in the region, which had only cattle farms. Moosrivier's grapes and wheat were the first crops under irrigation in the district.

Moosrivier was initially known as Mosesriviermond, named after the Moses River that forms one boundary of the farm and joins up with the Olifants River. Another river in the area is called the Aaron River. The biblical brothers Moses and Aaron led the Israelites out of Egypt to the promised land of Canaan. The Schoeman Boerdery's emblem, the big bunch of grapes carried by Joshua and Caleb, symbolises faith in God and the fertility of Canaan.

When Grandpa Karel wanted to register this emblem, he was unable to do so because it was already being used by Israel's department of tourism. 'Then he reversed the direction in which the two men are walking with the bunch of grapes, and they couldn't object any longer,' Kallie says laughingly. The wording below the image of the grape carriers reads: 'Die Kanaän van Transvaal'.

Today there are still giant 'bunches', Kallie believes, but now in the form of droughts, hail, rising input costs, a dysfunctional public service, thefts, corruption and so on. 'But, you can't be scared and farm. You must have faith in God and have to receive much grace from Him to keep farming in Africa.'

As a result of the depression in 1933, many destitute families approached Karel for help. He allowed them to become sharecroppers and grow wheat on condition that they cleared a patch of land on the farm for that purpose and build a *hartbeeshuisie* (a wattle and daub hut). In this way a small farming community developed on the farm.

Karel had to transport the wheat he bought from the sharecroppers with a buck wagon and oxen on the sandy road to Bronkhorstspruit where the only mill was. This trip took three days. The miller would often label the wheat as 'only good for chicken feed', just to pay a low price. Holding the whip hand, he exploited many farmers. To counter this problem, Karel and a few other farmers founded the Delmas Cooperative, which later became OTK and is now the agricultural services company Afgri.

In 1923, Schoeman bought the farm Witklip on which the town of Delmas was laid out. Hendrik senior, Kallie and Hendrik junior grew up here, and this is where Schoeman Boerdery's headquarters are situated. At Witklip, Karel established a mixed-farming operation, comprising a dairy, crop farming and a butchery in Delmas, to extend his value chain in the cattle industry.

The grapes produced at Moosrivier were the first commercial grapes outside of the Western Cape. The grapes in 'the Canaan of the Transvaal' were prone to many diseases, which led to the establishment of the Institute for Agricultural Research at Roodeplaat for research on fruit in the summer-rainfall area. Karel was the speaker at the launch.

In 1945, Hendrik Schoeman (1927–1995) started farming on Witklip at the age of eighteen and worked for his father, who still farmed full time until 1954. Karel subsequently devoted himself to his work for the then IDC, Foskor (the Phosphate Development Corporation) and the Bantu Development Corporation. Hendrik then took over the farming business, which expanded enormously under his leadership. He started farming with citrus.

'Hendrik had to fork out a lot of money for trees, equipment, buildings and implements, and he had to borrow it,' Kallie recounts. 'So he was constantly chasing cash flow to repay the loans by running different facets of farming, such as sheep, pigs, turkeys, a dairy, beef cattle, avocados, pawpaws, mangoes, litchis, tomatoes, prickly pears, tobacco, cotton, potatoes and watermelons. He expanded the grape-farming operations to the benefit of the current Loskop Valley.'

Hendrik entered politics and became the MP for Standerton in 1966. In 1968, he was appointed deputy minister of agriculture before becoming minister of agriculture in 1970. This was a pattern set by his grandfather, Commandant General Hendrik Schoeman, and his great-grandfather, General Stefanus (Stormvoël) Schoeman. All three of them were both farmer and politician. The popular Hendrik was later also minister of transport. Almost 25 years after his death, his famous response to a complaint about the food quality on SAA flights, '*Wil jy vlieg of wil jy vreet?*' (Do you want to fly or do you want to eat?), resurfaced during an AgriSA conference where the current drought crisis was highlighted.

Hendrik's son Kallie started farming in November 1974 after two 'interesting years' at the University of Pretoria's faculty of agricultural economics. He did not take his academic studies seriously and studied the patterns of the social behaviour of students instead, he recounts jokingly.

'Where could I find a better agricultural training school than at my father's farming business? There wasn't a management position for me on the farm. Pa gave me 10 hectares to produce vegetables for our farm stalls and the municipal market in Springs.'

The farming enterprise had purchased more farms over the years, and after a year as vegetable farmer Kallie had proved himself sufficiently to be awarded a management position on one of the farms. Hendrik only farmed on Saturdays, as he was in Parliament during the week. To some extent there was a lack of direction because of this, Kallie says. 'Pa realised it, and one day in 1978 while I was busy digging up potatoes, he stopped next to the field and told me the business had grown too big for him to handle. I had to take over. So I took over the reins of Schoeman Boerdery as a 24-year-old,' he relates. 'Because of all the expansions we had a large debt, and suddenly both the management and the debt of the farming business fell into my lap.'

He knew that a turnaround was required but had no idea where to start. So he paid a visit to Professor Ekhard Kassier, a former agricultural economist from Stellenbosch University, who was known for his innovative thinking. Kassier's observation was that the farming enterprise had no specific focus because of the many different crops they grew.

Based on Kassier's advice that he should focus and specialise, Kallie's turnaround strategy was to stop every branch of production that made up less than 10 per cent of the farming business. A number of branches were phased out and poor land was sold. Specialisation, modern management principles and financial control received attention. 'Budgets used to be done on the back of a Lexington cigarette box, and that had to change,' he says with a smile.

Today the Schoeman Group consists of four divisions: the Highveld farming operations; grain handling at Delmas; Moosrivier Citrus; and, also on Moosrivier, the Agron fertiliser plant. The crop farming in die Delmas district extends over 10 000 hectares (maize, small white beans for canning, and soya beans); the citrus orchards are on 1 400 hectares under irrigation (navels, Valencias, mandarins and lemons), and then there is also the 1 700 hectares of land at Zoetwater that was recently added.

The new strategy worked: within four years, Kallie had paid off all the debt. 'I never wanted to be in such a predicament again, and since those years we've only incurred debt to buy land. We're wary of borrowing money to finance expensive equipment and don't make use of production loans either. Even new orchards are established with cash,' he explains.

Kallie's approach has helped to expand Schoeman Boerdery further in a focused manner to the point where it is now easily twenty times bigger than when Hendrik passed the reins to Kallie in 1978. 'The business could have been considerably bigger if I wanted to take the chance of borrowing money for expansions, but the intrinsic risks of agriculture make me cautious,' Kallie says.

At Delmas they specialise in the production of maize, soya beans and white beans. Grain handling has expanded greatly, because the business also buys, sells and hedges other farmers' grain. The grain is stored in silos with a capacity of 78 000 tons at Witklip, from where the marketing and distribution are done, just like an agricultural cooperative did in the past. Many farmers do contract farming for Schoeman Boerdery, including black farmers as part of an empowerment programme.

The farming business has 903 permanent workers who are provided with housing, water and electricity. There are two nursery schools, two primary schools and a high school with 1 108 learners, a permanent clinic and a mobile clinic, soccer fields and a church building on the farms to meet the needs of the farmworkers and their families. A sewing centre (picking bags and uniforms) and a popular bakery (bread and vetkoek) are exclusively for the benefit of the workers, as well as unemployed people, who run them. A carpentry factory is currently in a planning phase.

One of their latest projects, Zamukele ('adopt' in Zulu), was started to help guide emerging farmers towards commercial farming. They identify and settle emerging farmers, and support them with advice and assistance to advance towards becoming sustainable, commercial dried-bean producers. A division dedicated to these initiatives, Schoeman Grondhervorming (Land Reform), was established within the business, and is managed by Jacques Roos.

On the Moosrivier farm – which has a subtropical climate – Schoeman Boerdery specialises in growing citrus under irrigation. 'To follow Professor Kassier's advice, I first had to do financial analyses of the 23 different crops,' Kallie recounts. 'We didn't have individual systems for each production branch. Everything was in one pot. There were no computers in those days … we had to make intensive sums. We got rid of many branches, and the citrus replaced the other crops. The most emotional decision was to ditch the table grapes, our pioneer crop. Having grapes and citrus on the same farm doesn't work for us.'

In 2008, Kallie's son, Hendrik junior, joined the family-owned farming enterprise as the fourth generation. After obtaining a BCom and an honours degree in industrial psychology at the University of Pretoria, he had gone to work at a citrus and fruit importer in the

United Kingdom. Eurodix sent him to a family business in Peru that also produces and exports citrus.

At the request of Hendrik junior, Kallie and his wife Elna flew to Peru, and they were just as impressed as Hendrik by the way in which the Masias family had survived and persisted after Peru had gone through a period of land expropriation. The family retained only 70 hectares of their 2 000-hectare property, but Masias successfully transformed the unowned stony mountains around him into terraces and started farming with layer chickens, avocados and citrus on terrain that had been classified as unusable. This enabled them to buy back the land that had been expropriated from them. Today they are among the largest farmers in Peru.

Hendrik junior's first position at Moosrivier was that of orchard manager in the production division. He was therefore only one of the cogs in one of the parts of the engine room. After the death of the marketing manager in 2011, Kallie appointed Hendrik to this position, in which he distinguished himself. In 2013, he was promoted to CEO of Moosrivier.

Kallie says Hendrik is the man who has brought sustainability into the business. The focus is on international markets, as they are in the export industry and offer the modern, international housewife a premium basket of citrus. 'Moosrivier's climate offers an opportunity to produce almost the entire citrus range. We focus particularly on varieties that offer the housewife something special, such as a sweeter taste quality, seedlessness and easy peeling.

'The choice of rootstock, as well as the soil type, orchard gradient and micro-climate have a big influence on the above – the wine industry talks about terroir. To this end, we gather the necessary expert knowledge and endeavour to have a well-considered planting strategy in order to offer the entire "basket" at high quality and scale to the international and local market,' Hendrik explains.

Kallie says they are serious about making a difference and believe that the restoration of dignity and entrepreneurship can be achieved through agriculture. Besides the business's dried-bean project for small farmers, Hendrik has a vegetable garden project that is run with the assistance of Umsizi ('helper' in Zulu). It is aimed at sustainable social solutions. They encourage families to start vegetable gardens in their backyards, along with which they learn the basic principles of business and entrepreneurship. This transformation initiative is inclusive and focuses on Schoeman Boerdery's employees as well as the families in villages close to Moosrivier.

To date, 501 vegetable gardens have been established in 14 villages in the former Lebowa. On Moosrivier itself there are 189 gardens of which 89 produce surpluses that they sell. 'Our dream is to have a material influence on unemployment and poverty in every community within a 200-kilometre radius of Moosrivier. We believe this model with its exponential influence can really impact the masses and give hope to those who are currently without hope,' says Hendrik.

On the same day that Hendrik started working at Schoeman Boerdery, Kallie's sister Madel's oldest son-in-law, Brent Parrot, started at Witklip. He heads up the grain production, processing and storage in the Highveld. Five years later, another son-in-law, Jacques Roos, took up the reins, and he manages the transformation process and non-agricultural commercial business.

Madel's husband, Kobus Fourie, acted as the financial director of the business for the past 36 years, and currently serves on the board as a non-executive director.

Kallie regards the development of centre pivot irrigation as the first major technological advance he experienced as a farmer. The old drag lines were very labour intensive. Centre pivot sprayers made irrigation much easier and more efficient.

Another key development was equipment that graded fruit electronically according to colour, size, weight and blemishes. Information technology has also made life much easier for a farmer. Today a farmer can use apps on laptops, cellphones and tablets to look at weather reports, keep an eye on markets, schedule irrigation, bid at auctions and read publications, says Kallie. The advent of satellite navigation – and also of drones – has taken precision farming to the highest level.

In this way, Schoeman Boerdery has grown, adapted and improved as a family business over a period of a hundred years. Today their vision is: 'Throughout the generations, we have been and will remain a blessing to our people, our community and our country.'

Louis and Cora de Kock: Wildeklawer

The world is heading towards a food shortage. Which means the wheel is going to turn so that farmers will no longer be price-takers on both the input and the sale side.

This is the view of Louis de Kock of Wildeklawer near Barkly West, a new-generation precision vegetable farmer regarded by some as the largest onion farmer in Africa and one of the largest in the world. All of this he accomplished within three decades with mostly borrowed money and own initiative, 'but an abundance of grace from God'.

To De Kock, with his agricultural engineering background as a former lecturer at the University of Pretoria, farming is his passion and hobby, not just work. His farm Wildeklawer is situated within an almost perfect U-shape of a section of the Vaal River approximately 50 kilometres northwest of Kimberley. The farm is virtually surrounded by the river. In the 1990s, he started rebuilding the barren and underdeveloped farm completely, with some of his lands having been ploughed up and levelled to such an extent that they are now flatter 'than many rugby fields'.

The Wildeklawer brand is a leading producer of crops such as onions, carrots, potatoes, beetroots, watermelons, sweet melons and squashes, but also maize and wheat. Everything is produced according to international standards with advanced equipment and facilities, for both the local and the export market.

Today, the De Kocks farm on close to 4 000 hectares of land. The group's operations are divided into three production units: Wildeklawer, Romance and De Bron (situated 130 kilometres southwest of Kimberley). The Wildeklawer Group comprises six companies that focus on the farming, packing and marketing of fresh vegetables and grains.

De Kock is renowned as an engineer-inventor-entrepreneur-farmer who had his own workshop built where qualified artisans can manufacture his own designs and modify expensive imported equipment to suit his needs. On top of that, he is a practical perfectionist. He believes he needs to know about and utilise everything in the farming enterprise: the soil, the climate, and also the human potential. 'You must be able to live in harmony with your environment.'

On Wildeklawer, there is a construction team working with concrete and cement to build pump stations, for example, and in the workshop they build their own conveyer belts for the packhouse.

As for how he creates his near-perfect precision lands, De Kock says: 'You have to do everything right.' When they started on the farm, irrigating their crops was done with only two centre-pivot systems and irrigation lines moved by hand. His father helped them to first plough the lands, at a time when they had to hire tractors from neighbours to supplement their own ageing fleet of three tractors.

'When we replanned and rebuilt the farm after the first five years, we actually started creating the perfect lands. We flattened our centre pivots and basically created open-air factories. By the time you plant, everything already needs to be 100 per cent right. Then incredible yields are possible. We moved millions of cubic metres of soil. Dongas were filled up. A seedbed has to be fine enough.'

Under each individual centre pivot – of which he now has more than 100 – there is the same type of soil, a metre deep everywhere, because when the rains come, there has to be space for the water under the crops.

De Kock imported special laser-levelling equipment from the United States to lay out the lands. He designs the land on his computer and then programs the equipment. Then tractors work day and night to move the soil, with the land being shaped at optimal gradients to ensure maximum water infiltration with ideal run-off conditions. The advantage of his technique is that all his lands have equal value in all respects – size, soil quality, gradient; everything is uniform. Because he had very little money in the beginning, he had to devise plans and build equipment himself from scratch.

He notes proudly that every bag of onions he sellls is numbered. If someone calls him and gives him a number, he can tell the person exactly on what day and where he purchased the seed in America, when these onions were planted, irrigated, harvested and had their tops cut off, and by which machine they were packed. There is a complete record of traceability of what people bought. They pack 45 000 to 50 000 bags of onions (500 000 kg of bags) daily, and each of those bags can be accounted for.

De Kock says in addition to the precision cropfields created, complex systems had to be developed, such as those for finance, marketing, technical support and transportation. In the busy three weeks before Christmas 2019, a truck was loaded or unloaded (with various vegetables, seeds, fertiliser and so on) on average every 8,6 minutes during a working day of nine hours. If the crops that are hauled in with tractors and wagons from the fields are added, a truck was uploaded or unloaded at the warehouse at Wildeklawer every 3,1 minutes. For each of those loads, negotiations were done with the recipient or the shipper, a truck was scheduled for a specific time, loading or unloading was overseen, freight letters were issued, fees were received and payments were made.

Asked whether he intends to expand in order 'to keep up' due to increased costs, De Kock replies that every year something should happen that makes one more creative. 'We learnt a lot from the drought. On many days it was hotter than 40 degrees, but we had to plant because we needed to deliver on contracts. At times beetroot was replanted five times, but the fifth time you learn how you should plant beetroot and potatoes when the temperature exceeds 40 degrees. One should constantly keep developing one's methodology and techniques. Farm size is indeed an important factor for economies of scale, but it's not about size, it's about relevance. If you only have 60 hectares you should plant strawberries because then you're relevant, but maize on 60 hectares is irrelevant.'

The people at Wildeklawer are future-oriented, and everything they do ultimately revolves around the idea of how to develop and advance the business. He reckons they have some of the most productive land in the world; not land that he inherited, but that he himself has developed into that state, with systems that have been put in place to maintain it. Because, he says, he believes in the future of agriculture.

Nonetheless, De Kock notes that no other industry operates like agriculture, where a farmer has to pay the asking price for his purchases (inputs), and when he delivers his product, 'you have to put up with the price the guy gives you'. Specifically in the case of vegetable and fruit, he believes, there will be such a shortage in future that the chain store that wants to have these products on its shelves will have to pay for them.

With his background as an agricultural engineer with a precision mindset and an urge for practical solutions, he explained his standpoint about the changing scenario for agricultural producers and the anticipated rise in food prices as follows: If he buys a bottle of drinking water at a shop, he pays R34 for 10 litres (prices as in 2015). In 2015, the average price a farmer got for a 10 kg bag of potatoes was just over half the price of the water. The person who sells the water merely puts the bottle under a fountain, screws a lid on top and gets R34.

'I have to buy a farm, obtain water, put up a centre pivot, get Eskom to supply power, cultivate the land, pay through the nose for seed, buy fertiliser, a lot of the product is stolen, there's drought, the potatoes have to be washed, sorted and packed, and I have to transport them to the market, but I get much less than the guy who sells water. That bag of potatoes is actually so cheap. A family can live on it for a month.

'We will have to think differently. Why should the person on the farm work at half price compared to the person in the factory who makes toys for you? But the person who makes food for you, he's battered by the hail, he's outside in the rain, wind and sun. We need to look at how such disparities can be corrected in the future. Agriculture has always been a kind of stepchild in a certain sense, but that's changing.'

De Kock says he once asked the head of John Deere who his largest shareholders were. It is Bill Gates of Microsoft fame, with the investment guru Warren Buffett close behind him. 'Just look at how many farms Bill Gates bought recently in America. And those guys have good advisers, don't they? So, I really think if there's one thing that's certain, it's that there are major changes in the offing for agriculture. Positive changes.'

During a panel discussion at a recent Stellenbosch Woordfees,

De Kock told the agricultural expert Mohammad Karaan and the academic Piet Croucamp the country would have to think quite differently about the land question. Karaan specifically wanted to know how De Kock was coping with 'political pressure, drought, tension and political turbulence', because according to Karaan agriculture is like a heavy truck that is driving uphill but has to gear down to get power.

De Kock replied that farmers were faced with cumulative tensions. Firstly, there is the tension caused by land reform, because the farmer is in total uncertainty about his survival (there is just constant toing-and-froing about the issue). Then there are the tensions resulting from the drought (the worst in recent times), as well as labour problems, wages and strikes (which have become life-threatening for families in the Western Cape), and, fifthly, the economic downturn. This is the total package the farmer has to carry, he said. Many other people are only worried about the fifth element (the economy).

'There will have to be realism from the side of the government.' He noted that because of the drought in particular, 'we're now seeing farmers committing suicide – as in the Free State where the farmer first shot his last 20 cattle and then himself. It's a new phenomenon.

'And yet we're the best farmers in the world. At one stage, I asked a minister of agriculture (after we'd been run down yet again) to give me the profile of who he saw as the ideal farmer. What does he look like? You travel all over the world. Tell me: is it a Japanese farmer; an American farmer? Who do you idealise as the person who should be here? Because then we'll know how we should get ourselves right. The reply was that he hadn't yet come across better ones, and that we were the ideal farmers.

'So, if that's the case, there would have to be realism about the issue, not so?'

The reason why everyone should look realistically at the land question, De Kock said, is that the government is faced with a truly massive and complex problem. Small (emerging) farmers will have to be established. The government, too, realises that is not the perfect solution for the country, yet emerging farmers will have to be assisted.

'In Rwanda, small farmers are doing incredibly well. That country is the size of Gauteng, but those farmers produce more potatoes than

South Africa does. The [SA] government therefore looks at Rwanda and thinks it can work here, but the government will have to transfer land. Land transfer started initially at a rapid tempo but was basically unsuccessful, which has slowed down the process. It has dawned on the government that it's not just about transferring land; expertise and technology also need to be transferred.'

De Kock believes commercial farmers possess incredible intellectual capital. In his own case, he can 'write three Bibles' about vegetable farming and everything it requires, but this knowledge is currently unrecorded. 'Anyone can read up a lot about maize and grain, but many aspects of agriculture you can't read about. In the end, the government is faced with that problem [of knowledge transfer].

'My question to people is: is it realistic to think that 35 000 farmers have to shoulder the burden of this national problem, an apartheid problem that developed over many years, alone? Precisely because the majority of them are already under such economic pressure that they're unable to make any contribution. To then leave this problem on the shoulders of only 1 000 or 2 000 farmers is not realistic. Beware of the spillover effect, where food prices could be affected.'

De Kock suggests that various solutions for the funding of land reform should be considered, including international funding. It may even be necessary to consider a land tax of some kind.

In 2018, he stated at a public hearing on land reform in Kimberley that it was the British governor of the Cape Colony, Sir Henry Barkly, who had forced the Griquas off their land in the 1870s. 'We should ask the British government to assist with the funding [of land reform]. The contentious question can be used as an opportunity to unite the country, if it's done in a responsible manner. We received worldwide recognition for resolving the first problem – apartheid. Now we should strive towards doing the same with the land question,' De Kock said.

His wife Cora, a qualified attorney, says she and her husband have an incredible passion for their employees. 'We're amazed at how loyal our people are. Things don't always go smoothly. At times there are patches where politics play a role. We also make mistakes. But what one reads outside, especially in the press, isn't always true. We care for our people and they care for us.'

According to De Kock, he started farming 30 years ago with 12 workers. Today he employs 1 400 workers. 'At one stage we didn't lose a single worker for six years in a row.'

Wildeklawer is involved in a multitude of social projects and sponsorships. The De Kocks are committed Christians, and Louis chairs the De Kock Trust that also owns the well-known Pro Regno and Deo Gloria Christian camping sites. People who visit their farms say they regularly see bakkies loaded with vegetables that are not perfect for the market standing ready to distribute the food to surrounding communities.

16

The mega-farmer as ultrapreneur II

Charl Senekal, Estelle van Reenen,

Milaan Thalwitzer, Nick Serfontein, BP Greyling

– by Jacques Dommisse

Charl Senekal: Senekal Suiker Trust

When the Libyan dictator Muammar Ghaddafi and his entourage of three huge trucks and 60 Land Cruisers drove away from Charl Senekal's farm in 2002, one of the filling stations in the small town of Mkhuze in northern KwaZulu-Natal was without fuel for two days.

Ghaddafi had been in Durban for an African Union summit and had heard from the then minister of water affairs, Ronnie Kasrils, that Senekal had built a R60-million pipeline to bring water from the Pongolapoort Dam to his farm and the surrounding community. As a result of his initiative, more than 300 000 people had access to clean water for the first time. At the time, Ghaddafi had been constructing a man-made river of some 5 000 kilometres through Libya, and he spent two days with Senekal to see what he had done.

Senekal is regarded by some analysts as the largest private sugar producer in Africa, while others consider him the largest in the southern hemisphere. Innovative thinking – and a mindset of putting his money where his mouth is – earned him the Agricultural Writers' Association of South Africa's National Farmer of the Year Award in 2002. With 4 500 hectares irrigated sugar cane in Mkhuze and Pongola, his Senekal Suiker Trust produces approximately 360 000 tons of sugar cane annually. His aim is to produce 600 000 tons annually.

Fifteen years after Ghaddafi's visit, the controversial former water affairs minister Nomvula Mokonyane took a sideswipe at Senekal by claiming that he acted like the owner of the dam even though it had been built by the state. 'People only started getting access in 2015, and today 36 settlements have access to the water. There is much hatred in the area because households were forcibly removed without compensation when the dam was built. These communities were there before Senekal, but they are now, after 48 years, the last to benefit from the dam,' Mokonyane alleged.

The minister also said water-use rights should be converted to licences granted at the discretion of the minister. Mokonyane added that those who had been the most privileged in the past were predominantly white and predominantly male. This had to be 'redressed' in the water sector as well. She referred by name to some of the country's largest farmers such as Senekal, but also the Van Zyls of ZZ2.

Senekal said in response that he did not want to attack the government, but he had an excellent relationship with the communities around him. Some of the community projects in which he was involved included water provision to the towns of Mkhuze and Ubombo, assistance to distribute water to an estimated 300 000 people and farm animals in the Mandlakazi area, and sugar cane cultivation in collaboration with farmworkers on 300 hectares. He also completed a bridge for a water pipeline of millions of rands so that black farmers would be able to plant sugar cane on 4 000 hectares.

The Senekals farm on about 20 000 hectares, of which around 4 500 are under sugar cane. 'As soon as the sugar price recovers again, I'd like to plant another 6 500 hectares of sugar cane. Lately we've been trying to counteract the low sugar price by planting 1 000 hectares of citrus and 1 000 hectares of macadamia trees. We're serial developers, we won't stop. We have a water quota we need to utilise. The water authorities in our area have a "use it or lose it" policy,' he said at the end of 2019.

Because he believes in diversification, the family has also long been engaged in game farming and ecotourism. Expansion at the 7 000-hectare Zimanga Private Game Reserve is ongoing, with more lodges under construction.

Senekal agrees that some of the country's biggest farmers should rather be called 'ultrapreneurs' and not mega-farmers, since farmers who farm on such a scale need to know more than just how to farm. The range of their skills is vast – like their academic knowledge (formal and sometimes informal, which they have to update daily). They are people who can make provision for water and electricity themselves, 'because a farmer makes a plan'.

Their practical approach, entrepreneurial thinking, staying power, forethought, humanity, plain common sense and pursuit of innovation and improvement all play a role; not to mention their qualities as negotiators, counsellors, educators and philanthropists – more than in any other (often 'one-dimensional') business field. All of that has enabled them to become super-farmers.

As far as the fourth industrial revolution is concerned, he believes the future of farming lies in technology, regardless of what type of farming enterprise it is. Technology has to become a farmer's best friend. 'In the next few years, cellphones are going to take over farming businesses. You'll be able to control everything from your phone, even if you're sitting in America. You'll be able to do your banking, switch on your irrigation systems, and see what your workers are doing. If you think you were born "BC" (before computers), I'm sorry for you. You'll simply have to catch up.'

Senekal says there is a close bond between farmers and agricultural journalists. Without really being aware of it, they are the distributors of technology globally. A good example of this was the world congress of the International Federation of Agricultural Journalists where 160 agricultural writers from more than 30 countries were gathered in South Africa. 'You tell us what farmers are doing in other countries, and we select that which we can utilise locally,' he told *Landbouweekblad* in 2017.

He says the rest of Africa is also hungry for food, knowledge and technology. According to Senekal, the role of big commercial farmers in South Africa is changing. 'We're looking at Africa and Africa is looking at us. They say, come and help us produce.'

Consequently, his sons have already become involved in countries like Zambia. In South Africa, 17 per cent of the population goes to bed hungry. In Zimbabwe, it is 47 per cent. This puts the value of a large-scale producer into perspective. Senekal is on record as saying he believes that if 10 of South Africa's so-called big farmers ('ultrapreneurs') had to move into Zimbabwe, Zambia and Namibia, all food problems there could be resolved within two years.

Although the low sugar price thwarted some of his expansion plans temporarily, 'drought hasn't affected us much … I farm with water and pipes,' says Senekal. 'We irrigate night and day if necessary. But we have our own weather station on the farm and keep a close eye on the rain.'

As far back as 2010, he said if he could switch off his pumps for just one day, he would save R30 000 in electricity. 'Irrigation is by a computerised drip system, known as open hydroponic irrigation. Metered quantities of nutrients are released and dissolved in the water tanks before irrigation, which places the nutrients right into the root zone for maximum uptake.'

At R25 000 per hectare, the initial irrigation infrastructure was already expensive in 2010. At that time Senekal's fertiliser bill averaged about R2 100 per hectare per year, while a rain-fed sugar cane farmer's cost was about half of that. Today the input costs have doubled. 'I spend more, but get twice the yield,' he explained in 2010. 'Our cane stalks are probably 2,5 times higher than those on the North Coast.'

His inventory of machinery is unusually long, because it includes earth-moving equipment, bulldozers, front-end loaders and tractors – some of them 450-horsepower eight-wheel tractors. His cane-hauling company Sentrans owned 50 Nissan trucks plus trailers. Although some R80 million had been invested in these trucks, it was cheaper than contracting out the job and the trucks paid for themselves in about four years, he said a decade ago.

Charl, who has lived in Pongola for most of life, recounts that he wanted to farm with sugar cane since his childhood. After his military service, he made a half-hearted attempt to study, but soon went in search of other pastures. In Kempton Park, he worked in a laboratory where he was trained as an analytical chemist. Later he became chief chemist at a sugar mill in Empangeni.

When someone else was appointed to the CEO position that had been promised to him informally, he resigned, sold his house and bought his first farm for about R150 000, of which he had only

R40 000 and had to borrow the rest. He wanted to buy the first farm they came across, but his wife Elize said: 'Buy something that can take us into the future.'

Charl and Elize had met each other in Pongola and were married for ten years before they had children. Elize worked at the university in Empangeni, and during that time they tried to save most of what they earned. This was how they got together the R40 000 with which they could buy the first farm. Eventually they raised four children – three sons and a daughter – on their land, and today all four of them are involved in the expanded business.

Charl employs about 1 200 permanent workers, with 14 managers and approximately 100 truck drivers. 'I know every man on the farm personally, and my children know everyone's name.' Years ago, his employees wrote a letter to the land commissioner in which they stated that they had job security on the farm and asked whether they would keep their jobs if the state took over the land.

Charl is not only concerned about the effects expropriation would have, but also about the thousands of hectares of farmland that are lying fallow on the Makatini Flats, for example, in which the government ought to get involved.

In his view, the interests of big and small farmers are reconcilable, because they come down to the same things: food production, decent wages and survival. The more big farmers there are, and the stronger they are, the more assistance they can give to smaller farmers who do not have the economies of scale. They should not let their land be cut up and parcelled out. Those farmers make a major contribution to the provision of food in South Africa and Africa. He says he often gets the impression that the government wants to get out of its responsibilities in an inexpensive way.

Senekal is part of a handful of successful farmers who are regularly asked for their opinion by the government. He feels strongly that the big farmers should continue to exist, and says the government generally underestimates farmers' goodwill. Farmers are only too aware of their responsibility as food suppliers of the country. 'We feed the nation,' he says, 'and have to do it as affordably as possible, at the highest quality possible.'

Estelle van Reenen: Sparta Group

When Estelle van Reenen's great-grandmother suffered the loss of three daughters in a British concentration camp in Winburg, she could not have imagined that a century later her great-granddaughter would be farming with 120 000 cattle – partly on the very family farm that had been burnt to the ground by British soldiers during the Anglo-Boer War.

Estelle's great-grandfather, Hendrik Marthinus Potgieter, had to subdivide his farm Middel in order to give each of his four surviving children a portion. Estelle's grandmother Hester was one of the beneficiaries. Ouma Hester later married Lou van Reenen (senior), the schoolmaster of the farm school.

Oupa Lou and Ouma Hester renamed their portion of the family farm Sparta, a reference to the ancient Spartans' industriousness as well as their strict and austere education system. Sparta lies a stone's throw from the Maluti Mountains, approximately 15 kilometres outside Marquard in the eastern Free State. Estelle and her sister Lynette (now Van Rooyen) reckon that with the name of the farm, their grandfather hoped to instil that discipline of the Spartans in his descendants.

Estelle regards her father Dirk, who lay the foundation for building a small cattle-farming concern into a mega family business, as a visionary. She remembers him as an excellent cattle buyer. He was no speculator, but unlike today, with animals' weight and other particulars being known beforehand at auctions, he could accurately determine many of an animal's traits merely by visual appraisal.

After graduating from the University of Natal with a BCom degree in 1953, Dirk joined his father Lou in a mixed-farming enterprise on Sparta. In 1960, Dirk married Betty Lombard from Clocolan and five children were born from the marriage. Today Ma Betty still lives on the family farm, Middel.

After reading about American farmers keeping cattle on grain feed all year round in a feedlot, Dirk started his own experiment in this regard with 30 cattle in 1966. This was the birth of Sparta's cattle-feeding business, which celebrated its 50th anniversary in 2016. In 1970, Dirk visited the United States to do further research on feed-lots. It was a huge step in those days, because as he said, when he was a little boy, 'America was as far as the moon'.

Estelle says her dad told her the biggest challenge of such an over-seas trip was building contacts. 'You know, nobody knows you. If you get an "audience" – as he called it – you must be able to sell yourself within two minutes so that someone is actually interested enough to tell you what they're doing.'

By 1974, Sparta was feeding 4 500 cattle. In 1981, the American feedlot specialist Dallas Horton visited Dirk on Sparta. This was the start of a lifelong professional relationship and friendship.

Today three of the children – Estelle, Lynette and their brother Lou – run a family business that is worth billions. Their brother Riaan, the youngest son, died in a car accident in 2006, and the eldest sister, Erika (now Kok), has a successful global accommodation business that she runs from Stellenbosch.

Estelle is the chief executive and Lou the chair. The siblings agree that, just as in the time when the late Dirk van Reenen started the Sparta Group more than 50 years ago, mutual trust is the fine thread that binds the family business together. But Lynette, the group director of business development, is quick to add: 'We're no lon-ger a family business, but a family that does business.' The children remember well what their father's approach was: ultimately, a business is nothing more than the quality of its people and the inter-actions between them. If we keep treating each other fairly and with dignity, we will flourish, he said.

By 1994, shortly before the disbanding of the South African Meat Board, Sparta began sending its cattle for slaughter to the Renown abattoir in Welkom. Two years later, more enormous extensions of the feedlots followed, and in 1999, when the industry was deregulat-ed, the family group bought the abattoir from Renown and named it Sparta Foods.

Dirk van Reenen's ideal had always been to control the full value chain from within the meat industry. It was realised when the abattoir became part of the value chain. For the first time, the group could now slaughter their own cattle, debone the carcasses, cut the meat into portions, and package it. In 2000, Sparta opened the first meat plant where carcasses were processed on a large scale – about three tons a day. By 2013, they were processing about 130 tons of meat per shift at the plant in Welkom.

Dirk stepped down in 2007 at the age of 76 and died the following year.

In 2013, equipment for a new deboning plant was imported from Ireland. This meant that the deboning capacity was almost doubled. The group succeeded in keeping up with new trends and consumer preferences for smaller portions and adapted their packaging accordingly. Since 2013, Sparta has been supplying packaged meat to retailers as well. The group now also produces processed products such as sosaties, beef cubes, hamburger patties and Texan steaks.

After another feedlot was acquired near Potchefstroom in 2015, Sparta had the capacity to feed about 120 000 cattle on its farms and feedlots. Over the years, several farms were acquired to expand the business to around 16 000 hectares. Sparta's abattoir plant in Welkom can slaughter about 270 000 cattle annually.

The Van Reenens expanded into gourmet meat in 2016 by entering into a joint venture with Brian Angus from Woodview farm, who specialises in the breeding of sought-after Wagyu cattle. According to the Angus family, thanks to this collaboration the Woodview Wagyu brand now benefits not only from Brian's superior breeding skills but also from Sparta's expertise in feeding cattle to their optimum potential. Sparta also launched the Sparta Angus brand, which is aimed at the high-end market.

Estelle mentions that their father had a unique management style. Even so, she has moved away from the so-called 'Stetson, boots & buckle' management style of 'I talk and you listen'. Estelle, a lawyer, says that as CEO, she has brought in a more inclusive management style, which lies in listening to people, involving the management team in decision-making, and consulting experts where necessary. She believes nonetheless that a firm and quick decision should be taken once the information has been gathered. In Estelle's view, employees take more ownership in the implementation of a decision if they were part of the process.

In line with the latest technology, the entire system of the farms and the abattoir is computerised and integrated. Estelle can say at any given moment where an animal was bought, how much it weighed on arrival, what it should weigh now, what medication it was given, and when it would be ready to go to the abattoir. This is achieved by attaching an electronic ID tag to the animal's ear from where all data is stored. The process is about traceability, and it is very important for their production purposes, because it means rapid adjustments in respect of feeding and other factors can be made.

Besides supplying meat to the local market, Sparta exports to various countries in Asia, the Indian Ocean Islands, the Middle East and parts of Africa. The meat produced by Sparta is halaal-certified, and the abattoir and meat-processing plant are internationally accredited by Certification Partner Global.

Maize and other crops are grown on Sparta's farmland as feed for calves and cattle in the feedlots. Most of the feed, however, is purchased externally. Sparta's cattle consume more than 1 000 tons of feed a day. Feedlot manure is used as an organic fertiliser and also to combat erosion, a major problem in the eastern Free State. Good feedlot management practice is a priority for the Van Reenens. 'We know that animals that are well cared for perform better and yield a better profit,' says Lou.

The future of the business depends on the availability of good-quality water. Proper water management and conservation is therefore an integral part of the business. Water run-off from the feedlot is treated by being passed through a series of oxidation and evaporation dams before the more purified water is used for irrigating pastures. The business does everything in its power to ensure that no run-off water enters the natural water system or groundwater, and the groundwater is tested regularly.

Sparta employs around 1 300 people, and the business is involved in various community projects. 'We care about our employees, community and environment. Every person who walks into the workplace isn't only that one individual, it's an entire family. And we have to see where we can help.'

It is noticeable that the business employs many women. The empowerment of women is close to Estelle's heart. She says women, firstly, have to believe in themselves – therefore she does everything in her power to send women in her employ for training. She believes it is easy to earn a few rand, but that it requires much more to make a difference.

The group also has a policy that family members need to be 28 years old before they are employed. 'One should be careful not to confuse ownership and management in a business.'

South Africa has its own unique challenges, and the drought is but one factor that complicates matters for the group; still, Sparta's people remain positive. 'We hope we can keep playing a role in the country's economy for longer than the next 50 years … It's a huge privilege to continue building the business into which my mom and dad put so much hard work,' says Estelle.

Milaan Thalwitzer: The Komati Fruit Group

From humble beginnings on about 100 hectares in the Lowveld just over half a century ago, the Komati Fruit Group of the Thalwitzer family has built its farming enterprise into a conglomerate that some experts describe as the biggest citrus business in the southern hemisphere.

'There are people worldwide in the industry that compare figures and production, but I don't really look at that. I've only heard that they talk about us as being the biggest,' says the second-generation owner and chair Milaan Thalwitzer – evidently faithful to the farming group's motto: '*Doen wat ons kan ten beste, vertrou op ons vennote vir die res*' (Do what we can to the best of our ability, rely on our partners for the rest).

Thalwitzer's Komati Fruit Group, which changed its name from the Bosveld Group to Komati Fruit a while ago, consists of 15 structures, as well as several empowerment initiatives and workers' trusts.

All the companies are landowners or production companies that farm primarily with citrus and subtropical fruit or related businesses. Eight companies in the group structure are 100 per cent owned by Bosveld Sitrus, while the group is in partnership with seven other groups in which its interests vary from 25 per cent to 68 per cent.

The group is owned outright by the Milaan Thalwitzer Family Trust. It is a 'family business' that attaches great value to the principle of such a business whereby the owner is directly involved in the management while the importance of corporate governance is understood and integrated in order to pursue sustainability and social accountability. The previous group name, Bosveld Sitrus – which used to be the 'parent company' – is now merely one of the production units, with Komati Fruit as the holding company. Komati Fruit is also the group's own export company, and the changed name is in alignment with this brand.

The group originated in 1954 when Theodore Maximillian (Mannetjie) Thalwitzer senior settled in the Letsitele Valley on the farm Die Vlakte along the banks of the Great Letaba River. In 1965, Theodore Maximillian (Milaan) Thalwitzer junior joined his father. The group operates largely in Limpopo and Mpumalanga, particularly around Malalane, Hoedspruit, Tzaneen, Louis Trichardt and Lydenburg.

Milaan Thalwitzer was born in Brakpan on 1 June 1942. He obtained a BSc (Agric) degree at the University of Pretoria in 1964, and has been involved in citrus farming since 1965. He is also a director and chair of two retail businesses – a Total filling station and a Spar grocery group in Letsitele. Besides his contribution to the establishment of Houers Koöperatief and Granor Passi – a highly successsful carton manufacturer and a fruit juice processor, respectively – he is involved in various community councils as well.

Thalwitzer is married to Antoinette and has four daughters. Three of his sons-in-law who farm with him serve as directors of the board.

The group's orchards and fields under irrigation cover approximately 5 500 hectares. Despite the persistent drought of the last few years, as well as a planned diversification to other crops such as soft citrus, macadamias and avocados, Komati Fruit's 5,5 million export cartons of citrus in 2013 still easily exceeded 5 million in 2019. The annual production of other crops includes sugar cane (about 80 000 tons), mangoes (about 3 400 tons), bananas (more than 2 000 tons), avocados (about 700 tons), macadamias (about 200 tons), blueberries (about 40 tons) and litchis (more than 500 tons).

The group is fully cognisant of the value of agricultural land, especially in the current political climate where land and the unproductive use thereof is increasingly used as an economic (and hence also a political) football. Komati Fruit is therefore geared to maximum utilisation of available land and the improvement of soil quality and yield on the land it utilises. The sons-in-law frequently refer to the new slogan: 'Nurture nature'. The aim is to farm sustainably so that future generations can farm here successfully.

Since not all their land is suitable for irrigation, the land use has been diversified and non-irrigable land of about 2 000 hectares is used for game farming on Riverside at Malalane, where they breed with buffaloes, blue wildebeest, giraffes, zebras, sable antelopes, kudus, waterbuck, impalas and other plains game. On the Olifants River Estate near Hoedspruit, they also farm with game on mountainous areas away from the Olifants River, and the game is captured and sold from time to time. The group has its own foundation for rhino conservation.

The group also owns a commercial herd of a few hundred cattle that is kept on non-irrigable sections of farms near Letsitele and Hoedspruit. It rents land that is unsuitable for growing citrus from community groups, where the Richmond Kopano production unit cultivates maize, potatoes, beans and pumpkins. In the winter months, unutilised tracts of the group's land are rented out to black farmers who graze their cattle on the land.

To Komati Fruit, responsible utilisation of soil and maintenance of 'soil health' are of crucial importance. This is achieved through proper soil preparation, particularly where long-term crops are grown; it is only once in every 20 to 30 years that one gets an opportunity to cultivate the soil beforehand. Before new orchards are planted, or existing orchards replanted, the soil is properly evaluated and prepared to improve root growth and water uptake.

Organic fertilisers play a major role, and during the planting process compost is worked into the soil. Compost and cattle manure are administered annually, especially where water uptake is a problem.

Huge quantities of cattle manure are also applied annually to avocado and banana plantings. Banana waste from the packhouses is chopped up and strewn on orchards. Gypsum and lime are used to counteract soil densification and salinisation. The group aims to farm in a manner that is as environmentally friendly as possible, but also understands the limitations, the financial impact and negative effect organic farming can have on yield and quality. Even so, they constantly strive to consider alternatives to chemical fertilisers and pest management strategies.

In light of the cost squeeze caused by the stagnation in product prices and the increase in input costs, the group realises the necessity of a constant improvement of its yield. To this end, they have a replanting programme whereby 5 per cent of the total area of planted hectares is replanted annually. This basically means that every orchard is fully replanted every 20 years and that they farm with relatively young trees to ensure a maximum yield. The negative aspect of this policy is that about 20 per cent of the planted hectares is unproductive annually, and it carries the risk that accelerated replanting may cause this figure to rise disproportionately. The practice is strictly managed, however, and evaluated on a regular basis.

Thalwitzer says that in the citrus industry, there is a constant search for new varieties and rootstocks with distinctive traits in respect of resistance to disease, yield, eating quality, seedlessness, demand, price and various other factors that are influenced by production and consumer needs. In order to farm sustainably, the group devotes serious attention to these aspects. Accordingly, there are experimental sites on Karino Farms (a 50/50 partnership with Johann Rupert) and other farms of the group where new cultivars and rootstocks are evaluated for their suitability for a specific production area and climate together with researchers from Citrus Research International.

The group has its own nursery, which is run on Karino Farms. The Ngwenya Nursery is accredited annually by Citrus Research International and also meets the demand for new plant material. In the litchi industry, too, Karino Farms' nursery is a leader in this field with the evaluation and propagation of new litchi varieties that ripen earlier.

In the citrus industry, the pursuit of a higher yield per hectare has led to the planting of high-density orchards. This, in turn, creates the challenge of getting enough sunlight among the trees to ensure proper fruit set and vegetative growth. Trees are pruned annually, primarily by means of selective hand pruning, in order to limit unnecessary regrowth. Water management is also critical; not only because of the shortage in the country, but because the trees' roots need a healthy balance of water and oxygen. Water application is done most efficiently with micro- and drip-irrigation systems.

Recent comparative studies have shown that the Komati Fruit Group outperformed participating producers by the following percentages in respect of particular crops: oranges (+6,6 per cent), grapefruit (+7,3 per cent), litchis (+13 per cent), mangoes (+10 per cent), avocados (+12 per cent) and two banana types (+20 per cent and 11 per cent).

Advanced software is used in the group's packhouses to ensure that fruit is packed correctly and can at all times be traced back to the block in an orchard where it was picked. Each orchard's profitability can be measured. The data is also used to evaluate which specific varieties do better in certain areas (soil and climate).

Risk is constantly measured at group level and thrashed out by way of regular management meetings in the respective companies in order to determine whether it fits into the strategic objectives of the group. An annual strategic meeting is held where the farming business is evaluated as a whole. Among the aspects that are analysed are geographic location – including logistics and the cost of transport to packhouses and markets – and the risk of natural disasters such as, for example, frost and hailstorms in an area like Groblersdal, pests and plagues, water resources and water management, varieties and rootstocks, as well as marketing risks such as, say, an export market's currency situation.

At board meetings and treasury committee meetings, international and national economic factors are taken into account so as to position the group correctly for the market. Executive directors annually attend the top international fruit shows, including Fruit Logistica (Berlin), Asia Fruit Congress (Shanghai) and WorldFood Moscow.

The group markets its products in some 50 countries globally – in regions such as Canada (1 per cent), Britain (7 per cent), Europe (27 per cent), the Middle East (7 per cent), Russia (18 per cent), China (10 per cent), South Korea (3 per cent), Japan (18 per cent) and South East Asia (9 per cent). Diversification is carefully considered in terms of these markets' individual economies, which ultimately determine prices, as well as risk associated with political instability. The entire group structure is positioned to take quick decisions in order to adapt to market conditions.

As an example, one can note the Russian markets of 2013 and 2014. Russia was very unstable at the time, but on account of the group's good client base there and strong sales structures, it was decided to remain involved and invest further in Russia. Other South African competitors withdrew, however, which strategically put the Komati Fruit Group in a healthy long-term position.

A great deal of attention is devoted to getting the right clients and achieving a good spread of risks in terms of the clients' profiles. The group has a very healthy exposure to supermarkets in Britain and the rest of Europe. Except for supermarkets, where a fixed volume and prices are agreed upon, it ensures that no product is shipped without a minimum guaranteed or fixed price being used. Much attention is also paid to expansion to markets that were traditionally inaccessible to South African citrus, such as China and South Korea.

Foreign exchange management is done formally by the group's elected treasury committee, which meets monthly. At these meetings, the internationally recognised economist André Cilliers from Treasury One is at the helm to take decisions about forex hedging.

Risk in respect of the availability of transport for taking export fruit to South African and Mozambican ports has been obviated through a management system within the group's Zest Fruit company, a system that brings about fast turnaround times from packhouses to ports, gives a proven advantage to transport companies that can make more vehicles available, and which allows them to negotiate lower tariffs.

The risk of rising energy costs is mitigated by using solar power, as well as a 350-kilowatt turbine generator on Riverside and power regulators at large installations such as packhouses and pump stations – installations that use electricity only outside of peak hours.

Regarding land reform, the group is actively involved in national committees, banks and the government's imbizos. Milaan Thalwitzer and other directors of the group focus especially on putting alternative suggestions on the table, such as practical ways in which the group's involvement has taken tangible form in empowerment projects such as those of Mabete Citrus, GFC, Letsitele Valley and the Calais Group.

The group conducts continuous training through its training facilitators Riverwalk Training and Agri IQ. Every year, not only permanent staff but also temporary employees receive training within their work environment. The group's human resources department also pays attention to the training of middle management.

Thalwitzer, his board and their staff actively participate in their immediate community, at different levels and in a variety of ways, by taking on roles in church councils, school governing bodies, community organisations, business chambers and empowerment initiatives. The group strives to employ South African citizens as far as possible, and specifically from communities in the vicinity of the group's farms. Thalwitzer was instrumental in the creation of community businesses such as Granor Passi and Houers Koöperatief, which are of great value to all farmers in the area and the broader community.

A wide variety of community-focused projects have been undertaken to date, which include the formation of sports clubs and the building of a community centre on the Riverside farm in 2014, and the group is involved in projects offering skills development and music training through the Waitrose Foundation. In addition to housing, the group provides its workers with child care and medical services. During the peak season, the group employs up to 3 500 people. Through a combined effort with foundations such as Waitrose, the Albert Heijn Foundation and others, the Komati Fruit Group strives to make a difference by running 36 projects to the benefit of its workers and the local communities where it conducts business.

In reality, for its thousands of employees and the broader community, Komati Fruit has created an independent social support network of employment, housing, medical care, training and recreation.

'Within the citrus fraternity, production and marketing, we don't want to be seen as followers, we want to be the leaders,' says Thalwitzer.

Nick Serfontein: Sernick Group

In mid 2018, Nick Serfontein wrote an open letter to President Cyril Ramaphosa in which he advised him that the government should start seeing the commercial farming sector as an ally and include commercial farmers in plans for effective land reform. Serfontein believes that the only way to establish successful black commercial farmers in South Africa is by selecting those with an ability to farm and then providing them with training, access to finance and mentorship.

The advice came from a successful farmer who bought a 250-hectare piece of land in 1983 and started farming with 30 cattle. Today Serfontein's Sernick Group – with an integrated business model of large-scale cattle and beef production right through to the end consumer – has a turnover of about R2,5 billion.

When it comes to land reform and the problems experienced by emerging farmers, Serfontein knows what he is talking about. His idea of empowerment in the agricultural sector has resulted in an initiative in which his group, together with other roleplayers, is training 660 emerging farmers. About R500 million has been raised to ensure that the farmers receive accredited training and resources in order to start farming themselves from mid 2021. Sernick has also been acting as a financial intermediary for black farmers without collateral since 2016.

In his open letter, Serfontein said land reform should be elementary: 'We select the people with potential and passion, people with access to land. We then train them, we assist them with cattle and infrastructure, we mentor them continuously and we monitor them. Most important of all is that it should be sustainable and create jobs.'

He believes his initiative can serve as a blueprint for other empowerment initiatives in agriculture. What political leaders do with his advice will determine not only the fate of farming in the country but also that of politicians: voters who have no bread to eat, opt for a change of government.

Serfontein was born in 1948 on the farm Liebenbergstroom near Edenville in the Free State. This is where the farm operations of the Sernick Group (a combination of a part of his surname and his name) are now located.

His family had a mixed-farming enterprise, and Nick grew up with a keen interest in and love for cultivating the soil and rearing animals. He had a dream to become a farmer, but was deterred by his parents who knew from experience that farming was a hard life. Eventually they convinced him to study engineering at the University of Pretoria after school.

After completing his studies in 1970, he started working at Sapekoe Tea Estates as chief engineer, where he was responsible for the planning, design and construction of dams, irrigation schemes and tea-processing factories. In 1977, he joined Eksteen, Van Der Walt & Nissen – an engineering firm in Mafikeng (now Mahikeng) – as consulting engineer. Only six months after being appointed, he became a director of the firm.

Serfontein finally found himself in a position where he could pursue his passion for farming while still working. In 1983, he bought a 250-hectare piece of land and 30 commercial Bonsmara heifers, and started his Bonsmara stud. This was the realisation of a lifelong dream and the start of what would become the Sernick Group.

In 1991, he founded EVN Consulting Engineers, which was restructured in 1999 to become the Bigen Africa Group he led as chair. Serfontein decided in 1990 that cattle farming alone was not enough – he felt compelled to do something that added value to the farm and the community and which made farming more cost-effective. Over time he acquired more land, including the family farm, and expanded the stud. He went on to add a Phase C bull testing station, a feed factory and a feedlot, and bought the Kroonstad abattoir.

In 2003, he retired from Bigen Africa to devote all his time to Sernick.

The value chain was completed with Sernick's entry into the retail market in 2010. Today the group consists of an integrated value chain of Bonsmara cattle, a feedlot, feed factory, abattoir, meat-processing plant and retail butcheries. The group employs more than 600 people and the annual turnover has climbed to about R2,5 billion. In 2016, Serfontein's stud won the Agricultural Research Council's Herd of the Year Award, while he was named both Free State Farmer of the Year and Mentor of the Year. In 2018, the *Beeld* newspaper named him their Newsmaker of the Year after his open letter to President Ramaphosa went viral.

Serfontein, who farms with his son Carel (chief executive), believes that everything he has achieved through the years can be ascribed to his faith, the belief that dreams can come true and his decision to surround himself with like-minded and dynamic individuals who are passionate about agriculture.

'Every person needs a bit of luck in life. My first bit of luck was that I grew up relatively poor. At school I only got a new set of clothes on one occasion, as I always wore my deceased elder brother's old clothes. My second bit of luck was that I chose engineering as a career. And my third bit of luck was that I established a successful business practice in Mafikeng, which enabled me to buy the land and 30 cattle. This was the start of my dream.'

He attributes his entrepreneurial mindset to three elements. Firstly, that he is a dreamer who believes everything in life starts with a vision of the future. Secondly, that he can make quick decisions based on a hunch. If you wait until you have 100 per cent of the information, you'll never make a decision, he says. 'Thirdly, any project I decide on is planned thoroughly and executed with urgency. But just up to a point; once a project has been set up, I hand it over to someone who can put in the systems and processes because I get bored with the detail.'

Regarding modern farming practices, he points out that there is an ever-increasing gap between input costs and commodity prices. Most of the input costs, such as vehicles, implements, fuel, fertiliser and medication, are linked to the dollar exchange rate. This is why farms are becoming bigger and farmers fewer. The number of commercial farmers in the country has declined from 120 000 in 1960 to 35 000 in 2016. It amounts to an annual decline of 1 500. This has nothing to do with politics, but everything with the realities of a modern farming enterprise.

'Today you can produce more on the same piece of land with the help of technology. You can diversify (and many farmers are doing that extremely effectively), or you can add value. At Sernick we do a bit of everything, but the emphasis is on value addition. The future of agriculture lies with the value chain, because you have to connect as closely as possible, and preferably directly, with the end consumer; that's where the profit lies,' says Serfontein.

As far as the potential of the country's meat industry is concerned, Serfontein notes that internationally South Africa is in 22nd place in terms of cattle numbers. When it comes to meat production, however, we are in 11th place. This means that the agricultural sector is dynamic, despite the fact that 40 per cent of our national herd is in communal areas where production currently takes place in suboptimal conditions. Much potential is therefore not being realised. If the production in the communal areas could be doubled, an additional 300 000 tons of meat would be produced.

Feed efficiency will become increasingly important, as it has a high impact on profit. Approximately 75 per cent of the country's slaughter animals go through a feedlot phase. With a 1,5 kilogram improvement in feed efficiency, profit can rise by R3 billion. Sernick is engaged in a series of tests to improve feedlot efficiency and also in the implementation of an own system for grading and traceability.

To Serfontein, his time on President Ramaphosa's land reform advisory panel was a traumatic experience. The panel was run like 'a spaza shop', he said at the annual Green Day of the Broodsnyersplaas Boerevereniging, a farmers' union. 'The chaotic process that was followed frustrated me enormously. The potential existed to arrive at the end as a team, with differences, but the way in which the panel was managed, sunk the ship. The total misconceptions about the realities of agriculture were extremely frustrating. Still, the end result, namely the panel's report and the supplementary report by Dan [Kriek] and me, was the best we could hope for, and the president has already said on three occasions that the report compiled by Dan and me will be considered, as it contains good suggestions.'

Serfontein is deeply concerned about the decay in the country's rural areas. In his local community, unemployment exceeds 70 per cent. A large percentage of farmers endeavour to do something to assist, but receive scant recognition for their efforts. The decay is the consequence of a dysfunctional government. The report of the Ramaphosa land reform panel talks about local authorities that have to make land reform happen, but in Serfontein's view this is 'laughably naive'.

'It will take years to get local authorities to work. However, we can say the country is in tatters; I'm leaving. For such people I have respect, because they make a decision. We can also say: I'm sitting on the fence and waiting to see what happens. For those I have no respect. Or we can say: there are solutions, and I want to be part of them. For such people I have enormous respect.'

According to him, South African agriculture has the best farmers in the entire world, a fact that is openly acknowledged in other countries. He believes that the recently launched South African Agricultural Development Agency – the one-stop-shop he talked about in his letter to Ramaphosa – can transform the agricultural landscape with the support of the private sector, farmers, agribusinesses, commodity groups and commercial banks, in collaboration with the government and other roleplayers such as educational institutions.

'I have no doubt about a bright future in agriculture, but then the government needs to start seeing the commercial farming sector as an ally. There are positive changes on the political scene, as well as recognition of the important role of commercial agriculture. I also foresee that the number of big commercial farmers will continue to decline, but that we'll see many small farmers making a contribution with the help of subsidies.'

Serfontein says his personal motto is: if you can dream it, you can achieve it. And that the true meaning of life is to plant a tree in whose shade you do not expect to sit.

The Sernick Group owns its complete value chain in the meat industry and considers this a defining component of the company. Sernick strives to add value wherever they can so as to grow by offering high-quality and diversified agricultural products, dynamic processes and client-oriented services.

BP Greyling

The secret to a successful farming enterprise lies not only with the farmer but also with his people on the farm and the people in his community, says BP Greyling, an ultrapreneur from Wakkerstroom in Mpumalanga and a former Farmer of the Year (SA Agricultural Writers).

He and his son Ghini farm with soya beans, maize, green feed, certified ryegrass, wool, sheep and cattle. In 2019, one of the biggest privately owned grain silos in South Africa was erected on his farm.

Greyling grew up as a farmboy and after completing a BCom degree at the University of Pretoria, he started farming on the farm Langfontein in 1988. In that year, he had 167 cattle and approximately 2 000 sheep. By 2016, Greyling had about 5 800 cattle and 21 200 sheep, *Landbouweekblad* reported. The numbers of the livestock have since increased.

In the meantime, he has bought five more farms, which brings his landholdings to about 20 000 hectares, plus he rents another farm of about 4 500 hectares. He believes that to get the best out of his farm, he has to use the natural environment to his benefit in the management of his operations. Diversification is important too; for instance, he not only runs a sheep stud but breeds his own rams as well.

Greyling has been passionate about sheep since his young days, and by the time he was in grade 10 he had supervised the shearing and classed wool himself. In 2011, he made the news with a Merino ram called Barrier he had bought for R250 000. A jaw-dropping price that some farmers described as 'foolishness'. Greyling said that the purchase of Barrier, a fine-wool sire, put his sheep farming on a totally different level. His aim was to breed a finer wool in their entire Merino flock by using this ram. The higher income from the finer wool, as well as sheep sales, would enable him to recover his investment, he believed.

Wynand Dreyer, who visited Greyling on his farm, wrote in his book *Megaboere* that the farm is in the deep rural areas, and one wonders how a farmer can make a living in an environment that from a political perspective is not necessarily the friendliest for a farming enterprise. For the most part, however, nothing goes missing.

Greyling says when you have been farming in a place for a long time, you become part of the community. You are not farming alone. The success of his enterprise is proportional to the loyalty and the quality of the people around him. He reckons everything is about feeling safe and secure. 'My workers have to feel safe, then I also feel safe.'

When any of his livestock disappears, some of the Zulu farmers in the area jump in and help search for it. Likewise, Greyling will go all out when any of these farmers' cattle is stolen. He uses his plane for aerial searches, and he has a good relationship with the local police.

Greyling is still a captain in the police's reserve force. His workers and the people who know him address him as 'Kaptein'. He says the secret lies in joining hands across cultural and colour lines. Regarding crime, his philosophy is that no one is more important than anyone else, no matter how big your farming operation is. It is not for nothing that Langfontein's motto is 'Sibambisene', which means 'We join hands' in Zulu.

In the Wakkerstroom area, the summers are short and the winters long. Greyling says it is vital to manage matters in such a way that you are ready for feeding the livestock in winter and have the right crops on the lands. 'But it's not only about maintaining a balance in how everything is managed; you also need quality people. My success is due to all the people who are loyally involved in the farming operations,' he told Dreyer.

Problem species such as jackal and bushpig are a big threat on Greyling's farm. In 2007, he decided to keep hunting dogs as a predator control measure after they had lost almost 400 lambs in one flock of sheep in one season. The flock had included 989 certified pregnant ewes.

As part of his integration plan for his farming operations, he sows ryegrass seed between the maize and by the time the maize is harvested, the grass is just high enough to go into the next growth phase.

Successful farming is about using nature to your benefit, he believes. For that reason, he lets the cattle graze on the ryegrass before winter's veld fires arrive. Veld fires are the farmer's biggest threat, and 170 kilometres of controlled burning annually ensures that the fire stays out of pastures.

Greyling reckons that one should also guard against over-capitalising. 'At a point I thought I had perhaps stuck my neck out too far, because if you want to become more efficient and want to expand, you need capital. Fortunately, up to now, the gambles have seldom failed.'

In 2019, his storage capacity for maize increased from 11 000 tons to 21 000 tons, thanks to the biggest silo built to date on a farm. The silo was built by the silo company GSI Group South Africa, according to the silo builder Dave Ohlmesdahl.

Greyling says the purpose of his new silo is to enable them to: harvest their maize earlier; let their thousands of cattle and sheep graze sooner on the maize stover; save money on unnecessary high transport, handling and storage costs; and add value to the grain by marketing it at higher prices.

The new grain dryer can dry 600 tons of maize a day. The maize is also husked at 120 tons an hour. The animal-feed factory is situated right next to the silo complex. It was designed by the engineer Sarel Kritzinger, and the machinery was designed and built by Willie Jones from Koster. The factory manufactures feed for cattle, sheep, horses and dogs, and produces feed pellets as well. 'At this stage, our focus is on our own use and sales of prescription and tailor-made mixes. The plant is designed in such a way that it can expand,' Greyling told the journalist Charl van Rooyen at the launch.

Greyling was as tight-lipped about the cost of the new complex as he is about the size of his herds, but he mentioned that the cost of the new silo and animal-feed complex exceeded that of the five additional farms they had acquired in the past five years. He believes, however, that the benefit and value added for the farming business will also be four times more.

About political uncertainty, which is any farmer's other major challenge, Greyling is quick to say that it holds certain promises and opportunities for farmers as well. 'It opens up new horizons and opportunities for new partnerships and new friends.' He is involved in nine empowerment initiatives in his area, and assists with capital, labour, raw material and entrepreneurship. He told Dreyer that he had already financed R32 million's worth of assets and inputs, of which he carried the risk, to start projects in partnership with empowerment farmers. They then farm together. He does not rent from the farmers, but enters into a 50/50 partnerhip. The risk is his.

He is proud of the fact that, together with his black neighbours, he managed to rebuild infrastructure such as dams, roads and cattle kraals.

Greyling says he is not farming for himself but for his ancestors: his father, his grandfather and his great-grandfather, who died at the Battle of Colenso. But he is also farming for his son Ghini, who will take over from him some day. He realises that every generation brings something new to agriculture. Building on economies of scale requires new technology and new thinking. Ultimately, farming is not about sentiment but about profitability.

It is amazing what you can do with your cellphone today, he says. 'I measure out my lands on my cellphone. I sit in my office and I go into programs and I know my land sizes, and I can plan everything accordingly.'

Greyling sees himself as the steward on Langfontein. He owns nothing; everything has been lent to him, he says. His father gave him opportunities and taught him how to farm. He is proud of that and honours it. According to Dreyer, he has devoted his life to teaching his son how to farm and in turn giving *him* opportunities to make him a better farmer, because his son will one day be the new steward on Langfontein.

17

Country of givers

MANY AFRIKANER businesspeople are among the country's most prominent benefactors. They, like other internationally renowned philanthropists, are following in the footsteps of the American steel magnate Andrew Carnegie – perhaps the first super-rich individual to state publicly that the rich have a moral obligation to give away their fortunes. Carnegie, who funded the building of Carnegie libaries worldwide, inter alia in Stellenbosch, wrote in 1889 in *The Gospel of Wealth* that 'the man who dies leaving behind many millions of available wealth, which was his to administer during life, will pass away "unwept, unhonored, and unsung", no matter to what uses he leaves the dross which he cannot take with him'.

The mega-farmers' investments in their workers and their neighbouring communities, as well as the benefactions of a great number of the country's businesspeople, bear out research findings that South Africa is a nation of givers, regardless of income brackets. According to the 2010 Barclays Culture of Philanthropy Report, South Africans are the second most generous people in the world (after the Americans), measured by the part of their income individuals donate to community causes.

Some are standard bearers of capitalism with a social conscience. Three recent reports in this regard were cited by Shelagh Gastrow, director of GastrowBloch Philanthropies. The *South Africa Giving 2017* report showed that the vast majority of South Africans (88 per cent) had participated in charitable activities, and that 81 per cent had given money. The most popular cause was aid to alleviate poverty, followed by donations to religious organisations and, thirdly, support for children.

Among high-net-worth individuals, there was a revealing perception. 'When asked what sectors they most trusted to effect social change in South Africa, they showed greater confidence in the corporate sector and religious institutions with "hardly any" confidence in government as a "change-maker". However, non-profit organisations were supported by 64 per cent of respondents, whilst advocacy groups and political parties were the least likely to receive funding (3 per cent),' Gastrow wrote.

François van Niekerk

A farmboy who quietly became one of South Africa's foremost philanthropists learned his first business lessons as well as important life lessons as a child in his father's farm store in the Agter-Paarl area. The success he achieved as a businessman eventually led to his being named Africa's top philanthropist.

François van Niekerk's remarkable business career was at a point on the verge of bankruptcy, but then a watershed moment in his life occurred. A desperately needed order was cancelled unexpectedly, and that had been his last hope for financial survival, he recounts. While walking to the offices of the client in question, he paused for a moment in front of the Land Bank building in the city centre of Pretoria and promised God 30 per cent of his company (Infotech, later the Mergon Group) if He helped him. Within minutes of his arrival at the client, an inspired new alternative emerged and the company was saved.

This narrow escape ensured that from then on he has consistently lived up to his promise and donated large sums to charity. Today the Mergon Group, which moved its head office from Pretoria to Stellenbosch a few years ago, has an investment portfolio consisting of significant interests in companies operating across multiple industries both locally and internationally. These sectors include property, various types of technology, hydroelectricity generation, coal mines, luxury goods and short-term insurance.

Though François's parents were poor, he and his brother Van Wyk, who started farming on the farm at 16 and later owned eight farms, grew up in a happy home. Their father, who had started school during the Anglo-Boer War, remembered how the British colonial authorities sought to thwart the growth of his home language, Afrikaans. Schools were exclusively English; yet he related without bitterness how children who were caught speaking Afrikaans had to wear a wooden board around their necks with 'Dutch Donkey' written on it in big letters. Their parents had received a patch of land in

COUNTRY OF GIVERS 369

Agter-Paarl as a wedding gift, but their mother had to contribute her pension money so that they could build a house. François recalls that for his parents, 'life was a never-ending balancing act between "the bank" and "the mortgage".'

Since there were no shops in the area, his father fitted out a small building next to the farmhouse as a store to earn extra income. From the age of eight until his matric year, François worked in the store over weekends. He matriculated at Paarl Boys' High, but as a boarder he could not participate actively in sport like most of the other boys because of his weekend duties in the farm store.

Here he learned that the client always came first, regardless of whether it was a rich landowner dealing with the lowliest of migrant labourers. The influence of his father, with his almost fanatical emphasis on the client, stuck with him throughout his career. A second lesson was that others should be treated with the same respect you expect for yourself. Thirdly, business is based on trust, with uncompromising honesty as first principle.

This was also where he learned the benefits of partnership. Two years before he entered high school, he asked his father to help him buy a camera with which he took photos of the clients. This venture was followed by bicycles he sold to the same people, and later at the South African Naval Gymnasium he sold irons to fellow cadets. The income was meagre but the business experience invaluable.

The seed for the idea of his 30 per cent gift to God had been planted in his schooldays when he read a biography of the American business magnate RG LeTourneau, a prolific inventor of earthmoving machinery and a Christian philanthropist.

Van Niekerk completed his BEcon degree at Stellenbosch and obtained an MBA at Unisa, which would later award him an honorary doctorate as well. His first job in 1965 was at Castle Wine & Brandy/EK Green, a family concern in Cape Town that was acquired by Distillers (later Distell), a subsidiary of the Rembrandt Group, in 1967.

He joined Bruynzeel Plywoods (Bruply) in 1970, a company in the timber industry in Cape Town, while he also worked on a dissertation for his master's degree at Unisa. During this time he wrote to *Rapport* the only letter he would send to a newspaper in the course of his career. It was published on 1 August 1971 under the headline 'We close our eyes to this "disease"'. A fierce battle was raging in the National Party between the *verligtes* and the *verkramptes* (progressive and conservative factions) at the time. In his letter, he expressed his concern about Afrikaners' relations with other race groups, a disease he likened to cancer.

'How readily we look past our responsibility with regard to human relations between ourselves and other race groups. We flatter ourselves that there is nothing wrong. Meanwhile the symptoms are unmistakeably there – symptoms of a social disease that has long threathened to undermine South Africa's good health.'

Regrettably, he wrote, the patient's health had already been jeopardised by an overlong passage of time. 'I personally believe the Afrikaner is facing a battle that will be just as decisive as that of Veg-kop or Blood River or any others of the past. This one is just much harder. Physical prowess won't help us this time, for the enemy to be conquered is not standing before us – this time the victory we have to achieve is over ourselves.'

To Van Niekerk, apartheid was wrong. Full stop.

His Unisa dissertation dealt with the extent to which top management should centralise or decentralise. Bruply, which was acquired by Anglo American shortly afterwards, had served as the guinea pig for his study in which he analysed how the company had gone downhill under the leadership of an autocratic managing director. He completed his dissertation shortly before he accepted an attractive offer and joined Armscor (later Denel) in Pretoria as an internal consultant.

Soon afterwards, the Unisa School of Business Leadership informed him that Bruply had lodged a formal complaint against the awarding of his degree. His former boss, to whom Van Niekerk had given a copy of his magnum opus, had evidently read it and was outraged by the youthful presumptuousness. He referred his allegation of 'misrepresentation, character defamation and related legalese' to Anglo American's head office. Unfortunately for him, a senior manager found that the dissertation's views on Bruply basically coincided with Anglo's own views about the company. The complaint was withdrawn and the managing director got rid of.

In the late 1970s, a reorganisation of Armscor offered Van Niekerk the possibility of accepting a settlement agreement that ensured pension benefits and a few months' salary. He was 38 years old when he entered the uncertain territory of being his own boss in September 1978.

At this point, he wrote down the key principles that applied in the corporate world: Firstly, optimal organisational success heavily depends on the entire spectrum of management expertise that is available and utilised to ensure the maximum contribution on the part of each employee. Secondly, 'business is all about the client, stupid'. Thirdly, the difference between failure and success is less than a hair's breadth, and, lastly: centralised control primarily serves the interests of only one person – and then usually only for a limited period.

Van Niekerk spent almost a year exploring various opportunities. In hindsight, he thought he might have acted rashly, as his family's meagre cash reserves were almost depleted. But he did see an opportunity in securing the local distribution rights for Wang, an American electronic word-processing system that was used by the Institute for Maritime Technology. With his knowledge of administrative systems, he realised it was a quality product.

On 1 January 1980, he started his one-man business – with a cash amount that would today just about cover a meal for four in a good restaurant. He was now the distributor of Wang computers in Pretoria and the surrounding area. Afterwards he heard that Wang's importers and distributors only awarded him the agency because they had not managed to sell anything in that area for years.

The offices of BF van Niekerk & Partners were in a backroom in a run-down building in Pretoria. There was no direct access to the offices through the main entrance; prospective clients were met in the street and had to walk through the parking lot. Though it had precious little business experience, the enterprise did have two fundamental success factors: an excellent product and first-rate employees.

They gradually made some progress, and the monthly salaries could be paid. Van Niekerk and his colleagues sensed a turning point when Gerard Heij walked into the offices one day and requested a demonstration of the computers. Subsequently they realised that Heij was the sales consultant of their biggest rival. Van Niekerk phoned Heij's boss to object, but then reconsidered and made Heij a job offer that he accepted.

For eight months things went relatively well, and then September 1980 arrived. An order from Van Niekerk's previous employer had to be confirmed after the negotiations had been finalised. Payment of his staff's salaries depended on this order, as the bank manager's patience had run out and all other sources of financing had been exhausted. Then came the call from his former colleague, Johan Nel: 'I have bad news and good news. We have decided to buy the equipment, but only in March 1981, when the new budget commences.'

It was the news any entrepreneur dreads most: that bankruptcy is imminent and the doors have to close. Yet there was also a sense of resignation because they all thought they had done their best, and if that was not good enough, there was nothing more to be done.

Van Niekerk asked if he could come over for coffee. Nel replied: 'I will give you all the coffee you want, but the decision is final. Senior management has decided and I am not going to argue the point.'

Van Niekerk was devastated. The client's premises were half a block away, and he set off on foot. He had no idea what to do, who or what he should turn to, or what strategy he should follow to avert an impending catastrophe. Halfway there, he was walking past the Land Bank when the thought came from nowhere: 'Why not ask God for help?'

I don't know God well, Van Niekerk thought, but surely He would consider helping me if I prayed. 'I stood under a large jacaranda tree and simply asked God to help me. Maybe due to unfamiliarity or because I felt I needed to bring something to the table, I offered Him 30 per cent of the company if He answered my prayer. At the time, I failed to realise that 30 per cent of a soon-to-be-liquidated company was a "negative gift".'

He carried on towards Nel's office still thinking he was a dead businessman walking. Once there, Van Niekerk heard himself say to

Nel: 'So you definitely want to buy the system, but only six months from now, in the new budget period? How about renting it in the interim six months?'

The fact that neither the supplier nor his own business had rental facilities was at that stage a minor consideration. 'Yes,' Nel replied. 'We actually need it immediately. I have money in my rental budget and can give you a rental order right away.'

This event in Van Niekerk's career became the core of his testimony; that a new Power, far beyond his expectations and human weaknesses, started dominating his life and took ownership of his company. The conviction has been strengthened by the extent to which he, his family and his employees have been blessed since then.

Back at the office, they immediately set about persuading their suppliers to conclude a rental agreement and securing bridging finance. The business started growing, despite the instability of the technology industry and the scarcity of trained technical staff. In order to recruit the very best people for a fledgling enterprise, preference was given to women up to management level. In addition, much time was devoted to the training of staff.

Before long, the trade name was changed as well. Infotech (Pty) Ltd was registered and launched in 1983. The company expanded to a staff complement of 150 as it gained a reputation as the leading supplier of word-processing technology and minicomputers.

By 1988 it began dawning on Van Niekerk that he was perhaps no longer the best CEO for the company in uncertain times. It was rumoured that he found it hard to recruit and retain 'techies'. They thought their career prospects were limited because the founder was below the age of 50 and might still be the boss for a long time. Hence he decided to resign and to appoint the marketing director, Jim Alexander, in his place.

Suddenly he was at a loose end. But then the idea arose to build offices for Infotech. A suitable site was found in Hatfield in Pretoria, and an agreement was reached with a developer group. The new company, Infoprop, became the principal tenant for a three-storey building with a basement for parking, with the right to build another storey that would increase their shareholding to 50 per cent.

Property development, which would in time become a major

building block in the Mergon Group, opened up new horizons. At this stage Louis van der Watt, a young articled clerk from Deloitte who audited Infotech's financial statements, asked Van Niekerk to start a joint venture with him in the property market. Initially the timing was not right, but when Van der Watt came with the proposal again a year later, they started as equal partners.

Each partner acquired a third share of the new company, Atterbury Property, while they also decided to establish the Atterbury Trust with the remaining third of the shares. The trust was aimed at assisting promising young South Africans who could not afford tertiary education. For five years the two partners were Atterbury Property's only employees, and the first two years they earned no salary.

Their partnership would last for decades, in spite of adversity they inititally had to survive amid the economic downturn of the 1980s and bankcruptcies of several companies. In such times of uncertainty, Van Niekerk relied on the unconditional support of his wife Miems, to whom he was married for 53 years. On more than one occasion he had to tell her that the bank wanted to register a full mortgage bond over their home as security. Her unqualified consent in each case would forever be etched in his memory, he stated.

At some point, Absa Bank instructed them to sell Infoprop's half share in their building. Van Niekerk recounts that he 'will never forget when, at the last of several meetings with the bank, the tall head of the Credit Committee stood up behind his sizable desk to underscore his final verdict: "Listen, buddy, the bank is not asking you to sell the building, we're telling you to."'

Eventually the building was sold for R23 million. The buyer's agent was Investec Bank, and at a final meeting in Johannesburg two Investec bankers tried to force the price down to a 'non-negotiable' R22 million because that was supposedly what top management had decided. Van Niekerk immediately stood up and said: 'OK, then there is no deal, and I'm going back to Pretoria.' They knew his financial position was critical and had sought to exploit it. He considered it a painful insult, but after making a few calls they informed him that the original agreement still stood.

The financial predicament was so acute that he had sold Infoprop shares in the building to Infotech employees. After the sale of the building, it was particularly gladdening that everyone's investments had multiplied. Infoprop made a reasonable profit of R4,3 million from the deal, and that helped to carry the company through a taxing period. Political uncertainty exacerbated the instability in the business sector prior to the settlement of 1994.

In the late 1980s, Wang's head office in Boston in Massachusetts imposed sanctions against South Africa, despite the fact that South Africa was the biggest Wang franchise among 153 countries outside the United States. This was a near insurmountable setback. Infotech's clients included the office of President FW de Klerk and some of the most strategic organisations in the country. Rival companies started snatching up the shrinking numbers of Wang users.

Prayers that were answered and the investment in and retention of excellent employees bore fruit. Fanie Marais, a senior colleague with a doctorate in information technology, formulated a strategy whereby Infotech's service division was turned into a separate company. The new company, Technicare, was a success from the outset; notably thanks to a breakthrough to deliver a technical one-stop-service for Absa Bank's more than a hundred kinds of computer-related equipment.

Technicare was the first step towards diversification of the group. Eventually Atterbury began expanding strongly with buildings for BMW/Nissan and Rover/Ford and an office building for the South African Revenue Service. The main focus was on the development of shopping centres and commercial buildings. The Atterbury Value Mart was started in Faerie Glen in Pretoria in a period of great political uncertainty, but in time it became the cornerstone of the property portfolio, as well as Mergon's single biggest investment category, which made the subsequent diversification programme possible.

Further lasting partnerships and outside associations were entered into with respected figures in the property industry like Louis Norval, Neno Haasbroek, Gary Steinberg and Dirk Hensen. In 2002, Atterbury co-founded Attfund Retail with Norval. Norval was the executive chair of Attfund that provided management services for property development and investments in shopping centres, retail buildings and corporate office parks.

After the successful launch of Atterbury Value Mart three major shopping centres were completed in Pretoria, Johannesburg and George, followed by other property developments across South Africa – including more than 20 shopping centres in recent years. Among these is Waterfall City in Midrand, where the Mall of Africa was built as the largest shopping centre in the country.

Atterbury Investments Holdings was listed on the JSE in 2013 as Attacq (Atterbury Acquisitions). Attacq has since partnered with Sanlam Properties to develop Waterfall City with further expansions into the largest corporate headquarters destination in Africa. The auditing firm PwC moved into a 26-storey office tower, while other big corporates such as Group Five, Premier Foods, Massbuild, Cipla, Altech, Diageo, Novartis, Cell C, Medtronic and Honda also decided to situate their headquarters in the Waterfall precinct.

Diversification beyond South Africa's borders started in 2008. By this time, Van Niekerk and Van der Watt, to whom the management control of Atterbury had been transferred over time, were firmly convinced that the group should not do any business with a government. Uncertainty about economic policy in South Africa, which would worsen alarmingly under the Zuma regime, convinced them that it had become risky to do business with a corrupt government that plotted with tenderpreneurs. According to Van Niekerk, political events and trends were by far the main cause of Mergon's intensive diversification programme.

A partnership with a private equity and venture capital investment business in the European Union, Argosy Capital, led to the establishment of MAS Real Estate plc in 2009. MAS is a real estate investment and development company that is listed in Europe with a secondary listing on the JSE.

The offshore expansion, from which most of the Mergon Group's income is derived, has brought an umbrella group into being. It consists of about 200 companies, many of which are partnerships, that are active in ten industry sectors globally. Those sectors comprise technology, property, short-term insurance, logistics, coal mines, hydropower generation, health, specialised agricultural engineering and marine engineering with a combined market capitalisation of more than R10 billion in 2017. A few of the companies are listed on the JSE and the Luxembourg and Sydney stock exchanges, and business is done in Africa, Britain, Europe, Australia, the United States and China.

As an investment group, Mergon focuses on viable business relationships, partnerships and a decentralised management structure. Some of the specialised companies that use advanced technology are Mobile Data, Enermatics and The 4PL Group. Mertech Marine is the pioneer in the recovery and recycling of out-of-service submarine telecommunication cables. Renewable Energy Holdings is a leading developer of hydroelectricity in South Africa. WildFig Grow's first investment is in Nilo, a company that focuses on the luxury-goods market and has become the world's biggest breeder of Nile crocodiles, while Bössi produces rooibos iced tea that is marketed as a health drink for children in the United States.

As founder of Mergon and Mertech, which comprises the group's commercial activities, Van Niekerk stepped down as CEO of the Mergon Group in 2008 at the age of 69. His successor, Pieter Faure, who had been the financial director of Infotech as a 33-year-old, then put together a management team of five colleagues to control the group and invest in it. While visiting Cape Town six years later, he walked out of a Cape guesthouse on a beautiful summer's day when the idea occurred to him to establish Mergon's headquarters in the south.

On 5 January 2015, after 35 years in Pretoria, the new head office was opened in Stellenbosch. The relocation was well considered and timely, as Mergon had moved from involvement in local firms to an international investment organisation in diverse geographic regions. Above all, Stellenbosch had started developing into the primary centre for investment capital in the south.

The extensive diversification had by then already necessitated an earlier restructuring that resulted in two broad divisions in the Mergon Group. All business activities are conducted under the banner of the Mergon Group, while the Mergon Foundation deals independently with aid.

Van Niekerk's original promise of 30 per cent of the shareholding in Infotech, and later Atterbury, was increased over time to 70 per cent of the shares in Mertech. In 2010, this share portfolio was transferred into the Mergon Foundation as an independent trust. Of the remaining 30 per cent of the shares, 15 per cent was allocated to senior management while the founding family also owns 15 per cent. The founding family of François and Miems van Niekerk, including their spouses and legal dependants, have the right to appoint two trustees to Mergon's boards of trustees. In 2018, the Van Niekerk family representative trustees were François and his only child, Carla van Rensburg, a chartered accountant with a master's degree in tax.

The name Mergon is derived from the Greek words 'nomè' (the area where the flock graze) and 'ergon' (effectiveness). The dividends fund the foundation's charitable activities across Africa and the Middle East. 'The focus is on effective ministries, education, poverty alleviation and social upliftment,' says Van Niekerk. 'The sole beneficiary is Christian community work, and it follows logically that God is our controlling shareholder.'

Forbes magazine reported in 2011 that François van Niekerk was Africa's top philanthropist. According to the magazine, he had donated $170 million to charity, more than the continent's richest man, Alika Dangote from Nigeria, and other rich South Africans on Africa's A-list of the wealthy. In 2013, he received the Philanthropist of the Year Award from the UK-based organisation African Achievers International.

Van Niekerk, who married Louise Neethling after the death of his first wife Miems, stresses that he is by no means an adherent of prosperity theology: 'You don't receive if you give with the aim of receiving.'

Moreover, he does not think of himself as a philanthropist. 'Philanthropists normally share self-made success. My business and personal philosophies and practice are based on and guided by my Christian faith, which was strengthened immensely by how God responded to my plea of desperation when faced with complete business failure about forty years ago. Now, sharing with others offers me inspiration and direction.'

He points out that Marie Antoinette and her French husband King Louis XVI fell victim to the guillotine a mere 224 years ago. 'We're approaching that point again. It's simply not sustainable that fewer than 200 rich people own more than the bottom 3,5 billion of humanity. Dr Anton Rupert believed that he who wishes to retain all, will lose all. In Africa in particular it is crucial that the business community fulfils its social responsibilities. Every business is largely dependent on a sustainable environment, after all.'

The independent Mergon Foundation's shared ownership in the Mergon Group provides close to R10 million a month that is allocated to some 135 established community organisations that run about 800 upliftment projects in Africa and the Middle East. On top of that, each group company is encouraged to run its own community trusts. Atterbury trusts, for example, built a world-class community theatre, the Atterbury Theatre, in Pretoria.

The Atterbury Trust provides bursary loans for tertiary study and related support to disadvantaged matriculants. The average pass rate over more than a decade is 97 per cent. Atterbury also gives large-scale support to schools in financial distress and runs clinic services in impoverished communities.

Contributions to the cause of bolstering Afrikaans include a personal donation of R5 million each by Van Niekerk and Van der Watt for subsidisation of the Atterbury Theatre in Pretoria. The Atterbury Trust has assisted about 700 Afrikaans-speaking graduates to date, while several other trusts in the group focus on the Afrikaans-language community (medical clinics, schools, children's homes). Van Niekerk, who was named Business Leader of the Year by *Die Burger* in 2018, has also personally supported the establishment of the new digital RoepTV with a loan of a few million rand.

Van Niekerk emphasises that success in a business enterprise indicates that a much wider obligation rests on the business community and the wealthy to reduce inequalities in the world. With a view to inspiring and equipping the business community to lead social change, the Muthobi Trust is one of several institutions that were established in recent years to enable Mergon to broaden its footprint by giving businesspeople easier access to the group's kaleidoscope of projects. One of these Muthobi initiatives is Nation Builder, which seeks to be a catalyst for a new wave of leadership to reduce inequalities and ensure the long-term future of South Africa.

'Nation Builder embodies my conviction that South Africa will be built up and strengthened when there is active cooperation between the church, civil society, the state and business,' says Van Niekerk.

Johann Rupert

The Ruperts rank among the best-known benefactors in the country. Johann Rupert, who annually donates his salary to the amount of an estimated R40 million to charity, and his sister, Hanneli Rupert-Koegelenberg, both serve on the boards of long-established family foundations that were set up by their father, Anton Rupert.

Rupert senior is often quoted because of a pronouncement that has lived on as one of his best-known sayings: 'In southern Africa you cannot escape being your brother's keeper; we cannot sleep peacefully if our starving neighbours cannot eat.'

Despite his philosophy of co-partnership and coexistence, he was nonetheless strongly opposed to handouts. He believed people should be helped to help themselves, as he considered self-development the only lasting development. In the case of deserving projects, he therefore set the condition that the applicants had to find the first half themselves, and he would fund the second half. 'They do something themselves and feel grateful towards you, but then you are not in a position of superiority,' he stated.

There are five Rupert foundations that have for years been making substantial contributions in the fields of nature conservation, art, music, education and historical homes. Among these are the preservation of Cape Dutch homes in Stellenbosch and in Tulbagh, where hundreds of houses were restored after the destructive earthquake on 29 September 1969. In Graaff-Reinet, the town with the most historical monuments in the country, the façades of more than 250 houses in the Karoo architectural style were restored and preserved. In 2019, Johann Rupert offered on behalf of Historical Homes of SA to assist with rebuilding the heritage of the historic mission town of Wuppertal after 53 of the 113 houses on the terraces, and other buildings, had been gutted by fire.

Besides support given to the performing arts, which includes assistance for musical recitals and operas, the Rupert Museum in Stellenbosch houses a large collection of valuable artworks, among others, paintings by Irma Stern, Jean Welz and JH Pierneef, sculptures by Auguste Rodin and Anton van Wouw, and tapestries by Jean Lurçat. Rupert senior was a founder member of WWF South Africa, and his ideal of establishing transfrontier peace parks is continued in the Peace Parks Foundation under the chairmanship of Johann Rupert.

The Rupert descendants are generous benefactors in their own right. Johann donates considerable sums for education and training and also assists people to obtain title deeds for their homes. His sister Hanneli has established extensive upliftment projects on her farm La Motte in Franschhoek.

In response to attacks by radical black groups such as Black First Land First, Johann disclosed in 2017 that he and his wife, Gaynor, had donated more than R600 million to various bursary and training schemes in that year. In addition, in Graaff-Reinet his family was feeding more than 10 000 children from eleven schools in the black and coloured communities on a daily basis. The project was run by Litha Yaya, and with the assistance of the Rupert family the black-controlled company Nutriwell delivered the food parcels that were prepared for the children by women from the communities.

In November 2018, against the backdrop of heated debates in Parliament about expropriation of property without compensation, Rupert made an impactful contribution to effective land reform. He handed over 70 title deeds to their homes to residents of Aberdeen, the town that has a close association with his wife Gaynor. Her father was a master builder who had built the magnificent Dutch Reformed church in Aberdeen. At the event, the speaker of the Graaff-Reinet town council, Tembisa Nonnies, praised the Ruperts for their care and concern 'to give back to the people'. She said: 'I have evidence! Twenty-four schools in the area have computers and internet. Nobody goes to school hungry.'

The handover ceremony took place in Graaff-Reinet at the SA College for Tourism, of which Gaynor is the chair. It followed after the graduation ceremony of 92 hospitality students from disadvantaged communities who had been trained for careers in the tourism industry. Besides the ongoing hospitality training, the college's Tracking Academy trains trackers for game parks, while the Herding Academy trains herders for the livestock industry.

The Rupert couple are also sponsors of Khaya Lam (My Home), the empowerment project of the Free Market Foundation, which facilitates the transfer of municipal rental homes to the occupants.

In December they handed over 326 title deeds in Stellenbosch as well.

In 2018, Johann Rupert was given special recognition for his 'humanitarian efforts and generosity' by the Appeal of Conscience Foundation, which awarded him the Appeal of Conscience Award alongside Christine Lagarde, managing director of the International Monetary Fund, who received the foundation's World Leader Award.

GT Ferreira

At a birthday party, GT Ferreira told the guests that you should divide your earthly possessions into four piles. 'The first pile is for your personal use, and you have to spend it before you die. The second pile is only for when you spend the first pile too soon. The third pile you should donate to charity, and your children inherit the fourth pile.'

He awards bursaries to financially challenged students at Stellenbosch University, especially those from previously disadvantaged communities who do not necessarily all have to be black or coloured, but with the criterium being that they do not need to have achieved seven distinctions in matric. 'That guy can look after himself. Someone will give him a bursary. So get a person who has at least jumped over the hurdle, but who won't have the opportunity to go to university unless he gets a bursary.'

He does set the condition, however, that two of the bursary holders should be former pupils of the Volkskool in Graaff-Reinet, which he attended. Ferreira likes to quote the American billionaire Bill Gates, the founder of Microsoft: 'Charity comes from the heart, not the head.'

An event from his schooldays has stayed in his memory. When a group from his school had an opportunity to go to Die Burger Strandhuis in Muizenberg for an educational seaside holiday, he desperately wanted to go. Each child had to pay R200, but his parents just said there was no money for the Strandhuis. 'So these kids come back and can't stop talking about how nice it was at the seaside, and so on. You're very angry with your mom and dad, and to this day my heart is still sore about it ...

'Funnily enough, about two, three years ago I received a letter from the coloured school in Graaff-Reinet that had been given an opportunity to send a group to Die Burger Strandhuis. Not all the kids had enough money for the trip, and could I please make a contribution? And this is where it touches your heart.'

He then phoned the principal and said he would help, but on one condition: 'Stop asking any other people for money, I want to sponsor the whole thing, from start to finish, the bus, the lot, and the kids have to get extra ice cream. Yes, the principal said, but the kids also don't all have the same clothes, so I said: okay, we'll have tracksuits made for them so that they all look the same. I mean, that's the kind of thing that makes you feel good.'

Ferreira would be one of the last among the wealthy that was able to sponsor such a seaside holiday for children from small-town schools. In October 2018 it was announced that Die Burger Strandhuis would close down – yet another victim of the financial quandary in which newspapers found themselves.

Koos Bekker

Despite being a media billionaire, Koos Bekker is not someone who likes to broadcast his philanthropic activities. On the contrary, he is outspoken about public declarations in this regard. 'The older I get, the more cynical I become about people who boast about their altruism: the biggest scum and slyest crooks in the world have always been those who parade themselves as a Mother Teresa.

'The role of business is to create jobs, and jobs, in turn, generate economic growth, tax and so on. It's the role of the state to then use that tax in the most socially effective way. If people wish to do good deeds in their private lives, the biblical advice is that your left hand should not know what your right hand is doing,' he stated in an email.

Nonetheless, *Die Burger* did report on 12 March 2018 that Bekker had donated his directors' remuneration from Naspers and Tencent to the value of R3,4 million to the Simondium Primary School, which is situated in the vicinity of his Babylonstoren estate. According to Bekker, South Africa can only compete if schools are strengthened: 'Countries that put emphasis on education do very well in the world. Job creation is vital in our country, but for jobs to be created, people first need to be trained.'

Ton Vosloo states in his memoir, *Across Boundaries*, that Bekker's 'good deeds are never publicised'. Among other things, he has made the publication of significant books with a historical element possible. Through personal sponsorship of refresher projects for lecturers and bursaries to students, he contributes to the advancement of training and education.

Bekker, who has studied Mandarin himself, sponsors a chair in Mandarin at Stellenbosch University. He was sharply criticised about this association by the columnist Sonja Loots, who responded in *Rapport* to an announcement that the university was expanding its ties with the Chinese government and the Confucius Institute by means of this sponsorship. She regarded it as a worrying threat to the university's academic freedom.

In the United States, the National Association of Scholars has called on US universities to close their Chinese government-backed Confucius Institutes. According to the *New York Times*, they are a propaganda vehicle in the Chinese government's 'most ardent effort at image-polishing' in a disguised power play to gain influence through the forging of cultural ties.

Michiel le Roux

Michiel le Roux's philanthropic grant-making is mainly done through the Millennium Trust, which was established in 2010 as a non-profit organisation. This trust sees the challenges it seeks to address as the country's need for sustained economic growth, high-quality education, informed public debate, independent democratic institutions and efficient service delivery.

The emphasis of the trust is on education and teaching, which includes support for initiatives such as the Afrikaanse Spelfees, as well as the strengthening of democracy in the country. Among other causes, the trust helps to fund the amaBhungane Centre for Investigative Journalism, which played a decisive role in exposing large-scale corruption and state capture during the Zuma regime. Wide-ranging reporting under the #GuptaLeaks banner revealed thousands of damning emails and documents.

Funding also goes to Corruption Watch, as well as Freedom Under Law – the organisation chaired by Judge Johann Kriegler that has instituted several court cases against the state to ensure and stabilise the rule of law.

Hendrik du Toit

As a benefactor, Hendrik du Toit makes a clear distinction between his personal life and his business and corporate life. 'Being at the helm of a big public company is exactly that: public. What the company does, is there for everyone to see. I come from an Afrikaner background where we were taught not to shout about everything from the rooftops and where you don't brag about your good deeds ... But because the question has been put to me directly, I can't keep quiet.

'I like to give, and I give significantly. My wife and I support a few educational institutions, nature conservation and deserving individuals who will make good use of an opportunity in life. We endeavour to leave the world a better place than we found it. I like giving through others and try to keep my name out of it where we are involved. I don't give in order to get back, but because I genuinely would like to help out of gratitude for the grace and abundance I receive from Above on a daily basis.'

Regarding Investec's sponsorships, he firmly believes in the principle that they should boost the value of the brand. Sponsorships are not welfare or corporate social responsibility. Sponsorships, which can change from time to time, support the ability of the business to live up to its brand proposition. Investec supports excellence (sport, art) and sustainable development (maths tuition, job creation via the Yes Project and environmental conservation).

He believes sponsorships should be decided on professionally; they fall in the domain of the marketing team and business units. 'The chair, board members and top executives shouldn't use sponsorships to support their personal interests. Sponsorships are one of many techniques to promote the business in the communities it serves. Nothing more and nothing less.'

Christo Wiese, Renier van Rooyen and Whitey Basson

Many business leaders emphasise private property ownership as a means of building up wealth. Like Johann Rupert, Christo Wiese attaches great value to funding title deeds that are transferred to occupants of homes. He is a sponsor of the Free Market Foundation that works with FNB in the Khaya Lam (My Home) project, which aims to help previously disadvantaged people secure their property rights. He believes these title deeds will ensure that young people have a roof over their heads when their parents or grandparents pass on, and he encourages people in his companies to initiate such projects everywhere.

The ANC was initially opposed to the concept, and Jeremy Cronin, a deputy minister, wrote in an article that it was a trick because people with title deeds could trade with their properties, which would then be bought up by white capitalists. Wiese pointed out that millions of people across the world own assets worth trillions of dollars, yet the land on which their homes have been built belongs to the municipality or the state. The occupants can do nothing with it, because they do not have legal title to the property.

The first municipality where Wiese handed over 100 title deeds was Parys in the Free State. According to him, the mayor, a black woman, was 'a real go-getter – she just cut through everything and said, let us, the municipality, do it.' Wiese says he listened to heart-rending stories in the Tomahole township. He believes the project will have both an economic and a psychological impact: 'That people are able to say "my house is modest, but it's mine", is important. Others don't realise how it helps make people feel they have human dignity; being property owners.'

The Red Cross Children's Hospital in Cape Town was the project the Wiese family became most involved in. They created considerable facilities that did not previously exist at the hospital. 'This is something that touches me because the facilities are there for everyone, also children from elsewhere in South Africa.'

He also sponsors the South African Academy for Arts and Science's Christo Wiese Medal for emerging entrepreneurs, which is awarded to young businesspeople (45 years and younger) who have excelled.

Wiese's predecessor at the Pep Group, Renier van Rooyen, was also one of the early private philanthropists in the country. A cause that was close to his heart was the upliftment of impoverished coloured communities. In 1974, he made a personal donation of R500 000 to a foundation for community development that still exists today. The poet Adam Small was the first executive director, and Franklin Sonn became the chair a few years later. The economist Eltie Links also became a director of Weswok, which was subsequently renamed the Foundation for Community Work (FCW). One of the people who was assisted to further his studies in his youth was Professor Jakes Gerwel.

A trust for education is an important objective for the retired Shoprite boss Whitey Basson. Under his leadership, Shoprite embarked on a different initiative: mobile soup kitchens consisting of about twenty large vehicles that regularly distribute hot soup to children in need. Every day, the group also donates left-over food from its stores to non-profit organisations that make it available to poor communities.

Empowerment of women is another of Shoprite's projects, with one of the initiatives being to support women to become suppliers to the group.

Douw Steyn

Douw Steyn is also known for his generosity. Over the years he not only assisted various family members and other people financially but was also very good to the Mandela family.

Gert Grobler, a former South African ambassador to Spain and Tokyo, was once driving with Steyn in his car in Bloemfontein when they saw woman in ragged clothes begging at a robot. 'Douw rolled down the window and said: Madam, you can't stand here like this in the hot sun. She said yes, but she had no food to eat. And he asked Bossie (his assistant) to hand him the money bag, took out a bundle of banknotes and handed them to her. The woman stood there, totally dumbfounded ... Douw had given her R2 000,' Grobler recounted.

Most of the donations made by Telesure, the holding company of the companies Steyn founded in South Africa, go to Diepsloot, the informal settlement next to Steyn City. The aim is to transform the Itirele-Zenezele High School into a school with a 100 per cent pass rate, reduce youth unemployment, promote adult education and combat gender-based violence. Telesure employed 3 000 residents of Diepsloot when they moved into the new head office in Auto & General Park.

Steyn's wife Carolyn has gained renown in her own right with her 67 Blankets for Nelson Mandela Day campaign that she started at the instigation of Mandela's personal assistant Zelda la Grange to distribute blankets among those in need. Thousands of people in South Africa and other countries, in old age homes and other institutions, as well as prison inmates, have helped to crochet, knit and sew blankets in Carolyn's charitable movement that captured international attention.

Jannie Mouton and Laurie Dippenaar

Both Jannie Mouton and Laurie Dippenaar have a partiality for education as a deserving cause for philanthropy. In 2016, Mouton started the Jannie Mouton Foundation with a billion rand when he sold his shares in Steinhoff International. It happened after he had watched a television interview with Warren Buffett during which the American investment guru smiled broadly as he talked about giving away most of his wealth to charity. 'He looked happy. That inspired me.'

In 2019, Mouton donated R50 million in the form of PSG shares to Stellenbosch University for a learning centre. The centre is named after his father, Jan Mouton, for whom he has 'incredible respect'.

A sequel to Mouton's donation was that the university's fundraiser, Neil Krige, thought a cash donation would be more convenient. Mouton then bought back the shares at R190 apiece, after which the share price rose. He recounts that he then phoned Krige to thank him jokingly for the 'favour' he had done him, as those shares were now worth R19 million more.

Mouton also manages a bursary scheme at Stellenbosch University 'that has already put 100 children through university, and then I'm not even talking about the bursary scheme we have for black children to attend Curro schools'. He mentions that the PSG Group – if one includes Curro and Capitec – has given R20 billion for black empowerment. His daughter Charité opened a coffee shop in Khayelitsha. She trained three black entrepreneurs who later took over the business from her.

Laurie Dippenaar, for his part, makes it possible for South Africans to study at international universities. Every year he awards bursaries to the value of R800 000 to students with excellent academic and leadership track records. Known as the Laurie Dippenaar Postgraduate Scholarship for International Study, the bursaries are available to South African citizens for postgraduate study at any internationally recognised university for a maximum of two years. In addition, the Dippenaar Family Trust has to date supported more than 350 Stellenbosch students who would otherwise have had to drop out due to a lack of funds.

Louis Norval, Frik Rademan and Johan van Zyl

Several Afrikaner business leaders also contribute generously to art and culture.

An art museum that brings together the visual arts and nature conservation has been created by the property billionaire Louis Norval in Constantia in Cape Town – the first of its kind in South Africa. The Norval Foundation museum, which houses one of the largest private art collections in the country, has also been designed to rehabilitate and maintain the sensitive Steenberg wetland with its endangered indigenous flora and fauna, including the rare western leopard toad. Works of renowned artists, such as Gerard Sekoto, Edoardo Villa, Alexis Preller and Irma Stern, are on display in the museum and sculpture garden.

As chief executive of Avbob, Frik Rademan, unlike many other businesspeople, has a special open-door policy: he speaks personally to every policyholder of the society because they are put through directly to him when they call, and he becomes personally involved in all complaints.

Under his leadership, the Avbob Foundation was established in 2012 to drive their corporate social investment initiatives. The flagship project is to donate container libraries to schools in disadvantaged communities. Constructed from shipping containers and refurbished and designed to be comfortable reading spaces, the mobile libraries are fitted with solar PV systems and stocked with 3 000 books and educational games. Avbob staff themselves and some of their brand ambassadors have donated additional books and equipment.

An exceptional initiative under Rademan's leadership is the Avbob Poetry Project and its online poetry competition, which attracts entries from all regions of South Africa. Every year the project publishes an anthology of poems in all eleven official languages as well as others such as the N|uu language, which is on the brink of extinction. The anthology, *I Wish I'd Said ...* , deals with themes of death, mortality, loss and consolation, and three volumes have appeared so far.

As a director of Sanlam and co-CEO of Ubuntu-Botho, Johan van Zyl is well positioned when it comes to charitable activities. Sanlam's corporate social responsibilities range from sponsorships for educational and cultural activities to contributions towards both entrepreneurship and job creation as well as welfare and other community programmes. Education is the core of Sanlam's community programmes, which include the *Takalani Sesame* TV series, which promotes school readiness in children and the Thuthuka Bursary Fund, which awards bursaries to black aspirant chartered accountants.

Sanlam is a sponsor of the Woordfees in Stellenbosch, the WOW initiative (Words Open Worlds), the annual Radio Drama Competition in conjunction with Radio Sonder Grense, and the Sanlam Prize for Youth Literature. The Sanlam Foundation was established in 2011 to support communities, promote enterprise development (particularly entrepreneurship), and improve financial literacy.

Ubuntu-Botho, chaired by Patrice Motsepe, is the owner of African Rainbow Capital (ARC), which consists of the Motsepe Family Trust, the Sanlam Ubuntu-Botho Community Development Trust and BEE groups. Van Zyl and his former Sanlam colleague Johan van der Merwe are the joint CEOs. The Community Development Trust was founded to support and empower the poorest of the poor. Schools, clinics and other public facilities are built in rural areas, and in a national schools programme stationery and library books are supplied to schools countrywide.

Johannes van Eeden

A striking innovation in the philanthropic sector is GivenGain, whose office in South Africa is run from Stellenbosch. This organisation that manages charitable donations in some sixty countries is the brainchild of Johannes van Eeden, an entrepreneur who started his career as a composer-poet.

Van Eeden, who studied music, languages and philosophy at Stellenbosch University, was a co-founder of Obelisk, an organisation dedicated to the advancement of contemporary music. After completing his studies, he first taught at a school in Pretoria and then worked as a librarian at Unisa while he wrote music reviews for *Beeld* and provided opportunities for South African composers to have their work performed through Obelisk. He lived a rather bohemian lifestyle, but he married at an early age and soon discovered that bohemianism lost its charm once there were children in the house.

He also realised that building a business was 'in itself a highly fulfilling creative action'. He was appointed as marketer and sales agent of GNLD, a multi-level marketing company. Things went so well there that at the age of 26 he was able to retire and move to Stellenbosch, where he rented a small farm.

As an entrepreneur who also cares for his fellow human beings, Johannes wanted to apply and execute a simple idea: 'to enable global philanthropy by empowering individuals and non-profits to break down the barriers between and within ourselves'. He and his brother Jaco, an IT specialist, had always wanted to do something together. They considered various possibilities before turning the idea of GivenGain into a reality in 2001.

Both of them spent much time outside South Africa and the company was registered overseas, with the first office in Ticino in Switzerland. It was therefore an international enterprise from the outset, although some of the development work was done in Stellenbosch. Johannes, who retained his South African passport, obtained

Swiss residency. Besides Stellenbosch, branches were in time also established in Britain and Canada.

As a non-profit organisation, GivenGain earns only a small income, a 5 per cent admin fee, from its advanced technological system for philanthropic donations. 'Our sole aim was to make the world a better place and to help people fundraise on behalf of non-profit organisations,' Johannes recounted. 'We realised after a few years that it's not so simple to create a sustainable business model for the philanthropic market. We tried to do it, but we were very naïve.'

A new idea emerged one day when Johannes went to pay his monthly rent at the estate agent Anna Basson in Stellenbosch. He told the receptionist there had to be a better way of paying rent than all tenants having to come to their offices monthly to give her a cheque.

This was the start of PayProp, which was launched in 2004 as a one-stop-service for the property management industry: a bank-integrated and automated payment and settlement platform to simplify and expedite rental payments and related transactions such as agents' commissions. The easier payment method expanded rapidly, because 'PayProp is revolutionary in the sense that it automates a process that took days and was heavily manually driven, and it reconciles to the cent. It then became transactions of quite a few billions per year, and I think PayProp eliminates a lot of inefficiencies and red tape and also brings a chunk of trust and integrity into the market,' Van Eeden states.

'I don't see myself as being in the property industry; I see myself as being in an industry where I automate transactions for people. We feel we have a unique ability to simplify complex things.'

PayProp Holdings, a fully owned subsidiary of the parent company, Humanstate, owns subsidiaries in South Africa, Britain, Canada and the US. PayProp Capital provides property managers with risk management solutions, inter alia through insurance and capital market strategies. PayProp's Rental Index is a research tool that provides the latest information on trends in the residential rental market.

Johannes is the chief executive of Humanstate, which has its head office in London. There is an office in Villars-sur-Ollon in Switzerland, and branches in Stellenbosch, Toronto and Miami. Johannes insists on four board meetings a year where the entire top management is present. The meetings are held in an old castle in France, among other venues, and in this 'island situation' they 'speak bluntly'.

In 2009, the GivenGain Foundation was founded to manage all donations made to charitable projects listed on GivenGain. More than 100 000 donors from 193 countries make use of his services. Among the organisations that use the hypermodern technological platform for fundraising are Unicef, Médicins Sans Frontières, the Red Cross, the WWF and many more.

The foundation's chair is Frans Stroebel, who was the CEO of Stellenbosch Farmers' Winery before he became the personal assistant of Anton Rupert. The Van Eeden brothers serve on the board of the foundation along with several experts in the field of philanthrophy.

According to the founders, without the starting belief that it is more blessed to give than to receive, nothing would have happened. They regard the welfare of others as a universal truth, and their altruism is also practised internally. All employees are given twelve days' leave a year to volunteer for a non-profit of their choice. 'I think the people feel part of something that's not only about making money, but something that changes the world. It's the DNA of our business and it will stay that,' says Van Eeden.

'We have some of the top programmers in the world working for us in Switzerland and in England, and I often think we pay well, but we're not necessarily paying Google's salaries, so why do the guys work for us? I think they experience something different; they experience a company that is built on a philanthropic foundation, a company with a soul that's not only extremely profitable but also gives special meaning and purpose to everyone who works there.'

18
Farms and follies

AFRIKANER BILLIONAIRES who have risen to the top in the South African economy since 1994 are a diverse group. Quite a few of them know each other well, but it is a myth that they operate like a mafia and support each other all the time. Often their interrelationships are rather characterised by intense rivalry.

Nor are they limited to a single geographic location, as the 'Stellenbosch Mafia' label suggests. Some of the leading figures who are typecast as such do not even live in Stellenbosch. Laurie Dippenaar, for instance, resides in Johannesburg, Christo Wiese and Koos Bekker have been Cape Town residents for decades, and Johann Rupert lives in Somerset West.

Still, Stellenbosch, often celebrated in the past as the cradle of Afrikaans culture, has for the past few decades been the prime spot where Afrikaners make money. Unlike the group of Afrikaner businesspeople who gathered in the town more than a century ago to found *Die Burger* in 1915, a meeting that spawned Naspers and institutions such as Sanlam and Santam, the new generation is no longer driven by *volkskapitalisme*. Ethnic mobilisation has been replaced by capitalism and the free market, although most of them are still involved in charitable support for community causes.

Most of the contemporary super-rich have maintained a strong connection with the country after the transition of 1994 and many own farms, notably wine estates and game farms. While some have a more modest lifestyle, the majority live in swanky houses in exclusive suburbs with assets that speak of big money: select paintings, expensive furniture, Persian carpets, wine cellars and the like. They travel overseas, mostly business class, stay in five-star hotels and are able to book a table in Michelin restaurants. They visit playgrounds of the rich and famous such as the French Riviera and the Swiss Alps, and quite a few own an exotic vehicle or two that make motorheads drool.

Some also openly admit to a folly.

Several of the new generation of Stellenbosch businesspeople got to know each other in their student days. One of the country's rugby legends was a contemporary. The former Springbok wing Jannie Engelbrecht, a former Matie who had attended Paul Roos Gymnasium like some of these men and started farming on the historic Rust en Vrede wine estate in 1977, points out that Stellenbosch University was small in those days. 'We all knew each other.'

As a student, Engelbrecht stayed in the Simonsberg residence on the same floor as Jannie Mouton of PSG and GT Ferreira of FirstRand.

'Many of us gained our business experience in Johannesburg,' recounts Chris Otto, who had been in Johannesburg for 25 years when he decided together with Jannie Mouton in a house in Parkview to establish PSG. Mouton suggested that they open an office in Stellenbosch. 'It took me 30 seconds to say yes.'

Despite the close ties, Otto stresses that it is a misapprehension that they do business deals with one another. He maintains that people prefer doing business with those they know well, but in Stellenbosch such deals are not necessarily made with each other.

Otto's roommate in the Eendrag men's residence was Michiel le Roux of Capitec. They started their university careers in the same year as Edwin Hertzog, who later became the head of Mediclinic in the Rembrandt Group. Other residents of Eendrag were Koos Bekker and Cobus Stofberg of Naspers, who were there at the same time as Gys du Toit of the Dutoit Group from Ceres.

Hertzog had gone to school at Paul Roos Gymnasium in the town. Other prominent former Maties who are also PRG Old Boys are Johann Rupert, Jannie Durand, who became the head of Remgro, Jan Scannell of Distell, Riaan Stassen of Capitec and Michael Jordaan of Montegray.

A popular meeting place of the Stellenbosch business elite is the town's golf course, said to be the only golf club in the country where more wine than beer is consumed.

Another regular hangout for many of them is Decameron, the Italian restaurant in the town centre where Mario Ladu's menu has become legendary. Lunches can at times run into the late afternoon when the table talk is engrossing. Mario makes sure that a table is available for his regular customers, just as for years he reserved a corner table for Anton Rupert when he did not eat at the Volkskombuis.

A Friday lunch at Decameron happened to be the prelude to a narrow escape one of Stellenbosch's most prominent women, Erna Meaker, had with Steinhoff shares. On that day, she and her husband Paul were enjoying a meal in the smoke-free section of the restaurant when they smelled smoke. Paul got up to investigate and saw Markus Jooste chatting to people with a cigarette in his hand. The staff were loath to take action against the VIP guest, but Erna was outraged.

She decided on the spot that she did not want to own shares of something owned by someone who showed so little regard for other restaurant-goers. The following Monday she instructed her broker to sell all Steinhoff shares in her and her children's trusts. A few days later, Steinhoff collapsed.

One of the important business decisions taken in Decameron concerned the merger of the liquor companies Distillers and Stellenbosch Farmers' Winery. The new company needed a new name. A team of experts tasked with the job eventually agreed on Distell, a combination of the two names. The proposal was submitted to Anton Rupert, who was not very happy with it. Rupert, widely regarded as the oracle of trademarks, wanted to see something of the history of the wine industry reflected in the new name.

The team then returned on a Friday with the name Van Rijn, derived from the Van Ryn Wine and Brandy Company, one of the building blocks of Distillers. Delighted with this name, Rupert said he would talk to his tobacco colleagues to arrange that the tobacco brand Rembrandt van Rijn would in future be known simply as Rembrandt. The following Sunday, while the Rupert family were assembled for lunch at Decameron, the proposed new name was among the topics they discussed. Huberte Rupert, who regularly act-ed as her husband's sounding board, objected strongly: 'But Van Rijn is tobacco!' Early on Monday morning, Johann Rupert notified the team: 'Van Rijn is out.' Rupert senior eventually gave his approval that they could proceed with Distell.

The Decameron building was also the scene of a conflict be-tween the Stellenbosch businesspeople that kept tongues wagging for months. It happened when plans were submitted for alterations to the four-storey building in which the restaurant is situated in Plein

Street in the town centre – strategically close to the offices of a number of the businesspeople. There were half a dozen investors in the building, including Jannie Mouton and GT Ferreira, but along with the restaurant owner Mario Ladu they did not feature prominently in the disputes.

The group of developers met with opposition after the announcement of the building plans that, among other things, made provision for five storeys and included a penthouse for Markus Jooste. The resistance was spearheaded by the Stellenbosch Interest Group, led by three women who were opposed to the envisaged development on aesthetic grounds, inter alia because height restrictions were exceeded. The Interest Group received support from the side of the Ruperts, particularly from the Rupert Historical Homes Foundation and Historical Homes of South Africa.

The battle ended up in court, and later in the Appeal Court. Some Stellenbosch residents recounted gleefully that Johann Rupert once bumped into Jannie Mouton and admonished him about the dispute: 'Jannie, if you want to play cat and mouse, you have to ensure you're the cat.' Mouton withdrew from meetings with the group of developers after talks with Anton Rupert, but did not his relinquish his investment or his lunch-time seat in the Decameron restaurant.

After months-long delays with court cases and a struggle to get the plans approved by the municipality, some of the smaller investors started feeling the pinch. Then GT Ferreira, who more than once had been the peacemaker in Stellenbosch, contacted the Rupert camp again to mediate after earlier attempts had failed. Finally, in February 2008, a settlement in which the municipality was involved was reached between the warring parties. New plans that conformed to the requirements for the town's historic core were approved. The building was limited to four storeys, and Markus Jooste lost his penthouse in the process.

Some of the business elite live in the upmarket suburb of Mostertsdrift, where old homes have been razed and flashy houses erected that are so prominent that long-time Stellenbosch residents who are averse to ostentation sneeringly refer to the 'Mostertsdrift syndrome'. Here and there a culture of conspicuous consumption made inroads into the once fairly unpretentious university town with its academics whose salaries were nothing to write home about.

Thys du Toit, the former Coronation boss and a former chair of the KWV, is one of the well-known residents of Mostertsdrift. He believes he and his family are very privileged to own properties in 'the three best places in the country': Stellenbosch, Hermanus and Leopard Creek (the golf estate Johann Rupert developed on the banks of the Crocodile River next to the Kruger National Park).

In Stellenbosch he lives a stone's throw from Anton Rupert's old house in Thibault Street, on the banks of the Eerste River in a house he bought from Rupert's brother Jan. Because of the proximity of their houses on the river bank, Du Toit once had a run-in with the formidable Huberte Rupert, Anton's wife, of whom Anton himself said she did not mince her words.

At the time measures had to be taken to protect the banks of the Eerste River from erosion, and Du Toit had called on Professor Albert Rooseboom, a hydrologist from the university, to give advice on river bank protection. Wire cages filled with stones had to be packed along the river bank. When Mrs Rupert saw this, she was highly upset. So Du Toit and his wife invited the Ruperts to dinner 'just to give them some context and to say we're also inviting Professor Rooseboom, since he's the expert'. As Mrs Rupert came walking up to the front door with her cane, she saw the professor standing there. Brandishing her cane at him, she said: 'I know more about water than you.'

Albie de Waal, a former Springbok rugby player who made his fortune in the north, now lives in Stellenbosch. So does the former Springbok coach André Markgraaff, who himself manages a business empire of millions. Other well-known residents of Mostertsdrift are the former Sanlam chair Johan van Zyl, the former Pep CEO George Steyn, Chris Otto of PSG fame and Mof Terreblanche, the broker who had to break the news to Jannie Mouton when he was fired from SMK.

A number of the best-known Western Cape businesspeople own wine farms, an asset considered to be one of the ultimate status symbols among the world's super-rich. Wine farms are some of the most expensive agricultural land in the country. According to industry experts, the prices of the approximately 600 Cape wine farms vary between R10 million and R100 million, depending on where the farm is situated and how well the vineyards, the land and the buildings have been developed.

CHRISTO WIESE regards wine farms as his folly. He bought his first wine farm, Lanzerac, in 1990 – it is the third-oldest farm in Stellenbosch. After having made considerable improvements to the property and vine-growing in the course of two decades, Wiese sold Lanzerac in 2012 to Pavilion Estates, a company of which the British property developer Malcolm King and his wife Paula King are directors. It was long speculated that either Bruno Steinhoff or Markus Jooste, who lived on the neighbouring farm Jonkersdrift, bought the hotel, since King is a business friend of Jooste's and a creditor of his Mayfair Speculators.

In 1998, Wiese acquired the farm Lourensford, a historic 4 000 hectare estate on the outskirts of Somerset West that had been established by Governor Willem Adriaan van der Stel in 1709. The estate is a popular tourist destination with attractions that include its winery, microbrewery, restaurant, coffee roastery, outdoor market, music concerts and other activities such as luxury weddings and film shoots.

However, wine farms are seldom a very profitable investment. Wiese himself says: 'There are people who make money from wine; I'm not one of them … We're now starting to lose less money on our wine business at Lourensford, which is progress.'

Cognoscenti view wine farms in any case as a way of life rather than a way of making big money. An anecdote about Wiese and GT Ferreira illustrates this.

In its early days, Rand Merchant Bank (RMB), of which Ferreira was the co-founder, sought to increase a 20 per cent stake they held in the Natal Building Society (NBS) with a view to establishing a retail bank, but their attempt failed. RMB was outmanoeuvred by Wiese because he wanted to buy RMB's fifth share in order to merge NBS with Boland Bank.

He and Ferreira met for a business breakfast at Lanzerac, which Wiese owned at the time. Ferreira told him it was highly unlikely that NBS would agree, as they had already rejected RMB's offer. Wiese smiled and suggested they make a bet on it for a bottle of wine.

A wary Ferreira, who 'knew Christo well enough', insisted on a local wine. Wiese agreed to a bottle from his own estate for which he would ask the cost price rather than the retail price. Ferreira had reason to be suspicious, for it turned out that Wiese was already negotiating with NBS. 'Well, the deal was completed and I went to see Christo to pay for the wine,' Ferreira recounted.

Wiese had selected a Lanzerac Chardonnay with a retail price of R35. 'But the cost price of the bottle – and he offered to show me the statements – was R10 643,' Ferreira said laughingly. He had paid up with good grace. Ferreira, too, eventually embarked on a wine farm, despite the lesson about the cash-flow implications he had learned from Wiese.

At a point Wiese bought the imposing Ellerman House above Bantry Bay, which once belonged to the British shipping magnate Sir John Ellerman. At a dinner the Wieses attended, one of their business acquaintances remarked in front of everyone that Ellerman House 'suited Christo's status'. An upset Caro Wiese retorted that someone's status was not determined by the house he lived in.

In any case, she flatly refused to move there. The Wieses continued living in their house on Clifton's Fourth Beach and raised their children, Clare, Jacob and Christina, there. Caro's parents, Japie and Clarence Basson, lived next door.

Wiese also has a private game reserve, the Kalahari Oryx, 85 kilometres from Upington, which he visits regularly in his private jet. There are about 17 000 head of wildlife on the farm that stretches over 85 000 hectares. Nearly all types of antelope and predators are kept on the sprawling reserve in the Kalahari, except cheetahs and elephants, as in Wiese's view they do too much damage. He enjoys clay pigeon shooting on the farm and allows hunting expeditions since animal numbers need to be controlled. The farm has a landing strip for planes and luxury accommodation in a five-star lodge. In April 2018, Wiese wanted to sell two of his family's private planes, a Dassault Falcon 900C and a Boeing Business Jet, because he did not need two and intended to buy a different one.

Known for his cost curbing in his business operations, Wiese is equally thrifty in his private life. He keeps a little bottle in his Lexus

SUV in which he collects spare change. 'Christo is stingy,' says his friend Whitey Basson. 'He'll give me the nicest bottle of champagne as a present, and I'll open it up, and I'll see he forgot to take out the message: It's a bottle from Lord So-and-So. He's a regifter.'

But Wiese also has a liking for games of chance. When he lunches with friends at his favourite restaurant near his workplace, Magica Roma in Pinelands, they regularly play matches to determine who will have the privilege of paying the bill.

GT FERREIRA is about equally renowned as FirstRand banker and as owner of the wine-and-olive farm Tokara outside Stellenbosch. Ferreira once jestingly made a comment about wine farms that some wine farmers took amiss. He says he was just joking when he remarked 'that in banking ROE means a "return on equity", but in the wine business it stands for a "return on ego", that's all we get'.

He believes the wine industry has not come into its own. 'There are various reasons: too many brands; you sometimes buy bottles of wine for less than you pay for water. The competition is simply too huge. On the other hand, a wine farm doesn't go bankrupt; you just sell it to another idiot who thinks he can do better. But as a way of life, it's fantastic.

'My only problem is that my ego's so big, I actually want to make money. It's the easiest thing in the world to run a business and make a loss. Anyone can do that. But not everyone can make a profit.' People tell him he should not take it so seriously, it is just a hobby. 'I say no, it's not a hobby, this thing has to make money. We're now very close, and I'm going to pull it off before I die ... '

He supposes his wife Anne-Marie would say his real folly is sporting events. He enjoys all types of sport, so much so that he travelled to Italy in 2016 to watch the rugby test the Springboks lost. Goodness knows why he went, he says, '*that* was a folly'. He has attended eight Olympic Games, World Cup soccer, World Cup rugby, even the Super Bowl (American football) when he was on a visit to Texas. 'Also Wimbledon. This and that. I enjoy it.'

Another folly of Ferreira's is his six-wheeled SUV, a Mercedes-Benz G63 AMG. It is one of only ten right-hand-drive 6x6 models that were imported into South Africa after Ferreira expressed interest in such an off-road vehicle. The German aftermarket tuning company Brabus had upgraded fifty such vehicles for the German motor manufacturer. It is a massive but extremely powerful SUV, with a boot big enough to accommodate a small car. There were other buyers too, but Ferreira donated a G63 each to a few good friends – those he considered people who had helped him a great deal in his life – 'as a special gift he wouldn't buy himself, but which you knew he would appreciate'.

WHITEY BASSON of Shoprite fame has a penchant for classic cars, and he also likes 'beautiful cars' – he keeps his vehicle collection in a shed on his small wine estate Klein Dasbosch outside Stellenbosch. He has kept all the Porsche sports cars he has bought in his life. And he has all the cars that belonged to his father Captain Jack Basson, including his very first car: a Chevrolet Fleetline.

On Klein Dasbosch, the former Springbok flanker Boland Coetzee is his winemaker for a limited range of wines. A short distance from Klein Dasbosch is another farm he acquired, Mont Marie, which has a popular restaurant. In the Porterville district, Basson developed and revamped the family farm Dasbosch considerably after his brother passed away – the farm had been put in a trust for the sons after their father's death. In the Northern Cape, he owns a large game farm of 21 700 hectares between Brandvlei and Kenhardt that he bought at an auction. Guests he invites to the farm have to bring along a tree to be planted and cared for there.

Basson admits openly that he has a folly: he says what he likes, even if it may be undiplomatic. To many, his 'Whiteyisms' during the announcement of Shoprite's results were the cherry on top. He would regularly poke fun at the government and at competitors – and at himself. 'I always say we put our testicles out there, then people tell me: "No, it's the wrong word; you put your tentacles out there",' he once said.

'I'm unorthodox, emotional. All my life I've tried to think a bit outside the box … no, that's such a cliché. I've tried to feel a bit differently about things, which isn't necessarily right, is it. It makes you rather unpopular, because you touch on things people fear or with which they don't agree because they've never thought about it.

And then there are things that I do ... I don't go to audit committee meetings, for instance. Never. Why should I go there? Because then I don't know my business. I'd rather *not* do certain things, and make sure that my business is in good shape.

'So, I'm an oddball, but not to the extent that I would stand out as a loony. But I don't have fears about putting a foot wrong. Hence my circle of friends are people who are a bit more ... I don't know if the word is "daring", but who are a bit more entrepreneurial. I always say: when a businessman tells you they're appointing a new guy who says "We're going back to the basics", then you should know he won't last long. If you go back to the basics you're a goner, because the basics are 20 years old.'

It is true that he sometimes makes fun of Christo Wiese, he admits. 'Jannie Mouton always recounts that when my son Cornel asked him how one makes money, he told him: "Your dad says you should take lessons from Oom Christo. He's never done a day's work in his life, and look how rich he is."'

He jokes that since his retirement, it is not so easy for him to talk to other corporate bosses on the telephone any more because he is no longer the CEO of Shoprite: 'Nowadays I can't say things like that. Now I'm just Whitey. The telephonist will ask me: and what is it about? Then I say: Miss, this is very confidential, but your boss and I have the same girlfriend and there's a bit of a problem. Then I go through like a rocket!'

In the technological age, Basson is in one respect old-fashioned: he believes in a chequebook. Despite being a self-described 'terrific fan of technology', he pays accounts and creditors by cheque. He believes there are just too many risks attached to electronic payments. To him, a cheque is still documentary evidence with a foolproof trail.

JOHANN RUPERT is not only a businessman. He also farms on three historic wine farms in the Franschhoek valley – L'Ormarins, Fredericksburg and La Garonne – while his sister, Hanneli Rupert-Koegelenberg, owns a fourth estate, La Motte. Rupert took over the ownership of the L'Ormarins wine estate after the death of his brother Anthonij in a car accident in 2001 at the age of 50.

To Johann, winemaking is not just a hobby; it is personal cause because he wants to fulfil his younger brother's dream for the estate. To that end, Anthonij Rupert Wines has been developed on L'Ormarins in his memory. And Johann wants wine enthusiasts to enjoy the range of wines they produce: 'I look at people, and I would say there are sippers and there are drinkers. People who stir a salad around and sip a bit of Sauvignon Blanc are probably the same people who in the past would drink spritzers. They're not wine drinkers, and I'm not in that business. I want people who love wine.'

L'Ormarins is also home to the Franschhoek Motor Museum, an exclusive collection of vehicles that pays homage to more than a century of motoring history. Besides vintage cars, there are luxury sedans, racing cars, motorcycles and bicycles from the past hundred years, each with a distinctive history. One of the rarest vehicles is the 1956 Aston Martin DB2/4 Mk II Touring Spyder, a sports car model of which there are only three in the world. Apart from the exotic and rare vehicles, of which 80 at a time from the collection of 320 are exhibited rotationally in four halls, there are champion horses on L'Ormarins. Johann's wife Gaynor keeps her racehorses on the estate.

In 2011, Rupert purchased the neighbouring farm that had belonged to Graham Beck, one of the pioneers of South African wine production. This wine estate, La Garonne, has an imposing Cape Dutch manor house, as has other estates owned by the Ruperts.

On the third wine farm, Frederiksburg, the Rupert & Rothschild Vignerons partnership produces high-quality wines. Anthonij Rupert, who had farmed here as well prior to his death, substantially improved the rather dilapidated farm to the north of Simonsberg after buying it in 1984. Replanting of noble varieties started in 1986, the wine cellar was modernised and the manor house restored. In 1997, Anthonij and Baron Benjamin de Rothschild, only son of the late Baron Edmond de Rothschild, took over the reins of the partnership that was created by their fathers. Anthonij's game farm Welgevonden outside Graaff-Reinet was also taken over by Johann.

Johann Rupert is a noted sports enthusiast and a former cricketer. In 1990, he founded the Laureus Sport for Good Foundation, which funds 65 projects globally, with the goal of supporting underprivileged children by using sport to tackle social challenges. Among other contributions to sport, Rupert co-founded the Institute for Sports Science at the University of Cape Town.

He owned a stake in the English rugby club Saracens, and in 2019 he and Patrice Motsepe made a controlling investment in the Blue Bulls rugby team with a shareholding of 37 per cent each.

Rupert is a golf enthusiast and serves as chair of the South African PGA Tour and the South African Golf Development Board. One of his good friends is the champion golfer Ernie Els, who also owns a wine farm outside Stellenbosch and where Ernie Els Wines are produced.

The annual Alfred Dunhill Championship, a professional golf tournament, takes place at Rupert's picturesque Leopard Creek estate near Malalane. Several of Rupert's friends and business acquaintances, including directors of his companies, own holiday residences on this estate.

Rupert also has a holiday home at Onrus, near Hermanus. Among his overseas residences is a house in London's upmarket Belgravia district, as he has to spend much of his time outside South Africa.

KOOS BEKKER of Naspers is another businessman who is also a farm-owner. His particular hobby is gardening, something he considers a substitute for farming since he grew up on a farm. He still farms on his father's farm in Heidelberg too. Bekker reckons the nostalgia for farm life possibly offers him a counterweight for the cold technological world in which he has made his fortune.

He and his wife, Karen Roos, have visited most of the famous gardens of the world. As a result of their shared interest, they have created magnificent gardens with a great variety of plants and trees, inter alia on the farm Babylonstoren and at their Cape Town manor house, Waterhof.

In 2007, the couple bought Babylonstoren, a 200-hectare wine-and-olive farm near Franschhoek, for R35 million. Several trees with interesting histories grow in the garden on the estate. One was grown from a cutting from the apple tree under which Isaac Newton purportedly formulated his law of gravity. Bekker literally guards the first fruit of his own Newton-tree descendant like gold: the first apple it produced he had gilded.

The couple also obtained a cutting of the sycamore-fig tree of biblical times in which Zacchaeus the tax collector was said to have sat while awaiting Jesus' entry into Jericho. Another cutting comes from the oldest apple tree in South Africa, one that was planted by Jan van Riebeeck after his arrival at the Cape in 1652.

In fact, the original inspiration for Babylonstoren's fruit-and-vegetable garden, which was designed by the Italian-French architect Patrice Taravella, was the layout of the Company's Garden Van Riebeeck had planted. The vegetables and fruit produced on Babylonstoren supply the luxury hotel on the farm and the Babel restaurant. Wine is also produced on the farm, and the wording on the wine bottle labels is in Afrikaans, English and Mandarin (for the Chinese market).

Bekker's high regard for Emily Hobhouse, the British humanitarian activist who gained heroine status among Afrikaners during the Anglo-Boer War because the suffering of women and children in the concentration camps had moved her so deeply, played a role in another acquisition of a historic farm. In 2013, he bought the Hadspen estate, which had for many years been the family farm of the Hobhouses in the English county of Somerset. Emily interests Bekker 'as a fascinating and complex figure'.

According to the *Western Daily Press*, he paid £13 million for the Hadspen property. His wife has transformed it into a farm hotel similar to Babylonstoren. 'Karen is mad about design and styling. In the past she had to give up her career repeatedly and follow me – from Johannesburg to Cape Town, to New York, to Johannesburg, to Amsterdam, to Cape Town – and each time she had to resign as TV presenter, fashion editor, magazine editor. Now I'm following for a change, and I help her part-time,' he recounts.

A luxury hotel called The Newt, named after a salamander species endemic to the area around Hadspen, was opened in July 2019. The complex includes, among other things, a spa, a restaurant, an exotic walled garden and a garden café. When the grounds were opened for public viewing, Karen said: 'I would have been happy with a little courtyard. But my husband, he is different. He thinks on scale.'

A special train from London transports guests to the estate and back to the British capital in the evening. At £285 a head they can enjoy a stylish breakfast and supper on the train. The British travel writer Lisa Grainger described The Newt in *The Telegraph* as 'unlike anything any of us has seen since the heyday of the Victorians'.

Bekker owns a house in Amsterdam that he bought when the pay-TV service FilmNet expanded in Europe. As far as rumours about property investments in Tuscany in Italy or other regions of the world are concerned, he says he has 'a small partnership or interest here and there, but nothing of monumental or public interest'. The Tuscan interest is probably in Villa Vignamaggio, the historic wine estate where Mona Lisa's name appears on the villa.

Bekker is wary of admitting to any follies in public. 'Entrepreneurs typically have serious follies – some are certifiable – but I doubt that it is wise to advertise such defects,' he says.

JANNIE MOUTON of PSG lives on his farm Klein Gustrouw in the Jonkershoek valley outside Stellenbosch. He bought Klein Gustrouw in partnership with Markus Jooste with whom he was friends for years, and they made wine together on the farm that dates back to 1817. Jooste later sold his half of the farm to Mouton. When the Steinhoff scandal erupted, Mouton terminated their friendship: 'We're no longer friends.'

Mouton also owns the farm Koktyls near Barrydale and a seaside house at Plettenberg Bay. He has a predilection for luxury cars, like his snow-white, low Aston Martin, the first such model of the sports car of its kind in South Africa. His garage houses a Bentley as well. He shares his partiality for this luxury sedan with his long-standing PSG partner Chris Otto, who also drives a Bentley.

Mouton has a passion for Afrikaans, and he owns a private book collection that includes practically every Afrikaans novel ever written. He took over the collection of Afrikaans-language books from the private library of Professor Gerrit Kruger, a Stellenbosch classical and New Testament Greek scholar who never bought a car or other luxuries but spent all his money on books. Mouton had the collection catalogued and expanded it.

His folly is Sudoku. When he has finished reading a newspaper, he tackles the number puzzle and the crossword. He also likes to refer to a famous writer who discovered that all successful businessmen are thrifty. To him, thrift, which differs significantly from stinginess, means that you look after your things and use resources sparingly. He switches off the lights behind him when leaving his office in the evening. 'I don't leave the lights on – small things like that. Even at PSG we don't waste money.'

MARKUS JOOSTE's love of display involved, inter alia, posturing as a wine expert. In the process he had no qualms about humiliating even some of his own executives. At an event attended by the heads of all his companies, one of them had brought along a bottle of sparkling wine (Méthode Cap Classique, the Cape equivalent of French champagne), which Jooste picked up while exclaiming loudly: *'Nou watse kak is dit? Wie het dit gebring?'* ('What is this crap? Who brought this?')

In 2003, Jooste bought the farm Jonkersdrift, previously known as Bengale, together with two of his former confidants, Danie van der Merwe and Frikkie Nel, for R25 million. In contrast to Jooste's mansion, the other two homes on the property are much more modest: Van der Merwe restored the old homestead, and Nel had a house built. For 'security reasons', there is only one entrance to the property. The three owners, who live within walking distance of each other, used to braai together frequently, but after Steinhoff's collapse their relationship became strained.

After Jooste settled in Stellenbosch, where Steinhoff's head office was erected in Stellentia Road within sight of Remgro's headquarters, he purchased two double seaside plots in Hermanus. Preliminary construction work on one of the properties, where a palatial holiday residence with a panoramic sea view had been planned, stopped after the Steinhoff revelations.

On the other property, which was once Anton Rupert's holiday house, Jooste landed in controversy. Rupert senior used to direct visitors to this address by remarking that the highest tree in Hermanus stood in front of his house. In the course of expansions he made to the property, however, Jooste had five large Norfolk pines chopped down. An upset Johann Rupert confronted Jooste about this, saying that civilised people planted trees, while uncivilised people ripped them out. Jooste apparently just stared at him.

After the collapse of Steinhoff, Rupert did not make an offer for the holiday house that used to belong to his parents, as was rumoured in Hermanus. He did, however, at an earlier stage, when the house was put on the market, reject Jooste's initial offer; he wanted a million rand more. Jooste had then agreed to his price, but arrogantly told friends: 'He needs the money more than I do.'

Following the Steinhoff debacle, Jooste regularly had to call in painters to paint over graffiti such as 'Thief', 'Con artist', 'Pants on fire' and 'Psychopath' on the white wall around the house where he was holed up for most of the time.

Although racehorses were regarded as Jooste's hobby, they were actually much more than that because he ran his dozens of racehorses like a business. On his many overseas trips, he would switch on his iPad in hotelrooms at night to see how his horses were faring in races across the world. 'It's for relaxation – I participate in it as a sport,' he stated.

Some people wonder if Jooste's folly was his swaggering love of display. But perhaps his real folly was self-deception: the delusion that he would never be caught out.

MICHAEL JORDAAN lives on Bartinney, the family farm on the slopes of Botmaskop alongside the Helshoogte Pass, which he bought back on his return to Stellenbosch after retiring as an FNB banker in Johannesburg. The manor house, which blends Cape Dutch and English Tudor styles, dates from 1923. The house boasts features such as Delft tiles originating from the Castle in Cape Town and a sixteenth-century Elizabethan carved beam of black oak.

Jordaan's wife, Rose, an architect, runs the winemaking operation on the farm and does not allow him near her as far as the business side of the enteprise is concerned. He does have another foothold in the wine industry by means of Port2Port, an online wine marketplace that offers buyers more than 1 600 different types of wine.

Both are passionate about nature conservation and have planted more than 5 000 trees, proteas, pincushions and fynbos in what was previously a pine plantation. A sculpture by the sculptor Dylan Lewis called 'Elevage' graces the fynbos garden. Bartinney strives to be a sustainable farming operation that promotes biodiversity through working in harmony with nature.

JOHAN VAN ZYL's folly is a farm in the Karoo. The man from Sanlam and African Rainbow Capital says: 'Money and cars aren't my thing; my cars are old, so that's not something I care about. But what I enjoy are Afrikaans people, farm people. For that reason, I often go to the farm in the Karoo.'

He owns a farm on the slopes of the Nuweveld Mountains next to the Karoo National Park near Beaufort West. 'I have a mountain, vast open spaces – that's what I like. I like nature. I love getting out, going to the Kruger National Park, or Etosha, where there are no people. Most people here in Stellenbosch go to Hermanus, where they talk to the same crowd as at home. I have a little place at Boggomsbaai on the West Coast where there's not a soul. So I like open spaces, and that's the thing about Africa, you know? When you come from a farm and you had to live in London or in Washington or New York, you crave these places. So that's my folly – I spend too much money on it!'

Ironically enough, he has entered into another farm saga. Along with Willem Roos of OUTsurance fame and other businesspeople, he is part of a consortium that is negotiating to buy Jooste's Jonkersdrift – an initiative that will likely gladden the hearts of Stellenbosch residents who do not want to see Jooste near their town.

MICHIEL LE ROUX of Capitec lives in Stellenbosch in the suburb of Uniepark and does not own a farm. His right-hand man, Riaan Stassen, who succeeded him as chair of Capitec, however, bought the wine-and-olive farm Hidden Farm in the Stellenbosch district before he retired as CEO. Grape.co.za reported that Stassen had paid R60 million for the farm above Annandale Road on the slopes of the Helderberg Mountains where wine is sold under the Hidden Valley Wines brand, inter alia in the Overture restaurant on the farm.

Stassen is a racing car enthusiast who regularly attends Formula One races. He owns a Ferrari himself and has long been interested in motor racing and the people and organisations involved, either because of the excitement of the races or the business principles behind them. 'Ferrari has been inspirational for me,' he said in an interview. 'It is an organisation that really strives for perfection. I remember watching them at the Chinese Grand Prix, practising changing the tyres on a car over and over, trying to do it better and faster.'

FRANÇOIS VAN NIEKERK, who had a house built in the Stellenbosch suburb of Die Boord when he moved to the Town of Oaks in 2015 after 35 years in Pretoria, does not own a farm, but he did have a tractor on his smallholding in Pretoria. 'After all, one should at least have a mildly eccentric streak,' the Mergon founder said. 'I don't own any farmland, but I do have a rebuilt 1942-model McCormick Farmall tractor with which I used to drive around on my property in Pretoria over weekends.'

As businessman, he liked cycling, 10 to 20 kilometres three or four times a week, but his favourite pastime was being able to sail with Hobie Cats at Plettenberg Bay for nearly 20 years, until he bought a seaside house at Melkbosstrand. He also collects precision vehicle models (rather than the full-sized versions).

THE FIRSTRAND co-founder Laurie Dippenaar is not keen on extravagance but does have a plane of his own, which comes in handy when he has to travel. He and his wife live in Bryanston in Johannesburg, a city he loves. He says jokingly that everyone thinks he is a member of the Stellenbosch Mafia, which is by no means the case. 'Besides, I wasn't even invited!'

He is passionate about the Garden Route as well. He owns a holiday home in Plettenberg Bay, where he and his family regularly spend the summer holidays. 'It's a lovely, very beautiful place. You can swim safely, and the climate is excellent. I've been going there for fifty years.'

Dippenaar does not believe in investing in bitcoin; in his view, it is 'just gambling'. At a 'very liquid lunch' where he, GT Ferreira, Paul Harris, Jannie Mouton and others discussed the cryptocurrency, they pooled their collective knowledge of bitcoin. To them, there were simply too many areas of vagueness and uncertainty, albeit that some investors believe it can serve as a store of value and is comparable to 'digital gold'. 'The only firm anchor in the ground is the meteoric rise in the price. Anyone who buys bitcoin is buying it for that reason only,' Dippenaar summed up their conclusion.

HENDRIK DU TOIT reckons his 'self-identified folly, over and above stubbornness, is that I think far ahead and, according to some of my colleagues, sometimes build castles in the air. What is the world without dreams? Yes, successful businesspeople believe they can help change the world in which they operate and that they can win in a very competitive environment. They are generally creative and driven. This goes hand in hand with a measure of stubbornness.'

He spends most of his time in London and in aeroplanes. But Cape Town, where he owns a seaside house in Llandudno, is still his favourite city. 'After all, it's the city of my birth,' he says. In a busy life where one travels as much as he does, time with his family is very important. 'Weekends are family time. I'm also crazy about outdoor life and about participating in sport and watching it – mountain biking, skiing, time in the waves or on my kayak, swimming, or just walking with the dogs. And I love breaking away with my family to the silence of the Karoo or the Bushveld.'

19

Rainmakers

THE RAPID RISE of Afrikaner businesspeople since the political transition of 1994 has several implications for both the South African economy and our national politics, a twosome that has become inextricably linked in the modern world.

On the one hand, their rise illustrates the ability of a minority group to advance even within a political order that in practice does not set great store by minority rights. At the same time, it raises the worrying question as to how far this success will be tolerated under a government that strives for hegemonic top-down control over society as a whole: the party controlling the state and the state the economy. In a centralist model with scant protection for minority rights and plenty of opportunities for corruption, it may justly be asked: what is the role of the rainmakers – the entrepreneurs and businesspeople in the private sector who create jobs through enterprise and innovation?

In 2004, the ANC spokesperson Smuts Ngonyama spelled out a generally accepted ambition of the new ruling establishment: 'I didn't join the struggle to be poor.' Their manipulation of economic policy is geared to the enrichment of the rulers through a system of patronage that favours a small elite. The emphasis is on a consumption economy, not a production economy that generates wealth. Political connections are rewarded, not creativity and skills that unlock value.

Coupled with this, race-based affirmative action and black economic empowerment (BEE) benefited a limited elite group to whom public funds flow. In the process, the needy were most disadvantaged by politicians who pose as the representatives of the poor and the oppressed. Unemployment increased, and by 2019 the country's growth rate had reached the lowest downward spiral since the 1940s and fallen below the population growth rate of 1,6 per cent.

Prior to Jacob Zuma's election in 2008, the trade union leader Zwelinzima Vavi described the new ANC leader as a 'tsunami'. This was in the days when Vavi was still an ardent Zuma supporter in the company of Julius Malema, the ANC Youth League leader who had declared himself willing to 'kill for Zuma' before he became 'commander in chief' of the Economic Freedom Fighters. The grim irony is that the metaphor used by Vavi – who subsequently had to warn against a 'predatory elite' that was capturing the state – proved to be spot-on. For when the waters recede, a tsunami leaves behind a devastated wasteland.

The economy of the continent's most industrialised country was ravaged, the public service paralysed and the law enforcement agencies hamstrung by Zuma's lackeys. Corruption had reared its head early on during the Mandela administration with the Sarafina and Virodene scandals under the influential Nkosazana Dlamini-Zuma. The certainty of continued victories at the polls that prompted Jacob Zuma to boast that the ANC would rule 'until Jesus returns' was the root cause of the arrogance of power and the delusion of untouchability that made corruption increase hand over fist as tenderpreneurs ensured a flow of funds back into ANC coffers.

Damning evidence piled up in hundreds of incriminating emails in #GuptaLeaks and books about the gangster state became bestsellers, but at the time of writing the criminals have neither been arrested nor prosecuted. The three Gupta brothers left the country scott free with their colossal spoils and their families and everything, like hyenas slinking away from a stripped carcass.

The example set by Zuma as head of state – looting and plundering, economic illiteracy and reckless squandering of money – filtered through to the lowest municipal positions, the entry level for the cadre culture of self-enrichment that has been a contributory factor in the collapse of numerous municipalities and service delivery due to 'a lack of capacity'. Year after year, the Auditor-General had to report an increase in the misapplication of funds by government departments and municipalities as well as an increase in their debt levels. In 2019, it was reported that irregular government expenditure rose to R61,35 billion in the 2018/19 financial year, while only 21 of the country's 257 municipalities received a clean audit in 2020.

Credit rating agencies downgraded South Africa to junk status. Harri Kemp, an economist from Stellenbosch's Bureau for Economic Research, calculated that the ten disastrous years of the Zuma administration cost the country R1 trillion. The South African economy could have been been up to 30 per cent larger and have created 2,5 million more jobs had the country kept pace with other emerging markets and sub-Saharan African economies over that decade. According to Kemp's calculations, the government could have collected R1 trillion more in tax had the economy performed closer to those of its peers and had tax collection remained efficient. Another observer remarked that, as government, the ANC had caused greater damage to South Africa's infrastructure than during the time when it was the party's policy to blow it up.

By this time a fiscal cliff was looming: a stage where the state's income from taxes is less than the sums spent on social grants, the public sector wage bill and the interest on government debt. Debt service costs on the mounting government debt had risen to more than R2 billion per day in 2020, and according to finance minister Tito Mboweni, debt would 'stabilise' at 95,3 per cent of GDP by 2025 – provided that the country did not slide back further into the danger zone.

As a result of the ANC government's urge to exert greater control over the country's assets, South Africa, which in 2000 was ranked 46th in the annual Economic Freedom of the World Report, had dropped to 110th place out of 159 countries in the 2018 report. The state's interference manifested itself in all kinds of attempts to micromanage and manipulate the economy. Every point of control carried the risk of becoming an expanding point of corruption.

The once flourishing mining industry was gradually almost choked to death. In this regard, *Business Day* commented sardonically in 2018: South Africa, once the world's biggest gold producer, has in recent years been exporting more mine bosses than gold.

The race-based BEE policy framework is predicated on the race classification of the apartheid system that was abolished by the National Party as far back as the 1990s. The fears expressed by the perspicacious politician Van Zyl Slabbert in June 2006 have been realised: 'If you make yourself and others hostage to a racist past, you can budget generously for a racist future.'

This policy, like the patronage system and political connectivity, is not aimed at broad-based wealth creation and the eradication of poverty and unemployment. On top of that, it puts a dampener on the democratic dialogue, as white businesspeople are reluctant to express criticism of government policy for fear of being made out to be avaricious, unrepentant racists.

Employment equity programmes in terms of which workforces have to reflect the country's demographic profile were instituted in various spheres. The country's energy supplier was at the forefront. *Rapport* reported in February 2019 that Eskom intended to persevere with its affirmative action plan by reducing its number of white qualified employees by 1 308 by March 2020. From February 2014 to December 2018 a total of 4 356 employees, of whom 56 per cent were white, had left Eskom. According to *Rapport*, Eskom had additionally suffered an enormous loss of skills in the preceding five years because top employees of all races were forced out of the company by state capturers.

The extent of the mismanagement at Eskom, which had, in December 2001, garnered a prestigious award by being named the global power company of the year at the Financial Times Global Energy Awards ceremony in New York, was evident from the utility's own annual reports. In an analysis of the reports, Allan Gray's chief investment officer, Andrew Lapping, pointed out that in 2017, Eskom delivered the same amount of electricity as it had done in 2003, but with almost 50 per cent more employees, who were paid double what the salaries had been in 2003. Furthermore, load shedding was introduced at the beginning of 2008.

By 2019, when Eskom announced a loss of R21 billion for the financial year, its debt had risen to R440 billion. Eskom's total debt was equivalent to 9 per cent of the gross national product – the same size as the mining and agricultural sectors combined.

As a result of the loss of expertise and institutional memory, coupled with wide-scale corruption and the role of tenderpreneurs, Eskom had become a threat to the entire economy of the country Archbishop Desmond Tutu so hopefully baptised 'the rainbow nation of God' in 1994. The mismanagement at a state-owned monopoly was the cause, not 'white monopoly capital', Jan van Riebeeck, the supposed 'Stellenbosch Mafia' or other evil spirits in the air.

Tutu himself eventually condemned the ANC as 'scandalous'.

And in the midst of the Covid-19 pandemic Ramaphosa had to confess that in the tender scandal relating to personal protective equipment for combating the virus, the ANC had become Accused Number One.

Under the ANC regime – with a faction that became more like a criminal syndidate while the party dished out positions to card-carrying cadres like an employment agency – power dominance was reintroduced. Destructive policies and intentions to apply them even more strictly have not brought about sustainable development and a 'better life for all'; on the contrary, systemic decay characterises this new environment in which Afrikaner businesspeople find themselves in the private sector along with other minority groups.

As an expert in agricultural economics, Johan van Zyl says that much of the land debate in agriculture is actually a debate about yesterday's problems. 'Looking at Africa as a whole, we see that 80 per cent of the population will become urbanised within a decade or two. This is where the services have to be provided.'

In rural areas, there will be fewer services, networks, data and opportunities for the youth in particular. In Africa, people will speak of 17 or 18 mega-cities instead of 50 countries. According to Van Zyl, agriculture gains in importance in such a context because governments will have to be attuned to urban populations that require affordable food.

'When one looks ahead, the guys who want to stay in power and will come into power – who will control the media and the other things in the cities – will need to have expert producers on the land. I think landownership will become even more important, but it will become much more critical to keep knowledgeable people who can produce in the rural areas.

'Farming is becoming mechanised. It is about large farms. When you look back 30 years, it was almost impossible to become a mega-farmer, as the tractors were small and managing farms was difficult. With present-day implements and technology, scale has an incredible advantage – with equipment that operates day and night. At best, some small farmers will be able to survive, but only as a satellite of the large farms,' he said.

Johann Rupert also weighed in on the land debate after great uncertainty, even panic, was sparked among investors in 2018 following President Cyril Ramaphosa's announcement that property would be expropriated without compensation. He told the *Sunday Times* that there were misconceptions in the discussions about the land reform plans because 'land' was confused with 'property'. 'Without an inalienable right to private property, no person can build capital.' His argument was premised on the free-market principle that, globally and throughout history, institutions have always insisted on security before lending out their depositors' funds. 'South Africa is no different, except in South Africa black Africans were denied this basic human right,' he said.

In the Afrikanerbond's commemorative book *Broederskap*, he stated that, like his father, he believed that if Afrikaners were to survive, they had to make themselves indispensable in numerous spheres. 'I'm a farmer, among other things, and we should produce and supply food to such an extent that our inputs are indispensable: feed the nation so effectively that everyone takes note of it. If the Afrikaners all had to leave today, this country would fall apart – just look at one rural town after the other where people were removed at local government level. What is happening in those places? NOTHING.'

By 2019, two-thirds of the South African population (compared with 40 per cent in 1950) were living in urban areas, where 75 per cent of the labour force was located. Projections regarding the rate of urbanisation indicate that 71 per cent of the population will be urbanised by 2030, and 80 per cent by 2050. The number of farmworkers has declined by half since 1970. Mechanisation, technological advances and farming on scale will further accelerate this trend.

Between 1995 and 2014, more than 1,8 million individuals who had lodged land claims received compensation – the vast majority, more than 90 per cent, opted for cash rather than land. In the Eastern Cape, the state spent R1,4 billion on buying out farms that were handed out to aspirant farmers. Out of the 265 farms, only 26 are still in a working condition; 90 per cent of once flourishing farms have fallen into ruin.

The average age of commercial farmers in South Africa is close to 60, with fewer and fewer young people who want to farm. According to Dirk Hanekom of Agri All Africa, approximately 2 500 farmers have emigrated to the rest of Africa in the past decade (by now about 50 of Africa's 54 countries) and even to countries such as Georgia, where governments have mostly welcomed them with open arms.

Optimal land utilisation should be the leading route map in the reform of the agricultural industry. To achieve this, water is just as important as electricity for the stability and growth of the agricultural sector. Farmers should be able to rely on a government that can understand the commissioning and importance of dams and other infrastructure, and the meticulous and competent administration as well as maintenance of such assets. Ongoing electricity shortages have already caused great damage to agriculture, with more and more farmers asking to be allowed to produce electricity on their farms and sell it to the grid.

Accelerated urbanisation will in future be the determining factor of land utilisation and the resultant affordability and safety of food. Regimes that are unable to feed their supporters are brought down. The residents of the mega-cities will determine who are going to survive as the most productive farmers, not transitory and populist politicians.

The deteriorating economy, policy uncertainty and plodding public service have on occasion compelled businesspeople to offer their assistance to the government, but such attempts have not borne much fruit. By 2015, about two dozen of the leading Stellenbosch and Cape Town businesspeople started a movement with the aim of getting the government to function more efficiently. A confidential meeting was convened in Cape Town, and no one declined the invitation. They came with an idea that the government lacked integrity and transparency – aspects of cardinal importance in any business enterprise. The question was how they could assist.

'We then sat down with these companies and decided we could give the government people at no cost to them, to put on all the boards. We thought that would be an ideal contribution, and you're making such a contribution for free: people with experience on the boards of the Public Investment Corporation, the Reserve Bank, Eskom, state institutions … We became excited … We got incredibly positive feedback from experienced people – and nothing came of it;

the politicians didn't want it. It's sad, isn't it?' one of the participants recounted.

Wealthy Afrikaner businesspeople make a substantial contribution to philanthropy, as is evidenced in the chapter 'Country of givers'. Although there is widespread admiration for the success quite a few high-profile businesspeople have achieved, both locally and internationally, they regularly attract criticism. Particularly because their remuneration packages seem too lavish, and their compensation highlights inequality in a country that is known as one of the most unequal in the world.

Such business leaders defend generous performance bonuses and share options on the grounds that they reward accomplished individuals who create jobs for hundreds of people. Also, that top chief executives of that calibre can easily be lured to other countries with huge salary offers in more favourable currencies.

Yet the debate about the super-rich is nothing new. As far back as half a century ago there were concerns that Afrikaners might be getting too rich. In 1968, the academic-cum-newspaper editor Wimpie de Klerk, the brother of former president FW de Klerk, wrote in *Huisgenoot* that it would be an insulting generalisation to say that all Afrikaners had fallen prey to materialism. 'We have our rich people who carry their wealth gracefully and use it responsibly, but we also have the rich Afrikaners who are close-fisted when it comes to anything that is not in their own personal interest.'

De Klerk concluded with a warning: 'The Afrikaner will have to employ his wealth in service of greater things than pleasure and self-service … what does it profit us if we gain the whole world and lose our soul?'

The historian Albert Grundlingh cited De Klerk in an article '"Are we Afrikaners getting too rich?": Cornucopia and change in Afrikanerdom in the 1960s' in the *Journal of Historical Sociology* in 2009, which he wrote about the same phenomenon. He referred to Mandela's biographer Anthony Sampson, who described the prosperous years of the 1960s as follows: 'Mandela was out of sight and out of mind. And the way was clear for the biggest boom in South Africa's history since the gold rush.' Grundlingh pointed out that a more nuanced view was provided by the economist Jan Sadie from Stellenbosch. The restored business confidence was rather based on the assumption that it was unlikely that the political situation – although not completely resolved – would deteriorate to such an extent that profit margins would be seriously hurt.

Grundlingh attributed the stronger role of Afrikaners in the economy to, inter alia, the National Party's investments in education, including technical schools and medical and engineering faculties at Afrikaans-language universities. There was a new trend among Afrikaners: a shift from relatively low-paid unskilled and semi-skilled jobs to better-paid posts with stable career prospects.

Education also remained a highly topical issue after the transition of 1994. International institutions such as the International Monetary Fund have highlighted poor-quality education as one of the main reasons why South Africa was failing at improving social mobility and moving people out of poverty. In this regard, the ANC is following in the footsteps of most of the post-colonial African states where the former colonial languages are the official languages. Africa is also the only continent where education in one's mother tongue is not a given, despite it being strongly encouraged by international bodies such as Unesco.

Mother-tongue education became a major bone of contention in South Africa as Afrikaans was phased out in public life. From the early 2000s, one former Afrikaans university after the other began dropping Afrikaans as language of instruction. Educationalists were concerned about the survival of Afrikaans-medium schools if tertiary education had to anglicise completely.

Over the years, Afrikaner businesspeople have been involved in the language debate at Stellenbosch University (SU); from the time that the establishment of the oldest Afrikaans university in 1918 was made possible by the businessman Jannie Marais's donation of £100 000 on condition that Dutch (Afrikaans) would occupy 'geen mindere plaats' (no lesser place) than English.

The process of gradual anglicisation was not the result of a normal language shift, but occurred due to pressure from resolute politicians. Paradoxically, ideologues who were the most vociferous advocates of the decolonisation of curriculums went on the warpath against

Afrikaans – the hybrid, most decolonised indigenous language, one of only four languages in the world that in the course of the 20th century was standardised and developed to the highest levels as academic and scientific language.

The debate impelled the Naspers chair Koos Bekker, who was at a time a council member of SU, to write in *Die Burger* on 26 October 2005: 'If Stellenbosch were to anglicise, the university chooses the road of cowardice.'

The PSG founder Jannie Mouton resigned from the SU Council in 2009 because Stellenbosch had become 'too English and too white'. He could no longer stay on in a council where people treated Afrikaans speakers with suspicion and the campus became increasingly more English. He was also opposed to transformation as it was being implemented at the university – as if transformation could not take place in an Afrikaans environment, he stated.

However, university councils capitulated meekly to political pressure. Since 2015, Stellenbosch, under the leadership of a new vice-chancellor, Professor Wim de Villiers, has established English as the preferred medium of learning and teaching. Despite the constitutional provision that official languages enjoy 'parity of esteem', the Constitutional Court ratified the anglicisation. Jannie Marais's founding ideal was snuffed out.

Mouton, who received an honorary doctorate from SU in 2018 during the university's centenary year, eventually accepted the anglicisation of the university. He donated R50 million to SU for the construction of a learning centre named after his father.

It was expected of Afrikaner businesspeople to provide financial support for tuition in Afrikaans, a proven important empowerment tool. The extent to which businesspeople, who are already under so much pressure, can contribute to yet more areas where the state has neglected its duty and vast sums disappear because of corruption and misapplication of funds, remains an open question.

Job creation is still regarded by businesspeople as the country's top need. Laurie Dippenaar of FirstRand pointed out that, when it comes to poverty and inequality, everyone refers to South Africa's Gini coefficient of 0,65, which is the highest in the world. (The Gini coefficient is a statistical measure of economic inequality in a population.) 'Of course it will be the highest, because we have the highest unemployment figure. When you have an unemployment figure of 36 per cent, it has to be rotten,' he said.

FirstRand commissioned Pricewaterhouse to calculate its own Gini coefficient for its 48 000 employees. It was much better than that of South Africa, although the difference between the bank's lowest-paid and highest-paid was still big.

A similar study was done at one of the platinum mines. 'Their Gini coefficient is 0,34, ours is 0,42 and the country's is 0,65. The platinum mines' 0,34 is better than America's. It almost comes close to those of the Scandinavian countries, and that's an interesting insight you get,' Dippenaar stated.

He referred to an Oxfam study that found the world's 86 richest people owned as much as the poorest 3,5 billion. 'Then I said, okay, confiscate everything the 86 own, every dollar, and divide it among the three and a half billion. How much does each guy get? Only $500 – that's about R7 000, two months' minimum wage. What have you achieved? Nothing. Giving the guy a job, a good job, is much better than confiscating it [the wealth of the super-rich].'

Dippenaar's view is backed up by research by Johan Fourie, associate professor of economics at Stellenbosch University. The tragic fact, he wrote, is that redistribution would do very little for the poorest. If the wealth of all 38 500 dollar millionaires in South Africa (according to New World Wealth) had to be expropriated and distributed equally among all South Africans, each South African would have received R38 282.

'A one-off payment. One's year study for a BCom course at a good university costs more. The Gini coefficient would tumble, yes, and what would we have achieved? Even if we were to make the unlikely assumption that everyone would invest this amount and earn 10 per cent interest on it per year, it would still only increase our income by R319 per month. A quick history lesson will teach us that innovation is the most important building block of any economy and society. This kind of redistribution won't make us rich.

'There is, of course, a redistribution story that needs to be told, but which one seldom hears amid the din of the populist slogans:

the enormous redistribution that takes place annually through the fiscus. Here are the facts from Pravin Gordhan's mouth: The poorest 50 per cent pay 4 per cent of the tax, but get 59 per cent of the social expenditure. The richest 10 per cent pay 72 per cent of the tax, but receive only 6 per cent of the social wage. A group of World Bank researchers found recently that the Gini coefficient is reduced from 0,77 to 0,59 because of this redistribution; the biggest redistribution through any fiscus in the world. The focus on redistribution takes us away from the thing that creates wealth: economic growth. Gordhan knows it too. Redistribution through the fiscus is already the maximum it can be,' Fourie wrote.

Johann Rupert, who believes, like other top business leaders, that private enterprise and the free market have best succeeded in creating wealth and development for all people, said at Remgro's annual general meeting in December 2017 he had pointed out ten years before that in 1870 the world was more or less the same regardless of where you lived. The standard of living and quality of life were the same, whether in Buenos Aires or in Paris, with roughly the same per capita income. Then some countries made choices, and others did not. The winning nations have free markets and protection of private property, ownership incentives for capital formation – 'which we never did for the majority of people in this country' – and strong and convertible currencies. And flexible labour markets, because trade unions destroy jobs. Trade unions are there to protect those who have jobs, but for the unemployed there is a barrier. 'So it creates a new slave system, which is a mass of unskilled people who are unemployable in a modern economy. And, paradoxically, the countries that fire the most, hire the most,' he said.

Then there is entrepreneurship, which is essential for growth. But so are socioeconomic policies; democracy; free speech; honesty and transparency in government actions; respect for the rule of law; and subjection to the constitution.

'It's too late for us to try and create a new industrial economy. You need a very big home market. And we are at least two cycles behind in terms of technology.' The world is moving to an information and knowledge economy, hence brain power. And people's brains cannot be nationalised. You can nationalise banks and industries, but then you end up like Venezuela and Zimbabwe. 'The most critical component for economic growth today is between people's ears: innovation, brains,' Rupert stated.

Regarding job creation, Christo Wiese also quotes a saying his mother often used: You only buy things you can't do without, not things you need. 'And a job is something you can't do without.'

Thys du Toit feels strongly that the private sector will have to save the country. 'The state can't create jobs by employing people. Only entrepreneurs, only people who start businesses, can give people jobs.' With reference to the salaries the state pays – 40 per cent more for its officials than the private sector – his commentary was blunt: 'Lunacy! Lunacy!' This was before finance minister Tito Mboweni announced in October 2019 that there were 23 000 millionaires in the public service.

'There is only one Roger Federer,' says Du Toit. 'There are many other tennis players, but there is only one Roger Federer. Likewise, there are only a few rainmakers in the business world. Their names are Johann Rupert, Christo Wiese, Jannie Mouton. Look further: Elon Musk, former South African; Roelof Botha, former South African. So, the secret a country should have is to give rainmakers the opportunity to perform their magic in your country. You need those few top individuals, like Bill Gates. He started in his garage. Today he employs 250 000 people, and he has the largest charitable foundation in the world. But, most important, he raised the entire world's growth rate by half a percent as a result of technological advances.

'Now – we can either decide to take this cake, this pie, and we're going to divide it among all and eventually no one will have anything left, or we can grow it. *That's* the difference. So, we are fortunate in South Africa in that we *have* these people who can grow the economy, but they are distrusted.' They have all been forced to decide they will focus only on their own business, he says, 'because it's better to be out of the public eye than being on the public stage where you are a target'.

At Naspers's annual general meeting in August 2019, Koos Bekker levelled criticism at the government's distrust of the business sector. For the second year running he warned that policy uncertainty was discouraging investments in South Africa. Bob van Dijk 'wants to bring back his dollars to invest in South Africa', but the competition authorities put restrictions on what was possible. The authorities were in fact retarding investments because they do not see the global picture. Naspers cannot be limited in size and still be competitive against giants like Google, Amazon and Facebook.

One businessman who abandoned a large project summed up the reasons for the decision succinctly: the project was stopped because of the government's lamentable lack of consistency regarding network conditions, constantly changing BEE demands and lax payment culture. 'They have no concept of the principle that stability is an absolute requirement for business success.'

The predominant sentiment among businesspeople was reminiscent of what happened after 1948. After the National Party came into power, 'I don't like their policies, but they're efficient' was an oft-repeated refrain in the business world. Since the transition to ANC rule in 1994, businesspeople have been whispering, at first softly but increasingly louder and more unflatteringly: 'I don't like their policies *and* they're incompetent.'

One consequence of distrust of the government is the brain drain – the loss of skilled South Africans from all groups who head for foreign destinations. In 2019, AfrAsia Bank's South Africa Wealth Report indicated that the number of dollar millionaires living in South Africa had declined from 43 600 to 39 200 compared with the year before, and that the country had lost 130 high-net-worth individuals with assets of $10 million or more over the same period. The departure of such a large number of super-rich individuals means that people who could have created jobs have left the country.

In government circles, disdain for and envy of the business sector persists. Although business has occasionally been admonished 'to come to the party' – after the party has started looking more like a night vigil in a sick bay – the ANC under Ramaphosa persevered with the idea that the state has to take the lead with plans for economic revitalisation.

That notion might have had credibility if the state had not demonstrated its inability to implement the National Development Plan (NDP) and constantly had to rush to the aid of state-owned enterprises with taxpayer-funded bailouts. The NDP, as ambitious as the five-year plans in the former Soviet Union, proposed an annual growth rate of 5,4 per cent to create eleven million jobs by 2030, but the plan has gathered dust in bureaucratic drawers while the country headed for another recession.

Regarding Ramaphosa's new leadership, even sympathetic observers eventually concurred with Mmusi Maimane's assessment: 'He is just a new driver of the same doomed ANC bus.' Zuma promised 5 million jobs, Ramaphosa 2 million – but unemployment has reached record levels. Zuma wanted to create a hundred black industrialists – but the country deindustrialised and heavy industries such as Saldanha Steel and Highveld Steel decided to switch off their blast furnaces and close their doors.

Funding for research at universities – so vital for a country that has to keep up with rapid technological and economic advances – was cut by 90 per cent. It was a stupefying decision on the part of a country from where the idea of an African renaissance had still been propagated shortly before.

A prerequisite for the government's idea of a developmental state is a capable public service. This is true of some countries in the East such as China, which is regarded as a role model by the increasingly anti-Western government of South Africa. After the tyrannical regime of Mao Zedong, China switched to the free-market system under Deng Xiaoping, who believed it did not matter if a cat was black or white, as long as it caught mice. As has been the case elsewhere in the world, the free market's incentives freed millions of Chinese from poverty. All the same, the authoritarian state with its state capitalism, its suppression of civil liberties and its human rights violations is not an example that is worthy of emulation. Western hopes that stronger trade links with the totalitarian China would lead to more democratic changes – *Wandel durch Handel* (change through commerce), as the Germans call it – have faded in any case.

Besides, China's ambassador to South Africa, Lin Songtian, of all people, expressed the sharpest criticism of the ANC government. In 2019, he said on more than one occasion that projects proposed by the government had lacked feasibility studies capable of reassuring the Chinese government and banks of their profitability and sustainability.

Policies of extending incentives, including tax breaks, to attract foreign capital also did not do enough for Chinese investors, who wanted to see favourable conditions enshrined in an investment law. 'To date there are no major infrastructure projects from China here. Why? Because we don't only need the concept of a project,' he said.

In any case, Singapore with its heterogeneous population probably provides a better example of an economic model for South Africa. It is based on Lee Kuan Yew's three pillars: honesty, meritocracy and pragmatism. Honesty means that no corruption is tolerated; meritocracy that the best candidate is appointed in positions; and pragmatism that an economic policy of whatever ideological nature is followed as long as it best suits the country's needs.

Moreover, in the East there is a culture of shame. One pays a price for transgressions and failures; party cadres are not simply 'redeployed' to alight on a new perch.

The ANC government's inability to embrace and facilitate a modern economy does not mean that the business sector can be exonerated from its own responsibility. International auditing firms, banks, software suppliers and spin doctors took part in the bribing of the ruling kleptocracy. Apart from that, the Steinhoff scandal is a blot of shame on the private sector. Poor governance at other companies has contributed to the economic decline. Phenomena such as bonuses for managers of companies that perform badly or suffer losses are simply indefensible.

For Afrikaner businesspeople, the question has arisen as to how much they still attach importance to their bond with those who share their language and culture. Do they see themselves as merely commerce-oriented, intent on making huge profits, or still as part of a small group they have helped to advance to where they are today, and that as one of South Africa's minority groups can continue to play a meaningful role in the country of their birth?

Of relevance in this regard is what the great Czech writer Milan Kundera said in 1993 about the concept of small nations: 'The concept is not quantitative; it points to a condition, a fate; small nations lack that felicitous sense of an eternal past and future; at a given moment in their history they all passed through the antechambers of death; in constant confrontation with the arrogant ignorance of the mighty they see their existence as perpetually threatened or with a question mark hovering over it; for their very existence *is* the question.'

Threats to minority groups come from within the ANC's Afro-nationalist faction, but even more strongly from the ranks of its offshoot: the Economic Freedom Fighters. The leader of this party, Julius Malema, has threathened with impunity that 'we're not calling for the slaughtering of white people, at least for now', and he has frequently railed against Indians.

The hegemonic ideal of the ANC government and a reglemented, state-led economic model could not establish a cohesive vision in which all the abilities and expertise of a deeply divided society are harnessed. The 'enemy' is not 'whiteness' and 'white monopoly capital', but rather obsolete views.

Hence the biggest transformation should perhaps take place in the hearts of populist politicians in particular in order to unite the best and the brightest and escape the fate of struggling and failed states such as Zimbabwe and Venezuela. In a democracy, a capable state in any case requires an independent, competent public service; not one that serves as a refuge for professional politicians, the kind the historian Paul Johnson described as the scourge of the 20th century.

Anton Rupert's prescient insight after the first military use of the atom bomb in 1945 – that humanity has become like scorpions in a bottle and people will simply have to learn to live together – has become an even more compelling necessity by 2020 on account of the global economic crisis caused by the Covid-19 pandemic. Even before the declaration of the state of disaster in South Africa, the ANC's economic policy failed, the country was downgraded to junk status and doubt had arisen about the government's ability to reform and to modernise the economy.

In the stranglehold in which an interdependent globe finds itself, South Africa's economic regression and mounting unemployment indicate that the time has run out for politicians who want to divide and steal. The imploding state has become reminiscent of the Italian philosopher Antonio Gramsci's description of a similar situation: 'The crisis consists precisely in the fact that the old is dying and the new cannot be born; in this interregnum a great variety of morbid symptoms appear.' The question has been hovering over South Africa: how long will megalomaniac, corrupt rulers who violate their social contract with the citizenry be tolerated and endured by the citizens?

Systems thinkers' rule for this kind of problem, which has already forced the ANC rulers to hold out the begging bowl to international lenders, is that problems cannot be solved on the same level of thinking that created them. Many of South Africa's strongest assets are situated outside of the ANC government, which is why in such circumstances civil society tends to be self-sufficient in as many areas as possible rather than relying on the state. In the first decades of the 21st century it seems as if the 'helpmekaar' idea has found affinity with the black consciousness leader Steve Biko's call for self-reliance: communities that fix potholes in public roads, expand independent power generation and support neighbourhood watches and security companies for protection; community-based organisations and churches that provide social assistance; and farmers that distribute food to those in need.

Afrikaner businesspeople have made a significant contribution to innovation and the development of the country and will continue to do so, even within the space allowed them. If they are not regarded as fully equal and valuable citizens, however, they will perhaps rather invest in other countries.

The choices are stark and demanding. But through an inclusive value system that promotes creative modernisation as well as accountable leadership with integrity and steadfast action to eradicate state mismanagement and corruption, South Africa can indeed become an advancing country in which all South Africans will be able to reach for the stars.

List of sources and further reading

Books, theses and articles

Babiak, Paul, and Hare, Robert D. 2006. *Snakes in Suits*. New York: Harper Collins.

Barnard, Niël. 2015. *Secret Revolution: Memoirs of a Spy Boss*. Cape Town: Tafelberg.

Beukes, Wynand; Ehlers, Anton; and Verhoef, Grietjie. 2018. Sanlam-amptenare uit die volk gebore om die volk te dien? *Tydskrif vir Geesteswetenskappe*, Vol. 58, No. 3.

Bishop, Chris. 2017. *Africa's Billionaires – Inspirational Stories from the Continent's Wealthiest People*. Cape Town: Penguin.

Bovill, EW. 2013. *The Golden Trade of the Moors: West African Kingdoms in the Fourteenth Century*. Princeton, NJ: Markus Weiner Publishers.

Carnegie, Andrew. 1901. *The Gospel of Wealth and Other Timely Essays*. New York: Doubleday, Doran and Company.

Changuion, L. 2007. *A Farm Called ZZ2: The Bertie van Zyl Story*. Polokwane: Review Printers.

Davenport, TRH. 1977. *South Africa: A Modern History*. Johannesburg: Macmillan.

Davidson, Basil. 1966. *Africa: History of a Continent*. London: Weidenfeld & Nicolson.

De Kiewiet, CW. 1942. *A History of South Africa, Social and Economic*. Oxford: Clarendon Press.

De Klerk, W. 1968. Word Afrikaners te ryk? *Huisgenoot*. 12 July.

Die Burger. 2015. Agriculture supplement. 27 November.

Dommisse, Ebbe. 2005. *Anton Rupert: A Biography*. Cape Town: Tafelberg.

Dommisse, Ebbe. 2011. *Sir David Pieter de Villiers Graaff – Die Erfridder van De Grendel*. Cape Town: Tafelberg.

Dommisse, Jacques, and De Vynck, Dirk. 2018. *Reddingsdaad wat 'n Nasie Dien*. Pretoria: Avbob.

Dreyer, Wynand. 2017. *Megaboere*. Parklands: Penguin Books.

Du Plessis, EP. 1964. *'n Volk Staan Op*. Cape Town: Human & Rousseau.

Du Toit, Pieter. 2019. *The Stellenbosch Mafia: Inside the Billionaires' Club*. Cape Town: Jonathan Ball.

Ehlers, Anton. 2007. Renier van Rooyen and Pep Stores, Limited: The genesis of a South African entrepreneur and retail empire. *Business and Economic History Online*, Vol. 5.

Ehlers, Anton. 2012. Business, state and society – doing business apartheid style: The case of Pep Stores Peninsula Limited [report]. Stellenbosch: History Department, Stellenbosch University.

Ehlers, Anton. 2015. The Helpmekaar: Rescuing the 'volk' through reading, writing and arithmetic c.1916-c.1965. *Historia*, Vol. 60.

Ehlers, Anton. 2018. *Die Kaapse Helpmekaar c 1916-c 2018. Bemiddelaar in Afrikaneropheffing, selfrespek en respektabiliteit*. Stellenbosch: African Sun Media.

Ellis, Stephen. 2012. *External Mission: The ANC in Exile*. Jeppestown: Jonathan Ball.

Fanon, Frantz. 1963. *The Wretched of the Earth*. New York: Grove Weidenfeld.

Ferreira, OJO. 2018. *Broederskap – Eeufeesgeskiedenis van die Afrikaner Broederbond en die Afrikanerbond 1918-2018*. Pretoria: Groep 7 Drukkers en Uitgewers.

Fourie, Christel. 2016. The FirstRand founders' story: Exploring synergistic relationships. [PhD thesis (Industrial Psychology)]. Johannesburg: University of Johannesburg.

Fourie, Johan. 2013. The remarkable wealth of the Dutch Cape Colony: Measurements from eighteenth-century probate inventories. *Economic History Review*, Vol. 66, No. 2.

Fourie, Johan, and Swanepoel, Christie. 2018. 'Impending ruin' or 'remarkable wealth'?

The role of private credit markets in the 18th-century Cape Colony. *Journal of Southern African Studies*. Vol. 44.

Gastrow, Shelagh. 2018. Who gives in South Africa and to whom? *Daily Maverick*. 5 March.

Giliomee, Hermann. 2004. *Die Afrikaners*. Cape Town: Tafelberg

Giliomee, Hermann. 2008. Ethnic business and economic empowerment: The Afrikaner case, 1915-1970. *South African Journal of Economic Affairs*. Vol. 764.

Giliomee, Hermann. 2012. *Die Laaste Afrikanerleiers*. Cape Town: Tafelberg.

Giliomee, Hermann. 2016. *Historikus: 'n Outobiografie*. Cape Town: Tafelberg.

Giliomee, Hermann. 2019. *The Rise and Demise of Afrikaners*. Cape Town: Tafelberg.

Gramsci, Antonio. 1971. *Selections from the Prison Notebooks*. New York: International Publishers.

Grundlingh, Albert. 2009. Are we Afrikaners getting too rich? Cornucopia and change in Afrikanerdom in the 1960s. *Journal of Historical Sociology*. Vol. 21.

Harber, Anton. 2012. *Gorilla in the room: Koos Bekker and the rise of Naspers*. Johannesburg: Parktown Publishers.

Heese, JA. 1971. *Die Herkoms van die Afrikaner*. Cape Town: JA Balkema.

Johnson, Paul. 1983. *The History of the Modern World*. London: George Weidenfeld & Nicolson.

Johnson, RW. 2015. *How Long Will South Africa Survive? – The Looming Crisis*. Johannesburg: Jonathan Ball.

Joubert, Dian. 1972. *Toe Witmense Arm Was*. Cape Town: Tafelberg.

Kapp, Pieter. 2015. *Nalatenskappe sonder Einde: Die Verhaal van Jannie Marais en die Marais-broers*. Stellenbosch: Het Jan Marais Nationale Fonds.

Kestell, JD. 1918. Foreword. In: *Helpmekaar Gedenkboek*. Cape Town: Nationale Pers Beperkt.

Kruger, Joan (ed.). 2018. *Die Eeu van Groei, 1918-2018*. Cape Town: Tip Africa Publishing.

La Grange, Zelda. 2015. *Good Morning, Mr Mandela*. Johannesburg: Penguin Books.

Landes, David. 1988. *The Wealth and Poverty of Nations*. New York: W.W. Norton & Company.

Luyt, Louis. 2003. *Walking Proud*. Cape Town: Don Nelson.

Mbeki, Moeletsi. 2009. *Architects of Poverty: Why African Capitalism Needs Changing*. Johannesburg: Picador Africa.

McGregor, Andrew. 2018. *Who Owns Whom: Africa Business Information*. Johannesburg: Who Owns Whom.

Meades, David. 2019. *Afrikaner-kapitalisme: Van Brandarm tot Stinkryk*. Cape Town: Naledi.

Meredith, Martin. 2014. *The Fortunes of Africa: A 5000-Year History of Wealth, Greed and Endeavour*. London: Simon & Schuster.

Mouton, Jannie. 2011. *And Then They Fired Me*. Cape Town: Tafelberg.

Muller, CFJ (ed.). 1990. *Sonop in die Suide – Geboorte en Groei van die Nasionale Pers, 1915-1948*. Cape Town: Nasionale Boekhandel.

Myburgh, Pieter-Louis. 2019. *Gangster State: Unravelling Ace Magashule's Web of Capture*. Johannesburg: Penguin Random House.

Naudé, Piet (ed.). 2018. Business perspectives on the Steinhoff Saga [report]. Stellenbosch: University of Stellenbosch Business School.

O'Dowd, MC. 1976. An assessment of English-speaking South Africa's contribution to the economy. In: De Villiers, A (ed.) *English-speaking South Africa Today*. Cape Town: Oxford University Press.

Oliver, P James. 2013. *Mansa Musa and the Empire of Mali*. Scotts Valley, California: Createspace Independent Pub.

O'Meara, Dan. 1983. *Volkskapitalisme – Class, Capital and Ideology in the Development of Afrikaner Nationalism 1934-1946.* Cambridge: Cambridge University Press.

Pama, C. 1983. *Die Groot Afrikaanse Familienaamboek.* Cape Town: Human & Rousseau.

Pauw, Jacques. 2017. *The President's Keepers.* Cape Town: Tafelberg.

Pelzer, AN. 1979. *Die Afrikaner-Broederbond: Eerste Vyftig Jaar.* Cape Town: Tafelberg.

Pretorius, Fransjohan (ed.). 2012. *Geskiedenis van Suid-Afrika van Voortye tot Vandag.* Cape Town: Tafelberg.

Rabe, Lizette. 'n Konstante revolusie: Naspers, Media24 en oorgange. [Unpublished manuscript]

Renwick, Robin. 2018. *How to Steal a Country.* Auckland Park: Jacana.

Rose, Rob. 2018. *Steinheist.* Cape Town: Tafelberg.

Rose, Rob. 2016. End of the Wessels Toyota dynasty. *Leader.* 18 August.

Rosenthal, Eric. 1963. *Manne en Maatskappye.* Cape Town: Human & Rousseau.

Rupert, Anton. 1967. *Leiers oor Leierskap.* Stellenbosch: Pre-Ecclesia.

Sadie, JL. 2002. The fall and rise of the Afrikaner in the South African economy. *Annals of the University of Stellenbosch.*

Slabbert, F van Zyl. 2006. *The Other Side of History: An Anecdotal Reflection on Political Transition in South Africa.* Cape Town: Jonathan Ball.

Sparks, A. 1990. *The Mind of South Africa: The Story of the Rise and Fall of Apartheid.* Cape Town: Jonathan Ball.

Spies, Philip. 2019. *Afskeid van 'n Volk: Op Soek na 'n Toekoms.* Cape Town: Naledi.

Stals, ELP. 1998. Geskiedenis van die Afrikaner-Broederbond: 1918-1994. [Unpublished manuscript]

Strydom, TJ. 2019. *Christo Wiese: Risk and Riches.* Cape Town: Tafelberg.

Stukeley, William. 1752. *Memoirs of Sir Isaac Newton's Life.* London: MS/142, Royal Society Library.

Styan, James-Brent. 2018. *Steinhoff: Inside SA's Biggest Corporate Crash.* Pretoria: Lapa.

Terreblanche, Sampie. 2014. *Verdeelde Land: Hoe die Oorgang Suid-Afrika Faal.* Cape Town: Tafelberg.

Thomas, Harvey. 1993. *Sê Nooit Vaarwel: Die Storie van Toyota Suid-Afrika.* Sandton: Toyota.

Vance, Ashlee. 2015. *Elon Musk.* London: Virgin Books.

Van Vuuren, Hennie. 2017. *Apartheid Guns and Money: A Tale of Profit.* Johannesburg: Jacana Media.

Van Rooyen, Johann. 2018. *Renier van Rooyen, the Founder of Pep.* eBook, Kindle Edition.

Verhoef, Grietjie. 2009. Savings for life to build the economy for the people: The emergence of Afrikaner corporate conglomerates in South Africa 1918-2000. *South African Journal of Economic History.* Vol. 24, No. 1.

Verhoef, Grietjie. 2018. *The Power of Your Life: The Sanlam Century of Insurance Empowerment, 1918-2018.* Oxford: Oxford University Press.

Vorster, Theo. 2013. *Mind Your Business: Advice from South Africa's Top Business Leaders.* Cape Town: Jonathan Ball.

Vosloo, Ton. 2018. *Across Boundaries: A Life in the Media in a Time of Change.* Cape Town: Jonathan Ball.

Wassenaar, AD. 1977. *Aanslag op die vrye ekonomie.* Cape Town: Tafelberg.

Wassenaar, AD. 1987. *Op pad na luilekkerland.* Cape Town: Tafelberg.

Welsh, David. 1972. *The Roots of Segregation: Native Policy in Colonial Natal, 1845-1910.* New York: Oxford University Press.

Wessels, Albert. 1987. *Plaasseun en Nyweraar.* Johannesburg: Perskor.

Wolfe, Tom. 2008. *The Bonfire of the Vanities.* New York: Picador.

Interviews and email correspondence

Whitey Basson
Koos Bekker
Roelof Botha
Jonathan Butt
Tom Creamer
Laurie Dippenaar
Hendrik du Toit
Thys du Toit
GT Ferreira
Gert Grobler
Isabel Groesbeek

Markus Jooste
Meloy Horn
Hans Hawinkels
Tony Leon
Michiel le Roux
Jannie Mouton
Piet Mouton
Lizette Rabe
Frik Rademan
Johann Rupert
Dan Sleigh

Frans Stroebel
Mof Terreblanche
François van Niekerk
Johannes van Eeden
Chris van der Merwe
Hannes van Zyl
Johan van Zyl
Christo Wiese
A few colleagues of key
    figures (anonymous)

Mega-farmers

Theo de Jager
Cora and Louis de Kock
Gys du Toit IV
Pieter du Toit
Clive Garrett
BP Greyling
Dirk Hanekom

Elizca Kies
Kallie Schoeman
Charl Senekal
Nick Serfontein
Piet Smit
Hesti Steenkamp (media
    relations officer: Saai)

Milaan Thalwitzer
Estelle van Reenen
Lynette van Rooyen
Johan van Zyl
Philé and Tommie van Zyl

Newspapers, magazines and electronic media

Africa Check
African Millionaire
Annual reports of companies
Barclays Wealth Report
BBC Newsnight
Beeld
BizNews
Bloomberg
Bult
Business Day
Business Insider
Business Report
Businesstech
Business Times
Cape Times
Capital
City Press
Columbia Journalism
    Review
Country Life
Daily Friend
Daily Mail
Daily Maverick
Die Burger

eNCA
Financial Mail
Financial Times
Finweek
Fin24
Forbes
Fortune
Handelsblatt
How To Spend It.com
Huffington Post
Huisgenoot
ITWeb
Landbouweekblad
Manager Magazin
Moneyweb
Netwerk24
News24
New Yorker
New York Times
Noseweek
Politicsweb
Rand Daily Mail
Rapport

RSG
Sake24
South China Morning Post
Sporting Post
Süddeutsche Zeitung
Sunday Times
The Actuary
The Caterer
The Citizen
The Conversation
The Economist
The Guardian
The Telegraph
The Times
Top 500
Umrabulo
Volksblad
Wall Street Journal
Wallpaper
Wealth Manager
Western Daily Press
Wikipedia
YouTube

Index

About the author

EBBE DOMMISSE is the author of the best-selling *Anton Rupert –
A Biography* and *Sir David Pieter de Villiers Graaff: First Baronet
of de Grendel*, as well as several other books. After a 40-year career
in the media, he retired as editor-in-chief of the Cape Town daily
Die Burger.

He grew up in Carnarvon in the Karoo and matriculated at Boys'
High School in Paarl. Dommisse has a Master's degree from the Journalism School at Columbia University in New York and a PhD from
the University of Stellenbosch. Dommisse received the Phil Weber
Award, the highest accolade given by media company Naspers.

He also chairs the Cape branch of the Helpmekaar Studiefonds.